Gukurahundi
in Zimbabwe

Gukurahundi
in Zimbabwe

A Report on the Disturbances in
Matabeleland and the Midlands
1980–1988

HURST & COMPANY, LONDON

First published by The Catholic Commission for Justice and Peace in Zimbabwe and the Legal Resources Foundation as *Breaking the Silence: Building True Peace*, 1997

This edition first published by Jacana Media (Pty) Ltd., 2007

Published in the United Kingdom by
HURST Publishers, Ltd.,
41 Great Russell Street,
London, WC1B 3PL

ISBN 978-1-85065-890-0

Set in Sabon 10/13pt
Printed in India

www.hurstpub.co.uk

PUBLISHER'S NOTE

"All of Gaul has been pacified."
– *Julius Caesar*

It is ten years since the original publication of *Breaking the Silence: A Report on the Disturbances in Matabeleland and the Midlands*. In conjunction with the Catholic Commission for Justice and Peace and the Legal Resources Foundation, the report is offered again, now with an introduction by Elinor Sisulu, reflecting on her own and others' silence at the time of the massacres, as they celebrated a newly independent Zimbabwe; and a foreword by Archbishop Pius Ncube of Bulawayo, someone who has protested against the ongoing human rights violations by the Government of Zimbabwe and who has often paid a price for his outspokenness.

We have neither changed nor updated the text as it appeared in 1997. Particularly in the section dealing with the suggested payment of legal damages, all amounts are in 1997 dollars. Because the book had to be reproduced from an existing copy, and the printer's film could not be found, some photographs from the original book were not clear enough to be reproduced here.

It is hoped that this edition will find a wide readership, and that its availability will mean that more people will campaign for an end to human rights violations in Zimbabwe, and for restorative justice for the victims.

London, July 2007

CONTENTS

PART TWO: FINDINGS

PART THREE: IMPLICATIONS OF RESULTS

PART FOUR: RECOMMENDATIONS

APPENDICES

Appendix A
Interview forms

Appendix B
Interview forms

Appendix C
Findings

LIST OF PHOTOGRAPHS

LIST OF MAPS

FOREWORD TO THE 2007 EDITION

The report *Gukurahundi* is a study of human nature, especially its negative side. I took three weeks to read this shocking report. Three weeks of courage and perseverance to stubbornly go through it page by page. At the end of the report I was so sad, and I knelt down to pray and offer this shocking report to God. My soul was deeply hurt and disturbed by reading it.

On the surface, 5 Brigade, a crack unit of criminal elements trained by North Koreans, was tasked by Mugabe to sort out the 400 or so dissidents who broke away from the army and went around harming Government property, upsetting Government development and its tourism programme. However, we discover that over 20 000 people were killed by 5 Brigade. These were innocent, unarmed civilians.

Mugabe had a hidden agenda. The motive for these killings was to crush the people of Matabeleland so that they would conform to the ZANU-PF Government and give up their tribal identity and their attachment to ZAPU. This stemmed from grudges Mugabe held against Joshua Nkomo, grudges which now and then surfaced during their guerrilla warfare to liberate Zimbabwe. This revenge was finally carried out in a most cruel and inhuman manner.

This report is only partial. Some day we hope a fuller report will be made.

Archbishop Pius Ncube
Bulawayo, December 2006

INTRODUCTION TO THE 2007 EDITION

"All that is needed for the triumph of evil is that good men do nothing."
– *Edmund Burke, 18th-century British statesman and political thinker*

"Injustice anywhere is a threat to justice everywhere. Whatever affects one directly, affects all indirectly."
– *Martin Luther King Jnr, African-American civil rights leader*

"All humanity is one individual and indivisible family and each one of us is responsible for the misdeeds of all the others. I cannot detach myself from the wickedest soul."
– *Mahatma Gandhi, Indian freedom fighter and philosopher*

The Shona expression "Gukurahundi", meaning "the first rain that washes away the chaff of the last harvest before the spring rains", used to have pleasant connotations. For farmers in water-scarce environments, there are few things more pleasurable that the smell of the first rains on dry dusty soil, the coolness and freshness of the air afterwards and the promise of a new season of bountiful harvests.

In the 1980s, the term Gukurahundi assumed an entirely new meaning when the notorious North Korean-trained 5 Brigade murdered thousands of people in the Zimbabwean province of Matabeleland and parts of Midlands. Both the 5 Brigade and the period of mayhem and murder they caused were called Gukurahundi, which is why, since then, the word Gukurahundi invokes nothing but negative emotions among Zimbabweans, ranging from indifference, shame, denial, terror, bitter anger and deep trauma, depending on whether one is a victim, perpetrator or one of the millions of citizens who remained silent.

When I was asked to write this foreword, my first reaction was to refuse. "What right do I have to be given such a platform?" I asked myself. "Surely such an honour should be accorded to one of the survivors?" But then I recalled a writers' conference a few years ago where I listened to the testimony of Yolande Mukagasana, a Rwandan woman whose husband and three children were murdered in the 1994 genocide. In the aftermath of that catastrophe, Yolande has worked on healing herself and finding a purpose in life by taking care of Rwandan orphans and writing. I was profoundly distressed by Yolande's testimony. The title of one of her books, *Les Blessures du silence* (The Wounds of Silence) comes to mind whenever I grapple with the capacity of human societies to ignore gross human rights violations even if these happen right in their midst. Nelson Mandela commented on this tendency with reference to Rwanda: "The louder and more piercing the cries of despair – even when that despair results in half-a-million dead in Rwanda – the more these cries seem to encourage an instinctive reaction to raise our hands so as to close our eyes and ears." (Nelson Mandela, *In the Words of Nelson Mandela* by Jenny Crwys-Williams, Penguin 2004.)

It is no coincidence that this report is entitled "Breaking the Silence." Indeed, one of its main intentions is to get national acknowledgment of a "chunk of Zimbabwean history which is largely unknown except to those who experienced it first hand." The report points out that one of the most painful aspects of the Gukurahundi massacres was that the plight of the victims and survivors was and continues to be unacknowledged. They are still suffering from the wounds of silence. And who is responsible for inflicting these wounds? The perpetrators obviously have a vested interest in maintaining this silence. But what about the rest of us who lived through those years and continued our lives as if nothing was happening? Are we not equally responsible for the wounds of silence, both while the horrific events of Gukurahundi were unfolding, and in their aftermath? Even today many of us continue to be silent.

As I read this report I felt a deep sense of shame about my own silence. There are many in Zimbabwe who would give the excuse that they did not know what was happening, and indeed many of them would be speaking the truth. Emergency regulations designed by the Mugabe regime ensured a total media blackout of the affected areas. The activities of the dissidents were reported in much detail, but the operations of the army were a no-go area for the media. Consequently large parts of the population remained ignorant. But those of us who had family in Matabeleland had no excuse. Right from the start of the 5 Brigade campaign, news filtered out through family and community networks that there was something horrendous going on. When I visited my grandparents' home on the outskirts of Bulawayo, I recall the lowering of voices when there was discussion about relatives who had been forced to flee the terror in the rural areas, arriving in the city with little more than the clothes on their backs. We did what we could for them and shut our mouths.

As a young civil servant in Harare, I was conscious of the divisions between those who would engage in whispered conversations about this awful thing called Gukurahundi, and those who would simply pretend it did not exist. I recall an oft-repeated conversation, or various versions of it: "Does Mugabe know what is going on? His people cannot be giving a true picture of what is happening otherwise he would not allow it." What a naïve and ridiculous belief! The 5 Brigade did not fall within the army chain of command but was directly answerable to the highest office in the land. With hindsight we know without a doubt that President Robert Mugabe was fully aware and part of the campaign of mass murder in the Matabeleland hinterland.

At the time many of us were too enamoured of our great liberation hero to allow ourselves to confront all the evidence of his direct complicity. Zimbabweans were not prepared to see the fly in the ointment of their newly found peace. The ZANU-PF government did well in the first years of its rule, investing massively in education and health. A world of new opportunities had opened for the black middle class, and black peasant farmers for the first time had access to credit and extension advice. They made the most of these opportunities, and in the first few years of Independence they dramatically increased their agricultural production.

The eyes and ears of the international community were also closed. In contrast to the propaganda image of the radical Marxist leader, Robert Mugabe was moderation itself during his first few years in office. There was no nationalisation of industry and he won accolades for handing an olive branch to the white population. Zimbabwe was a problem that had been solved and no one was prepared to open a Pandora's box. The cries of the Ndebele people fell on deaf ears.

Reading the report after all these years, I am amazed by my own ignorance about a period that I thought I knew. The stories of physical and psychological torture, rape and other forms of sexual abuse, starvation of the population, burning of homes and granaries, disappearances, bodies thrown down mineshafts and murders are all familiar and consistent with what I had heard described by relatives. However, I was taken aback by the account of the mass shooting of 62 young men and women on the banks of the Cewale River in Lupane on 5 March 1983. The silence that greeted this massacre is in direct contrast to the 1960 Sharpeville Massacre, news of which reverberated around the world.

The Gukurahundi operations came to an end with the 1987 Unity Accord between ZAPU and ZANU. As at the end of the Liberation War in 1980, all those guilty of violations were covered by a general amnesty. The report notes the important fact that once more in Zimbabwe's history, those responsible for the most heinous acts against unarmed civilians were not held accountable for their actions, thus strengthening the culture of impunity that prevails in Zimbabwe. The human rights violations since 2000 are a product of this culture of impunity. The same tools of intimidation, physical and psychological torture and murder have been used, albeit on a lesser scale, in the recent violations. The difference is that they are targeted not at a particular ethnic group but at opposition leaders throughout the country.

The recent Operation Murambatsvina campaign in which the Government deployed police and army units to bulldoze or burn down the homes and businesses of people in urban areas around the country has echoes of Gukurahundi. Once again the imagery of cleansing is used, "murambatsvina" literally meaning to remove filth. Once again people are defined in terms that justify their removal – just as the Ndebele were the "chaff" to be washed away by the first rains, so the poverty-stricken urban masses are described by the police chief Augustine Chihuri as a "crawling mass of maggots bent on destroying the economy."

Some survivors of Gukurahundi have reacted cynically to the furore around Operation Murambatsvina. They comment that Murambatsvina "is absolutely nothing compared to Gukurahundi. They [implying the Shonas] are making a fuss because they themselves are affected. When it was happening to us they said nothing." This reminded me of German anti-Nazi theologian, Reverend Martin Niemöller's prophetic statement in 1945: "First they came for the Communists, and I didn't speak up, because I wasn't a Communist. Then they came for the Jews, and I didn't speak up, because I wasn't a Jew. Then they came for the Catholics, and I didn't speak up, because I was a Protestant. Then they came for me, and by that time there was no one left to speak."

Far from being a closed chapter, Gukurahundi has left a festering wound in the psyche of the Zimbabwean nation. As anti-apartheid campaigner and bomb survivor, Father Michael Lapsley, has pointed out: "The poison of hurt that has happened over generations continues to infect the present. The present has been infected by the past." (Statement made in a presentation at the Symposium on Civil Society and Justice in Zimbabwe, August 1983). The Zimbabwean people are speaking out, and as much as they would hope to bury the discussion, ZANU-PF leaders are forced to respond. President Robert Mugabe came as close as he could to an apology when he described Gukurahundi as "a moment of madness" that must never be repeated. A long moment indeed.

Veteran ZANU-PF leader Nathan Shamuyarira recently said he had no regrets about the operation because it had been necessary to deal with the dissidents in Matabeleland. Such comments underline the need for this report. It is absolutely crucial for the healing of the Zimbabwean nation to work towards some form of restorative justice. Giving death certificates to the families of all those who disappeared would be a good place to start. It is crucial for all Zimbabweans to read this report not only to understand and acknowledge the grief and trauma of their compatriots, but also to understand the violence of the past five years.

Father Michael Lapsley has noted that "if we have something done to us, we are victims. If we physically survive, we are survivors. Sadly, many never travel any further and remain prisoners of moments in history, psychologically, emotionally and spiritually. To become a victor is to move from being an object of history to becoming a subject once more." It is high time Gukurahundi survivors became subjects of their history by having their stories acknowledged.

The report is important not only for Zimbabweans but for others in the region, especially South Africa, which hosts the largest Zimbabwean diaspora. Speaking about Rwanda, South African President Thabo Mbeki said: "A time such as this demands that the truth, the whole truth and nothing but the truth should be told. It should be told because not to tell it is to create the conditions for the crime to recur." In the same statement he said: "Because we were preoccupied with extricating ourselves from our own nightmare, we did not cry out as loudly as we should have against the enormous and heinous crime against the people of Rwanda that was committed in 1994. For that we owe the people of Rwanda a sincere apology, which I now extend in all sincerity and humility." (Statement of the President of the Republic of South Africa, Thabo Mbeki, at the Commemoration of the 10th Anniversary of the Commencement of the 1994 Genocide in Rwanda, Kigali 7 April 2004.)

This statement could easily apply to Gukurahundi. The truth needs to be told "because not to tell it is to create the conditions for the crime to recur." The silence needs to be broken. Hopefully, one day the leaders of this region who have not cried out as loudly as they should have against the enormous and heinous crimes against the people of Zimbabwe that were committed in the past 23 years, will see fit to apologise to the people of Zimbabwe.

Elinor Sisulu, December 2006

PREFACE TO THE 1997 EDITION

The writing of the current report has been possible only because Zimbabwe is currently enjoying a period of stability and national unity that did not exist ten years ago. The country now known as Zimbabwe has, in the last hundred years, had a history marred by internal conflicts: the current state of peace in the nation is unprecedented. The signing of the Unity Accord in December 1987 brought an end to the disturbances this report documents. In 1990, the Emergency Powers Regulations, which had been in existence since the Rhodesian Government first instituted them in 1965, were finally lifted. Their removal ended the Zimbabwe Government's extra-legal powers, many of which had allowed for the infringement of basic human rights. Zimbabwe's current human rights record, while still not perfect, is better than it has ever been since Independence in 1980.

The disturbances documented in this report also need to be placed in a historical context. Zimbabwe did not come to Independence easily. The decade which preceded Independence was one which saw the fighting of an increasingly violent civil war, a war which cost many thousands of civilian lives and caused untold hardship and suffering. While the full number of casualties will never be known, it has been estimated that at least 30 000 people died countrywide, although real numbers of dead could be more than double this figure. Most of these casualties were in the northern and eastern regions of Zimbabwe, or in external training and refugee camps in Zambia and Mozambique, although there was no region of the country that was not severely affected by the Liberation War.

As in any conflict, damage cannot be measured in deaths alone: tens of thousands of Zimbabweans were displaced from their rural homes in northern and eastern Zimbabwe into "Protected Villages" (PVs), run by the Rhodesian Defence Forces. The relocation of people into these PVs was done in an effort to prevent rural civilians from feeding, and providing intelligence to, the guerrilla armies; conditions were cruel, and led to massive human rights abuses, including wide-spread malnutrition. The PV policy was combined with "Operation Turkey", the code name given to the policy of destroying crops in rural areas in an attempt to cut the guerrillas off from their food supplies. Needless to say, such a policy also impacted adversely on innocent civilians, exacerbating the starvation already being caused by life in the PVs. The placing of people in PVs was a form of state-organised violence against civilians: no doubt many, especially children raised in such places, still suffer the mental consequences of this experience.

Thousands of civilians were also detained indefinitely without trial during the 1970s, including many of those at the forefront of the nationalist movements, ZANU and ZAPU. President Robert Mugabe and Vice President Joshua Nkomo were both detained for many years.

Thousands of young men and women who left the country to train as freedom fighters also sacrificed their own opportunities to gain an education, while others ended the war with permanent physical or mental disabilities. While there are legal mechanisms in place through which war veterans can claim help and compensation, not all ex-fighters are aware of this, or know how to take advantage of the law. For many hundreds, possibly thousands, of war veterans and their families, the hardship continues.

It is also a fact that since Independence, Matabeleland and the Midlands are not the only parts of the country to have suffered as the result of internal disturbances. In the late 1980s, there were human rights abuses in the eastern districts of the country, as a result of MNR bandit activity. The South African-backed, Mozambique-based MNR bandits were responsible for serious human rights abuses, particularly in Mount Darwin in the northeast of Zimbabwe and in Chipinge in the southeast, from 1988 onwards. While these abuses involved only small areas of the country, their effects were extremely harsh for those civilians involved. Scores of innocent people in this region were murdered, mutilated, or had to live with daily insecurity as a result of this conflict.

The injustices and suffering caused by ninety years of colonial rule, and in particular by the ten years of civil war that brought Zimbabwe to Independence, have been well documented. The Catholic Commission for Justice and Peace (CCJP) has played an important role in this process. As one of the few independent human rights organisations active in the country, CCJP played an important, politically impartial role in the 1970s. They were able to collect evidence of human rights abuses committed during the Liberation War, and were able to publicise these abuses internationally. CCJP facilitated the international publication of several reports, including *The Man in the Middle* (May 1975), and *The Civil War in Rhodesia* (August 1976), both published by the Catholic Institute for International Relations (CIIR) in England. Since Independence, CCJP archival information has also been used to document the history of the 1970s. In 1992 *Reaching for Justice*, a history of CCJP, was published (Mambo Press), and in the same year, a CCJP video entitled *Caught in the Crossfire* was released: this detailed the plight of rural Zimbabweans in the Liberation War. Apart from CCJP, many other individuals and organisations have also recorded aspects of pre-Independence history. This process of documentation means that a crucial period in Zimbabwean history is on permanent record for generations yet to come.

The whole southern African region is now enjoying unprecedented peace and stability. The coming of Independence in South Africa drew to a close the colonial history of Africa. It also began a new process of accountability, and highlighted the realisation that true reconciliation between people who have traditionally been opposed, is often best facilitated by honest public acknowledgment of the past. This process need not be vitriolic, but it is important for victims to have their suffering publicly acknowledged. While the suffering caused by colonial rule is widely documented and internationally recognised, the suffering in Matabeleland and the Midlands in the 1980s is a history that is unknown except to those who experienced it at first hand. It is also apparent that while the signing of the Unity Accord in December 1987 was an important step towards national reconciliation in Zimbabwe, there nonetheless remains in rural Matabeleland a deep-seated mistrust of the Government, and a fear that events of the 1980s could be repeated in the future.

This report acknowledges the historical context within which events of the 1980s occurred, and does not seek to apportion blame. It merely seeks to break the silence surrounding this phase in the nation's history, by allowing over one thousand people who have approached the report compilers in the last several years a chance to tell the stories they want told. It is hoped that greater openness will lead to greater reconciliation. At the same time, the report alone cannot result in reconciliation. It is therefore accompanied by a Project Proposal, which puts forward some concrete suggestions as to how the hardship caused by the 1980s disturbances can now be redressed.

ROLE PLAYERS

CATHOLIC COMMISSION FOR JUSTICE AND PEACE IN ZIMBABWE

The Commission was formed by the national Catholic Bishop's Conference in March 1972 and was tasked with, among other things, education in human rights; research into areas of institutionalised violations; the monitoring, recording and reporting on violations; and action in the protection of the violated.

The Commission works through Church structures in seven dioceses, a national and two regional offices. It is affiliated to the Pontifical Council *Justitia et Pax* and has active contact with commissions in other countries. The Commission publishes research findings, legal and political rights, information and reports on human rights violations.

LEGAL RESOURCES FOUNDATION OF ZIMBABWE

The Legal Resources Foundation of Zimbabwe (LRF) is a charitable trust established in 1984. The LRF promotes human rights through its paralegal, educational and publication programmes. It operates through Legal Project Centres in Bulawayo, Gweru, Harare, Masvingo and Mutare, which in turn run Legal Advice Centres. The paralegal programme aims to provide indigent Zimbabweans with legal advice through a network of advice centres established in poor urban areas and rural areas. The Legal Advice Centres are manned by paralegals trained by the LRF. The educational programme aims to educate Zimbabweans regarding their legal and human rights. The publications programme facilitates an understanding of laws and the legal system among Zimbabweans, through the publication of legal pamphlets that simplify Zimbabwean law for lay people, and also the publication of law reports and legal textbooks.

ACKNOWLEDGMENTS

CCJP and LRF gratefully acknowledge the contribution made to this report by their research coordinator/editor, their chief interviewer and the more than a thousand Zimbabweans who came forward to share their experiences.

CHRONICLE OF EVENTS: APRIL 1980 – JULY 1990

1980

APR   Zimbabwe gains Independence. ZANU-PF wins 57 seats out of 100 and Cde Robert Mugabe assumes leadership of the nation. Before and after Independence there are sporadic outbursts of violence in the vicinity of Guerrilla Assembly Points (APs) all over the country.

JULY   State of Emergency, in place since 1965, renewed: it is further renewed every six months until July 1990.

OCT   Prime Minister Mugabe enters into an agreement with North Korea for the training and arming of a brigade of the Zimbabwe defence forces.

NOV   There is a battle between ZIPRA and ZANLA guerrillas, moved from rural APs to Entumbane near Bulawayo.

1981

FEB   There is a second, major outbreak of violence at Entumbane that spills over to Ntabazinduna and Connemara in the Midlands. More than 300 die.
        The *Dumbutshena Report* is commissioned by the government to investigate events surrounding the Entumbane uprising: to date its findings have been suppressed.

AUG   Inkomo Army Barracks are sabotaged by South African agents destroying $50 million in ammunition and equipment. North Korean instructors arrive to begin training the "5 Brigade", which will be used to "combat dissidents".

DEC   South African agents sabotage ZANU-PF headquarters, killing 7 and injuring 124.

1982

FEB   "Discovery" of arms caches in Matabeleland leads to arrest of ZIPRA high commanders and expulsion of ZAPU leaders from cabinet. Ex-ZIPRAs defect in large numbers and banditry increases.

JUNE   There is an abortive attack on Prime Minister Mugabe's residence. A ZIPRA connection is established, leading to curfews, detentions and weapon searches in Bulawayo.

JULY   Six foreign tourists are kidnapped and killed, although

	their deaths are only confirmed years later. Curfews are imposed in Matabeleland, troop numbers and detentions are stepped up.
JULY	Thornhill Air Base in Gweru is sabotaged by South African agents, and 13 military planes are destroyed.
JULY	Government reinstates the Indemnity and Compensation Bill first used in 1975, granting immunity from prosecution to government agencies.
NOV	CCJP sends a confidential report to the Prime Minister expressing concern at army excesses.
DEC	The 5 Brigade has its "passing out" parade and is ready for deployment.

1983

6 JAN	The Government allows farmers to rearm, to protect themselves against dissidents, after a spate of attacks killing six people on commercial farms. Between Nov 1982 and Dec 1983, 33 people murdered by dissidents on commercial farms.
26 JAN	The 5 Brigade is deployed in Matabeleland North. Reports of atrocities begin within days.
FEB	Atrocities continue and first documentation is presented to government.
MAR	Nkomo is placed under house arrest and flees to Botswana. A four-day cordon around Bulawayo leads to 1 000 detentions.
MAR	Zimbabwe Catholic Bishops' Conference (ZCBC) and Catholic Commission for Justice and Peace (CCJP) speak personally to Prime Minister Mugabe and present their paper "Reconciliation is Still Possible".
5 APR	The curfew is lifted in Matabeleland North.
22 JULY	5 Brigade is withdrawn from Matabeleland for a brief retraining session.
29 AUG	5 Brigade is redeployed in Matabeleland North.
SEPT	Chihambakwe Commission of Inquiry is set up to investigate atrocities in Matabeleland.

1984

JAN   It is announced in Parliament that since Jan 1983, dissidents have murdered 120, mutilated 25, raped 47 and committed 284 robberies.

JAN   The Chihambakwe Committee begins to collect evidence of army atrocities in Bulawayo.

4 FEB   A food embargo is imposed on Matabeleland South and 5 Brigade is simultaneously deployed in the region. Mass detentions follow, with thousands of civilians being incarcerated at Bhalagwe Camp in Matobo District.

7 APR   ZCBC expresses deep concern over conditions in Matabeleland South.

10 APR   The curfew is relaxed and the food embargo is lifted.

JULY   It is announced in Parliament that since Jan 1984, dissidents have killed 45 civilians, raped 37 and committed 253 robberies.

LATE 1984   The 5 Brigade is withdrawn and retrained and in 1985 it is redeployed in Matabeleland.

LATE 1984   Pre-election violence begins, mainly at the hands of the ZANU-PF Youth Brigades. Areas notably affected include Gweru, Kwekwe, Beitbridge and Plumtree.

1985

ALL   ZANU-PF Youth rampages continue before and after the July elections, resulting in 2 000 being left homeless and scores dead in Matabeleland, the Midlands and Harare.

FEB   The CIO orchestrates a spate of detentions of ZAPU officials countrywide. Many of those detained disappear permanently.

MAR   CCJP sends a confidential report to the Prime Minister condemning the bullying of opposition party members.

JULY   It is announced in Parliament that since January 1985, dissidents have killed 45, raped 40 and committed 215 robberies.

JULY   Zimbabwe has its second General Election and ZANU-PF wins convincingly, although ZAPU retains all 15 seats in Matabeleland. There is a spate of post-election violence targeting ZAPU supporters. Top ZAPU men, including five MPs, are detained on grounds of treasonous activity.

AUG	Dissidents target Shona-speaking civilians in an attack in Mwenezi, killing 22. CCJP is among those who condemn the attack.
NOV	It is announced that the Chihambakwe Commission's report will not be made public.

1986

MAR	Two ZIPRA commanders in jail for four years are released.
DEC	A ZIPRA High Commander is released, to facilitate unity talks.

1987

JAN	It is announced in Parliament that during 1986 dissidents killed 116 civilians, raped 57, abducted 20 and committed 210 robberies. CCJP releases a confidential report on Torture in Zimbabwe to the Prime Minister.
FEB	It is announced at a rally in Bulawayo that Unity is imminent.
APR	Unity talks break down.
JUNE	All ZAPU rallies and meetings are banned.
SEPT	ZAPU is effectively banned: offices are raided and officials detained.
OCT	Unity talks resume.
NOV	Dissidents murder 16 on a mission farm in Matobo.
DEC	The Unity Accord is signed by Joshua Nkomo and Robert Mugabe.

1988

APR	An Amnesty is announced for all dissidents, and 122 surrender.
JUNE	The Amnesty is extended to include all members of the army who committed offences before the Unity Accord.

1990

JULY	The State of Emergency is not renewed.

LIST OF ABBREVIATIONS

5B	5 Brigade
AAAS	American Association for the Advancement of Science
ANC	African National Congress
AP(s)	Assembly Point(s)
ASS	Assault
BLPC	Bulawayo Legal Project Centre
Byo	Bulawayo
CBD	Central Business District
CCJP	Catholic Commission for Justice and Peace
Cde	Comrade
CID	Central Intelligence Department (Police)
CIO	Central Intelligence Organisation
Col	Colonel
CONADEP	Commission on the Disappearance of Persons
c-r	Cross refer
CSC	Cold Storage Commission
DA	District Administrator
Detn	Detention
GSW	Gun shot wound
HB	High Court, Bulawayo
HH	High Court, Harare
HR Database	Human Rights Database
LCFHR	Lawyers' Committee for Human Rights
LRF	Legal Resources Foundation
LtCol	Lieutenant Colonel
MNR	Mozambique National Resistance
PISI	Police Internal Security Intelligence unit
PTSD	Post Traumatic Stress Disorder
PV	Protected Village
RDF	Rhodesian Defence Force
RF	Rhodesian Front
SADF	South African Defence Force
SU	Support Unit (Police)
UDI	Unilateral Declaration of Independence
UNHCR	United Nations High Commission for Refugees
WHO	World Health Organization
ZANU-PF	Zimbabwe African National Union – Patriotic Front
ZANLA	Zimbabwe African National Liberation Army (armed wing of ZANU-PF)

ZAPU	Zimbabwe African People's Union
ZIPRA	Zimbabwe People's Revolutionary Army (armed wing of ZAPU)
ZCBC	Zimbabwe Catholic Bishops' Conference
ZNA	Zimbabwe National Army
ZOC	Zimbabwe Omnibus Company
ZRP	Zimbabwe Republican Police

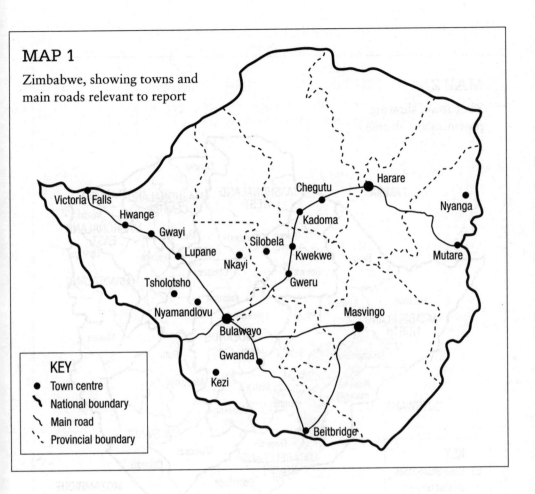

MAP 1

Zimbabwe, showing towns and
main roads relevant to report

KEY
- Town centre
- National boundary
- Main road
- Provincial boundary

Victoria Falls
Hwange
Gwayi
Lupane
Silobela
Nkayi
Tsholotsho
Nyamandlovu
Bulawayo
Gwanda
Kezi
Chegutu
Harare
Nyanga
Kadoma
Kwekwe
Gweru
Mutare
Masvingo
Beitbridge

MAP 2

Zimbabwe, showing
provinces and districts

ZAMBIA

Guruve

MASHONALAND
WEST

MASHONALAND
CENTRAL

Rushinga

Mudzi

MASHONALAND
EAST

Gokwe
North

Makonde

Mazoe

Binga

Zvimba

Nyanga

Gokwe
South

Harare

Chegutu

MANICALAND

Hwange

Lupane

Kadoma

MATABELELAND
NORTH

Nkayi

Kwekwe

MIDLANDS

Nyamandlovu

Bubi

Gweru

Mutare

Byo

Gutu

Bulilima-
mangwe

Umzin
gwane

Insiza

Masvingo

BOTSWANA

Mberengu-
wa

Matobo

MATABELELAND
SOUTH

Gwanda

Mwenezi

MASVINGO

Chiredzi

Beitbridge

MOZAMBIQUE

SOUTH AFRICA

KEY

Case Study areas

District borders

Provincial and
National borders

PART ONE
BACKGROUND

I
INTRODUCTION

When Robert Mugabe assumed office as the first prime minister of Zimbabwe on 18 April 1980, he was faced with the task of uniting a country that had been subjected to 90 years of increasingly repressive racist rule. There had also been over a decade of escalating military activity, which had served not only to accelerate the process of liberating the majority, but also to create some divisions within it. In addition, the new Zimbabwe had a powerful and hostile neighbour, South Africa.

It was obvious that integrating a community that had serious divisions within itself would be no easy task. Mugabe himself had long been an assassination target, and attempts on his life continued. He escaped an attempt on his life near Masvingo during the election campaign. He and others narrowly escaped a "Rhodesian" assassination attempt planned to coincide with Independence Day in 1980. In December 1981 South African agents attempted to kill him by blowing up the new ZANU-PF headquarters, and in July 1982 there was yet another abortive attempt on his life, involving ex-ZIPRA combatants, when shots were fired at his residence in Harare.

In addition, there were sporadic outbreaks of violence emanating from the guerrilla assembly points (APs) countrywide. Such outbreaks began before Independence and continued throughout the early 1980s. This violence was committed by both ZANLA and ZIPRA ex-combatants, sometimes against civilians and quite often against each other; the causes of this were complex.[1]

The net result of the unstable situation was that by early 1982, Zimbabwe had serious security problems in various parts of the country, particularly in the western half.[2] Bands of "dissidents" were killing civilians and destroying property.

The Government responded with a massive security clamp-down on Matabeleland and parts of the Midlands. What is apparent in retrospect, and will be shown in this report, is that there were two overlapping "conflicts" going on in Matabeleland. The first conflict was between the dissidents and Government defence units, which included 4 Brigade, 6 Brigade, the Paratroopers, the CIO and the Police Support Unit. The second conflict involved Government agencies and all those who were thought to support ZAPU. This was carried out mainly against unarmed civilians in those rural areas which traditionally supported ZAPU; it was also at times carried out against ZAPU supporters in urban areas. The

Government agencies that were engaged in this second conflict were primarily 5 Brigade, the CIO, PISI and the ZANU-PF Youth Brigades, as shown in this report. These units committed many human rights violations, which compounded the plight of civilians who were, once more, caught in the middle of a problem not of their own making.

The Government's attitude was that the two conflicts were one and the same, and that to support ZAPU was the same as to support dissidents.[3] Rural civilians, the ZAPU leadership and the dissidents themselves all denied and continue to deny this allegation. Whatever the ultimate truth on that issue, it is indisputable that thousands of unarmed civilians died, were beaten, or suffered loss of property during the 1980s, some at the hands of dissidents and most as a result of the actions of Government agencies.

1. THE INTENTIONS OF THIS REPORT – AN OUTLINE

A) NATIONAL ACKNOWLEDGMENT

One of the most painful aspects of the 1980s conflict for its victims is their perception that their plight is unacknowledged. Officially, the State continues to deny any serious culpability for events during those years, and refuses to allow open dialogue on the issue. In effect, there is a significant chunk of Zimbabwean history which is largely unknown, except to those who experienced it at first hand. All Zimbabweans, both present and future, should be allowed access to this history.

Only by fully exploring how the 1980s crisis developed, can future Zimbabweans hope to avoid a repetition of such violence.

It is only once all Zimbabweans have acknowledged this part of their history, that it can be put aside. The belief that *truth and reconciliation are not mutually exclusive* is the belief of those who have motivated this project. In fact, it is believed that lasting reconciliation is contingent on truth.[4]

Those who would rather that events of the 1980s remain shrouded in secrecy have claimed that discussing them will "reopen" old wounds. However, it was clear during the interviewing procedure that, for thousands of people, *these wounds have never healed*: people still suffer today, physically, psychologically and practically, as a result of what they experienced in the 1980s. Far from "reopening" old wounds, the victims' being allowed to speak out and having their stories validated by a non-judgmental audience has begun what is hoped will be a healing process, after more than 10 years of people suffering in fear and isolation.

Critics of this project have been quick to point out that in April 1980, Mr Mugabe made a magnanimous speech, in which he "drew a line through the past", and forgave those whites and others who had persecuted the black majority in the country, particularly during 10 years of increasingly bitter war in the 1970s. Why, then, it is asked, does this report seek to hold the very Government, which was so forgiving, accountable for its own shortcomings in the next decade?

It is not the intention of this report that its evidence be used to hold individual human rights violators accountable. The report seeks rather to promote greater openness to certain truths, currently denied, in the belief that this will lead to greater reconciliation of communities and will help victims to rise above their memories of pain and any desires for retribution.

There may be individuals, not only among victims but also among the dissidents and security agencies responsible for violations, who need an atmosphere of truth-telling in order to purge themselves of their memories of events.[5]

It also needs to be pointed out that while the perpetrators of offences in the war for Independence have not been held accountable as individuals, many documents exist, including a substantial body of academic books and memoirs, ensuring that this part of the nation's history is accessible to those who wish to know it.[6] These have been written not only by those who once opposed the colonial order, but also by those who were part of this old colonial order, as well as by international academics. While far from complete in its documentation, an important record of events surrounding the Second Chimurenga has been produced over the years. For example, the names Nyadzonia and Chimoio arouse deep emotions in all Zimbabweans, not only those who lost loved ones in the raids on these external guerrilla camps. While nobody was ever held accountable for the terrible killings, Zimbabweans have access to details of these events if they wish to know more.[7]

But many, both nationally and internationally, are unaware that the name "Bhalagwe" arouses similarly deep emotions for people who live in Matabeleland. It is only those in affected areas who attach significance to this name.

That many parties were at least partly culpable in the unfolding of events is clear. These include ZANU-PF, those ex-ZIPRAs and others who became dissidents, those remnants of Rhodesian state agencies which sought to disrupt unity, and South African agents who both actively disseminated misinformation and who also trained and equipped dissidents.

It is the intention of this report to broaden the debate on how these events unfolded, which has so far been restricted to a very small number of academics and human rights activists,[8] and to allow all concerned parties to enter into healthy public debate over issues they dispute, so that a more complete picture of the truth can emerge.

B) RECONCILIATION – A CHANCE TO BE HEARD

There is a need for a deeper and more lasting reconciliation in Zimbabwe. This is only possible when the magnitude of the happenings in the affected areas is more widely understood by all those concerned. Only when those who inflicted untold hardship are prepared to acknowledge that they did so, can a lasting reconciliation take place between all who live in Zimbabwe. Only then can bitterness and fear finally be eased. Once the fact that thousands suffered atrocities during those years has been acknowledged, once fear has finally receded, then victims will feel able to speak out about their experiences without dreading retribution.

What those we have spoken to in Matabeleland want more than anything else is lasting peace in Zimbabwe.

They do not want a witch hunt, just a chance to be heard.

They have survived two terrible civil wars in as many decades, and they have received no guarantee that it will not happen again. Only one senior minister in the last 13 years has expressed public regret for what happened. In fact, ministers are on public record as saying they will never apologise.[9]

The single exception to this is Minister Mahachi, who said in the *Sunday Mail* of 6 September 1992 that "events during that period are regretted and should not be repeated by anybody, any group of people or any institution in this country."

However, if most people do not know in the first instance what it was that happened, and why it happened, how can a repetition be avoided?

Part of the process of psychological healing, for any victim of abuse, is being given the opportunity to recount that suffering to a supportive, non-judgmental audience. It is at least partly in recognition of this principle that truth commissions have taken place in other parts of the world in recent years.[10] Those involved with taking testimony for the South African Truth and Reconciliation Commission have noted:

> "In many instances the act of telling their stories to a
> sympathetic statutory body which acknowledges their pain
> has proved a cathartic one for witnesses. A common thread

running through their testimonies is an extraordinary capacity to forgive, if they can only know the truth."[11]

One of the most tragic effects of events in the 1980s is that it served to harden "ethnic" differences in Zimbabwe, resulting in what could be referred to as "quasi-nationalism."[12] Recent events in Sri Lanka, Rwanda and Yugoslavia provide sad testimony to what happens when such conflicts are not satisfactorily resolved. Recent conflicts in all these countries have their roots in previous, unsatisfactorily resolved internal conflicts. While the signing of the agreement of National Unity in 1987 was an important step towards reconciliation, there are many issues that still need to be aired by ordinary citizens of Zimbabwe and taken into account by its national leadership, if we are to prevent a recurrence of violence between future generations of Zimbabweans.

More than a thousand ordinary citizens came forward in the last five years to relate their experiences to the compilers of this report. People often travelled long distances to give evidence, and waited overnight to tell their stories. For many, this was the first time they had been given the opportunity to have their experiences formally recorded. Many wept, or expressed anger, or voiced confusion as to why the violence of the 1980s ever took place.[13]

Many expressed pain at the memory of how senior officials had refused to acknowledge events at the time: the disappearances of people were repeatedly denied in the 1980s, and death certificates were denied for corpses who officially had not been murdered. Others related how their pain at the loss of a loved family member was compounded by a death certificate with a fallacious cause of death filled in; for example, one murdered person had "stomach injury" recorded as the cause of death.[14]

All evidence was given entirely voluntarily, and without suggestion of reward or future compensation. The need to document events historically was explained as the primary intention of this report, and the desire to help set the record straight was apparently motivation enough for witnesses.

While those who came forward gave evidence freely, some told of other victims who were still too afraid to tell their stories. That this fear was not unjustified was borne out in our second case study area, where the CIO made what were perceived as intimidatory appearances at interview sessions, and interrogated at least one person who helped the data collection process, and where certain councillors also actively discouraged their ward members from giving statements.

According to the South African Truth and Reconciliation Commission, enabling the victims to talk freely and not to be dismissed as liars without being given due consideration is an important aspect of "restoring the dignity and honour as well as the good names of victims."[15]

C) SYSTEMATIC COLLATION OF INFORMATION

A substantial body of evidence, some published and most previously unpublished, has long been in existence detailing the broader historical events and the abuses suffered by individuals in the 1980s. This report aims to bring together data collected in the 1980s, when the disturbances were taking place, as well as information from interviews, conducted in the 1990s.[16]

Claims of casualty numbers have varied dramatically over the last decade, with the then-ZAPU opposition party leader Joshua Nkomo mentioning a figure of 20 000 dead,[17] and other sources putting the figure as low as 700. There is a need to resolve these disparities by methodical investigation, in order to set the historical record straight.

Data sources have been used to reconstruct a chronicle of events and, more importantly, to detail the reported impact of these events on communities and individuals. Sources document atrocities across most of Matabeleland and in parts of the Midlands.

Interviews in 1995-96 were centred on two case study areas, as time and funding did not allow for comprehensive research across all affected areas. The case studies aim to quantify as accurately as possible, within the acknowledged limitations of the data available,[18] the extent of the abuses, and their perpetrators, in the two specified areas between 1982 and 1988. Research in the case study areas was extensive in the first targeted area, and less extensive but nonetheless very revealing in the second targeted area. It has resulted in a much clearer picture of the nature of abuses in these two areas, and in the process much evidence of atrocities in other districts has also been documented.

While the precise number of dead will almost certainly never be known, more accurate estimates are now possible.[19]

Apart from murders, many other atrocities took place in Zimbabwe between 1982 and 1988, such as the destruction of homesteads or even entire villages, mass detentions of civilians, and the physical torture of civilians, including rape and the phenomenon of mass beatings.

The findings in the two case study areas are documented in Part Two. The pattern of abuse in all areas of Zimbabwe as revealed by a variety of sources is also summarised in this section, in the form of tables and graphs. Part Three discusses some of the implications of these findings.

D) THE LEGACY OF THE 1980S FOR THE VICTIMS

The full scale of the impact of the civil conflict on those who survived it has yet to be forensically established. However, from interviews now on record, it is apparent that those years have left people with a legacy of problems that include physical, psychological and practical difficulties. Some of these negative legacies, as apparent from the database, are listed below.

• Families were left destitute, without breadwinners and without shelter.
• Many people, possibly thousands, suffered permanent damage to their health as a result of physical torture, inhibiting their ability to seek work, or to maintain their lands and perform daily chores such as carrying water.
• Possibly hundreds of murder victims have never been officially declared dead. The lack of death certificates has resulted in a multitude of practical problems for their children, who battle to receive birth certificates, and for their spouses who, for example, cannot legally inherit savings accounts.
• Others who fled their homes to protect themselves were considered to have deserted their employment without due notice, and forfeited benefits including pensions as a result.
• Many people, possibly thousands, who were either victims of physical torture, or forced to witness it, continue to suffer psychological disorders indicative of Post Traumatic Stress Disorder (PTSD). Disorders such as unexplained anxieties, dizziness, insomnia, hypochondria and a permanent fear and distrust of senior government officials are evident in victims. Typically, such victims pass on their stress to their children and create a heavy extra burden on existing health care structures.[20]

2. TIMING OF THE REPORT

The timing of the report is significant: enough time has now elapsed that many victims have been able to overcome the memories of fear sufficiently to tell their stories. At the same time, to have delayed any longer would have meant increasing difficulties in locating source documents and people. Much of this data has already been lost, destroyed, or thrown out. People who were involved at the time have died, moved away from Zimbabwe, or have begun to forget precise details, such as dates of events. This report attempts to rescue and order a substantial proportion of what information remains, although there are doubtless documents that have not been located.

During the 1980s, the continuing disturbances and the fact that the Emergency Power Regulations were in place, severely limiting freedom of movement, freedom of association and freedom of expression, made the prospect of actively canvassing information from victims impractical.[21] However, in July 1990, the state of emergency was repealed and Emergency Powers were dropped for the first time since 1965. Also in 1990, the Bulawayo Legal Projects Centre (BLPC) opened its first paralegal office, in Lupane in Matabeleland North. Almost immediately, reports of practical problems arising from events in the 1980s were brought to the attention of this paralegal office. People who were in need of death certificates for relatives said to have been murdered began to seek help. People wanting to know their rights in terms of claiming damages for losses suffered at the hands of government agencies also began to report their experiences. As other paralegal offices opened in other parts of rural Matabeleland, similar requests and reports began to come in.

It was also apparent that the Government had decided that there would be no compensation given to people who suffered as a result of Government action during the years 1982-88.[22] However, the data base reflecting the present consequences of events in the 1980s continued to grow. The decision to order this data base, first and foremost to establish an accurate historical record, and secondly to suggest ways of helping victims on the strength of it, was made by BLPC in conjunction with CCJP in 1993.[23] The process of establishing funding and personnel, and the devising of suitable interview forms and a computer database, took some time.

It was in 1995-96 that the archival material was examined in detail and also in 1995-96 that interviewing took place in earnest in the two case study areas. The interviews conducted in the 1990s reflect how the more than a thousand people who reported to project personnel currently perceive the years between 1982 and 1988. This report is therefore focused on events of the 1980s both as a history and as a part of the present.

II

DATA SOURCES AND METHODOLOGY

A substantial body of largely unpublished evidence has long been in existence detailing thousands of atrocities perpetrated by both dissidents and the security forces in Matabeleland and the Midlands of Zimbabwe, between Independence in 1980 and the Amnesty in 1988. This report has collated and analysed this evidence, which includes data records that were contemporary to the 1980s, as well as information from interviews conducted during the 1990s.

As well as tabulating available data for all areas, this report also provides a comprehensive outline of abuses within two chosen case study regions of Zimbabwe.

The report also draws attention to the legacy of practical and personal difficulties that continue to affect those who suffered human rights abuses in the 1980s.

1. SELECTION OF CASE STUDY AREAS

Archival material provided evidence that human rights abuses were widespread throughout Matabeleland North and South, and also at times in the Midlands of Zimbabwe. It was decided to actively canvas additional data, but time and funding excluded collection on a national scale. After consideration, it was decided to concentrate data collection in two administerial districts only; Tsholotsho/Nyamandlovu in Matabeleland North and Matobo in Matabeleland South.

Data on record made it clear that the two parts of Matabeleland had qualitatively different experiences of the Government action, with Matabeleland North being subjected to a massive 5 Brigade onslaught in 1983, and Matabeleland South experiencing an extremely long and harsh food embargo, together with mass detentions, in 1984. The decision as to which administrative district to target in each province was made partly with practical criteria in mind: the two chosen areas are near to Bulawayo, and readily accessible from it. CCJP also already had a substantial number of interviews from Tsholotsho on their files. The presence of Bhalagwe Camp in the second chosen area, Matobo, was an important selection criterion.

The two areas targeted for the case studies were:

Tsholotsho/Nyamandlovu
In the early 1980s, Tsholotsho Communal Land north of Bulawayo was administered together with the more sparsely populated commercial farmland of Nyamandlovu adjacent to it. (This adjacent commercial farmland has since been incorporated into an administerial district known as Umgusa; the map of Zimbabwe on page xxxii designates district boundaries as used in this report, which in a few cases do not coincide with district boundaries recognised in 1996). Atrocities by Government agencies were known to be severe in Tsholotsho in 1983: the adjacent commercial farmland of Nyamandlovu was known to have been hard hit by dissidents. Making Nyamandlovu part of the case study area allowed for the inclusion of data on dissident atrocities in the commercial farming and forestry resettlement areas of Nyamandlovu: there was almost no information on dissidents forthcoming from people based in the Tsholotsho Communal Lands.

Matobo (known as Kezi District prior to the 1980s)
A largely communal area south of Bulawayo, where atrocities were known to be severe in 1984. In particular, there was already substantial data on record of detentions, beatings and killings at Bhalagwe Camp, near Maphisa (previously called Antelope).

Further evidence of atrocities in other parts of the country came to light during this process, and tables showing known atrocities in all affected areas can be found immediately following the two main case summaries in Part Two of this report.

2. A SUMMARY OF DATA SOURCES

"Reliable statistics [of human rights abuses] are extremely difficult to come by in Zimbabwe. It is often all but impossible to verify reports of army abuses. The reports one hears in Harare about atrocities committed by dissidents often sound indistinguishable from the reports one hears in Bulawayo about atrocities committed by the security forces; neither side acknowledges any legitimacy in the other's version of events."[1]

This report has sought to overcome the difficulties in collecting data on human rights abuses by relying upon a variety of data sources. The nature and quality of these sources are very varied and, in the case of press reports, at times conflicting, but together the data provide a complex picture of the 1980s conflict, and probably as complete a record as there is now ever likely to be. An outline of main sources follows.

a) Catholic Commission for Justice and Peace in Zimbabwe (CCJP) archival material, collected in the 1980s.

b) Bulawayo Legal Projects Centre (BLPC)
   i) Archival material, including records of legal clients,
   ii) BLPC current material: current paralegal clients with legal problems arising from the 1980s, and interviews conducted in the case study areas in 1995/96.

c) Human rights reports, including:
   i) Zimbabwe: Wages of War – A Report on Human Rights, published by the Lawyers' Committee for Human Rights, New York, 1986. (Referred to in this report as LCFHR).
   ii) Zimbabwe – A Break With the Past? Human Rights and Political Unity: An Africa Watch Report, Richard Carver, October 1989.
   iii) Amnesty International Reports and Memoranda.
   iv) CCJP Report on Torture in Zimbabwe, presented to the Zimbabwe Catholic Bishops' Conference, January 1987.

d) Media reports contemporary to the 1980s, both local and international, including newspapers, magazines and video clippings. The most comprehensive source here proved to be *The Chronicle*, Bulawayo's daily newspaper. As well as detailing much dissident activity, *The Chronicle* provides useful insight into the "official view" of events, recording the opinions and pronouncements of Government office bearers as events unfolded.

e) Academic research, including most notably:
   i) Two conference papers written by Jocelyn Alexander and JoAnn McGregor. These are part of a broader collaborative research project undertaken with Terence Ranger, which will cover a wide range of twentieth century history in Matabeleland North.
   ii) Richard Werbner, *Tears of the Dead: The Social Biography of an African Family*, Baobab, Harare, 1992.

f) Selected interviews with CCJP officials, commercial farmers and others.

g) Medical and other material evidence. Medical records and evidence from three sets of exhumed bodies.

3. A DISCUSSION OF DATA SOURCES

A) CATHOLIC COMMISSION FOR JUSTICE AND PEACE

CCJP provided invaluable archival files on atrocities, compiled when the 1980s disturbances were taking place. As data were being collected simultaneously with events occurring, CCJP accounts remain the most accurate and valuable source, particularly in terms of dates; they also capture the horror of those years in a way less contemporary accounts cannot. Priests and doctors were recording events and noting the broader picture as well as the details, such as the movement and numbers of troops, as well as civilian casualties. CCJP files provide a firm framework within which data from other sources have been placed in context.

Strict curfews prevented the movement of all civilians in Northern Matabeleland during parts of 1982 and in early 1983, and in Southern Matabeleland in early 1984. This meant that resident mission staff were among the few who observed closely and recorded the unfolding of events during these years. They also made strenuous efforts at the time to protect people and to bring an end to the atrocities.

TSHOLOTSHO has three Catholic missions: Pumula Mission in the southwest, Magama Mission in the east, and Gwayi Mission in the north. In addition, there is Regina Mundi Mission, on the Tsholotsho-Lupane border, whose parishioners are all from Tsholotsho as there is only forestry land on the Lupane side of this border. Reports on events filtered back from all these missions. St Luke's Mission, which is also in neighbouring Lupane, has a hospital, and recorded some Tsholotsho victims among its patients.[2]

MATOBO has two Catholic missions: St Joseph's Mission in the southwest, and Minda Mission in central Matobo. In addition, there are several Catholic schools – Guardian Angel School, St Thomas School and St Mary's School – along the western border of Matobo and Bulilimamangwe. There are also Brunapeg, Embakwe and Empandeni missions in Bulilimamangwe. Again, mission staff at all these missions monitored events in their regions and kept invaluable records.

Presentation of CCJP data is of various types, and includes the following:

- Seventeen very detailed statements, sworn and witnessed in front of lawyers, which were prepared for the Government Committee of Inquiry into alleged atrocities by security forces in 1983 and 1984. These are each several pages long and are accompanied by copies of medical records in a few instances. In all instances they give full details of victims, times, perpetrators and places where events occurred.[3] There are also other well-documented and prepared statements by civilians, which were not notarised, as they were not ultimately selected for presentation to the Committee.

- Detailed hospital records from mission hospitals, recording precise name, age, date of arrival, village of origin and the nature of injuries suffered by hundreds of victims.[4] Injuries include evidence of beatings, bayoneting, burnings and gun-shot wounds. There is a long statement of events in early 1983, made by a doctor at St Luke's. In addition there is also a long written statement from a government doctor working at Tsholotsho District Hospital, sent in February 1983 to the CCJP, detailing information given to him by patients, as well as his own observations of events in the village of Tsholotsho itself. There are also details of victims beaten and shot by soldiers from a doctor at Embakwe Mission, in Matabeleland South in 1984.

- A significant database, known as "Matabeleland Case Files", listing names and other details of approximately 1 000 victims. There are several thick interview files that contain some, but not all, of the source interviews for this database.

- Letters written by priests at the various missions, recounting their horror at what they were witnessing and appealing for intervention and help.

- Many other letters from Catholic priests or parishioners appealing for help in locating missing family members, or detailing other atrocities. Some of these are written by priests resident in Bulawayo or elsewhere, who have had news of events affecting their friends or families in the rural areas of Matabeleland.[5]

- General reports that were submitted to the Government at various times during 1983 and 1984, giving evidence of human rights violations by both security forces and dissidents, and appealing for a more humane approach to the security problem.

- Files with lengthy legal documentation concerning specific people detained without trial, including requests for information as to their whereabouts, requests for detention orders to be reviewed, requests for medical treatment for certain detainees. There are also other files on detainees listing page after page of people known to be in detention at Chikurubi, or other centres, at certain points in time.

- Statements taken by CCJP members based in Bulawayo in the 1980s, made by refugees from the rural areas.

Taken together, the CCJP raw data amount to well over 1 000 pages, providing a comprehensive record of what happened in those years.

Shortcomings of the CCJP data

- Letters or accounts written when atrocities were ongoing frequently do not name victims or informants, in order to protect them from further harm should the evidence be intercepted. There is one recorded instance of a person being murdered subsequent to making a phone call to Bulawayo reporting atrocities, and other instances in which people were detained and tortured after making phone calls, and told this was the reason for their detention; concern for the safety of informants was very real. However, it makes it difficult to decide whether events described, perhaps by three or four different sources in February 1983, are all referring to the same set of victims or different ones. For example, there are four accounts among CCJP records of two pregnant girls being bayoneted to death by 5 Brigade in Tsholotsho in February 1983. In all four accounts the victims are not named and the exact location is imprecise. This was treated as one case validated from several sources, probably the one given in great detail in BLPC interviews 1146-1168 incl. It is impossible now to try to validate such CCJP accounts independently. A conservative approach has always been taken when trying to quantify atrocities: it is always assumed accounts overlap unless there is a very good reason for not doing so, such as clear difference in location or timing of the alleged events. For this reason, many brief accounts of atrocities had to be completely disregarded as they lacked the detail to enable their distinction from other atrocities on record.

- No follow-ups on file to a letter of inquiry about a "missing person" occur often. Many young men in particular fled the country for Botswana or South Africa, or moved into town with relatives, but were too afraid to write and inform their families, so it is possible that at least some "missing" persons turned up, perhaps even years later. Many may have turned up in detention centres and been released, or may have joined a gang of dissidents, but there is no way of knowing from available evidence. Again, a conservative approach has been taken, so that people are not presumed missing unless the report of their disappearance is substantiated by other evidence suggesting they remained missing. Numbers of actual missing may therefore be higher than numbers given in the case studies.

• Information on those in detention is incomplete. Typically, all one can say is that a person with a certain name was in a certain jail during a certain month. Where that person was originally detained, how long he had already been in detention or remained in detention, and who originally detained him, are details that are usually not given. For example, there is a large file on Chikurubi detainees from 1985, merely listing names of those in Chikurubi at the time. Some people were in detention for three or four years, and others for a few weeks. Many were tortured. Certainly, the vast majority of those detained never made an official report of their detention and release to an independent body such as the CCJP: figures of those in and out of detention between 1982 and 1988 run to thousands, according to some sources.[6] "Detention" is therefore not a uniform experience with the same implications for every detainee, and the actualities of every individual case, or real numbers of detainees, will remain speculative.

• The Matabeleland Case Files also had shortcomings. Many names were ultimately discarded as being accompanied by too little information to make them useful. In some cases, information consisted of a name only, with no clear indication of alleged offence against that person, or district or perpetrator. Other entries contained some of the relevant information, but not enough for this project. Entries had to be accompanied by details of at least the offence, and year to be entered into the HR Database.[7] This is the name of the main database for this project. At the same time, many hundreds of entries contained full details, and 431 victims were added to the HR Database from the Matabeleland Case Files.

B) BULAWAYO LEGAL PROJECTS CENTRE

The Bulawayo Legal Projects Centre (BLPC) is one of six Project Centres run under the auspices of the Legal Resources Foundation of Zimbabwe (LRF). It was established in March 1987 and is responsible for implementing the LRF's programmes in Matabeleland North and South provinces. It has established Legal Advice Centres in Lupane, Hwange, Nkayi, Plumtree, Gwanda and Beitbridge, as well as in the poor urban areas of Bulawayo itself.

i) Archival data

Legal cases: The BLPC original database consisted of approximately 100 legal cases. The bulk of these cases involved representation of people by lawyers working for private law firms, who made their data available to BLPC. Most clients were people who had been detained under the Emergency Powers legislation. Several involved "missing persons".

ii) Current data

Paralegal cases: Approximately another 100 cases, predominantly deaths, were brought to the attention of the BLPC by their paralegals who, from the time paralegal offices began opening in rural Matabeleland in 1990, started receiving requests from clients for help in obtaining death and birth certificates.[8] These cases involved people from all districts in Matabeleland.[9]

Interviews: CCJP personnel had already collected many interviews from Tsholotsho residents in 1993-94, and this data had been incorporated straight into the BLPC database.[10] This base was extensively increased by further interviews in 1995-96, using the combined resources of CCJP and LRF.[11]

TSHOLOTSHO

Data was collected in Tsholotsho on a ward-by-ward basis. Tsholotsho is divided into 16 administrative wards, and all were visited in the course of 1995. Twelve visits were made, each lasting two days and taking in one or two wards. In most cases only one person was available to record the interviews, although on a few trips, a second interviewer was able to dramatically increase the number of cases processed in the short time available. Interviews were conducted in Ndebele, and written up simultaneously in English. Arrangements were made in advance with the ward councillors, who were asked to inform the inhabitants of their ward that the interviewer would be attending a certain central point in the ward on a certain day. Councillors and people giving evidence were told that the interviewer wished to collect data relating to what happened in the 1980s, to document any injuries or losses suffered by people during those years, whether at the hands of security forces or dissidents.

All evidence was given entirely voluntarily, and without suggestion of reward or promise of future compensation. Speaking about those years was visibly traumatic for many of its victims. While those who came gave evidence freely, some told of other victims who were still too afraid to come forward and tell their stories. A number of key witnesses made appointments to speak to the researcher and then felt they could not do so, and stated that it was fear of possible harm to themselves that had made them reconsider.

An examination of the data base also makes it apparent that while some victims are reportedly too afraid to speak out, there are others who have now told their story to various different bodies in the last 13 years. The same interviewee names and details of events are, in a few dozen cases, on file in CCJP archives, on BLPC paralegal files, recorded in interviews conducted by CCJP personnel in the early 1990s and/or recorded in interviews in 1995-96.

In other instances, many different interviewees recount the same incidents, naming a constant list of victims, particularly in incidents involving substantial numbers of deaths, such as hut burnings. These collaborating accounts span more than a decade and are often collected from widely distanced parts of the country.

The number of people who turned up to give evidence varied from ward to ward: in certain wards, particular councillors were inefficient about informing residents about the impending visit in good time. In one ward of Northern Tsholotsho, virtually no information was forthcoming on the first visit, and this appeared to owe to lack of information given to residents. In 1996, the interviewer conducted a final series of visits to all the wards to identify some of the people who had been unable to give evidence the previous year. This brief trip resulted in a further 160 named victims, and once again, the small area in Northern Tsholotsho produced very little data. It therefore seems reasonable to conclude that 5 Brigade missed this area in their initial sweep through Tsholotsho, as the reported cases only refer to 5 Brigade passing through the area in pursuit of dissidents in August 1983.

However, data collection in Tsholotsho remains far from complete: those who gave evidence in the final round of sessions in 1996 spoke of yet others who had not come forward. It was also noteworthy that out of all the testimonies collected on this last round, fewer than a dozen of the named victims were already on record.

A total of 910 *named* victims in Tsholotsho was collected through these interviews, many of whom suffered more than one human rights violation. The interview data also indicated huge numbers of *unnamed* victims. A more detailed discussion of this can be found in Methodology (see section 4 of this chapter), and in the case studies themselves. While the data collection process was *far from exhaustive,* it helped provide a clearer picture of the scale and nature of the violations of human rights in the 1980s.

MATOBO

The process of data collection here followed a similar pattern to that used in Tsholotsho. However, time ran out before interviewing had been carried out in all wards. Only 10 weeks were devoted to data collection in Matobo, with most of this time being devoted to publicising the project and setting up sessions. The Matobo Case Study is, therefore, more of an extended pilot study than a complete record of events in all areas. Interviewing was limited to nine one-day sessions at six different venues. Local councillors were not always supportive of the exercise, and in some cases actively undermined it, ordering people not to come forward. The CIO also put in what was perceived by the interviewers to be an intimidatory appearance at some sessions. Despite this, a total of 350 named victims were identified, and thousands of others were implied by witnesses.[12]

Shortcomings of BLFC interview data

• Inadequate interviews. Of the interviews made by CCJP personnel in Tsholotsho in 1993, approximately 50 left serious gaps in their accounts. Interviewees assumed local knowledge of places, which were therefore not always named. Interviewees would also be primarily concerned with their own experience, and so fail to provide general details of events on a certain day. For example, an interview might read: "They came and took everyone in the line to the school. They beat us and then they shot people dead, including my brother, named XX."

Such information produces more questions than answers, and only one named victim. Fortunately, these interviews all referred to events in the Pumula Mission area, an area which was well covered by other data sources, in particular File H.[13] Forty names from BLPC sources coincided with more comprehensive accounts of events in File H, and many other names coincided with events in villages documented by CCJP. Cross referencing of these multiple data sources allowed for a clear picture of events in the case study areas.[14]

A revised interview form devised by BLPC and used thereafter by CCJP personnel, provided more comprehensive data. This form required precise details of the perpetrator, including clothing, weapons etc, and precise details of where the alleged incidents took place and who else was involved or witnessed events, and caused a dramatic improvement in the quality of information collected.[15] A further handful of interviewees nonetheless were unable to give adequate details, usually because they were now very old and forgetful, and in a very few other cases because interviewees were mentally confused. In these cases the interviewer always noted his assessment of the interviewee. For example, one old man whose child went missing in 1983 was only able to keep repeating: "I want my son."

- Time lapse. The BLPC interviews were conducted a full 12 years after the bulk of atrocities occurred in early 1983. While people interviewed were very clear as to the nature of their loss or injury, other details were forgotten. A person might know that on a certain day, his entire homestead was burnt down, or that his son was killed, and remember the perpetrators clearly, but not know whether this event happened in February or March, or even what year it happened. While dates have been recorded as given, there is likelihood that some are inaccurate. Fortunately, data collected closer to events (such as CCJP files) have frequently cross-referenced with data collected in 1995-96, and has helped clarify the timing of certain events.

- Rape remains dramatically under-reported. While CCJP reports – and *The Chronicle* – referred to widespread rape at the time, people are not willing, 12 years later, to report it. This is understandable and reflects a general reluctance of women to report rape under any circumstances. Many victims will now be married with families and will have put the incident behind them: to probe too deeply would be counter-productive. Reading between the lines, some interviews pointed to rape having occurred, but when interviewees were asked directly by the interviewer if rape took place, this was denied. The following extract is one such instance:

> "The 5 Brigade came after dark when we were sleeping. They forced their way into the house and asked if we had any daughters. When we said our daughters were only young and were sleeping, they went to the bedroom, and took our two daughters aged 12 and 14 to the forest,

> where they beat them for half an hour, then brought them
> home..."

This interview was coded in the HR Database as a beating, not a rape, in accordance with the interviewees' assessment of the event.

In Matobo, men referred to widespread rape, especially in Bhalagwe, although the number of women admitting to rape remained far smaller than the men's accounts suggested.

- False information. This of course cannot be entirely ruled out, but it seems improbable that many people would be motivated to bear false witness at this stage. People do not easily invent dead relatives, and were not led to believe they stood to benefit by doing so. Interviewers were careful to point out that the data collection process was for the historical record only, and not for purposes of individual compensation.

  There are often more than 30 interviews testifying to events in a small area, and on occasions, some of these reports are made many miles away from the concerned village, by somebody who has been resettled or married away from that village in the last decade. It seems almost impossible for such witnesses to have colluded, so many years later and at comparatively short notice. There is also the obvious distress – and fear – that many people show in recounting these times, indicative of real, as opposed to invented, suffering.

  In addition, recent interviews have often served to confirm events on record in CCJP files since the 1980s. People giving witness also provided full personal details, so knew they were not making statements anonymously. Some interviewees even submitted death certificates or medical records to the interviewer for photocopying and returning.

- Dissidents. Information on dissident atrocities was barely reported in Tsholotsho. Yet other sources indicate that dissidents were indeed a menace in the area. In particular, dissidents coerced food from villagers, and also committed rape. For the reasons described above, rape was under-reported; furthermore, 10 years after the event, people may not feel it is worth specifically reporting occasions on which they were coerced into killing chickens in order to cook for and feed dissidents.[16] The degree of sympathy for dissidents during those years and the role this might play in under-reporting, is discussed at greater length under "The Dissident Problem" in Part One, III: on the whole, there was apparently little sympathy for dissidents.

  Independent research in adjacent districts of Northern Matabeleland suggest dissidents did not commonly murder villagers, unless they were considered sell-outs, were ZANU-PF officials, or had informed on dissident movements. In Lupane, for instance, independent researchers estimated a minimum of 750 deaths during the 1980s, of which only 25 were thought to have been committed by dissidents: of these 25, some were considered to have been committed by Government agencies in disguise.

In Tsholotsho, among an estimated 1 000 dead, a total of 18 murders by dissidents were reported to interviewers. In addition, 21 deaths were inflicted by dissidents in the commercial farming area of Nyamandlovu adjacent to Tsholotsho. There were, however, many other references to army members disguising themselves as dissidents and committing crimes. This phenomenon is reminiscent of the war for Independence, when the Rhodesian Selous Scouts used to dress and pose as members of the guerrilla forces.[17]

BLPC data: evidence of atrocities committed in the 1970s
While it was not the primary intention of this report to collect data on events relating to the 1970s war of liberation, some information on people who went missing during the late 1970s was reported both to paralegals and to those interviewing specifically for this report. A total of 23 such reports were made, involving people who left the country for guerrilla training and never returned. The relatives of such "missing persons" are eligible for compensation under the War Victims Compensation Act (see final section of this report for more details), and these reports were accordingly dealt with by paralegals.

In total, BLPC data amounted to more than 5 000 pages of raw information.

C) HUMAN RIGHTS DOCUMENTS
i) Lawyers' Committee For Human Rights: Zimbabwe: Wages of War, New York, 1986
The Lawyers' Committee for Human Rights (LCFHR) has served as a public interest law centre since 1978. The committee works to promote international human rights and refugee law and legal procedures in the United States and abroad. Their Zimbabwean report was compiled after two visits to Zimbabwe in 1985 and 1986, during which committee members interviewed a wide range of Zimbabweans, including a large number of Government officials. Wherever possible, information given in interviews was independently checked and verified. The final report was written in May 1986.[18]

This report provides a well-documented account of the conflict in Zimbabwe during the years following Independence. Its findings coincide to a useful degree with those of the current report. In addition, it provides an overview of various aspects of those years which it has not been possible for this project to research independently, and which would now be difficult to research, a decade after the events. For example, the timing and magnitude of various mass detentions and events in the Midlands, in particular in 1985, were well covered by LCFHR. Their scholarship is thorough and their estimates conservative: this is now apparent in the light of the evidence used for the present report, which indicates far larger numbers of dead and injured people and destroyed homesteads in the case study areas than LCFHR suggested. This makes the consideration of LCFHR estimates in non-case study areas seem reasonable.

The main shortcoming of the LCFHR report is the fact it was written in 1986: the disturbances continued for a full two years after its publication, until the Amnesty in 1988. This means potential key interviewees were in detention, or were hesitant to come forward at the time. The committee therefore had to rely on Government versions of figures for example of damage caused by dissidents, there being no other data source. It also means that there is no information in the report on events during the last two years of the disturbances, including the second Treason Trial in 1986 and the wave of detentions that accompanied this.[19]

ii) Richard Carver, Zimbabwe: A Break With the Past? Human Rights and Political Unity: An Africa Watch Report, October 1989.

iii) Richard Carver, Zimbabwe: Drawing a Line Through the Past, Amnesty International, June 1992.

iv) CCJP Confidential Report on Torture in Zimbabwe, January 1987.

v) Memorandum to the Government of the Republic of Zimbabwe, Amnesty International, May 1986.

All the above human rights reports contributed both to the database and to the overall historical record of events in Zimbabwe in the 1980s. They added a limited but well authenticated number of named torture victims to the HR Database, and also provided names of prisons where torture and other human rights violations took place. Carver's reports gave a useful insight into the human rights violations in Zimbabwe as being a partial consequence of Rhodesian personnel having been retained in government agencies after Independence.

D) THE CHRONICLE

This report deals with *The Chronicle* as a separate entity, with a separate database of recorded victims and perpetrators. The picture resulting from this can be seen in Part Two, III and IV.

The Chronicle, Bulawayo's daily paper, remains one of the primary sources of dissident atrocities during the 1980s. There was without any doubt a serious dissident problem at the time, although it is also now clear that there were several separate groups of "bandits", with varying motivations. (For a more detailed discussion of dissidents, see Part One, III).

A total of 562 offences, committed between June 1982 and March 1988 and involving mainly dissidents but also some Government agencies, were identified from approximately 1 500 media reports extracted from *The Chronicle*.[20] Those media reports that did not refer to offences contained a record of public statements by Government officials and running details on various trials of dissidents, politicians and government agents.

The Chronicle records many attacks by dissidents on civilians, tourists, Government construction projects, and Government resettlement programmes. There were also many robberies and rapes perpetrated by dissidents. However, certain aspects of *The Chronicle's* reporting suggested it was better kept as a separate entity: in particular, it was difficult to cross-reference the incidents it reports with other data sources.

General observations

- Peasant victims are seldom named, but tend to be referred to as a number of victims: e.g. "Five peasant farmers in Tsholotsho were killed by dissidents since the beginning of the month." As names are not given, or precise villages, it is impossible to cross-reference these sorts of statements with, for example, BLPC interviews or CCJP data.
- The perpetrator is almost invariably given as "dissidents" or "bandits", with very few acknowledgments of atrocities by security forces. It is only in instances where individual members of the security forces were prosecuted, which were rare, that the newspaper reported such atrocities. Most references to security force atrocities take the form of vociferous denials.
- When acknowledged, deaths of civilians at the hands of security forces are at times referred to as being "deaths in crossfire", implying the

unintentional killing of innocents where dissidents were the target. This is reminiscent of the statements made by security force headquarters during the 1970s, where civilian deaths were invariably accounted for in this way. Of the approximately 3 500 named victims on file from other sources, there are in fact only seven interviews which refer to five people killed and two homesteads destroyed in genuine crossfire.

• Detainees were named only if they were prominent members of society, or were white. Similarly, white murder victims were invariably named.

• The political nature of the disturbances is very clear from *The Chronicle* reports. Speeches made by Government office bearers and quoted in the press make it apparent that it was ZAPU the ruling party sought to destroy, as well as the handful of dissidents operating at the time. This issue of the two overlapping conflicts has been referred to above, and is further explored in the Historical Overview. In general, there are many statements referring to supporters of ZAPU and supporters of dissidents as being one and the same menace, deserving of one and the same fate – "to die or go to prison", as Minister Enos Nkala put it.[21] The LCFHR also makes a strong case for the perception of the problems as being primarily political.[22]

• *The Chronicle* lists atrocities in two ways:
  - Specific reports: there are weekly or monthly news reports, detailing incidents during these periods. These could be considered "Specific Reports", as there is often some accompanying detail as to location and events, such as precise date and value of property stolen or destroyed from a particular store or mine. In articles listing "bandit" or "dissident" activities, large and small incidents are often given almost equal coverage.
  - General reports: The second listing of atrocities occurs in reports of speeches made in Parliament, stating general totals of atrocities, usually for the previous six months. These were read out as evidence for the need to continue the state of emergency, which had to be renewed by Parliament every six months.

    It is very noticeable that the numbers of atrocities announced in Parliament is always *significantly higher* than the sum of the Specific Reports for the same time-span (see Part Two, III Tables 7 and 8, p 299). Particularly noteworthy here is the disparity for "murders" reported in 1986. "Specific Reports" record only nine murders by dissidents in that year, while the "General Report" for 1986 refers to 116 civilian deaths. A further confusing factor, when Government statistics are considered, is the phenomenon of Government agencies committing crimes "disguised" as dissidents (see below). As all official information and sources for Government figures on dissident atrocities were state controlled, it is impossible to resolve these discrepancies now.

• Incidents which occur in very different parts of the country are not always clearly distinguished from each other, but may be listed together in one article. In fact, there were atrocities being committed by the Mozambique-based MNR in northern and eastern Zimbabwe during the 1980s and an analysis of Specific Reports shows that 10 per cent of atrocities were not committed in Matabeleland or the Midlands.

It is not always clear to a casual reader which events occurred where, and whether ZIPRA-sympathetic, Renamo (MNR) dissidents or ordinary criminals were responsible. This type of reporting seemed to confuse the foreign press at times: for example, in the *Sunday Times* of London, 6 March 1983, there is a report called "Timetable of a Massacre". In it, the murder of a white farmer in Chinhoyi, the raiding of an armoury in Mutare, and the murder of three British tourists in Nyanga are included in a list of "dissident" atrocities that the foreign journalist represented as giving some justification to the Government's decision to send 5 Brigade into Matabeleland. All the above events actually took place in northern and eastern Zimbabwe and the murder of the three British tourists strongly implicated 5 Brigade itself, which was training in Nyanga at the time.[23]

• Once *The Chronicle* reports had been collated for all issues between June 1982 and March 1988, with victims' names (where possible), dates and perpetrators extracted, these were cross-referred with names collated from other sources into the Human Rights Database. *The Chronicle* Specific Report data amounted to 562 entries, and other sources amounted to 3 534 entries. It was discovered that fewer than 40 names could be cross-referenced. (If time and money allowed, no doubt many more cases could be verified: the 40 coinciding cases are merely those that overlapped without every newspaper reference being actively pursued.)

Of the names and incidents that could be cross-referred, 21 involved murders by dissidents in the commercial farming area of Nyamandlovu. Here all data sources agreed the perpetrators were dissidents in every case. Approximately 10 other cross-references involved the detentions of prominent ZAPU leaders, some of whom were in detention for many years. Here all sources agreed on obvious aspects of the detentions, such as who detained the men and when, although the sources may have disagreed on other aspects, such as allegations of torture of victims in detention.

In the remaining seven incidents, which included a bus burning, the murders of three chiefs in Matabeleland, a shoot-out at a rural shopping centre in Inyathi, and the murders of health clinic staff in a car ambush in Nkayi, there were glaring disparities between eyewitness accounts given to independent sources, and the official version of events as represented in *The Chronicle*. In every one of these cases, *The Chronicle* attributes events to dissidents, but eyewitnesses put forward convincing arguments that the perpetrators were in fact government agencies.

Usual arguments for concluding that Government forces were the perpetrators include:

- The inability of perpetrators to speak Ndebele fluently (all dissidents were, by both the dissidents' and the Government's own definition, Ndebele speakers).

- The fact that victims were often known to be hostile to the Government or have other political significance. For example, the Inyathi shopping centre shoot-out involved a prominent opposition ZAPU party member.[24] While the party member in fact survived, seven others died, including several from the his family.

- The police and CIO either did nothing to prevent events taking place even if they were on the scene of the crime, or showed no interest in solving the crimes, even when perpetrators were positively identified to them by witnesses.

- The perpetrator was personally recognised as a specific member of a Government agency, known to the witness due to prior contact. On occasions, for example, members of 5 Brigade would parade as dissidents, then appear as 5 Brigade the next day, and punish villagers for having failed to report their own "disguised" presence the previous day.

However, as previously mentioned, most of *The Chronicle* reports did not specifically name victims. If the reports which specify *location* of atrocity are totalled for the first case study area, *The Chronicle* attributes 50 murders to dissidents in Nyamandlovu and Tsholotsho as a whole, *including* murders on commercial farms. This is fairly similar to the total of 39 murders arrived at via the HR Database. However, as most of *The Chronicle's* victims in Tsholotsho are unnamed, specific cross-referring of victims is not possible.

Reports in *The Chronicle* do not always indicate where murders took place, and the official view was certainly that Tsholotsho was a hot bed of dissident activity, which does not correlate well with the mere 14 murders in Tsholotsho that *The Chronicle* specifically identifies. The impossibility of reconciling such disparities at this stage is a major reason for keeping *The Chronicle* data separate: the two sets of data results are presented in parallel in Part Two, III, and readers of the report must draw their own conclusions. While dissidents are seldom regarded as perpetrators of crimes by villagers interviewed, *The Chronicle* almost never acknowledges atrocities by the army.

In summary, it seems fair to say that while there is certainly much substance in *The Chronicle's* portrayal of the "dissident menace", there are also contradictions and apparent inaccuracies within its reports, which justify maintaining its data in a separate base.

E) ACADEMIC RESEARCH

There is very little published academic research dealing with the history of events in Zimbabwe in the 1980s. Most historical research still seems to be concentrated on the less politically contentious task of establishing a more complete picture of the War of Liberation and the colonial years that preceded the war. However, there are a few key documents on the 1980s which have provided invaluable background for this report.

• Richard Werbner, *Tears of the Dead: The Social Biography of an African Family*, Baobab, Harare, 1992. This anthropological work provides a comprehensive history of one extended family, based on interviews conducted in 1960-61 and further interviews in 1989. The "family", which consists of almost 500 people in all, is primarily located in Matabeleland South, in an area immediately adjacent to the second case study area. This document therefore provided an invaluable insight into how the arrival of 5 Brigade was perceived by those in the Bango chiefdom in 1984.

• Key research is currently being conducted into events in Lupane and Nkayi. This research is part of a broader research project in which Jocelyn Alexander, JoAnn McGregor and Terence Ranger will document the social history of this region for the last one hundred years. Events of the 1980s are therefore a small aspect of their research, but it has produced two papers of particular interest. These are:

- Jocelyn Alexander, *Dissident Perspectives on Zimbabwe's Civil War*, Seminar Paper, St Antony's College, Oxford, 1996.

- Jocelyn Alexander and JoAnn McGregor, *Democracy, Development and Political Conflict: Rural Institutions in Matabeleland North after Independence,* presented at the International Conference on the Historical Dimensions of Democracy and Human Rights in Zimbabwe, Harare, September 1996.

This research is based largely on first hand interviews with civilians, including those who were dissidents in the 1980s, and has been of key importance in reconstructing the history of those years.

• Various other academic documents have contributed to the writing of the Historical Overview in this report, including:

- D Martin and P Johnson, *The Struggle for Zimbabwe,* ZPH, Harare, 1981.

- D Martin and P Johnson (eds), *Destructive Engagement: Southern Africa at War,* ZPH, Harare, 1986.

- Bhebe and T Ranger (eds), *Soldiers (Vol 1)* and *Society (Vol 2) in Zimbabwe's Liberation War,* UZP, Harare, 1995.

- J Hanlon, *Beggar Your Neighbours: Apartheid Power in Southern Africa,* Indiana University Press, 1986.

- K Yapp, *Voices From the Conflict: Perceptions on Violence, Ethnicity, and the Disruption of National Unity,* paper from The Britain Zimbabwe Research Day, St Antony's College, Oxford University, 8 June 1996.

Other written sources were used for very specific information, for example in the chapters on "Legal Damages" and "Implications of Organised Violence". These references are cited in the appropriate chapters.

F) INTERVIEWS

A few selected, in-depth interviews were conducted in 1995-96 by the research coordinator, to answer specific questions which needed clarification after other data had been analysed. In particular, commercial farmers were approached, as it was hoped their evidence could shed some light on *dissident activities* in the case study areas. Remarkably little evidence of dissident presence or activities was apparent from other data sources, yet there were, without question, dissidents committing atrocities during the 1980s. Farmers were in fact able to confirm dissident atrocities in the commercial farming areas.

A few interviews were also conducted with CCJP officials to clarify aspects of troop movements, and some gaps in the chronicle of events. These interviews were for general background purposes.

Interviews were also conducted in Johannesburg in September 1996, with a few individuals who it was hoped might know details of the extent of South Africa's involvement in destabilising Zimbabwe in the early 1980s. These included two journalists, and two ANC officials, one of whom works for the Truth and Reconciliation Commission. To date the South African role in Zimbabwean events still remains largely shrouded in mystery, although some new details are gradually coming to light.[25] Hopefully more details will surface from the Truth and Reconciliation Commission.

Shortcomings of interviews
As with the BLPC interview data, the time lapse has taken its toll on what people can now remember of events. The interviewer was, on occasion, more in touch with those events, having better cause to be so, than those who were more involved at the time. People also destroyed key documents, having felt such documents were endangering their personal safety during the years when house searches and detentions were commonplace. Other documents have been destroyed more recently, in the belief that they were no longer of interest to anyone.

These shortcomings notwithstanding, personal interviews with people with a "larger view" of events proved very enlightening.

G) MATERIAL EVIDENCE

Project personnel established that corroborating evidence for claims of epidemic violence in 1983-84, now made by over a thousand victims, exists in bulk in some places: some rural hospitals have, on their admission records, listings of hundreds of civilians admitted to their wards during the 1980s, suffering from beatings, bayoneting, gunshot wounds and burns. Some of these records have already been referred to under CCJP data above. Hospitals where such records are known to exist include Catholic and other mission hospitals.[26]

The Government hospitals in Bulawayo and rural Matabeleland and the Midlands are also known to have admitted such patients, some of whom were referred to these better-equipped hospitals, such as Mpilo in Bulawayo, by mission doctors unable to treat seriously ill patients adequately. Doctors who were employed in Government hospitals during the 1980s have independently confirmed this. An orthopaedic surgeon who was at Mpilo in the 1980s has confirmed that from mid-1982 onwards, he saw patients suffering from gunshot wounds. The 1982 patients were army personnel and "dissidents" allegedly wounded in shoot-outs. The latter were kept under armed guard in the wards. In early 1983 this same surgeon became alarmed at the sudden influx of gunshot wound and assault cases affecting civilians: at the request of colleagues, in March 1983 he compiled a list of current patients including their names, injuries and treatments and submitted it to the Minister of Health. These included gunshot victims, and patients so severely beaten by soldiers that some later died of renal failure. He also took photographs of patients and submitted a set to the Minister, who insisted that the photographic negatives be surrendered too. A duplicate set of prints had been made by the surgeon, and these are still on file in the Netherlands, as is a complete duplicate set of these medical records.[27]

There are a few individual cases well substantiated by medical records, notably victims whose cases were prepared for the Committee of Inquiry by CCJP in 1984.

Apart from these cases, there are currently on project files only a handful of medical records substantiating claims made by interviewees, although many other victims claimed to have such records, but did not bring them to the interviewing venue. In other cases, victims brought records with them, but there were no photocopying facilities in the rural areas where interviewing took place, and interviewers, having no medical background themselves, were not in a position to note relevant details from such records. They were also hesitant to take such records away with them, as the logistics of returning them to remote rural dwellers were daunting. In any case, such records were in some cases needed on a current basis, by people paying regular visits to clinics.

In many other cases, victims did not have medical records, or had never had them, having been too afraid to seek medical attention at the time.

There were also very few post-mortem or death certificates issued which acknowledged violent causes of death, although a handful of death certificates acknowledging violent deaths are on project files.

There has to date been no large-scale, co-ordinated exhumation of the bodies of those persons whom others claim to have been murdered, in order to conclude independently their cause of death. However, bodies were exhumed from mine shafts in the Midlands and Matabeleland South in the 1990s, with coins in their pockets dating their violent deaths to the 1980s: bodies exhumed at Cyrene Mission in 1984 showed clear evidence of recent gunshot wounds.[28] There is thus a handful of cases which have forensic post-mortem evidence to substantiate the types of atrocities claimed by many hundreds of people.

Other material evidence is the existence of many mass gravesites, throughout the curfew areas of 1983-84. Many such sites were indicated in the interviews in the two case study areas, and were also brought to the attention of report personnel by those doing independent research in Matabeleland North. A few such sites were actually visited by project personnel, to confirm their location.[29] People in both Matabeleland North and South also refer to the way in which bodies were thrown down mine shafts by Government agencies, and the findings in the two mines mentioned above point to the probable truth of this claim, and also to the possibility of many other shafts which still contain bodies not yet exhumed.

People who had homesteads burnt down have also often not rebuilt on the identical foundations to the missing huts: the floors and foundations of such destroyed huts are recognizable in the case study areas.

The lack of specialised examination of such material corroboration of claimed abuses is a shortcoming readily admitted to by this report, which operated under severe funding and personnel constraints. It would have been unethical for personnel involved in this report to try to conduct forensic investigations, and to have thus tampered with potential evidence. This report seeks merely to bring to the attention of properly authorised and qualified personnel the existence of material evidence that could be used to corroborate or contradict the report's claims, if the State so decided.

Similarly, claims of psychological disturbances still experienced by victims of the 1980s upheavals have to remain inferential in this report, based on what victims themselves said in their interviews, where they frequently referred to insomnia, anxieties, dizziness, headaches and other possibly psychosomatic symptoms which they date as having onset after particular events in their lives. Inferences can also be made based on known psychological consequences, which have been forensically established in work with civilians who suffered similar types of trauma in Zimbabwe during the 1970s. That those who experience psychological and physical torture suffer recognizable types of stress in consequence has been widely established, but to date there are no studies forensically corroborating this for 1980s victims in Zimbabwe.[30]

4. METHODOLOGY

A) NAMED VICTIMS – HUMAN RIGHTS DATABASE

The names of victims were collected from all the above-mentioned sources. With the exception of *The Chronicle* data, names were collated in the HR Database, which included all named victims from all districts of Zimbabwe.

The bulk of the named victims in the HR Database are from BLPC sources, with CCJP archival material providing the next largest number of victims. Human rights documents and academic sources provided a small number of named victims, which frequently validated names from other sources. In approximately one thousand cases, names would ultimately be validated from more than one source, with three or more confirmations occurring for more than three hundred victims: additional sources on any name were noted on the file print-outs.

Each victim was categorised and had the following information recorded in a running table:

1. A NUMBER was allocated.
2. The SOURCE of data was indicated by a set of letters, such as CC for Catholic Commission, or PL for paralegal: the initials of lawyers, authors or persons conducting interviews were also used.
3. The OFFENCE was indicated by a further set of letters, with most serious offence listed first in cases of multiple offences. More than half of the victims suffered multiple offences, such as physical torture and detention, or death and homestead destroyed. A complete key for offences is given on page 35.
4. The NAME of the victim, including his or her surname and first names, was recorded. If the victim's own name was not completely indicated, the name of his or her spouse or parent was included.
5. The DISTRICT in which offence took place.
6. The PERPETRATOR, as alleged by interviewee.
7. The YEAR and MONTH of the offence.
8. The AGE of the victim was recorded if the victim was under 18 years of age.

The sex of the victim was not recorded in the running table, although the distribution of male to female victims was separately assessed by returning to the raw data in the first case study area. (Sex is usually apparent from the names of victims in any case.)

Periodically, data were sorted by the computer alphabetically according to districts and names, including first names, to eliminate the same victim being listed several times from different sources. At times, more than one person with the same name was established as having died or suffered injury, but this was only concluded after returning to the raw data, to compare the complete circumstances allegedly surrounding each incident.

Code for offences

X	Dead
M	Missing
P	Property loss
AS	Physical torture: assault with sticks, gun butts or blunt object
AB	Physical torture or injury resulting from burns
Aby	Physical torture: assault with bayonet, knife or sharp object
AG	Gunshot wound
T	Physical torture: including electrocution, water torture and other tortures not covered by above
D	Detention
R	Rape

It will be noted that various types of physical torture have been differentiated: in the case study areas, the phenomenon of "mass beatings" is also dealt with as a separate entity. This is to draw attention to beating, and in particular "mass beating", as the preferred means of physical torture during those years, in particular by 5 Brigade.

Sub-sections of HR Database

When it became apparent that the database was going to run to several thousand victims, it was sub-divided:

1. HR.1 consisted of 2 152 entries, including all data collated up until February 1996, from BLPC and CCJP sources.
2. HR.2 consisted of 411 entries, including data collated from academic and human rights sources, and two files of CCJP interviews conducted in the early 1990s.
3. HR.3 consisted of a severely reduced version of the CCJP "Matabeleland Case Files", excluding all those names already listed from other sources

35

and all those without sufficient details. Remaining names amounted to
a further 431 entries.
4. HR.4 consisted of 540 entries, representing all data collected from
interviewing from July 1996 to October 1996.
5. HR.5 was a temporary database constructed by moving all named
victims from Matabeleland South already listed in HR.l, 2 and 3
into a sub-section, to facilitate comparing of names coming in from
interviews in the Matobo region in late 1996 and being filed in HR.4,
with those already on file from Matabeleland South.

The HR Database, inclusive of sub-sections HR.1, 2, 3 and 4 consists
of 3 534 names, inclusive of all sources and districts of Zimbabwe.

The database was closed at the end of October 1996 in order to
facilitate graphing of existing data. However, data continued to be
submitted to the BLPC, through the paralegals. Within a week of the
database being closed, a further eight deaths were reported to BLPC.
In seven cases, 5 Brigade were allegedly the perpetrators and in one
case dissidents were blamed. In the same week reports came in of one
gunshot wound caused by dissidents, four cases of property losses (two
allegedly caused by ZANU-PF Youth and two by 5 Brigade), and two
cases of assault, allegedly by 5 Brigade. This serves to highlight once
again both the continuing problems facing people in areas affected by the
1980s disturbances, who continue to seek legal help, and the fact that the
database collated for this report is far from complete.

B) THE CHRONICLE DATABASE

All *The Chronicle* news reports relating to the 1980s disturbances were
extracted from June 1982 to March 1988. Information about alleged
victims was entered into a database separate from, but identical to, the
HR Database, for reasons already discussed.

As previously mentioned, these reports could be referred to as
consisting of either "Specific" or "General" information. Only "Specific
Reports" were entered into the database. "General Reports" were treated
separately (see Part Two, III for comparative tables and graphs).

As victims were often not named, the number of victims in a news
report frequently had to be entered instead of names. The names of
farms, stores and bus companies were entered when these were available
and names of actual persons were not given. The value of property lost
was entered if specified.

The Chronicle database consists of 562 entries.

C) UNNAMED VICTIMS – HUMAN RIGHTS DATABASE

Apart from named victims, there were vast numbers of unnamed victims evident, not only from the interviews, but also from CCJP archival material, where victims were more often represented as numbers than names. Certain other documents, such as the LCFHR account, also referred at times to numbers of people injured or detained, without naming everyone.

In addition, in all districts apart from the two case study districts, named victims on file were from unsolicited sources, either archival CCJP names, or the names of legal clients with problems pertaining to these years. Most districts are therefore considerably under-represented on the named database.

It became obvious that while it was important to keep the database of named victims running, additional ways of assessing numbers of victims had to be found, if a realistic picture was to emerge.

On the HR Database, a number of victims unsubstantiated by every name was therefore occasionally entered. This was only done when the collator was certain that those victims were not already on the database as named victims, and where the source seemed reliable. For example, several CCJP archival files refer to "two school-teachers shot dead at Dete Road turn-off" in February 1983. No interviews of named victims on file described these conditions for any death, so it seemed reasonable to assume these were new victims, and to include them in the database. On the whole, very few cases involving purely unnamed victims in the CCJP archives were included in the HR Database, because of the problem of double-counting victims.[31]

Occasionally numbers from other sources were included, such as those from the LCFHR document. This report often uses broad numbers to indicate people detained or injured, or property destroyed in a certain city within a given time span. For example, in its account of the disturbances in Matabeleland South in 1984, there is the following statement:

> "An American doctor, Davee Boyd, reported that he had treated more than a 100 assault victims with broken bones and stab wounds at his mission hospital [in Gwanda District] between February and the end of April [1984]."[32]

The HR Database had no named assault victims from Gwanda, although it had named deaths from Gwanda on record. This above statement was therefore entered into the HR Database, as "100 assault victims, Gwanda".

Similarly, the LCFHR document refers to numbers of properties destroyed in the Midlands during the 1985 disturbances. Compilers of the LCFHR document visited some of the affected areas in the immediate wake of these disturbances, and were therefore in a position to comment reliably. The HR Database had comparatively few of the Midlands offences on record, particularly from Silobela, so these figures were also introduced into the HR Database.

The LCFHR document was well researched and substantiated, and only those figures which the compilers considered fair were included in the HR Database. If the compilers were not sure that a certain figure could be substantiated, they said so. For example, when commenting on the post-1985 election wave of detentions in Bulawayo, LCFHR states:

> "A ZAPU spokesman... said that 415 ZAPU members had been detained during the month of August, but this number could not be independently confirmed. Repeated attempts to obtain the names of those whom ZAPU claimed to be in detention were unsuccessful."[33]

This figure was therefore not included in the HR Database. There are, however, some named detainees from other sources included under Bulawayo in the HR Database, supporting at least in part the contention that detentions took place at that time.

The LCFHR general figures were also not included for Tsholotsho and Matobo, the two case study areas, because of the different and more detailed way in which these two areas were analysed.

D) UNNAMED VICTIMS – THE CASE STUDY AREAS

As mentioned in the discussion of data sources, BLPC interviews always included the *names* of victims, while CCJP records tended to deal in *numbers* of victims, rather than consistently naming victims. However, both CCJP and BLPC records of victims tended to record "village" where events took place[34] in the case of each victim. In the two case study areas it was, therefore, decided to use "village" as the common parameter across data sources. In this way, it was possible to integrate information on both named and unnamed victims, without counting the same victim twice.

i) The "village by village" summaries

This method involved going back to all the raw data in the case study areas, and rearranging it in terms of villages where offences took place, rather than in terms of overall district, or type of offence.

The "village by village" summary of events proved to be a very productive strategy when analysing data on Tsholotsho and Matobo, and helped reveal broader patterns of events. The locations of army units at different times, in particular 5 Brigade, was also apparent with this approach.

The presence of dissidents was also indicated, but they were comparatively rarely referred to as perpetrators. Those statements indicating dissidents were therefore highlighted in the summaries by four asterisks.

As villages were mentioned in source data, they were located on a map, and a section on every village was opened in the "village by village" summary. Interview data on each village was included in highly abridged form, and this data was added to as new details came to light.

Total offences were included at the end of each village summary, once all data had been processed in this way.

A conservative approach was taken when assessing numbers of victims. For example, if CCJP recorded eight deaths in a given village in February 1983, and BLPC had 10 named victims for that village, BLPC's victims were assumed to coincide completely with CCJP's, and 10 deaths were considered the total. In such cases, the CCJP archival record served as corroboratory evidence of statements being made in the 1990s. A reading of the case studies themselves will illustrate more precisely how different sources were used in conjunction with each other. CCJP sources are indicated by two asterisks, while source interviews are indicated by their HR Database file number.

As there was a high level of corroboration between sources throughout the case study areas, CCJP numbered victims were included for villages where there had been no information gathered in the 1990s.

In many of the interviews conducted in 1995-96, witnesses tended to concentrate on a few named victims, without specifying more general numbers of victims exactly. For example, an interviewee could comment: "besides my father, many, many people died that day". No attempt has been made to quantify such statements: they are merely indicated in the Total Offence summary at the end of that village as "one known victim, plus others".

ii) Physical torture

Mass beatings of villagers was a significant 5 Brigade activity. Interviews and CCJP files refer repeatedly to its occurrence, but what this means in terms of actual numbers of victims is difficult to assess. Many interviews refer to "all the people in their line" being marched at gun-point to a certain point and then being beaten.

39

The term "line" can mean very different things, in terms of population. Generally speaking, it refers to the way villagers were made to lay out their settlements when they were forcibly resettled in Tsholotsho by the colonial Government in the 1950s and 1960s. Homesteads were literally arranged in long lines, along the dirt tracks in the area.

A "line" can indicate anything from three "sabuku" areas, to an entire school catchment area, running for several kilometers. A "sabuku" is an official who is sometimes elected, but is more usually hereditary or appointed, and who presides over six to ten families. So a "line" could be from about 20 to 30 families, to at least treble this number. Each family could conservatively be estimated to have five members (two adults and three children), although in reality most families are larger than this. This means numbers of people present at a mass beating could be anything from 100 to several hundreds.

The problem remains as to what is meant by "everyone" being beaten. In some cases, even the elderly were beaten, and certainly women were beaten: interviews refer at times to women being allowed to take turns holding the babies between beatings. Children aged 12 and upwards were also frequently beaten.

The number of villagers forced to witness mass beatings runs to thousands, and includes all ages. Everyone present at such beatings was a victim of torture – either physical, if they were actually beaten, or psychological, if they were forced to witness the beating of others. For a full discussion of this, see Part Three, I.

A conservative estimate of 50 present at such beatings has been made.

iii) Detention

Detentions have proved difficult to quantify; at one level, anyone who is held at gun-point or translocated against his or her will can be said to have been detained, and to have experienced intimidation and trauma. At another level, there were many hundreds of people who were detained for long periods of time in police or army camps or buildings of one sort or another. Again, it is not easy now to quantify how many.

The number of "detainees" indicated in this report can therefore be assumed to be substantially lower than those actually detained.

5. SUMMARY

This report makes use of all currently available sources, both archival and contemporary. These sources include human rights documents, legal records, academic sources and media reports. These have all been assessed as *conservatively as possible,* in order to prevent exaggerating events or double-counting victims.

III

HISTORICAL OVERVIEW

1. THE LEGACY OF THE 1970s

In the last 15 years much has been written about the liberation war and its legacies: it is not the intention of this brief overview to re-enter this complex subject in great depth.[1] However, some understanding of the problems facing Zimbabwe at Independence helps elucidate the events that followed in the 1980s. For the purposes of this summary, the legacy of the 70s will be dealt with as two-fold.

• First, the legacy of colonial rule, which included not only a vast array of repressive legislation, designed to silence political opposition at the expense of human rights, but also a number of personnel in the armed forces and the CIO, who had committed human rights abuses in the 1970s, and who were also ideally placed to work as double agents for South Africa in the 1980s.[2]

• Second, the legacy of antagonism between the two guerrilla armies, ZIPRA and ZANLA. Up until Independence, ZIPRA was the military wing of the political party, ZAPU, which was under the leadership of Joshua Nkomo, and ZANLA was the military wing of ZANU-PF, which was under the leadership of Robert Mugabe.

A) THE LEGACY OF COLONIAL RULE

The new prime minister, Mr R G Mugabe, was highly acclaimed for his magnanimous speech at Independence, in which he agreed to "draw a line through the past", in order to achieve reconciliation of all parties involved. This speech did much to build up confidence in all those who were outside ZANU-PF. It also enabled the new nation to maintain economic stability and attract investment and aid from abroad. It was perceived as an important and laudible gesture.

This speech had been preceded by the Amnesty Ordinance 3 of 1979 and the Amnesty (General Pardon) Ordinance 12 of 1980, both of which had been passed during the interregnum of Lord Soames. These ensured that no prosecution could lawfully take place for any acts done either by members of the former Government, or security forces, or persons or forces acting in opposition to that Government.

However, the policy of forgetting the past, as well as the general amnesties granted by the governor during the interregnum before Independence, meant that those who had committed crimes and human rights abuses in the 1970s, were not made answerable for their actions.[3] Many of the old Rhodesian guard resigned and emigrated after Independence. Others remained, and in many instances became key personnel within the ranks of the Zimbabwean forces and secret services. Here some personnel continued to commit human rights violations on behalf of the new Government in the 1980s, before once more being granted immunity. The message to armed personnel first in Rhodesia and then in Zimbabwe has remained the same for two decades: you will seldom, if ever, be held accountable for your actions.

Repressive legislation can be dated back to the beginnings of colonialism, with various pass laws, tax laws, land laws and a myriad of other racially biased laws, all of which served to ensure the economic and educational supremacy of a small white elite, which was never more than 6.2 per cent of the population,[4] at the expense of the black majority. These laws, their purposes and consequences have been dealt with at length by others.[5] One of the main results of 90 years of colonial laws was that ordinary blacks came to see the law as their enemy:

> "It never occurred to them to seek redress of their grievances
> through the courts. It was absurd. They knew it would be
> fruitless, that the deck was always stacked against them.
> Since then, that attitude toward the law has remained."[6]

Even where awareness of possible legal redress existed among victims of abuse in first the 1970s and then the 1980s, *fear of further retribution* was an overriding factor in keeping people away from suing government agencies. In the 1980s, ZAPU leaders who were well aware of their supposed legal rights, were being persecuted and were in hiding. They feared making their whereabouts known by seeking legal redress. In addition, people faced economic constraints: legal advice was often beyond their financial reach.

The policy of protecting Government personnel was established during the rule of the Rhodesian Front (RF). As the war for majority rule intensified, so did the repressive legislation. Before UDI was declared in 1965, a State of Emergency was announced. This gave the Government the power to legislate by regulation, rather than through Parliament. Regulations included the Emergency Powers (Maintenance of Law and Order) Regulations, which gave sweeping powers of arrest and detention without trial, the right to control meetings, and so on. Using emergency powers, the Government had the right to override almost all fundamental rights in existence under the Constitution, if this was deemed necessary to maintain law and order.[7]

Rights that the State could curtail under these powers included personal liberty, freedom from arbitrary search or entry, freedom of expression, freedom of assembly and association, freedom of movement and freedom from discrimination. These laws were used to ban political parties and meetings, detain people without trial for indefinite periods, and enforce extensive curfews, to mention some of their applications.

The State of Emergency had to be renewed every six months by Parliament, and remained in force from shortly before UDI in 1965, until ten years after Independence, being finally lifted in July 1990. During those twenty-five years, emergency powers were used to authorise many infringements of human rights by both the RF and ZANU-PF governments.

Both the RF and ZANU-PF governments also passed indemnity laws. These were, respectively, the Indemnity and Compensation Act 45 of 1975, which was repealed in 1980, and the Emergency Powers (Security Forces Indemnity) Regulations 1982 (SI 487/1982), which fell away when the State of Emergency was lifted in 1990.

In terms of these laws, all State officials and members of the security forces were granted immunity from prosecution, if their actions were "in good faith" and "for the purposes of or in connexion with the suppression of terrorism" (the 1975 law) or "for the purposes of or in connexion with the preservation of the security of Zimbabwe" (the 1982 law). These laws, together with the presidential amnesty for all dissidents and security forces declared in 1988, meant that human rights abusers were once more not held accountable, no matter how severe their crimes.

In addition to inheriting a formidable array of repressive laws from the previous regime, Zimbabwe also inherited an army and CIO that retained some men well versed in the techniques of torture. Emmersen Mnangagwa, the Zimbabwean minister responsible for the CIO in the 1980s, would point out to his visitors the old CIO members who had personally tortured him when the RF held power.[8] While, on the one hand, this points to extraordinary powers of forgiveness, on the other hand it also could have conveyed to the old guard the message that they were not to be held accountable.

The very men who had been responsible for inhuman and degrading torture in the 1970s used exactly the same methods to torture civilians in the 1980s. This has been well documented by Africa Watch, Amnesty International,[9] the CCJP Confidential Report on Torture (1987) and the Lawyers' Committee for Human Rights.[10]

Maintaining old members of the CIO also laid Zimbabwe wide open to espionage. In fact, several members of Smith's CIO became double agents for the South Africans, and were in an ideal situation to inflame the brewing troubles in Matabeleland.[11]

Minister Mnangagwa maintained that he had no option but to retain the old CIO agents, as ZANLA did not have a well-developed intelligence unit to replace it, and the "old CIO guard" had key information in certain areas.[12] However, ZIPRA had a well established intelligence unit which it was not asked to make available to the new Government, and consequently the unit was dismantled.

B) THE LEGACY OF ZANLA–ZIPRA ANTAGONISM

While it has been pointed out that too much can be made of antagonisms between, and differences in the modus operandi of ZANLA and ZIPRA,[13] there was nonetheless a legacy of unease between the two armies of liberation and their respective political followings which played an incontrovertible role in the events of the 1980s.

In 1963 there was a political rift within Joshua Nkomo's ZAPU party, which until then had been the main liberation movement. This led to a split and the setting up of ZANU, under the leadership of Ndabaningi Sithole. The causes were multiple, and involved not only policy, but personal differences between members, such as Enos Nkala and Nkomo. The dislike between these two men in particular was to be exploited by the ZANU-PF government in the 1980s.[14]

During the 1970s, there were outbreaks of fierce fighting between ZIPRA and ZANLA, both in training camps in Tanzania and within Zimbabwean borders. These incidents were frequent, resulted in many casualties and left a legacy of distrust between the two guerrilla armies.

The training and mobilisation of ZIPRA and ZANLA also differed in some respects. While the two were united in wanting an independent Zimbabwe, ZIPRA was Russian-trained, and ZANLA was Chinese-trained. ZANLA had a policy of politically mobilising the masses by the use of the "pungwe", or night-time meetings, involving a combination of song, dance and politics. ZIPRA did not use pungwes. ZIPRA prided itself on superior military training, and by the end of the war, ZIPRA had operational, tank and air units, in addition to ground forces, which ZANLA did not. ZIPRA also had a very well established intelligence network, unlike ZANLA. ZIPRA and ZANLA also traditionally recruited from different parts of the country, with ZANLA relying on the eastern half, and ZIPRA on the western parts, and also on black Rhodesians working in South Africa.

ZAPU and ZANU, and their military wings ZIPRA and ZANLA, were not tribalist by policy, and both Shona-speakers and Ndebele-speakers could be found in both groups, but increasingly regional recruitment, together with mutual antagonism, led to a growing association between ZAPU and Ndebele-speakers.

Many would claim that regional antagonisms in Zimbabwe date back to the very arrival of the Ndebele in Matabeleland, in the middle of the nineteenth century. They believe that the Ndebele were intensely disliked and feared by the Shona, whose tribes were raided and whose cattle were stolen by the Ndebele. Other historians have contradicted this view of "the Shona" and "the Ndebele" as existing as dual tribal entities dividing Zimbabwe in the nineteenth century.[15] According to these historians, the opposition of the Shona to the Ndebele is, in fact, of very recent origin and most significantly the product of competition for followers and leadership positions among the nationalist parties.

The former view that such antagonism has old historical precedents nonetheless remains a prevalent one, and it took perhaps its most virulent form in 5 Brigade's justification of its violence as revenge for nineteenth-century Ndebele raiding.[16]

The differences and similarities between ZIPRA and ZANLA, and the manipulation of popular belief about antagonism between Shona and Ndebele are contentious topics.[17] Suffice it to say, first, that there were some differences between ZIPRA and ZANLA in training and outlook, and some negative memories of one another which added to the complexity of integrating the two forces into one army after independence. And, second, that divisions created by recruitment patterns and party loyalties played all too easily into oppositions between Shona and Ndebele speakers.

The partial failure of this integration process is one important factor in the outbreak of disturbances in the 1980s. There were major outbreaks of violence between ZIPRA and ZANLA guerrillas awaiting integration into the National Army near Bulawayo. The first of these was in November 1980, followed by a more serious uprising in early 1981. This violence led to the defection of many hundreds of ex-ZIPRA members back to the bush, and the general atmosphere of instability and suspicion led to the concealing of arms on both sides.[18] (Arms had also been concealed by both ZANLA and ZIPRA forces before they entered APs prior to Independence. They had done this as a safeguard in case Independence failed, or one of the main external parties did not win the 1980 election.) The antagonisms between the two guerrilla armies hardened into hostilities between their political parties, as ZANU-PF became convinced that ZAPU was supporting a new dissident war in order to improve its standing in the country. ZAPU, in turn, has expressed its belief that ZANU-PF used the pretext of the disturbances as a long-awaited opportunity to crush ZAPU once and for all.[19] There is no denying the political nature of events as they unfolded in the 1980s, as the Shona-speaking, ZANU-PF-supporting 5 Brigade ruthlessly persecuted the Ndebele-speaking, ZAPU-supporting residents of Matabeleland.

Indeed, one of the tragedies of the 1980s was that events served to harden regional differences along tribal and linguistic lines. While the Unity Agreement has, on the face of it, healed the rift, some would contend that Ndebele-speakers have neither forgotten nor forgiven 5 Brigade. Richard Werbner in his book *Tears of the Dead*,[20] refers to 5 Brigade as being a symptom of the "catastrophe of quasi-nationalism" in Zimbabwe. Werbner states that the polarisation that occurred in Zimbabwe in the 1980s cannot be solely explained as the consequence of mythically hostile tribes invented by colonial settlers in their policy of divide and rule, although the existence of such a history could be seen as a necessary but not sufficient basis for what followed.[21] Rather, quasi-nationalism should be seen as the product of the new Zimbabwean nation-state's struggle to assume power and moral authority. Werbner also argues against events being interpreted as simplistically "ethnic" in nature.

While mainly Ndebele speaking, people in Matabeleland and targeted parts of the Midlands in 1980 were representative of many "tribal" and linguistic backgrounds; what they had in common was that there was widespread support in these regions, both historically and in the 1980 elections, for ZAPU.

> "The catastrophe of quasi-nationalism is that it can capture the might of the nation state and bring authorised violence down ruthlessly against the people who seem to stand in the way of the nation being united and pure as one body... it is as if quasi-nationalism's victims, by being of an opposed quasi-nation, put themselves outside the nation, indeed beyond the pale of humanity."[22]

In Zimbabwe in the 1980s, a certain sector in the nation had been identified as "other": the purging of this other became necessary for the purification of the rest of the nation. It is surely no coincidence that 5 Brigade was also called "Gukurahundi", which means "the rain that washes away the chaff from the last harvest, before the spring rains."[23]

C) SUMMARY

In the 1980s, the ZANU-PF Government came to draw on an array of legislation from before Independence. It also installed personnel from the former Rhodesian intelligence services in key positions, and some of these personnel used their continued influence to further South African interests by destabilising Zimbabwe. One of their most significant achievements was to enhance distrust between ZANU-PF and ZAPU and their respective military wings. Inter-party tension pre-dated Independence, but notions of traditional hostility between the "Shona" and the "Ndebele" played into and were consolidated in the conflict of the 1980s.

2. SOUTH AFRICAN DESTABILISATION POLICY

As countries in southern Africa began to gain their independence from 1975 onwards, white-ruled South Africa began an increasingly coherent policy of destabilising these nations, in order to prolong its own power. Independent nations most notably affected by South African destabilisation in the early 1980s were Angola, Mozambique, Zimbabwe and Lesotho. This policy and some of its ramifications for Africa have been admirably documented in Joseph Hanlon's *Beggar your Neighbours: Apartheid Power in Southern Africa.*[24] As the current Truth and Reconciliation Commission progresses in the now democratic South Africa, further details of these events are coming to light.

A) A TWO-FOLD APPROACH

South African intervention in Zimbabwe in the 1980s was basically two-fold: it consisted of the systematic supply of misinformation to the Government, and also of military attacks on the government and on the country's infrastructure. Many ex-members of the Rhodesian army, police and CIO became integrated into the South African armed forces. Some remained in the country after Independence and actively recruited people for sabotage duties or to act as double agents.[25] Some became trusted Government informers, ideally placed to exacerbate tensions between ZAPU and ZANU-PF by the use of misinformation. ZAPU was often blamed for various events which were in fact, at least partly, the work of South African agents. This created an atmosphere of escalating distrust and dislike between ZANU-PF and ZAPU.

Physical attacks by South Africans in Zimbabwe included the destruction of a huge arsenal at Inkomo Barracks near Harare in August 1981; an attempt to kill Mr Mugabe in December 1981; and the sabotage of the Thornhill Air Base in Gweru in July 1982, which resulted in the destruction of a substantial percentage of Zimbabwe's Air Force aircraft.[26] This last attack was probably coordinated by ex-members of the Rhodesian Special Air Services working for South Africa, although this has never been confirmed.[27] Initially, local white officers (including the Chief of Staff) in the Zimbabwe Air Force were accused of the crime and tortured. They were later acquitted by the High Court of Zimbabwe but were promptly detained once more and only released on condition they immediately left their country.

In addition to these major bombings, there was a steady stream of minor incidents. One of these resulted in the killing of three white members of the South African Defence Force in a remote part of Zimbabwe near the eastern border, in August 1981. They were part of a bigger group of 17, and their deaths were incontrovertible evidence of South Africa's forays into Zimbabwe. Of the three dead, two were former members of the Rhodesian armed forces.[28] They were believed to be on their way to sabotage a railway line from Zimbabwe to Mozambique when they were intercepted and killed.[29]

Major arms caches which were discovered in early 1982, and which caused the final rift between ZANU-PF and ZAPU, were almost certainly engineered by a South African agent, Matt Calloway. Calloway was in fact head of a branch of the Zimbabwean CIO at the time the arms were stockpiled, although he later defected to South Africa. South Africans were also implicated in the timing of the "find", and in the subsequent trial of Dumiso Dabengwa and Lookout Masuku.[30]

The kidnapping of six foreign tourists in July 1982 was also blamed on ZAPU and Joshua Nkomo. Recent confessions by ex-Rhodesian CIO members now indicate that South African agents may have kidnapped and killed these tourists, with the direct aim of fuelling antagonisms between ZANU-PF and ZAPU.[31] According to these South African agents, the operation took three weeks to plan and involved eight ex-members of Rhodesia's notorious Selous Scouts, armed with Kalashnikov rifles. From the time of the tourists' disappearance, the Zimbabwean Government referred to the kidnapping as the work of dissidents.

The final truth in this matter has yet to be established. This latest report and those who make this claim may well prove to be unreliable, but convincing evidence either proving or disproving the claims may come to light in the course of the South African Truth and Reconciliation Commission.[32]

B) OPERATION DRAMA

"Operation Drama" was the South African code name for the undercover support of Zimbabwean dissidents. It was carried out under the direction of Col Moeller and Col Jan Breytenbach.[33]

Operation Drama's primary role was the formation and funding of "Super ZAPU". This was a small band of dissidents, recruited from refugee camps in Botswana and trained in four camps in the former Transvaal province of South Africa. Super ZAPU operated in southern Matabeleland in 1983 and 1984, exacerbating the security situation already in existence.[34] Precise numbers of Super ZAPU and the degree of material support offered by South Africa to Zimbabwean dissidents remain largely conjectural, although it is clear the Zimbabwean operation was far less extensive than those in Angola and Mozambique, which operated concurrently.[35]

Those interviewed about the South African involvement in Zimbabwe all commented that it is noteworthy that far less is known about South Africa's military destabilisation policy in Zimbabwe than about its Mozambique or Angolan operations. The lack of knowledge suggests that fewer personnel were entrusted with information about Operation Drama, which in turn suggests that the Zimbabwean operation was not only smaller, but regarded as more highly sensitive than the others.[36]

C) SUMMARY

South Africa's policy of simultaneously destabilising Zimbabwe by military means, while blaming ZAPU for the actions of South African agents whenever possible, helped escalate the irrevocable breakdown between ZAPU and ZANU-PF in the early 1980s. This in turn led to the decision of Zimbabwe's Government to retain the State of Emergency throughout the 1980s, and more significantly, to impose massive troop numbers and restrictive curfews on Matabeleland.

3. "THE DISSIDENT PROBLEM" – AN OVERVIEW

A) A SUMMARY OF CONTRIBUTING FACTORS

Factors contributing to the growth of dissident numbers are complex. The relative importance of these factors has been variously highlighted in existing accounts of these years, depending in part on the implicit agenda of researchers, and in part on their sources.

Some explanations as to why dissidents became an entity include:

- The view of the Government and ZANU-PF that the dissidents were actively sponsored by ZAPU leaders, who were hoping to gain through renewed fighting what they had failed to gain in the elections.[37]
- ZAPU's view that the heavy-handed Government reaction to the dissident issue, and its targeting of ZAPU as solely responsible, expressed a long-held desire either to punish ZAPU, or crush ZAPU totally and create a one-party state.[38]
- The well-established view that South Africa exacerbated events by training and funding dissidents, known as Super ZAPU, with the intention of disrupting the newly Independent Zimbabwe.[39]
- The dissidents' view that they were driven to desert the National Army by the persecution of ex-ZIPRA members within its ranks, and that once outside the army, they found themselves further persecuted and on the run.[40]

While there is evidence to support the last three views, at least in part, to date there is no documentary or material evidence to support the contention that ZAPU leadership concretely supported or instructed the dissidents, apart from an abundance of Government rhetoric at the time, insisting on links between ZAPU and dissidents. Two lengthy treason trials, one in 1982 and one in 1986, both failed to prove ZAPU–dissident collusion.[41]

The political and military violence of the 1980s resulted in huge losses for the citizens of Zimbabwe, in terms of human life, property and economic development in affected areas. The dissidents themselves became answerable for this in no small measure, and are certainly known to have committed deeds of heinous cruelty against their fellow Zimbabweans during these years. Civilians who lived in the rural areas and came into contact with them describe them as "cruel, uncontrollable, leaderless."[42] Their activities led to the abandonment of around 200 000 hectares of commercial farmland in Matabeleland, the murders of scores of civilians, the destruction of many homesteads, and scores of robberies.[43]

At the same time, the dissidents were few, numbering no more than around 400 at their peak, and experienced large numbers of deaths, captures and desertions. It is also now clear that many dissidents consider themselves to have been driven to lead the lives of fugitives by the partial failure of the Army's integration process, and the persecution of all former ZIPRAs as the conflict escalated.[44]

Whatever the initial causes of the rising numbers of "dissidents", the Government certainly had a serious security problem on its hands by mid-1982. The situation needed a military response but, unfortunately, the Government launched a double-edged conflict in Matabeleland. The first offensive was against the dissidents, and involved the use of various ZNA units and the Police Support Unit. However, the Government also launched an offensive against the ordinary civilians of Matabeleland, through 5 Brigade. This served both to increase dissident numbers and to exacerbate the plight of those most vulnerable to the dissidents. These two conflicts escalated into what has been called, even by Government itself, a civil war. While there is little love for dissidents in the memories of those who lived with them, it must be acknowledged that it is 5 Brigade that people remember with the most intense hatred and fear.[45]

B) THE DISSIDENTS' PERSPECTIVE

One contributing factor to escalating dissident numbers, according to the dissidents themselves, was the ZNA's initial failure successfully to integrate ZANLA and ZIPRA into one army. The task facing the ZNA at Independence was unprecedented: its role was to integrate three armies, all of which had long-standing animosities towards each other, and form one army with a conventional military background.[46]

The animosities between ZIPRA and ZANLA have already been dealt with. Not only did these two antagonistic forces have to integrate with each other at Independence, but they had to be integrated with the existing Rhodesian Defence Forces (RDF), which had fought to preserve white supremacy in Zimbabwe. There were obvious long-standing political and military antagonisms between the RDF and both the guerrilla armies.

From the time of the negotiated ceasefire in Zimbabwe, ex-guerrillas were held in APs throughout the country, from where they were gradually integrated with the RDF, or demobilised. Many ex-guerrillas from both sides resisted entering the APs, fearing the consequences, or rejecting the negotiated outcome to the war. In the APs, after Independence, there were several minor skirmishes between ZANLA and ZIPRA forces in different parts of the country, and also outbreaks of bad behaviour in the vicinity of the APs, as ex-combatants spent long months waiting for integration to take its course.

In February 1980, *The Chronicle* reported approximately 200 guerrillas roaming the north-west, campaigning for ZAPU and committing crimes.[47] In Nkayi and Gokwe, in northern Matabeleland, there was a group of ZIPRAs operating under a man called "Tommy", who had been renowned for refusing to obey the ZIPRA High Command structure in the 1970s. In addition, there was a group of ZIPRAs in Tsholotsho who refused to enter the APs, as they rejected the ceasefire. In May and June 1980, four hundred ZIPRA guerrillas were rounded up in Northern

Matabeleland and taken to Khami Prison near Bulawayo.[48]

ZANLA was considered as much of a problem as ZIPRA, if not a worse one, in these early months.[49] ZANLA was involved in armed attacks in Mutoko, Mount Darwin and Gutu. *Both sides* were involved in the concealing of weapons outside the APs.[50]

i) Trouble at Entumbane

At the end of 1980 only 15 000 out of 65 000 ex-combatants had been integrated into the army, and the decision was made to remove some of the remaining ex-combatants into housing schemes near the major centres.[51] Under a rehousing scheme in Entumbane, a suburb of Bulawayo, ZIPRA and ZANLA found themselves living in close proximity to each other, and also with ZIPRA's civilian supporters.

Coinciding with this development, in November 1980 there was an inflammatory speech by Enos Nkala, a Government minister, in which ZAPU was referred to as the enemy.[52] This contributed to the first Entumbane uprising in November 1980, in which ZIPRA and ZANLA fought a pitched battle for two days before being brought under control by ZIPRA and ZANLA commanders. Five hundred more ZANLA soldiers were moved to Entumbane, and ZAPU officials were arrested.[53]

The fighting between ZIPRA and ZANLA was not restricted to Matabeleland, but led to deaths in holding camps in Mashonaland as well.

In February 1981, a second outburst of fighting started in Entumbane, which spread to Ntabazinduna and Glenville, in the vicinity of Bulawayo, and also to Connemara in the Midlands. ZIPRA troops elsewhere in Matabeleland North and South headed for the city to join the battle, and Prime Minister Mugabe called in former RDF units to quell the uprising, but not before more than 300 people had lost their lives.

ii) The Dumbutshena Report

The Government instituted a Commission of Inquiry into events surrounding Entumbane, conducted by Justice Enock Dumbutshena. However, Mr Mugabe complained about its findings, and the Dumbutshena Report has never been made public.[54]

iii) Army defectors

The Entumbane uprising led to mass defections of ZIPRA members from the APs. Defectors interviewed in the 1990s have stated they saw their decisions to leave the APs as life-preserving, or alternatively as reflections of their disillusionment with their experiences in the APs. Some of this disillusionment was with what was perceived as a political bias in the army towards favouring ZANLA, especially where promotions were concerned. ZIPRA members also commented on the growing number of ZIPRA soldiers who seemed to be disappearing under mysterious circumstances from army ranks, and to a growing paranoia among ZIPRA members who, for example, began to imagine plots to poison them in the army. It was thus disillusionment and fear, rather than any strong political motivation, that led ZIPRA soldiers to defect from the army and hence to a life on the run.[55]

Those who defected took their weapons with them, and armed banditry increased. The "discovery" of large arms caches in Matabeleland in February 1982 had major political repercussions for ZAPU. The ZANU-PF leadership now openly accused ZAPU of planning an armed revolt, to make up for ZAPU's comparatively poor showing in the 1980 General Elections. ZAPU Cabinet ministers Nkomo, Chinamano, Muchachi and Msika were dismissed from the Government, and ZIPRA's former military leaders Dumiso Dabengwa and Lookout Masuku were arrested with four others, and subsequently tried for treason.[56] The High Court later acquitted all the men on the treason charges, and referred to Dabengwa as "the most impressive witness this court has seen in a long time" and "the antithesis of [a person] scheming to overthrow the government."[57] However, Dabengwa, Masuku and the four others were re-arrested and held in detention for many years. The seriously ill Masuku was released into hospital in March 1986, to die in April, and Dabengwa was released in December 1986.

The harsh treatment given to ZAPU leaders in the wake of the finding of the arms caches – at least some of which were later found to have been planted at the instigation of white former members of the CIO working as South African agents[58] – convinced many more ex-ZIPRAs that they could not expect fair treatment if they remained in the APs or in ZNA units. Many – possibly thousands – of ex-combatants deserted at this time: the exact number remains speculative.[59]

The perception among ex-ZIPRA soldiers that they were being increasingly persecuted as 1982 progressed, led to more defections. For example, six dissidents made the decision to leave the ZNA after their company commander announced in Lupane, in the late 1982 search for dissidents, that he would kill "dissidents" – meaning former ZIPRA guerrillas – in the company first.[60] By the end of 1982, there were many hundreds of ex-ZIPRA soldiers who had deserted the ZNA for one reason or another, and the availability of weapons in the bush helped snowball dissident growth. At first, dissident operations were piecemeal, and complicated by the existence of Super ZAPU, although how active Super ZAPU was, in particular in Matabeleland North, is still partly a matter of conjecture.[61] They appear to have used southern Nyamandlovu as a corridor into the country at times, but whether they committed any crimes in that area or further north is not clear.

The Government increasingly used the anti-ZIPRA and anti-ZAPU rhetoric that had become apparent as early as 1980, and there was a change in semantics at this time, so that all armed robberies in Matabeleland became referred to as the work of bandits or dissidents. There were also repeated speeches by Government officials linking ZAPU to dissidents.[62] In addition, from 1982, ex-ZIPRA combatants – and not just deserters – increasingly faced persecution: ex-ZIPRAs who had been formally demobilised and those still in the army were increasingly subjected to arrest and harassment. Detention camps were established at St Paul's in Lupane, at Tsholotsho, at Plumtree airstrip, and at Bhalagwe in Kezi, where the CIO interrogated ex-combatants. Within army battalions, tensions ran high: ZANLA and ZIPRA each suspected the other of concealing arms, and ZIPRA members noticed the escalating arrest and disappearance of cadres from their ranks. The response of ZIPRA ex-combatants and ZAPU officials to this was varied: many fled the country to become refugees in Botswana or Zambia, or to find work in South Africa, and some formed bands of armed dissidents. Some of those who fled to Zambia were assisted by the UNHCR to escape to various European countries, while others were pursued and killed by Zimbabwean Government agents. Those who left frequently lost property left in the country, and many have never returned.[63] According to Alexander:

> "...interviews with ZIPRA guerrillas consistently indicated that their persecution at this time, rather than the political rift, was the key in causing mass desertions. Many felt they had little choice but to flee or take up arms again to save their lives."[64]

The dissidents themselves reveal that the 1980s war was one with no clear goal or direction. In the words of one dissident:

> "...in the 1980s war, no one was recruited, we were forced by the situation, all of us just met in the bush. Each person left on his own, running from death."[65]

Another researcher who interviewed dissidents in the 1990s, recorded comments which confirm the idea that *self preservation* was the strongest motive ex-ZIPRAs had in becoming dissidents:[66]

> "We wanted to defend ourselves personally. Our lives were threatened."

> "Apart from defending ourselves, there was very little we wanted to achieve."

> "We were threatened. That was why I decided to desert."

Those who deserted or demobilised with the simple intention of going home to start their lives again found themselves driven away by the arrival of 5 Brigade:

> "They were hunting ex-ZIPRA members... and if they found [them], they killed those people."

> "If you say that you have been in the army, they would take you."

> "Some of us who demobilised, thought it best to return home because at least you could live in your own house. But little did we know that we were coming to a much worse situation. I did not even have time to spend my demob money before I had to leave to go to this second war... Since you were a demobilised ZIPRA ex-combatant, they would immediately find you guilty and level you [kill you] as a dissident."[67]

In direct contrast to the Government's claims that dissidents were being supported by ZAPU, dissidents express a sense of "abandonment by their leaders, who were often in jail or who actively dissociated themselves from, and condemned, their activities." At the same time, the dissidents "maintained their loyalty to ZAPU and tenaciously clung to their liberation war identity as ZIPRA guerrillas."[68] This loyalty expressed itself in the attempts of the dissidents to echo ZIPRA command structures and ethics, even though they lacked high level political or military leaders and were few in number.

iv) Operational zones

In late 1983, the dissidents divided Matabeleland and parts of the Midlands into three operational regions, in accordance with ZIPRA principles. The existence of Super ZAPU was a factor which encouraged the other dissidents to organise themselves along the lines of ZIPRA command structures, in order to help undermine and separate Super ZAPU from themselves.[69] The regions were as follows:

1. The Western Region, mainly Tsholotsho and Bulilimamangwe, which ran from the Victoria Falls railway line to the Plumtree railway line, and was under the command of a dissident called Tulane.
2. The Northern Region, mainly Kwekwe, Lupane and Nkayi, which ran from the Victoria Falls–Bulawayo railway line east to Silobela, and was under the command of three successive dissidents, first Gilbert Sitshela, then-Mdawini, then Masikisela.
3. Matobo, Insiza, Gwanda and Beitbridge formed the Southern Region, from the Plumtree railway line east to Mberengwa. One dissident interviewed commented that a Matobo unit was allowed to make contact with this southern structure only in 1986, because of fears of Super ZAPU. This region was under the command of a man called "Brown" in 1987.

Each region had a commander and a few platoons of 15 to 30 men, with sections of about five men each.

The dissidents faced operational problems: shortage of ammunition was a major concern, and this in turn led to a defensive strategy, with most dissident activities being restricted to night-time attacks or forays into villages for food, followed by hurried retreats and then lying low during hours of daylight to avoid being detected by troops. "What is five bullets against an army?" commented one dissident.[70]

The dissidents' commitment to seeing themselves as ZIPRA throughout this time, in spite of the absence of direct instruction from ZAPU, was instrumental not only in the swift demise of Super ZAPU, but also in the quick and orderly surrender after the Amnesty, when the dissidents obeyed the call of senior ZAPU officials that they should lay down their arms.[71]

C) SUPER ZAPU

Super ZAPU was the group of South African-backed dissidents, which operated in southern Matabeleland from late 1982 until mid-1984. Super ZAPU consisted of probably fewer than 100 members who were actually actively deployed in Zimbabwe. They were largely recruited from refugee camps and led by ex-ZIPRA members, who had been retrained in South Africa, in the covert operation known as Operation Drama.[72] A Zimbabwean Government briefing paper on the situation in 1983 conceded "the recent efforts of the Fifth Brigade in Matabeleland have offered the South Africans another highly motivated dissident movement on a plate."[73] Some sources claim that it was once again Matt Calloway, an ex-member of the Rhodesian CIO who acted as a double agent for the South Africans, who was a key player in the campaign to recruit from Dukwe Refugee camp in Botswana.[74]

While they operated, South Africa provided ammunition for Super ZAPU, and some of this found its way to other dissident groups in the country: arms and ammunition used by dissidents frequently indicated South Africa as the source of origin, particularly during 1983.[75] Some think Super ZAPU were also directly responsible for the deaths of white farmers in southern Matabeleland, during their time of operation.[76]

However, other dissident groups treated them with suspicion because of their South African link. "We said we don't want to be UNITA", was the comment of one ex-dissident, who saw a connection between Super ZAPU and South Africa's involvement in the civil war in Angola. Loyalty to ZAPU ideals by local dissidents contributed to the fact that Super ZAPU was comparatively short-lived.[77] By mid-1984 Super ZAPU was collapsing, partly as a result of clashes with other dissident groups, and also because of official military response and complaints to South Africa from the Zimbabwean Government.[78]

Apart from its role as a destabilising force, Super ZAPU probably also played a minor anti-ANC role.[79] Since the 1960s the ANC had used Matabeleland as one entry point to South Africa, and placing Super ZAPU in Matabeleland would have helped provide a buffer zone against their infiltration.

While some sources contend that Super ZAPU had a brief revival in 1985, evidence in support of this is not well substantiated.[80]

D) OTHER "DISSIDENT" GROUPS

The ex-ZIPRA dissidents could be characterised as being motivated, in 1980, by political resentment, and by 1982, mostly by the desire to escape persecution.[81]

Super ZAPU were those who sought to destabilise the country at South Africa's behest.

There were also dissidents who were not ex-ZIPRA, although they might have had similar motives. Those fleeing persecution included not only ex-ZIPRA soldiers, but other 5 Brigade target groups such as ex-refugees and ZAPU youth. Most of these became refugees in Botswana, but some joined groups of dissidents.

A few others who became dissidents were motivated by revenge, especially in the wake of the "Gukurahundi", or 5 Brigade massacres.

Some were criminals capitalising on the situation, to rob and plunder.[82] These dissidents were not necessarily ex-ZIPRA members, and it is possible that some of these did not surrender at the Amnesty.

There was a final group of what has been referred to as "pseudo dissidents", including the gang led by Gayigusu in Matabeleland South, which was responsible for the murder of 16 missionaries in November 1987. This gang was allegedly the personal "hit squad" of politically powerful ZANU-PF officials in this part of the country.[83]

They were summoned by local squatters engaged in a land dispute with the missionaries who were trying to evict them. Sixteen men, women and children were axed to death.

It is difficult to estimate numbers of those who could perhaps more correctly be described as criminals rather than dissidents, particularly as it seemed to suit Government statistics to attribute every armed robbery in Matabeleland during the 1980s to dissidents, while such events were attributed to criminals when they occurred elsewhere in the country. (See comments on *The Chronicle* in section on Data Sources.)

However, after the Amnesty in March 1988, the official position was reversed: the Government no longer wished to view certain crimes which had at the time been called "dissident", as the work of dissidents. The trial of a man who allegedly murdered two German tourists in 1987 is an example of this policy reversal. While the crime was referred to as the work of dissidents at the time, and the accused considered himself to be a dissident, and therefore exempt from sentencing under the terms of the Amnesty, the State urged that he be viewed and sentenced as an ordinary criminal. He was in fact found guilty of criminal rather than dissident activity and sentenced to death accordingly. This was a heinous crime, but there was no evidence of theft. The ambush was clearly an act of terror, and others who had committed similar crimes went free, such as Gayigusu who headed a gang responsible for murdering 16 missionaries in November 1987. This case serves merely to illustrate the way in which officialdom would use or abandon the label dissident, depending on what suited their purposes at the time.[84]

E) DISSIDENT NUMBERS

The numbers of dissidents were probably no more than 400 at their zenith.

Their attrition rate was very high, with approximately 75 per cent being killed, captured, injured or fleeing to Botswana. At their peak, dissident numbers in Matabeleland South were about 200, but by the Amnesty they were reduced to 54. In Matabeleland North, dissidents numbered about 90 at most, but again, by the Amnesty, only 41 remained. In western Matabeleland, dissidents numbered 90 at their peak, and about 27 at the Amnesty. Ultimately, only 122 dissidents would turn themselves in, country-wide.[85] It is possible that a handful of people who were more correctly criminals than dissidents, and who had committed similar crimes, did not surrender at this time.

F) POPULAR SUPPORT

Dissidents frequently point out that, in direct contrast to the war for liberation, they had very little popular support in the 1980s. This they attribute to the comparative strength of the forces against them, and the dissidents' inability to protect civilians who fed them from being persecuted in turn: "quite the opposite: their activities drew Government crackdowns in which civilians suffered greatly."[86]

In addition, while civilians had been prepared to suffer to protect the armed comrades when liberation was the clear goal, there was no perceivable long or short term benefit for civilians in helping dissidents in the 1980s. In 1981, dissidents were sometimes greeted with sympathy, when they told how they had been persecuted in the army.

> "However, sympathy deteriorated rapidly, partly because of ZAPU policy regarding dissidents, partly because of the disrespect and violence with which dissidents treated local people, and partly because some blamed the dissidents for the heavy costs to civilians of the government repression which followed."[87]

While the dissidents themselves did not fear 5 Brigade much, considering it to be an inefficient fighting unit dedicated to killing civilians,[88] the local population feared the Brigade greatly. Locals therefore gave help only with reluctance, or at the point of a gun. The dissidents were particularly resented for their insistence that villagers kill chickens, a luxury food, to provide them with relish; they also raped young women. When help was given, the dissidents did not perceive this help as politically motivated: "They gave us support knowing our lives were at stake".[89]

Interviews in the case study areas make it clear that civilians saw themselves as once more "caught in the middle", as they had been in the

1970s liberation war. On the one hand, if they supported dissidents, they were likely to be punished, detained or killed by 5 Brigade or other army units, but if they refused this support, or if they reported dissidents, they were likely to be punished or killed by the dissidents. This phenomenon is marked in the resettled villages of Nyamandlovu. (See Village by Village Summary, under Eastern Nyamandlovu). Here dissidents burnt out two resettled villages. 5 Brigade saw the smoke, and drove over. The dissidents escaped, but villagers were left to face interrogation by 5 Brigade, resulting in the only death in this incident. There are on record from Tsholotsho interviews which report people being beaten or killed by 5 Brigade for going to 5 Brigade camps to report the presence of dissidents in their area.[90]

In Matobo too, especially in Khumalo Communal Lands, civilians reported how they often found themselves trapped between dissidents who demanded food and returned on subsequent occasions making ever more violent threats about what would happen to any villagers who reported their presence. Several families fled the area for Bulawayo or Botswana, rather than face the continual dilemma of what to do about the dissidents.

G) DISSIDENT ACTIVITIES

It is very difficult at this stage to quantify clearly the full extent of the damage caused by dissidents, because of the biased nature of press reporting at the time, and the fact that Government agencies such as 5 Brigade and the CIO were committing human rights violations concurrently, sometimes in the guise of the dissidents.[91]

It is, however, generally accepted by all parties that dissidents were responsible for all the murders of white farmers and their families in the 1980s. Between late 1982 and the end of 1983, 33 farmers or their family members were murdered. While the impact of dissidents on civilians in the communal lands was perceived as less harsh by far than that of 5 Brigade, the impact of the dissidents on the small commercial farming communities was dramatic. For example, in Nyamandlovu, which lies in the first case study area, ZIPRA had been responsible for killing only one white farming couple in Nyamandlovu during the 1970s, but in the 1980s, dissidents killed 21 people in this commercial farming area, inclusive of farmers, their families and at times their staff. Many farmers sold their ranches, or moved their families into nearby Bulawayo for protection, leaving productive farmland idle.

Nyamandlovu farmers themselves say they believe their farms provided a convenient corridor for dissidents wishing to get from parts of Zimbabwe further east or north, back to Tsholotsho or Botswana in the west. Farms here are huge, frequently 5 000 hectares or more, and being mainly ranches, are not labour intensive. It would therefore have been easy for dissidents to travel through the remote parts of the ranches without being detected. Farmers believe dissidents did travel to and fro, keeping a low profile in between their ambushes.[92]

Dissidents themselves talk of using the commercial farms as "hospitals" for their injured. However, the problem in staying for any length of time on these farms was lack of access to food and water.[93] Dissidents were also responsible for severely disrupting normal activities in Matobo commercial farming areas, where eight deaths were reported by *The Chronicle* as having occurred on commercial farms in this district. In addition, farming equipment was frequently burnt out, and livestock killed. In June 1982, a cattle sale was raided by dissidents, who stole $40 000. There were also other murders of commercial farmers, apart from those in the two case study areas – see Tables in Part Two, III for more detail. Super ZAPU, particularly in the southern and south-western part of Matabeleland, committed some of the murders. These murders involved the deaths of men, women and children.[94]

It seems likely that most of the multiple murders and ambushes were committed by a few bands of dissidents, while the rest of the dissidents confined their activity to petty crimes. For example, on 5 October 1983, *The Chronicle* reports the arrest of a gang of five dissidents, part of a larger gang which is linked to the murders of 28 commercial farmers and their families: these murders occurred in Gwanda, Bubi and Nyamandlovu, and included the murder of Senator Paul Savage. This latter murder was attributed by Martin and Johnson[95] to Super ZAPU on ballistic evidence. Minister Simbi Mubako is also quoted in the news report as having said it is "extremely difficult" in some cases to determine which people had died at the hands of dissidents and which had been killed by out-and-out criminals.

Apart from the murders on commercial farms, dissidents also murdered civilians in the communal areas, although they did not appear to do so as a matter of course.[96] Those murdered were often villagers regarded as sell-outs, who were believed to have informed the security forces of dissident movements. The dissidents also targeted ZANU-PF officials, in a retaliatory gesture for the large numbers of ZAPU officials being arrested or murdered by Government agencies during these years, and also as a protest against the ZANU-PF role in repressing civilians in Matabeleland North.

Exactly how many people were murdered by dissidents in the rural

Historical overview

areas will remain speculation. Government figures would place the murdered in the region of about 700 to 800.[97] But in areas where fairly exhaustive research has now taken place, these high casualty claims are not borne out. In Tsholotsho, for example, fewer than 20 murders of civilians are blamed on dissidents by residents, and in Lupane, around 25 murders are attributed to them, although this figure includes some murders in which witnesses believed the true identity of the perpetrators to be Government agents in disguise as dissidents. There was a further handful of dissident murders in Nkayi.[98] Yet Matabeleland North was allegedly a hotbed of dissident activity.

In Matobo, the second case study area, *The Chronicle* specifically reports the murders of 30 people in the district: this figure includes the 16 missionaries murdered, and several commercial farmers and their families, well over half this total figure. Civilians in the Communal Lands interviewed in 1996 attributed 11 murders to dissidents, between 1982 and 1987. Most of these were in Khumalo Communal Lands, a mountainous region where dissidents could readily conceal themselves from pursuing troops. In this area certain notorious dissidents were well known to villagers and greatly feared and hated. These included the "pseudo-dissident" Gayigusu, and also "Fidel Castro", "Danger" and "Idi Amin".[99] All these dissidents are referred to by name in *The Chronicle* at different times.

While murders of civilians in rural areas were not common, those that occurred were often exceedingly sadistic, as the following testimony shows.

CASE 2611 ABy, 2612 X
DISTRICT: Nkayi
PERPETRATOR: Dissidents
TIME: November 1985
WITNESS: Wife of murder victim
VICTIMS: 47-year-old farmer, married with eight
                   children – murdered;
                   wife – wounded with an axe and beaten

OUTLINE OF EVENTS: At about 5pm, eight dissidents came to our home, asking for my husband. I told them he was ploughing in the fields, and they said they would wait for him. When he came, they took us to a neighbour's and made us enter a hut. They accused him of being a sell-out, and of having reported the dissidents at the police camp. Then they beat him on the head.

63

> When he collapsed, they told me, his wife, to kill him with
> an axe. I refused, so they hit me on the head with the axe. When
> I regained consciousness, I was covered with blood. They had
> chopped my husband on his legs and back with the axe. They
> made me kill him. They made me chop him in the neck with the
> axe. They chopped his head right off. They put his severed head
> in a plastic bag and told me to take it to the nearest hospital the
> following day. The dissidents eventually left at 2am, and the next
> day I took my husband's head, in the bag, to the hospital as they
> had told me to do.

Apart from committing murder, the dissidents also destroyed property. In particular, they burnt out several resettled villages, where people had been moved by the Zimbabwe Government. They also destroyed dams, Government equipment, and Government-sponsored co-operative ventures.[100] It is this phenomenon which has led some to argue that the dissidents had a clear land policy, and were displaying a political awareness of the need for land redistribution. However, dissidents themselves deny that these actions were in keeping with an organised policy. They claim they murdered those white farmers they perceived as hostile, without a clear redistribution policy. They do claim their destruction of resettlement and other Government projects was a form of economic sabotage – "where Government put money we destroyed that thing."[101]

To the extent that the dissidents wished to undermine any Government-funded project, their targets and actions can be described as political. The dissidents themselves did not stress land or resettlement as issues. Particularly in Lupane and Nkayi, the dissidents usually operated in regions which were some distance from commercial farmland. One of their reasons for hostility towards resettlement schemes was the fear that they were being used to harbour people who were sell outs in the dissidents' eyes, and who would inform on them to the authorities.[102]

The dissidents also committed armed robberies of stores in rural areas. However, many of the robberies listed in *The Chronicle* are petty thefts, involving, for example, six dollars' worth of cigarettes, or two tins of jam, or a wrist watch. Such robberies have been counted in to the total numbers of specified robberies in the tables of dissident offences in Part Two, III.

H) SUMMARY

The dissidents portray themselves as a small but organised force on the run from the authorities, who attempted to remain loyal to their ZIPRA ideals, even though they were ultimately leaderless. They had no coherent policy or aims, apart from sabotaging targets they saw as hostile or threatening, and staying ahead of the authorities in order to survive.

Dissidents were not a homogeneous group. In addition to ex-ZIPRA members, there were young men with no previous military training who were on the run from 5 Brigade, the South African-backed Super ZAPU dissidents, and also common criminals capitalising on the situation to commit armed robberies and other crimes. The dissidents knew they had little popular support, and knew their actions, which included coercing food and raping young girls, were unlikely to build any. The dissidents claim persecution as ex-ZIPRAs as their primary motive for taking up arms again, rather than any political agenda: in fact, they felt they had been abandoned by their ZAPU leadership, who were themselves under political siege or in exile at the time.

The dissidents' loyalty to ZIPRA ideals was instrumental in Super ZAPU's ultimate failure to become well-established in Zimbabwe, and also explains the orderly surrender when the Amnesty was finally announced in 1988.

The Government view of the dissidents during the 1980s differed substantially from the one offered above. In particular, the official Government view was that the dissidents had a large popular support base, and this was responsible for the decision to send 5 Brigade into Matabeleland to intimidate civilians out of offering dissident support. Certainly 5 Brigade themselves offered the explanation that all "Ndebeles" supported/parented/were dissidents, as justification for their actions.[103]

The Government line was also that ZAPU was directly instructing the dissidents, and this was used to justify the persecution, detention and disappearance of thousands of ZAPU officials and supporters. There is no substantive evidence that ZAPU was in fact directing dissident activities.[104]

4. GOVERNMENT ACTION: 1980 – 1982

In the first months after the ceasefire, the Government did not hold the ZAPU leadership responsible for the outbreaks of violence in Zimbabwe. For example, on 27 June 1980, Prime Minister Mugabe condemned "organised bands of ZIPRA followers" for "openly flouting

[Government] rule", but absolved ZAPU leadership of blame.[105] At this time, ZANLA forces were also causing disruption within the vicinity of their APs. ZAPU leaders also repeatedly condemned disruptive activity, and supported Government efforts to curb it.[106] Even as late as May 1981, after the violence at Entumbane, Mr Mugabe again claimed unity was working at the level of Government ministers, despite the troubles in the country.[107]

A) THE ARMS CACHES

However, in the ensuing months, there was a gradual increase in government statements aimed against ZAPU and its followers.[108] This seemed to reach a point of no return, in February 1982, when Prime Minister Mugabe revealed the discovery of huge arms caches on ZAPU-owned farms. The arms caches were seen by him as clear evidence of a long-standing plot on the part of ZAPU's leadership to instigate a military coup. On their exposure, he announced: "These people were planning to overthrow and take over the government."[109]

Minister Nkomo responded that many caches of arms had been found all over the country since Independence, and that until these recent finds, "No-one shouted 'This is ZIPRA, this is ZANLA'."[110] In addition to the many ZIPRA and ZANLA caches countrywide, there were also some caches that belonged to the South African liberation movement, the ANC. The ANC had had historical ties with ZIPRA since the 1960s and had used Matabeleland as one corridor of entry to South Africa for some years. They had cached arms with the knowledge of ZIPRA in Matabeleland.

One of ZIPRA's high commanders, Dumiso Dabengwa, also denied a plot, saying the caches had to be seen against the background of distrust that followed Entumbane, and the belief by many ZIPRA members that they might face attack from ZANLA forces. He had also advised the Government against disarming troops after Entumbane, warning it would lead to nervous guerrillas on both sides concealing arms.[111] In addition, as discussed above, there was later evidence implicating a white CIO officer from the Smith regime, called Calloway: he had been instrumental in organising the large arms caches exposed in February 1982, and deliberately misled the Government into believing ZAPU was engineering a coup.[112]

Dumiso Dabengwa was part of an ad-hoc committee consisting of himself, Mugabe, Nkomo and Mnangagwa, who met in early 1982 to discuss how best to handle *the known existence* of these arms caches.[113] Before the committee had resolved on a course of action, the news of the caches was broken in a sensational article in *The Sunday Mail,* in the first week in February. It was apparent that ZANU-PF had decided to use the arms caches as the "point of no return" in the growing crisis between the two parties. Following the find, ZAPU leaders, including Nkomo and Dabengwa, were demoted or removed from the Cabinet or arrested and tried for high treason and hundreds, if not thousands, of ZIPRA soldiers defected back to the bush.

B) BANDITRY RISES

Whatever the combined causes of these defections, the result was a marked increase in armed banditry, now confined for the first time almost exclusively to the western area of the country, ZIPRA's traditional home ground. According to the day by day reports in *The Chronicle,* Bulawayo's newspaper, June to December 1982 had a comparatively high number of specified dissident offences, totalling 278, of which 49 were murders.[114]

There were also further statements made by various Government ministers during 1982, directly accusing ZAPU leadership of having subversive intentions, and saying that the dissidents were "centrally motivated" by ZAPU leaders.[115]

Dissident activity seemed to reach a peak mid-year, culminating in the kidnap and murder of six foreign tourists, an event which received much international publicity.[116] Dissident offences tailed off dramatically by year end, according to *The Chronicle's* day by day accounts.[117] The Government itself acknowledged the problem was more under control. In October 1982, Minister of Defence Sydney Sekeramayi made a statement to this effect, simultaneously revealing the Government's attitude to ZIPRA soldiers – "the National Army's purge of dissident sympathisers and disloyal elements within its ranks has dissidents on the run."[118]

However, December ended on a depressing note, with four major incidents involving dissidents. These included the murders of several commercial farmers and their families, the destruction of Government equipment in Tsholotsho, and an ambush on the Gweru–Bulawayo road, which left several dead and injured. At around this time, the South African-trained Super ZAPU had become an effective force, and some of these December atrocities were in fact committed by Super ZAPU.[119] Their actions, together with those of other groups of dissidents, were threatening the lives and security of innocent Zimbabweans.[120]

C) GOVERNMENT RESPONSE

As Government leaders rightly claimed throughout the civil disturbances, it was their responsibility to keep the country governable and safe for its ordinary citizens.

However, after the discovery of the arms caches and the increase in violence in Matabeleland, the Government instituted what was perceived by ordinary people to be a draconian combination of legislative powers, restrictive curfews, widespread detention and searches, and dramatic increases in the number of troops in affected areas.

The State of Emergency remained in place throughout these years, granting the Government extra-legal powers, such as the power to detain people without trial. There were curfews imposed in different areas at different times, to try to control the movements of dissidents. In March 1982, for example, a dusk to dawn curfew was imposed on the main road through Matabeleland South, after an upsurge of dissident activity in that part of the country.

Two months later, in June 1982, an armed attack on the prime minister's Harare residence prompted a security clampdown in Bulawayo, and some detentions, as a ZIPRA link was established. Road blocks and extensive searches began in Bulawayo's high density western suburbs, and there was a skyshout[121] over the city, advising people to surrender any weapons they might have. Some weapons were laid out on the sides of roads as a result of this appeal.

On 6 July 1982, a formal curfew was imposed on Bulawayo, restricting all movement between the hours of 9pm and 4am. People caught more than 50m from their houses during these hours risked being shot on sight. People had to pass through road blocks in order to move around the city, and anyone without an identity card was liable to be detained. The stated aim of Operation Octopus was to locate and seize weapons. Houses and people were searched, and road blocks were maintained for some days. The Government claimed to have seized many weapons, and detained people, as a result of this curfew, although no numbers were given.[122] The curfew remained in force until October 1982.

This clampdown in Bulawayo was accompanied by further security measures in Matabeleland. On 22 July 1982, the day before the tourists were kidnapped, the Matabeleland North Chairman of ZANU-PF, Dr Herbert Ushewokunze, announced at a Police Passing Out parade that 2 000 extra Police Support Unit (SU) members would be deployed shortly in Matabeleland to curb banditry. Deputy Minister of Home Affairs Mudzingwa confirmed that 400 SU troops were to be deployed in August, and another 400 in September.[123]

A medical specialist who was working at Mpilo hospital in Bulawayo in 1982 saw evidence of increased military activity among his patients.[124]

He treated several gunshot wound patients after mid-1982, usually members of the ZNA injured in crossfire with dissidents, and also some wounded "dissidents", who were kept under armed guard in the wards. The repression at this time extended to the hospital staff itself: the Ndebele-speaking hospital administrator was detained on a trumped-up charge of stolen property and held in jail for eight weeks. When a lapse in police security led to the escape of a wounded "dissident", all the nurses on ward duty at the time were detained. One nurse became ill with enteritis while in detention, and was sent back to Mpilo as a patient: she had one ankle handcuffed to the bed. In 1983, Mpilo staff were again intimidated: the entire nursing staff were detained one morning, and were taken away to Stops Police Camp for interrogation in two buses, leaving the hospital almost unstaffed. They were released later in the day. In 1983, after he had presented medical records of civilians injured by soldiers to the Prime Minister, the specialist himself was asked to resign by the Minister of Health, Mr Munyaradzi. The specialist submitted his resignation, but it was subsequently ignored.

D) THE ABDUCTION OF THE TOURISTS

On 23 July 1982, dissidents made international headlines by the kidnapping of six foreign tourists in the Nyamandlovu area. They were from Australia, Canada and Britain, and a huge international outcry ensued, as the ZNA and CIO tried to find the missing tourists. Their safari vehicle was ambushed at the 76km peg on the main road between Victoria Falls and Bulawayo.

As soon as the tourists were kidnapped, a special force under the command of Lt Col Lionel Dyke was immediately deployed to trace the tourists, further increasing the concentration of troops in the area. A curfew was imposed first on Tsholotsho and then Lupane, in Matabeleland North. This banned buses, private vehicles and reporters from these areas. There was a concerted wave of arrests, of ZIPRAs both within and without the ZNA. Youths were rounded up from schools and homes and also interrogated, often ruthlessly, as were ZAPU officials. Although the abduction was in Nyamandlovu, it was in an area which is closer to Lupane Communal Areas than it is to Tsholotsho Communal Areas.[125] Lupane was therefore targeted in the massive troop mobilisation that occurred, and a detention centre was established at St Paul's in Lupane. An interrogation centre was also set up at Tsholotsho, where there were allegedly as many as 700 people being held at one time.[126]

Arrests occurred elsewhere in Matabeleland North as well. In October 1982 alone, 77 demobilised ZIPRA soldiers were arrested in Bulawayo while trying to collect their pay. Many civilians with no ZIPRA connection were also detained at this time: *The Chronicle* also reports that 452 "dissidents" were detained at this time in Bulawayo.[127] The search for the tourists continued for the remainder of 1982 and subsequently, with much media coverage.

There were statements from ZAPU leader Joshua Nkomo throughout this year, appealing to the dissidents – "Whoever you are, stop it and stop it now."[128] However, antagonism between the two parties hardened: such appeals were treated as mere showmanship, as the belief that "ZAPU is responsible for this banditry and this is clear", took an unshakeable hold in Mashonaland.[129] There were statements from various ZANU-PF ministers during 1982, advising people in Matabeleland to cease supporting dissidents before "the wrath of the 5 Brigade"[130] was unleashed on them.

In addition, the Government accused civilians in rural Matabeleland North of being uncooperative and in league with the dissidents, as the CIO failed to find concrete leads on the tourists' whereabouts. For example, there was much media coverage given to a dissident found by the ZNA enjoying a friendly meal with local villagers in Matabeleland North.[131] The official view that everyone in Matabeleland North supported ZAPU, and that ZAPU supported dissidents and that therefore everyone in Matabeleland North supported dissidents, took firm root in the media at this time.[132]

The bodies of the tourists were discovered several years later, in March 1985, not far from the point of abduction.[133] They had been murdered within days of their disappearance. Very few civilians in Lupane, or elsewhere, could in fact have come into contact with the tourists.

Two ex-ZIPRA men, Ngwenya and Mpofu, were later tried and found guilty of having been part of the group of five which abducted and then murdered the tourists. In 1986 the two were hanged for the crime. However, legal experts observed at the time of the trial that Ngwenya was an unreliable witness, changing his story several times.[134]

In January 1984 a man called Jeffrey Siwela, who was alleged to be part of the abduction group, was shot dead "while escaping from custody" in Inyathi.[135] The number of dissidents involved in the abduction was variously reported over the years, as five, then eight, and then in January 1986, the gang had grown to 22. Press reports claimed that 18 of the 22 had by January 1986, been "killed in shoot-outs with the security forces", while two others (Ngwenya and Mpofu) had been hanged for the crime, and two more were still at large.[136] On 23 June 1987, a ninety-year-old man was charged with having fed the tourists on the day of their abduction, but two days later he denied his confession, saying he made it when being tortured.[137]

In October 1996, a new version on the abduction of the six tourists was publicised in Zimbabwe. According to former Rhodesian secret service operatives who also served in the ZANU-PF government after Independence, and who now live in South Africa, the tourists were abducted by ex-Selous Scouts who had been detailed to perform the task by a South African covert operation group.[138] The truth or falsity of this latest claim has yet to be established.

E) INDEMNITY REGULATIONS

After the kidnapping of the tourists in July, the Government enacted the Emergency Powers (Security Forces Indemnity) Regulations, similar to the indemnity law that had been passed by the Smith Government in 1975. This granted freedom from prosecution to Government officials and the security forces, as long as the action they had taken was "for the purposes of or in connexion with the preservation of the security of Zimbabwe."

The CCJP quickly condemned the move, as they had done on 6 September 1975 when Smith initiated the original law. They stated their belief that "such an act is designed to protect violent men and history has shown that no matter how well intentioned the government is, these regulations can and will be abused."[139] They also reminded the Government that South Africa was the only other country to have such regulations *indemnifying future unlawful acts,* and quoted Sir Robert Tredgold's statement made in 1975, saying that such a Bill "strikes at the very root of democracy."

F) DISSIDENTS OR ORDINARY CIVILIANS?

> *"Where men and women provide food for dissidents, when we get there we eradicate them. We don't differentiate when we fight, because we can't tell who is a dissident and who is not…"*
> Prime Minister Mugabe, April 1983[140]

The Government expressed increasing frustration over its perception of the lack of co-operation its forces were receiving from locals in Tsholotsho and Lupane in their attempts to find the tourists. This was the beginning of an ever-increasing tendency on the part of the authorities to blur the distinction between "dissidents" and alleged "supporters of dissidents". This reached a peak in 1983 and 1984, during 5 Brigade activities in Matabeleland.[141]

One example of the blurring of the difference between civilians and dissidents was the statement made in February 1983 by Member of Parliament, Enos Nkala, at a rally of civilians in Matabeleland South: he told them that if they continued supporting dissidents and ZAPU, "you shall die or be sent to prison".[142] This statement also implied that to support ZAPU was automatically to support dissidents, a view that had been advocated increasingly by several Government ministers.

There was a marked lack of Government sympathy for the plight of civilians, often ordered at gunpoint to feed dissidents. As discussed above, there was very little genuine support for the dissidents in the rural areas: it was the ordinary civilians who suffered at their hands, and who also knew that dissident tracks leading into a village could well bring the army, meaning further beatings and abuse. Villagers who reported dissidents also knew they stood a good chance of being killed by the next group of dissidents to pass through – most murders by dissidents were reprisals on perceived "sell-outs."[143] The situation of ordinary civilians was an impossible one during these years: whatever they did, they were likely to be wrong in somebody's eyes.

While the difficulty of distinguishing a dissident from an ordinary civilian was very real, and while there were civilians feeding and hiding dissidents, people subjected to detention or torture during these years were seldom brought to trial, suggesting most were innocent.[144] The basic human right to be assumed innocent until proven guilty was increasingly ignored by Zimbabwe's various Government agencies, who were now guaranteed freedom from prosecution themselves.

There was a growing number of complaints about the open abuse of civilians, including those who were obviously innocent. One example cited in Parliament by a ZAPU MP described a pregnant woman who was stopped by a member of the security forces and accused in Shona of having a gun in her stomach. When she said she did not understand, she was pushed to the ground and kicked.[145]

When Joshua Nkomo alleged in Parliament in February 1983 that 5 Brigade was murdering civilians, Sekeramayi acknowledged, in his response, that innocent people could well be suffering, and also that this was acceptable: "Can Nkomo identify a dissident, a dissident supporter and an innocent civilian?"[146]

On 5 November 1982, representatives of the CCJP met the prime minister and expressed concern at "the activities of some elements of the National Army." The Catholic Commission gave the prime minister a report they had compiled, documenting some of these activities. CCJP also condemned the dissidents, referring to them as "those unlawful elements who are wantonly causing hardship and distress even in those areas which are already hard hit by drought."[147]

Then in January 1983, the Government strategy to crush the "dissidents" finally culminated in the deployment of 5 Brigade. Since August 1981, Korean instructors had been training a special brigade, aimed specifically at curbing dissidents. With the deployment of 5 Brigade, the trend of failing to distinguish the possibly innocent from the possibly guilty was broadened from a presumption of guilt against ZAPU to a presumption of guilt against all Ndebele speakers.[148]

5. 5 BRIGADE MOBILISATION – "GUKURAHUNDI"

"The knowledge you have acquired will make you work with the people, plough and reconstruct. These are the aims you should keep in yourself."
Prime Minister Mugabe, December 1982, at the Passing Out Parade of the Gukurahundi Brigade[149]

A) THE COMMISSIONING OF 5 BRIGADE

The first indication of the intention to form a specifically anti-dissident force was on 12 August 1980. Prime Minister Mugabe stated on this day, in his Heroes' Day Speech, that former guerrillas would form a militia to be trained to combat "malcontents", who were "unleashing a reign of terror."[150] Subsequently, in October of 1980, an agreement was signed between Prime Minister Mugabe and President Kim Il Sung, in which North Korea offered to train and arm a brigade for the newly independent Zimbabwe.[151]

The first news of this agreement in the Zimbabwean media was almost a year later, in August 1981, when 106 Korean instructors arrived to begin training the brigade. Prime Minister Mugabe announced that the Korean-trained brigade was to be known as 5 Brigade.[152]

This brigade was "purely for the purpose of defence and not for any use outside this country", said Prime Minister Mugabe. It would be used solely "to deal with dissidents and any other trouble in the country." A day later, at a rally in Nyanga, he warned dissidents that the new force would crush them.[153]

ZAPU opposition party leader Joshua Nkomo immediately questioned the need for the formation of 5 Brigade, saying that Zimbabwe already had in place several "efficient forces of law, including the civil police, to handle any internal problems", and expressed fear that 5 Brigade "is for the possible imposition of a one-party state in our country." He stated that 5 Brigade "is obviously a separate army, since it has different instructors from those we publicly know."[154]

Prime Minister Mugabe responded to this concern by saying that those who planned to be dissidents should "watch out." He further announced that his crack squad would be called "Gukurahundi", which is a Shona expression meaning *the rain which washes away the chaff before the spring rains*.[155] This led to a retort from Minister Nkomo that the whole of the National Army was Zimbabwe's Gukurahundi, and that there was therefore no need for 5 Brigade.[156]

B) THE TRAINING OF 5 BRIGADE – 1981-82

The training of 5 Brigade began in the last few months of 1981 and continued until 9 September 1982, when it was announced by Minister Sekeramayi that the setting up of 5 Brigade was complete.[157] Training took place on the banks of the Nyangombe River in Nyanga.

The 5 Brigade soldiers themselves made it clear once they were deployed that they should be regarded as above the law, and those from the Zimbabwe Republic Police or other army units who queried their actions were frequently told – whether rightly or wrongly – that 5 Brigade was answerable to "nobody but Mugabe."[158] It is clear that 5 Brigade was not an integrated part of the Zimbabwean National Army, but was an extraneous unit that was not answerable to the normal ZNA Command structure. Nor did 5 Brigade itself possess any disciplinary mechanisms for its members when they first took to the field:

> "The instructors never invisaged [sic] any major indiscipline
> that would need policing, but in the long run they saw fit to
> introduce a disciplinary machine to curb indiscipline."[159]

In the Zimbabwe Defence Force Magazine (1992, Vol 7, no 1, page 33 ff), there is a long article entitled *"Gukurahundi" – Ten Years Later*, which outlines some of the ways in which 5 Brigade's training and equipment differed from that of other ZNA units. In addition to military training, Gukurahundi also received training in "politics." They were also skilled in operating as individuals, in "close quarter battle tactics". Their equipment was all Korean in origin, ensuring that they had to operate separately from other units.

In addition, 5 Brigade had completely different communication procedures: their codes and radios were incompatible with other units. Their uniform was also different, its most distinctive feature by the time they became operational in 1983 being their red berets. These red berets are referred to time and again in interviews pertaining to these years and conclusively differentiate 5 Brigade from other army units. The use of AK 47s, recognisable by their distinctive bayonets and curved magazines, is another distinguishing feature of 5 Brigade. In addition, 5 Brigade travelled in a large fleet of vehicles which were Korean in origin, although this fleet did not last long, falling to pieces on the rough Zimbabwean terrain.[160]

5 Brigade itself was made up mostly of Shona-speaking ZANLA forces, loyal to the Prime Minister. These were drawn largely from 3 500 ZANLA combatants at Tongogara Assembly Point. In addition, there were, in the early stages at least, a few ZIPRA combatants. However, most of these were withdrawn by the end of the training, and replaced with ZANLA members. One ZIPRA soldier who was demoted to another brigade soon after passout, referred to the Brigade Commander's instructions: "From today onwards I want you to start dealing with dissidents. We have them here at this parade... Wherever you meet them, deal with them and I do not want a report."[161]

Interviews with civilians also repeatedly refer to members of 5 Brigade, certain men who were "darker" and very different in appearance to "normal Zimbabweans", and who spoke some language completely foreign to Zimbabweans.[162] These men were possibly Mozambicans or Tanzanians who had become attached to ZANLA in the course of the 1970s.

There is no clear statement as to the precise number of soldiers in 5 Brigade. However, if it were a normal brigade, it would have had three battalions, and a total of around 2 500 to 3 500 soldiers.

C) EARLY 5 BRIGADE EXERCISES

While 5 Brigade was not formally deployed until January 1983, it was engaged in some practical exercises before this. In July 1982, there is a press report of "4-day operation units of 5 Brigade" having netted "several dissidents" in the Kezi area.[163]

Interviews with two ex-dissidents who were in 4:6 and 4:7 Battalion at Silobela in the Midlands maintain that in late 1982

"There was an all-out assault on the ZIPRAs based at Silobela by a unit from Connemara which they took to be

5 Brigade. It is not possible to confirm this story but it is clear that conflict at Silobela was extreme and resulted in mass desertions and the disbanding of several of the Fourth Brigade battalions.[164]

D) PASSING OUT PARADE

In December 1982, Prime Minister Robert Mugabe and President Canaan Banana attended 5 Brigade's Passing Out Parade. They were treated to "the biggest live firing" of mortars, rockets and anti-aircraft guns that they had ever witnessed.[165] Prime Minster Mugabe then handed over the brigade flag, emblazoned with 'Gukurahundi', to Colonel Perence Shiri, the first Commander of 5 Brigade. Instructing the Brigade to "plough and re-construct", Prime Minister Mugabe told them they were ready for immediate deployment. Indeed, within days of passing out, 5 Brigade arrived in Matabeleland North.

While the advice to plough and reconstruct may seem positive, taken together with the meaning of Gukurahundi – the rain that blows away the chaff before the spring rains – at least some victims of 5 Brigade were left in no doubt as to how they were perceived by their persecutors. Richard Werbner, in his book *Tears of the Dead*, relates how villagers in Chief Bango's area of Matabeleland South saw themselves as the rubbish which the Gukurahundi soldiers were intent on sweeping away, or ploughing under.[166]

With the arrival of 5 Brigade in Matabeleland North, troop numbers in the region totalled more than 5 000, inclusive of Police Support Unit and other army units. Dissident numbers in Matabeleland North never exceeded 200 – both the dissidents and official government figures confirm this estimate of dissident numbers.[167] In other words, the ratio of government troops to dissidents in Matabeleland North was now at least 25 to 1.

6. DEPLOYMENT OF 5 BRIGADE – MATABELELAND NORTH, 1983

A) JANUARY TO MARCH 1983 – INITIAL IMPACT

5 Brigade was destined to become the most controversial army unit ever formed in Zimbabwe. Within weeks of being mobilised at the end of January 1983 under Col Perence Shiri, 5 Brigade was responsible for mass murders, beatings and property burnings in the communal living areas of Northern Matabeleland, where hundreds of thousands of ZAPU

supporters lived. 5 Brigade passed first through Tsholotsho, spreading out rapidly through Lupane and Nkayi, and their impact on all these communal areas was shocking.

Photo 1: 5 Brigade troops arrive in Matabeleland, January 1983

Within the space of six weeks, more than 2 000 civilians had died, hundreds of homesteads had been burnt, and thousands of civilians had been beaten.[168] Most of the dead were killed in public executions, involving between one and twelve people at a time. The largest number of dead in a single incident so far on record was in Lupane, where 62 men and women were shot on the banks of the Cewale River on 5 March. By pretending to be dead, seven survived with gunshot wounds, while the other 55 died. The following account of the Cewale River Massacre is by witness 2409 AG, a girl who was 15 years old in March 1983.

> On 5 March 1983, four people were taken from our home. The youngest was myself, then a girl of fifteen. The 5 Brigade took us – there were more than a hundred of them. We were asleep when they came, but they woke us up, and accused the four of us – me and my three brothers – of being dissidents. They then marched us at gun point for about three hours until they reached a camp.
>
> We were lined up and had to give our names, before they took us to a building where there were finally 62 people. Then they took us out one by one and beat us. They beat me with a thick stick

about eighteen inches long all over the body. We were beaten until about 3am.

Then the 5 Brigade marched us to the Cewale River, a few hundred meters away. All 62 of us were lined up and shot by the 5 Brigade. One of my brothers was killed instantly, from a bullet through his stomach. By some chance, 7 of us survived with gun shot wounds. I was shot in the left thigh. The 5 Brigade finished off some of the others who survived, but my two brothers and I pretended to be dead.

After some time, we managed to get home. The 5 Brigade came looking for survivors of this incident at home – they found my brother R who was badly injured, but they left him. My brother had a gun shot wound in the chest and arm, and later had to have his arm amputated; first at the elbow, and then later at the shoulder. My brother had to have his foot amputated because of a bullet wound.

In another incident in Lupane on 6 February, 52 villagers were shot in the small village of Silwane, mostly in small groups in the vicinity of their own homes.[169] There were several incidents in Tsholotsho involving large numbers of casualties in single incidents, mostly the burning to death of entire families in huts.[170]

The Government had introduced a stringent set of curfew regulations in Tsholotsho, Nyamandlovu, Lupane, Nkayi, Bubi and Dete, all in Matabeleland North, to coincide with the arrival of 5 Brigade.[171] These regulations severely limited movement into and around the curfew areas. There was a dusk to dawn curfew, stores were closed and drought relief deliveries of food were suspended. All forms of transport were banned, including bicycles and scotch carts. People found breaking the curfew regulations in any way risked being shot, as the following testimony shows. The victim, a 39-year-old farmer (Case 762 X), was shot for riding a bicycle.

At 6am on the morning of 13 February 1983, a Sunday, Mr N was cycling to St Luke's Hospital to visit his wife in the hospital. He met the 5 Brigade on the way. I, his brother, was informed on the afternoon of this day that a person who lived nearby had seen Mr N shot dead by 5 Brigade. The following morning I went with two friends to the spot where N lay dead near his bicycle. He had gun shots on the stomach. I wanted to bury N at my home, so we collected his body on the donkey cart. We were met by 5 Brigade on our way back, and they saw N's body and the bicycle on the cart. They took the bicycle off the cart and broke it into pieces. They threatened me and my two friends with assault. We buried N at my home, and I have had to raise and educate his three children who were all under ten when their father was killed.

As there was a severe drought at the time, many were dependent on drought relief for survival, and the curfew exacerbated people's suffering: however, lack of food in curfew areas was less marked in 1983 than in 1984, when it became a deliberate weapon used by the Government.[172]

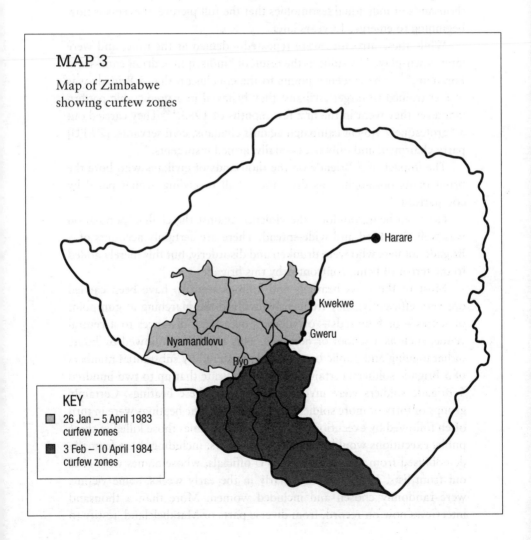

MAP 3

Map of Zimbabwe showing curfew zones

Harare

Kwekwe

Gweru

Nyamandlovu

Byo

KEY

26 Jan – 5 April 1983 curfew zones

3 Feb – 10 April 1984 curfew zones

Journalists were banned from leaving Bulawayo without permission, and no unauthorised people were allowed into and out of the curfew areas. There were road blocks established on all roads into these areas. In short, these measures, together with the curfew, ensured that there was a near-total information black-out, which ensured that word of atrocities took some time to leak out of the area, as terrified civilians fled to the relative safety of Bulawayo or Botswana. People within the curfew zones were also isolated even from neighbouring villages, so that most people within a given district had only patchy information on what was happening in their immediate vicinity, passed on to them by those fleeing in the wake, or ahead, of 5 Brigade. It is only by piecing together thousands of individual testimonies that the full picture of events is now beginning to emerge, 13 years later.

While these atrocities were repeatedly denied at the time, and were later down-played by some as the result of "indiscipline, drunkenness and boredom,"[173] the evidence points to the conclusion that 5 Brigade was in fact trained to target civilians: they behaved in a predictable pattern wherever they went in the first few months of 1983.[174] They carried out a "grotesquely violent campaign against civilians, civil servants, [ZAPU] party chairmen, and only occasionally, armed insurgents."[175]

The impact of 5 Brigade on the thousands of civilians who bore the brunt of its onslaught was dramatic – "all preceding armies paled by comparison."

Far from being random, the violence against the civilian population was well organised and wide-spread. There are certainly accounts of 5 Brigade soldiers who were drunken and disorderly, but this merely added to the terror of being confronted by this brigade.

Most of the mass beatings and killings seem to have been carried out very efficiently: they frequently involved the marching at gun point of scores – or hundreds – of villagers over large distances to a central venue, such as a school or borehole. This would be followed by hours of haranguing and public beatings, administered by substantial numbers of 5 Brigade soldiers: certain interviews indicate that up to two hundred 5 Brigade soldiers were involved in some of these beatings. Certainly groups of forty or more soldiers were common. The beatings were in turn often followed by executions of civilians. Sometimes those killed in these public executions would be ex-ZIPRA soldiers, including those formally demobilised from the Army, or ZAPU officials, whose names were read out from lists. However, particularly in the early weeks, some victims were randomly chosen and included women. More than a thousand interviews now on record, from diverse parts of Matabeleland, testify to such clearly coordinated and premeditated patterns of behaviour.[176]

At times, murders were not accompanied by mass beatings. 5 Brigade would arrive at a village with a list of known members of the ZNA, or demobbed ex-ZIPRAs, or deserters. If people on the list were found, they were shot. The following testimony, by the mother of victim 476 X, recounts such an instance:

> At the end of January 1983, 15 members of 5 Brigade arrived in our line and came to our homestead. They split into two groups and searched our homestead and the homestead of another young ZNA member home on leave. They said they were looking for weapons which these two might have brought with them from the army when they came home.
>
> They found nothing save personal clothing. They took my son out into the yard and told me, his mother, to go away. As I stood outside the yard, I heard a machine gun and they left. I got back to find my son riddled with bullets, with his chest shot wide open. We buried him.
>
> They also shot our neighbour's son. He was made to sit near the house. He was shot in the chest and with two bullets in the head. We buried him. He was also home from the army on leave.

One method used by 5 Brigade was a perversion of the "pungwe", a common ZANLA mobilisation method used during the liberation war, involving song and dance together with political education.

But in Matabeleland in 1983, "the songs were in an unfamiliar language, the dance was forced, the slogans were anti-ZAPU, and the 'festivities' were accompanied by beatings and killings."[177]

Villagers frequently report being forced to sing songs praising ZANU-PF while dancing on the mass graves of their families and fellow villagers, killed and buried minutes earlier.[178] The dissidents themselves provide further support for the argument that 5 Brigade's intention from the outset was to target civilians. In interviews in 1995, former dissidents commented:

"The Gukurahundi wasn't a good fighting unit – where do you see soldiers who sing when on patrol?... We would come across them singing and would just take cover. Soon after you'd hear people crying in their homes... We'd clash with them, but instead of following us they'd call for the villagers. That's where they'd take their revenge, that's where you'd hear bazookas and AKs firing into homes."[179]

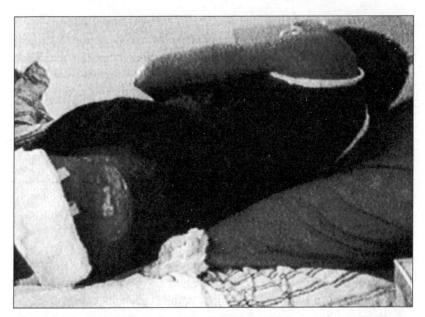

Photo 2: Victim of a mass beating, February 1983

It was the Police Support Unit (SU), the paratroopers and other army brigades which the dissidents respected as efficient fighting units. The dissidents' testimony is borne out by the – very few – interviews on record which refer to villagers injured in genuine crossfire between dissidents and government agencies: SU is invariably the Government agency involved, suggesting they were able to approach dissidents with stealth – and also with the co-operation of civilians – which 5 Brigade was not.

Commercial farmers interviewed also felt 5 Brigade was more interested in "politicking" than pursuing dissidents, and when farmers reported a dissident presence, 5 Brigade would show a marked lack of interest. Farmers agreed SU, the paratroopers and other army units were more active in pursuit of dissidents.[180]

It seems possible to identify the progress of particular 5 Brigade units, on the basis of interviews. While 5 Brigade behaviour uniformly targeted civilians, and the mass beatings and executions described above were reported wherever 5 Brigade went in 1983, there were some variations in accompanying details. For example, one unit, which operated in the Pumula Mission area of western Tsholotsho, routinely informed villagers as they were beaten and then selectively shot, that they were being punished "for having parented those responsible for Entumbane and Connemara."[181] This particular rationale seems limited to this area, although people in other areas were frequently accused in more general terms of having parented dissidents. The burning to death of men, women and children in their huts is also concentrated almost exclusively in this part of Tsholotsho. The burning of entire villages is grouped slightly further to the south and also in areas to the east of Tsholotsho.[182] In an area east of Sipepa in Tsholotsho there are several independent accounts, from at least three villages, of large groups of villagers of all ages being forced to strip completely naked before being beaten. Mass beatings were widespread wherever 5 Brigade went.

Victims from most areas report that 5 Brigade would forbid people who were badly injured by them from seeking medical attention. In some cases 5 Brigade would return the day after they had been in an area, to "execute" badly injured victims. Other interviews report victims who spent several days with agonising injuries, too afraid to leave their huts, before finally they were helped by fellow villagers to make harrowing journeys on back paths, with the victim in a wheelbarrow or scotch cart, to get medical attention.

The graphic representation of atrocities on the maps showing Tsholotsho by sub-region[183] indicates more completely the distribution of offences as revealed by interviews. While this report has concentrated on Tsholotsho, other areas – Lupane and Nkayi, as well as Silobela and Zhombe in the Midlands[184] – were also seriously involved in this first wave of 5 Brigade activity; other curfew areas were affected to a lesser degree.

The following testimony from a woman, witness 467 ASP, was made in western Tsholotsho and is not untypical of 5 Brigade behaviour in this region. The alleged events occurred at the end of January 1983, within a day or two of 5 Brigade deployment:

> The uniformed 5 Brigade soldiers arrived and ordered my husband to carry all the chairs, a table, bed, blankets, clothes and put them in one room. They also took all our cash – we had $1 500 saved, to buy a scotch cart. They then set fire to the hut and burnt all our property.
>
> They accused my husband of having a gun, which he did not have. They shot at him. The first two times, they missed, but the third time they shot him in the stomach and killed him.
>
> They then beat me very hard, even though I was pregnant. I told them I was pregnant, and they told me I should not have children for the whole of Zimbabwe. My mother-in-law tried to plead with them, but they shouted insults at her. They hit me on the stomach with the butt of the gun. The unborn child broke into pieces in my

stomach. The baby boy died inside. It was God's desire that I did not die too. The child was born afterwards, piece by piece. A head alone, then a leg, an arm, the body – piece by piece.

B) EARLY INDICATIONS OF EVENTS

Within days of 5 Brigade deployment, as early as 27 January, ZAPU MPs started claiming in Parliament that atrocities were being committed in Matabeleland.[185] These were denied, as the Government asserted its right to military action in the area.

By 12 February 1983, the first documented representations expressing alarm at what was happening had been made to senior army and government officials, including the Prime Minister and Lt Gen Rex Nhongo (now Mujuru), Commander of the Zimbabwean armed forces. These appeals included documents containing statements made by those in affected areas. An offer was made at this stage to arrange for Government and army officials to be shown mass graves in the area, but this offer was not taken up.[186]

There were several statements by Government ministers denying allegations of atrocities. In February, as clamour grew in the international press, the Director of Information, Justin Nyoka, arranged a trip for journalists to Kezi. This trip was clearly a smokescreen – Kezi is in Matabeleland South and more than a hundred kilometres away from the main curfew zones where the atrocities were taking place in 1983. Here Nyoka challenged journalists to find evidence of the "full-scale war" which he said was "no more than a figment of the imagination of foreign correspondents."[187] On 28 February, he again categorically refuted claims of atrocities.[188] When Nkomo alleged in the House of Assembly that there was a "reign of terror in outlying Tsholotsho District", he was told by the Minister of Home Affairs, Herbert Ushewokunze, that he would "win a Nobel Prize for fiction."[189]

In March, Nkomo was placed under house arrest. There was an armed raid on his house, which left two people dead, but Nkomo himself managed to flee to Botswana and then England, from where he continued to denounce 5 Brigade. Another four day cordon was placed around Bulawayo at this time, and many were detained.[190] Many of these were men who had fled from Matabeleland North to escape 5 Brigade, and Bulawayo is referred to by Nkala as "the fountainhead for dissidents."[191]

In March, Minister of State Sydney Sekeramayi announced: "a good number of dissidents and their collaborators have died."[192] Sekeramayi also told a press conference: "The foreign Press has been spreading malicious stories about the so-called atrocities committed by the security forces."[193]

C) ZIMBABWE CATHOLIC BISHOPS' CONFERENCE RESPONSE – "RECONCILIATION IS STILL POSSIBLE"

Missionaries in areas affected by the curfews were among the first to sound the alarm on what was happening in their parishes.[194] Priests kept records of events as they happened and forwarded these to CCJP in Harare. On 16 March 1983, Catholic representatives consisting of CCJP Chairman Mike Auret, Bishop Karlen and Bishop Mutume, met with Prime Minister Mugabe. They presented him with a comprehensive dossier of evidence. This dossier, as well as containing damning evidence of 5 Brigade atrocities, also included a statement by the Bishops' Conference (ZCBC) entitled "Reconciliation is Still Possible", making it very clear that the ZCBC continued to condemn dissident atrocities and to recognise the Government's need to maintain law and order in Zimbabwe.[195]

A few days after this, to coincide with the Easter weekend, the ZCBC released "Reconciliation is Still Possible" to the press. This document stated the ZCBC's recognition of the Government's duty to maintain order "even by military means", but said the "methods which should be firm and just have degenerated into brutality and atrocity." The statement pointed out that it is the man in the middle who was again suffering, and such violence "breeds bitterness, feelings of hatred and desire for revenge." The media was accused of grossly failing to reveal the truth about the "wanton killings, woundings, beatings, burnings and rapings." The document appealed to the Government to find ways of reconciling with involved parties and adopting less harsh strategies in areas of disturbances.

D) GOVERNMENT RESPONSE

While Prime Minister Mugabe had received the first documents detailing atrocities on 12 February, the face-to-face meeting with CCJP officials could well have been the first irrefutable indication he had been given of 5 Brigade behaviour. There certainly seems to have been a change in 5 Brigade tactics from late March onwards, with a marked decline in atrocities: it seems fair to attribute this to Mr Mugabe himself responding to prevent further mass killings and beatings.

The Government was by this stage surely aware that serious atrocities had occurred, and even seemed to be acting to prevent this continuing. However, their official response vacillated between denial and guarded acceptance of wrong-doings. A statement by Minister of Information Nathan Shamuyarira, responding to the CCJP press release, denied that the Government had "inflamed the situation" or committed wanton killing, and accused ZAPU of having made things worse. The Government said they would investigate the information given to them by CCJP, but said there would be no judicial commission.[196]

On 6 April, 1983, Prime Minister Mugabe once more refuted allegations of atrocities, and accused his critics of being "a band of Jeremiahs [which] included reactionary foreign journalists, non-governmental organisations of dubious status in our midst, and sanctimonious prelates."[197] He also accused the CCJP of condemning 5 Brigade, but not the dissidents. A few days later,[198] however, he spoke at Silobela as the curfew on Matabeleland North was lifted. He stated that charges of 5 Brigade atrocities would be thoroughly investigated and the culprits, if any, would be brought to book.

On 15 April 1983, the Catholic Bishops' Conference released a further statement in which they "welcome[d] promises by PM Cde Mugabe that action would be taken on allegations of brutality committed by the Zimbabwean security forces." They also welcomed the lifting of the curfews and the gradual improvement of life in the rural areas.[199] Statements denying atrocities, interspersed with some statements admitting and regretting "mishaps",[200] continued. Mr Mugabe said on 18 April 1983:

> "Obviously it cannot ever be a sane policy to mete out blanket punishment to innocent people, although in areas where banditry and dissident activity are rampant, civilian sympathy is a common feature and it may not be possible to distinguish innocent from guilty."[201]

While guarded statements such as this one were being made to the broader audience, in the communal areas themselves, Government ministers continued to make statements that indicated little desire to distinguish innocent from guilty, and indeed displayed a tendency to see all communal dwellers as potential dissidents deserving of punishment.

In March 1983, Emmerson Mnangagwa, who was Minister of State Security and in charge of the CIO, told a rally at Victoria Falls that the Government had as one option, which they had not yet chosen, the burning down of "all the villages infested with dissidents." He added: "The campaign against dissidents can only succeed if the infrastructure that nurtures them is destroyed."[202] In this same speech, he referred to the dissidents as "cockroaches" and 5 Brigade as "DDT" brought in to eradicate them.

At another rally in Matabeleland North in April 1983, Minister Mnangagwa told a huge, forcibly assembled crowd[203] that the army had come to Matabeleland like fire, "and in the process of cleansing the area of the dissident menace had also wiped out their supporters." He went on to state, in a parody of the Scriptures:

> "Blessed are they who will follow the path of the Government laws, for their days on earth shall be increased. But woe unto those who will choose the path of collaboration with dissidents for we will certainly shorten their stay on earth."[204]

Dissidents were paraded at these rallies, and were made to publicly declare their ZAPU allegiance. As a result of these rallies, more than 20 000 ZAPU supporters surrendered their membership cards, and bought ZANU-PF cards.

With unintended irony, Sekeramayi told an April rally in Matabeleland North: "The army will stay a long, long time... the majority of people now realise they have been misled by PF-ZAPU," and "understand the national character of ZANU-PF."[205]

Commission of Inquiry

On 14 September 1983, the Government announced that it would be setting up a formal Commission of Inquiry into 5 Brigade activity in Matabeleland North. Sekeramayi stated that the Commission would "report to the Prime Minister and everything would be made known to the people of this country."[206] The Committee of Inquiry ultimately consisted of four members, and they began taking statements in January 1984.[207] To date, the results of this inquiry have never been made known to the people of Zimbabwe.

E) APRIL TO DECEMBER 1983 – 5 BRIGADE IMPACT

On 4 April 1983, the curfew on Inyathi and Nkosikasi was lifted, and before the end of the month it was lifted in the rest of Matabeleland North. This brought some relief to residents, particularly as it was accompanied by a change in tactic on the part of 5 Brigade itself, probably at the instigation of the Government. The food supply situation eased, and civilians could try to resume some semblance of normal life, although some schools remained closed and 5 Brigade remained a dominating and intimidatory force in the area. Huge public rallies by ZANU-PF also became a feature of these months. School children as well as adults were forced to attend these rallies, which frequently involved public beatings and lasted for entire weekends.

It became a matter of personal safety to own a ZANU-PF card. As the vast majority of people in this region either carried ZAPU cards or no political card, the purchasing of ZANU-PF cards became a massive undertaking in the region. CCJP archives record how there were daily queues of many hundreds of people at ZANU-PF offices, where officials often made people wait overnight before selling them cards. During their period of waiting, they were commonly forced to sing songs praising ZANU-PF and denouncing ZAPU. People could then be told to come back the following week for the card receipts and once more be made to wait overnight and take part in pro-ZANU-PF mini-rallies. That this new allegiance to ZANU-PF was a protective rather than a genuinely political gesture on the part of locals, was clearly indicated in the General Election in 1985, when ZAPU was resoundingly returned in Matabeleland North, as it was in the District Council Elections of 1985.

From the end of March 1983, 5 Brigade became far more selective in terms of whom they beat and killed. The phenomenon of mass beatings which had been so widespread was replaced by a policy of removing chosen villagers to central 5 Brigade camps, where they were beaten, interrogated or killed. These involved mainly men, but also some women.[208]

Some villagers continued to be beaten or killed in their village settings, if they were caught engaging in activities perceived as subversive. For example, women found cooking meals were sometimes accused of cooking for dissidents, and were beaten. People found with food supplies, or returning from stores carrying food, were similarly treated.[209] If strange footprints were found leading through an area, or if dissidents were sighted in an area, the villagers could expect a beating. The incidence of 5 Brigade and other Government agencies disguising themselves as dissidents and committing crimes is also commonly reported in interviews.[210] There remained a number of beatings and killings which did not appear to have any clear motive, although the incidence had declined.

5 Brigade was withdrawn from Matabeleland North for approximately a month in mid-1983, for a "retraining exercise." However, they had a final flourish in July before their departure, and burnt to death 22 villagers, including women and children, in a hut in Solonkwe, a small village in western Tsholotsho.[211]

On 29 August, 5 Brigade were re-deployed in the area, and

disappearances and other offences at their hands occurred in Matabeleland North, through the rest of 1983 and 1984. The doctor at St Luke's Hospital in Lupane noted that during the month of 5 Brigade's absence, she admitted no patients with gunshot wounds, but once the brigade was re-deployed, she started to see such cases again.[212] In Tsholotsho, some of these incidents involved Mbamba Camp in the south.

F) DISAPPEARANCES

Throughout 1983, but particularly after March 1983, there was an increase in disappearances: 5 Brigade and CIO removed men from buses, trains, or from their homes, and they were never seen again. Such people were often taken because their names were on a list showing them to be either ex-ZIPRA, or some kind of ZAPU official. Others who were taken had failed to produce their identity cards when pulled from a bus or train by 5 Brigade. Some who were killed or detained were merely young men who were considered to be of "dissident age".[213]

The psychological impact of disappearances is dealt with in Part Three, I, of this report. The dead play a significant role in the well-being of the living in Ndebele culture, and the unburied dead return as "a restless and vengeful presence, innocent yet wronged, aggrieved and dangerous to the living."[214]

Not only those whose final fate and burial place is unknown are considered missing. People in mass graves are also culturally regarded as having aggrieved spirits, or as being in an unhappy state of "limbo." It takes the tears of the living, shed properly through a decent period of mourning, to release the soul and allow it to be at rest. It was a characteristic of 5 Brigade to insist that there should be no mourning for the dead. In some cases, the family of dead victims were themselves shot because they wept.[215] In other cases, burial of any kind was forbidden: families had to watch the bodies of their loved ones rotting in the sun and being scavenged, until the bones were finally removed by 5 Brigade. Some people in Matabeleland North have attributed recent droughts in their area to the large numbers of improperly buried dead, and there are still many mass graves which residents will indicate to those they trust. Some of these are almost indistinguishable from the surrounding terrain 13 years later, while others have been decorated and clearly demarcated by local residents, even though they do not always know all the victims buried in them.[216]

The phenomenon of disappearances was to continue throughout the emergency period until Unity in 1987, not only in Matabeleland North, but also in Matabeleland South where it was prevalent in 1984, and in the Midlands, where it coincided with the 1985 General Elections. In February 1985, as many as 120 civilians in Tsholotsho are alleged to have been taken in these night raids.[217] However, from 1985 onwards, most disappearances were at the hands of CIO and Police Internal Security and Intelligence unit (PISI), not 5 Brigade.

7. 5 BRIGADE DEPLOYMENT – MATABELELAND SOUTH, 1984

A) JANUARY TO MAY 1984

In January 1984, Zimbabwe was to witness a tactic which had been first used by the Smith Government – that of trying to starve out "the enemy". A harsh curfew was introduced in Matabeleland South, an area encompassing the districts of Gwanda, Matobo, Bulilimamangwe, Insiza, Umzingwane and Beitbridge. This was an area of 8 000 square kilometres, with 400 000 inhabitants, of which no more than 200 were dissidents.

This part of the country was suffering its third year of severe drought, and people in the area had no food stored. They were dependent on drought relief deliveries from humanitarian agencies as well as the Government, supplemented by food bought in local stores. The Government closed all stores, and halted all food deliveries to the area, including drought relief. This was done in conjunction with a blanket curfew, operating around the clock, restricting movement into, out of and around the curfew zones. It did not take long for people to begin feeling the acute effects of hunger.[218]

The troop deployment in Matabeleland South appears to have been even more extensive than in Matabeleland North in 1983: *Africa Confidential* estimated 15 000 troops from various units in the area.[219] From interviews and CCJP archives, these units included paratroopers, Greys Scouts (a mounted unit), Police Support Unit and various army brigades, including 5 Brigade. Widespread intimidation, beatings and killings by 5 Brigade began once more.

This was an area in which Super ZAPU had been very active during 1983 and by the year-end, government activity had been severely restricted over large areas of Matabeleland.[220] Veterinary services, civil administration and development projects had all ceased to operate, and police protection was non-existent. According to "Specific Reports" in *The Chronicle,*[221] in 1983 dissidents had committed eight murders, mainly of commercial farmers. This had led to the resignation of the entire Matobo Rural Council, which later reconvened and operated from the safety of Bulawayo.[222] It also led to most of the commercial farmers in this region abandoning their farms: by November only nine out of 41 farmers remained living in the area, in a state of siege.[223] In addition, in 1983 dissidents inflicted one gunshot wound and destroyed a ZOC bus. The dissidents may have been responsible for more than these acts of banditry in Matobo, but if so they were not specifically reported in the press.

However, by the end of 1983, Super ZAPU, the South African-trained group of dissidents, was in disarray. The ZIPRA dissidents interpreted the curfew as a direct consequence of the fact that the authorities knew Super ZAPU was fading, and knew that dissidents left in the country would now find it increasingly hard to survive without South African supplies of ammunition.[224] They believed the Government hoped the embargo on both movement and food, cutting off the dissidents' hope of asking – or forcing – villagers to feed them, would finally wipe the dissidents out.[225] However, the main result of the curfew was to reduce hundreds of thousands of ordinary civilians to a state of starvation and desperation.

According to the Lawyers' Committee for Human Rights, villagers were eating less than 20 per cent of the food they required.[226] Many children and elderly were brought to a "critical point", meaning that their lives were hanging in the balance, but it is very hard to assess how many people actually died of starvation. People had to resort to eating insects and grass seeds to try to survive.[227]

In addition to the food embargo, mass detentions became a deliberate strategy of 5 Brigade activities. At least 2 000 men and women, including adolescents, could be held at one time in Bhalagwe Camp, near Maphisa (Antelope) in Matobo.[228] People were detained for several days or weeks, in appalling conditions.[229] Many people died, and others suffered permanent injuries. It is likely that around 8 000 civilians were detained during these few months, possibly many more. Once more, it was mainly innocent civilians who suffered.

Approximately 6 000 civilians fled the curfew areas for Bulawayo,[230] risking their lives by doing so, as it meant breaking the curfew rules restricting people to within 50m of their homes. Some news of events became known through their stories, as well as through Catholic missions in this area.

Bones in Antelope Mine
There are also references in the foreign press at this time, to the stench of dead bodies from the mine shafts which abound in this part of the

country.[231] In 1992, skeletons were retrieved from Antelope Mine, near Bhalagwe Camp. In 1984 villagers within the vicinity claimed to have witnessed bodies being tipped down the shaft regularly, late at night. They also heard explosive devices being detonated down the shaft. Some villagers claim many more bodies remain unfound in the many mine shafts in the region.

B) 5 BRIGADE – RETRAINING AND DISBANDMENT

Later in 1984, 5 Brigade was withdrawn from active service, and had five months of intensive retraining in Mbalabala.[232] Certainly, when 5 Brigade re-entered active service for another brief period in 1985, they seemed a reformed brigade. Exactly where and when they operated thereafter is unclear, as a direct consequence of the fact that there were fewer complaints about their actions. The largest record of their activity is a report of mass arrests, torturing and interrogation of all the young men in seven villages adjacent to Dhlamini Rest Camp in Tsholotsho. This allegedly took place in November of 1985.[233]

In 1986, 5 Brigade was finally withdrawn,[234] and underwent conventional training in Nyanga under the guidance of the British Military Advisory Team and Zimbabwe National Army instructors. The members of the brigade were then disbanded and attached to other brigades on external operations in Mozambique.[235]

C) EXCEPTIONS TO THE RULE

Among the many accounts of 5 Brigade atrocities, there are a handful of accounts of 5 Brigade soldiers who showed tremendous courage by refusing to commit crimes against their fellow Zimbabweans. For example, in Ndawana village in Tsholotsho in early 1983, a 5 Brigade commander ordered the whole village into a hut, and set fire to it. As the burning thatch began to fall in on screaming villagers, the commander left, and another member of 5 Brigade immediately opened the hut door and released all the villagers before any were burnt to death.[236] He took a huge personal risk in undermining the orders of his superior by this action. J Alexander also reports a 5 Brigade commander who refused to take part in atrocities committed by his colleagues.[237]

Particularly after March 1983, there are also some reports of commanders who visited families of victims the day after a beating or killing had taken place at the hands of units under their instruction, and apologised for the event. In Nseze, for example, 5 Brigade soldiers shot and killed five young children who were sitting outside a hut eating sadza.[238] The commander came and apologised to the childrens' parents the next day. However, such apologies were exceptions to the rule, and probably offered little consolation to survivors.

In more recent years, a few members of 5 Brigade have been so disturbed by memories of their own actions that they have returned to the scenes of their crimes and begged forgiveness from the families of victims. These victims were apparently unable to grant such forgiveness at that time, demanding the return of their dead children before they could forgive their killers.[239] Others have suffered serious mental disorders, which they attribute to their own sense of guilt.[240] The families of the dead – and to a different extent their murderers – are psychological victims of the events that took place, and both are deserving of help to heal the damage caused by those years.

8. MILITARY RATIONALE FOR 5 BRIGADE

"You often have to be cruel to be kind. Had an operation like [the 5 Brigade's] not taken place, that battle could have gone on for years and years as a festering sore. And I believe the Matabele understand that sort of harsh treatment far better than the treatment I myself was giving them, when we would just hunt and kill a man if he was armed..."

"The fact is that when 5 Brigade went in, they did brutally deal with the problem. If you were a dissident sympathiser, you died. And it brought peace very, very quickly."

Lt Col Lionel Dyke, commander of the Paratroopers in 1983-84[241]

These statements and others like them are often used to justify the actions of 5 Brigade in Matabeleland and the Midlands in 1983-84. The argument is that without 5 Brigade, the dissidents would never have been brought under control.

However, the actual unfolding of events between 1982 and 1988 does not bear this out. It is worth noting that 5 Brigade was largely inactive after the end of 1984, yet the "dissident problem" continued, and in fact did not lessen in any perceivable way, until the signing of the Unity Accord in December 1987. Some have argued that 5 Brigade actually fuelled the growth of the dissidents, as previously unpoliticised youths living in rural Matabeleland became displaced and also motivated by desires for revenge in the wake of 5 Brigade actions.[242] 5 Brigade activity also caused a huge refugee problem, as thousands of civilians fled first from Matabeleland North and then from Matabeleland South to seek refuge in Bulawayo and in Dukwe refugee camp in Botswana. The refugees, particularly in early 1983, were then readily available to be recruited by South Africa for training as Super ZAPU.[243]

The Government's own figures for numbers of dissident murders and other crimes shows no measurable decline in the aftermath of 5 Brigade activity, as the following figures show. They are drawn from the Government's stated totals used to justify the renewing of the State of Emergency every six months, and quoted in the press. There were no figures quoted in the press for offences during the six months between July 1984 and January 1985.[244]

JANUARY 1983 – JULY 1984 (a period of 18 months)
Murders   165
Rapes   84
Robberies   497

JANUARY 1985 – END 1986 (a period of 2 years)
Murders   264
Rapes   184
Robberies   688

In addition, there were 66 murders specifically attributed to dissidents in 1987 in the press, although there was no general Government statement quoted in 1987.

Even taking into account the fact that the second period is six months longer than the first, it is apparent that, if anything, the dissidents were more active in the wake of 5 Brigade activity. Murders average less than 10 a month for the first period, and over 10 a month for the second period.

As in many armed conflicts, the situation was finally resolved by a political solution: it was the signing of the Unity Accord in December 1987 that brought an almost immediate halt to dissident activity, and not the actions of 5 Brigade.

Photo 3: Zimbabwean refugees in Botswana, March 1983

9. POLITICAL IMPACT OF 5 BRIGADE IN 1983 – 1984

One of the most tragic impacts of 5 Brigade on Matabeleland was the resulting perception among those civilians who suffered that they had become victims of an ethnic and political war:

> "The belief that the Fifth Brigade's particular brand of violence was not an aberration but part of a plan orchestrated by ZANU-PF's leaders changed people's perceptions of the goals of the 1980s war. They came to see it as a war fought not against dissidents but against the Ndebele and ZAPU."[245]

The 5 Brigade "war" hardened ethnic differences – "an attack on the Ndebele was an attack on ZAPU, an attack on ZAPU was an attack on the Ndebele. Such attacks struck at the root of people's most cherished social and political identity."[246]

This perception was a consequence not only of the 5 Brigade's Shona composition and indiscriminate picking of civilian targets – any Ndebele speaker, including women and children were liable to suffer – but also of their own descriptions of their orders. 5 Brigade commanders at rallies invariably expressed the conviction that "all Ndebeles were dissidents", and said their orders were to "wipe out the people in the area."[247] The Bible was often quoted to support 5 Brigade's claims to superhuman powers to judge and condemn. Certain 5 Brigade commanders referred to themselves as being the "Black Jesus": like the Biblical Jesus, they had the power to save or condemn others.[248]

The incidence of rape under 5 Brigade also became loaded with political overtones for those in Matabeleland, as "rapes committed by the Fifth Brigade were perceived as a systematic attempt to create a generation of Shona babies."[249]

While 5 Brigade largely failed in its attempts to change people's political allegiance by repression, as is evidenced by the 1985 election results, subsequent ongoing political violence continued to paralyse elected rural ZAPU leaders and led to much distrust at development efforts. The victory of ZAPU in the January 1985 District Council Elections brought punishment in its wake: "In Nkayi, the ZANU-PF Youth and soldiers assaulted the DA, councillors, and council and hospital staff under the watchful eye of provincial Governor Mudenda."[250] In national elections in July, ZAPU once more won in Matabeleland North, but District Councils could not function as their members fled to Bulawayo to escape detentions and beatings. The councils were then suspended in terms of the emergency powers legislation.

It was noteworthy in 1996 interviewing sessions, that as soon as the 5 Brigade was mentioned, people would spontaneously start to make political comments, such as "it is impossible to have more than one political party in this country, otherwise you will be punished." Whatever the intention of 5 Brigade's onslaught, this is the message that was extracted and learnt by those who suffered.

While there is indeed peace in the rural areas of Matabeleland in the 1990s, beneath this there remains both a "feeling of alienation from the national body politic", and a firm perception that Matabeleland continues to be neglected in terms of development.[251]

There is also a belief that a 5 Brigade-type onslaught could happen again at any time:

> "We can still be eliminated at any time... This wound is huge and deep... The liberation war was painful, but it had a purpose, it was planned, face to face. The war that followed was much worse. It was fearful, unforgettable and unacknowledged."[252]

Summary

The strategy of 5 Brigade varied in the two regions of Matabeleland, with Matabeleland North experiencing more public executions, and Matabeleland South experiencing widespread detentions, beatings and deaths at Bhalagwe camp: both areas experienced mass beatings in the village setting. The impact of 5 Brigade in Matabeleland North and South was profound. In both regions, 5 Brigade enhanced the notion of ethnic difference, produced a widespread fear, and developed a conviction that political freedom of expression was not permissible in Zimbabwe. This conviction remains today. In both regions, rural government in the 1980s continued to be incapacitated and subject to attack, even once 5 Brigade was withdrawn.

As 5 Brigade violence in both areas was very sudden and very intense, it was perceived as worse than anything ever experienced before. People retain the perception that such state inflicted violence could occur again in the future: having once witnessed the completely unexpected and inexplicable, it is not unreasonable to assume it could recur, particularly as the events of the 1980s have never been publicly acknowledged and no guarantees that it will not happen again have been given.

10. GENERAL BACKGROUND OF EVENTS, 1984 – 1988

A) CHIHAMBAKWE COMMISSION OF INQUIRY

From 10 to 14 January 1984, the four-man *Chihambakwe Committee of Inquiry* convened in Bulawayo and heard testimony from witnesses. The Committee stated that it was only hearing evidence relating to events between December 1982 and March 1983. The Committee consisted of: the Chairman, Mr Simplicius Chihambakwe, a lawyer; Major-General M Shute, a retired army officer; Mr P Machaya, a lawyer; and the Commission Secretary, John Ngara, who was a member of the CIO. Those who gave evidence mentioned the aggressive manner in which Ngara interrogated witnesses, but felt nonetheless that the Committee had been given ample proof of widespread army abuses.[253]

The Committee had initially expected a handful of people to turn up to testify, but were confronted by hundreds of potential witnesses.[254] On 14 January, the Committee left Bulawayo saying they would come back to take more statements. At short notice, the hearings were resumed in Bulawayo on 23 March 1984, and on 28 March CCJP gave its evidence.

The CCJP gave evidence for one and a half days, and produced 17 victims, who each gave evidence of multiple atrocities, including mass shootings, burning to death of people in huts, mass beatings, mass detentions involving various methods of torture, and general psychological harrassment. With more warning, CCJP could have produced more witnesses, but as witnesses were based outside of Bulawayo, locating them at short notice was not possible in all cases. For example, the survivors of the Lupane Cewale River massacre, who had already made sworn statements to a lawyer, were unable to attend the Inquiry in time.[255] Most of the Commission of Inquiry statements given by CCJP are referred to in the course of the village by village summaries, and some are reproduced in this report in full.[256] While evidence was supposed to be limited to events up to March 1983, by March 1984 the CCJP had a substantial dossier of events which had occurred in Matabeleland South in 1984, and some evidence relating to these events was also presented.[257]

In addition to the victims who gave evidence, CCJP Chairman Mike Auret also produced in evidence a skull from a mass grave, showing a clear gunshot wound. This victim was one of twelve men who had been pulled off a bus by 5 Brigade in January 1983, and shot and buried in two graves near Cyrene Anglican Mission in Matabeleland South. One of the graves was on Cyrene Mission property, and the other was on a farm across the road. The Anglican Vicar General and Bishop, Robert Mercer, had uncovered the grave.[258]

Once the Committee had gathered its evidence, no more was heard from it. On 30 May 1984, there was an editorial in *The Chronicle* appealing for the Committee to publicise its findings. In October 1984, Mr Chihambakwe was asked when the report would be made public. He advised that its publication had been held up at the printing house by papers being produced for the ZANU-PF congress, and that it would be published in due course.[259] Then in November 1985, Minister Mnangagwa announced that the Commission of Inquiry Report would not be made public. This decision has never been explained or revoked.

B) THE CURFEW IN MATABELELAND SOUTH

The curfew on Matabeleland South was imposed on 4 February 1984 and continued until 10 April 1984, after which some stores were re-opened and the curfew became a 6pm to 6am curfew. When the curfew was initially imposed, the State of Emergency was also renewed.

The eventual lifting of the curfew was probably partly the result of international pressure: foreign governments threatened to withhold financial aid on humanitarian grounds, as thousands of innocent Zimbabweans edged closer to starving to death.[260] The Catholic Bishops of Zimbabwe also issued a statement on 7 April, a few days before the curfew was relaxed, expressing "very grave concern... on current events in Matabeleland."[261]

A statement by the Minister of Home Affairs, Simbi Mubako, denying atrocities and blaming them on the dissidents, accompanied the lifting of the curfew.[262] This denial was reminiscent of the multitude of similar denials made in 1983. A week later, Prime Minister Mugabe dismissed CCJP claims of atrocities and accused the Catholic Church, in particular the Bishop of Bulawayo, of being politically sympathetic towards Joshua Nkomo. He said that just because "the holy of holies" had "sneezed" did not mean the whole nation should "catch a cold". He did agree to visit the sites of alleged atrocities.[263]

The Catholic Bishops responded immediately in defence of the political impartiality of all their members, but the following week, Sekeramayi accused the Bishop of Bulawayo of "spreading filthy lies" and of being "in league with Satan, Joshua Nkomo and other evil forces."[264] It was announced that Minister Nkala and the Minister of Parliamentary Affairs, Maurice Nyagumbo, were to go to Matabeleland to investigate atrocities. Two days later Minister Nyagumbo addressed a rally in Matabeleland South at which he threatened villagers that the Government might yet inflict worse things on them than the curfew, if they continued to support dissidents.[265]

International concern over events remained, and in May 1984 the Government arranged an abortive trip for foreign journalists to Matabeleland South. In the few days before the journalists were allowed into the curfew area, 5 Brigade organised the evacuation of all patients from hospitals in the vicinity, and also returned to the scenes of mass killings and burnt the bodies: they effectively destroyed as much evidence of their activities as they could, before allowing the journalists access.[266] The journalists' bus became bogged down in a river bed early on the first day, so the trip was extended to the following day, when journalists met alleged victims of 5 Brigade at a hospital. However, the doctor refused to allow the victims to speak in front of the army, for their own protection, and the army refused to leave the victims to speak in confidence with the journalists. After this, the journalists were taken to a spot where a mass grave was alleged to have been. There were no bodies, but there was evidence of a recent substantial fire through the area, suggestive of an attempt to destroy evidence.

Later in 1984, 5 Brigade was removed from Matabeleland South and sent for retraining.

In October 1984, there was an inquest concerning a group of four

5 Brigade soldiers, one of whom was a commander, who were accused of the murder of four people, an off-duty member of the army, his wife and another couple. They had been dragged from their car on the main Victoria Falls–Bulawayo road and killed in February 1983. In their defence, the 5 Brigade soldiers claimed the victims were killed "in cross-fire", in spite of the fact that three of the victims were killed by bayonets, and the two female victims showed evidence of rape. The inquest found the deaths were due to murder by 5 Brigade soldiers. The magistrate commented that the murder was "exceedingly cruel" and said the victims were "repeatedly stabbed with bayonets, much as a hunter slaughtering a wounded animal with a spear."[267]

The 5 Brigade soldiers were given into the custody of the Brigade, rather than awaiting trial in jail. Their trial was delayed until July 1986, when they were found guilty of murder by the High Court and sentenced to death. They were immediately granted a Presidential pardon. They were among the very few members of the security forces who were ever tried for crimes against civilians.

C) ZANU-PF YOUTH BRIGADES AND ELECTION VIOLENCE

From late in 1984, violence was related to the forthcoming elections. Once again, this violence had less to do with the pursuit of dissidents, than it had to do with the crushing of ZAPU. Zimbabwe's second general election was held in July 1985, and was accompanied by widespread intimidation of the opposition candidates and their supporters, starting in November of 1984, and continuing well after the elections in 1985.[268] This intimidation included mob beatings, property burnings and murders. While some of the rioting, especially in November 1984 and August 1985, was inspired by "dissident killings" of ZANU-PF officials; the victims of the rioting were chosen indiscriminately and were almost all town-based, or at district administerial centres, far removed from dissident activity. They were also almost invariably Ndebele speakers.[269]

Very few of those responsible for committing these crimes were ever formally accused of breaking the law or brought to trial.

Much of the intimidation was at the hands of the ZANU-PF Youth Brigades, who were a party-organised mob of young men, able to bully and destroy with virtual impunity. The ZANU-PF Youth were modelled on the Chinese Red Guard, and were supposed to promote national "development".[270] In Zimbabwe this seemed to mean primarily coercing people into buying ZANU-PF cards, forcing thousands of people on to buses to attend ZANU-PF rallies, and beating anyone who stood in their way. The ZANU-PF Youth were identifiable by their uniforms of khaki trousers and bright red and green shirts. The Youth Wing was a non-uniformed extension of ZANU-PF Youth that was also responsible for rioting and property destruction, particularly in Silobela and the Midlands.

The following is a list of some of the incidences of disorder caused by these ZANU-PF Youth Brigades, as accounted for by the Lawyers' Committee for Human Rights in their documentation of these years.[271] Many of the events they describe are confirmed by reports in *The Chronicle* or by CCJP and BLPC human rights interviews on record.

1984

June	Gweru	Mass beatings in Matapa and Mambu.
June	Kwekwe	150 injured by ZANU-PF Youth.
October	Gweru	66 homes, 3 stores, 6 cars destroyed by ZANU-PF Youth.
November	Beitbridge	Estimated 20 ZAPU supporters killed by ZANU-PF Youth.
November	Beitbridge	Estimated 200 injured by ZANU-PF Youth.
December	Plumtree	200 injured, 150 hospitalised by ZANU PF Youth.[272]

1985	Matabeleland/ Midlands/ Harare	Estimated 2 000 left homeless, mainly Ndebele speakers, after ZANU-PF Youth rampages destroyed homes in the following areas.
March	Tsholotsho	39 huts in 3 villages and 3 stores were destroyed by ZANU-PF Youth, leaving many homeless. At least one died and others were injured.
August	Silobela	166 homes destroyed, at least 4 killed, 1 500 left homeless.
August	Harare	"Scores" wounded, "several dozen" killed and hundreds left homeless after ZANU-PF Youth rampages.

It remains unclear to what extent this violence was sanctioned by the Government. Little effort was ever made by the police or army to prevent or intervene in ZANU-PF Youth activities, and attackers often seemed to have the tacit approval of the national Government.[273]

The violence up until the middle of 1985 was directed against ZAPU supporters in the pre-election campaign. The election itself was conducted in relative calm. ZANU-PF was once more the overwhelming victor. However, ZAPU retained all 15 seats in Matabeleland, much to the surprise and anger of the ruling party, which in the election run-up had predicted a clean sweep for ZANU-PF countrywide.[274]

In the celebratory aftermath of the elections, Prime Minister Mugabe made a broadcast in Shona in which he told his supporters to "go and uproot the weeds from your garden."[275] In Harare, vengeful mobs including the ZANU-PF Women's League seemed to take this advice to heart when they destroyed houses of suspected ZAPU supporters, and hacked a ZAPU candidate to death with axes, as well as killing several dozen others, including two pregnant women.[276] It was only on the third day of rioting and killing that the Government intervened to halt it.

The Beitbridge violence in November 1984 was in retaliation for the murder of Moven Ndlovu, a ZANU-PF MP: the last two ZAPU officials in Cabinet were also dismissed as Prime Minister Mugabe directly blamed ZAPU for the murder. Three members of the ZAPU central committee and an MP were detained by CIO, also in retaliation for this murder. Some believe that Ndlovu was in fact killed by his own party, and not by ZAPU supporters – CCJP's *A Place For Everybody* cites this possibility.

The Silobela violence was also inspired by the killing of three ZANU-PF officials by dissidents. After news of these murders in August 1985, busloads of ZANU-PF Youths, backed by PISI,[277] rampaged through Silobela, destroying properties and killing at least four villagers.

The response of ZANU-PF Youth and the tendency to take revenge on any ZAPU supporter for dissident murders of ZANU-PF officials was not surprising:

> "Time and again, the leaders of ZANU-PF, in their words
> and deeds, have equated support for ZAPU with support for
> dissidents. In those instances where they have condemned
> the violence and moved to curtail it, more often than not it
> has been too little too late, and not before lives have been
> lost and property destroyed."[278]

D) CIO: DETENTIONS, TORTURE AND POLITICAL KIDNAPPINGS

The Central Intelligence Organisation also played a role in the disturbances surrounding the 1985 general election, and at other times in the 1980s. A large number of ZAPU officials were detained in midnight sweeps in different parts of the country. It is assumed that most of these "disappearances" were at the hands of the CIO and PISI,[279] as the evidence points in their direction. Men wearing plain clothes and driving Government vehicles without number plates carried out the abductions. Some of the abductees later turned up in prison, confirming their captors had been agents of the State.[280] For example, 11 men from the Midlands who had been detained without trace in January were located in May 1985 in a Kwekwe prison. However, 13 others from the Midlands were among those who never turned up again.[281]

On 23 March 1985, CCJP once more sent a confidential report to the prime minister, deploring the abductions of ZAPU officials, and also the "brutal bullying" of opposition party members. CCJP claimed these actions were "threatening the legitimacy of the coming elections", and appealed for an end to politically inspired violence, so that people could vote freely.[282]

i) Detentions

The exact number of people who were detained in 1985 before and after the elections is not clear, but the Lawyers' Committee for Human Rights made the following estimates, based on interviews conducted close to the events of 1985:

February	Bulawayo	1 300 detained
February	Midlands	200 ZAPU officials detained
March	Matabeleland	80 ZAPU officials detained[283]
August	Bulawayo	200 City Council employees detained
August	Bulawayo	200 others detained

Some ZAPU officials claimed 415 of their members were detained in Bulawayo in the post-election round-up, but this could not be independently confirmed by LCFHR. Certainly, detentions were widespread, and may have involved thousands of people.

Photos 4 and 5: Homes destroyed by ZANU-PF Youth, Silobela,
August 1985

Photos 6 and 7: Stores destroyed by ZANU-PF Youth, Silobela,
August 1985

On 25 October 1985, Amnesty International sent a telex to Prime Minister Mugabe urging him to stop torture and incommunicado detention. It also called for an independent inquiry into torture, with the results made public. Amnesty International released a report on "Torture in Zimbabwe" on 13 November 1985. This referred to the upsurge of detentions after the elections, particularly in Bulawayo. They estimated that in November, 200 detainees were being held in Stops Camp in Bulawayo. Prime Minister Mugabe dismissed this report as the work of "Amnesty Lies International."[284]

Other evidence on file suggests that torture was also rife at Esigodini, where the CIO detention centre was known as "The Fort". In one well-known case, a CIO officer shot a detainee dead in front of witnesses.[285] A large group of ZAPU supporters detained in Beitbridge were also cruelly tortured at Esigodini: the CCJP pamphlet on torture highlights at least one of these victims, who had his legs tied to a tree branch, and his arms tied to the front bumper of a car, which was then reversed until the man was effectively "on the wrack". He was then beaten.[286] There are also detainees who claim to have been tortured in Goromonzi, near Harare, and at Daventry House in Harare.[287] Other interviews used in this report refer to torture as widespread throughout Matabeleland North and South, including police or army bases in Mbamba, Nyamandlovu, St Paul's, Sitezi, Bhalagwe, Sun Yet Sen, Gwanda, and elsewhere.

The CIO played a major role at Bhalagwe camp in early 1984. They interrogated all detainees, in the presence of 5 Brigade. The CIO also administered the more sophisticated forms of torture here, including submarine (i.e. asphyxiation by submersion in water) and electric shocks, and were regarded at Bhalagwe with even more fear, and considered even more deadly than 5 Brigade by some who have been interviewed in recent years.[288]

The Emergency Powers Regulations required that those being held in detention be informed of the reason within seven days. Within 30 days they had to be either charged with an offence or detained by a written order from the Minister of Home Affairs. Detainees were also entitled to see a lawyer. In fact, most detainees were never informed of the reason for their detention or detained by a written order. Most detainees also never had legal assistance.[289]

ii) Disappearances
It is difficult to verify how many of those who were detained in 1985 never reappeared: while estimated numbers run to scores, or even hundreds, there are only a handful of well documented cases. However, it is clear

from the case study areas that most families of the missing have not insistently approached the authorities, either through fear or the belief that it will make no difference. Relatives who reported missing persons to the police immediately after their abduction were frequently told the State knew nothing about it, or were sometimes told the abductee had since been discharged by the State. In many cases, the issue was not pursued by relatives after this, who feared reprisals against further family members if they continued to draw attention to themselves.[290] There were very few cases of Missing Persons in the case study areas before such information was actively sought in 1995-96.

However, in two cases, widows of two men who were abducted by State agencies on separate occasions and never reappeared, have been compensated by the State as a result of legal action.[291]

Among the few well-documented cases of disappearances is that of 11 men who were abducted from Silobela in the Midlands, on the night of 30-31 January 1985.[292] Other documented disappearances from the same area were attributed to CIO and included a further nine men abducted in August 1985. Some of these cases of Missing Persons were pursued by CCJP, but material evidence was impossible to locate years after the event, and CIO guilt could not be proven. The Silobela Eleven abducted in January 1985 have been declared "Missing, Presumed Dead." While the widows of the missing men have accepted their husbands will never return, they have expressed the desire to be issued with an apology by the State for what happened.[293]

Human remains in mine shafts

In 1992, CCJP was instrumental in arranging for bones to be retrieved from Old Hat Mine No. 2, in Silobela. These bones were positively identified as belonging to eight humans – six men and two women.[294] They did not appear to be the remains of any of the known Silobela abductees. Bones were also retrieved from Antelope Mine in Matabeleland South in 1992, and in 1995 there was a press report of human bones being found in a disused mine shaft near Filabusi, in the south of the country.[295] Rumours of bones in other mines are common, especially in Matabeleland South, where disused shafts abound.[296] Mines in Matabeleland North, including those in Nkayi, are also rumoured to hold human bones. When bones were first unearthed, the Government claimed they dated back to Smith's days: however, Zimbabwean coins in the pockets of some of the deceased's clothes placed their demise firmly in the 1980s.[297]

Photo 8: Bones excavated from Old Hat Mine No. 2, Silobela, 1992

iii) Torture

Of the thousands detained, the vast majority suffered physical torture, and all suffered psychological torture. People in detention were kept in appalling conditions, including over-crowding, under-feeding, and totally inadequate sanitary facilities and bedding. Detainees were also often kept within earshot of those being tortured, causing them extreme emotional distress. In their report on torture in Zimbabwe, Amnesty International describes how detainees at Stops Camp were kept in three large "cages" which were open to the weather. Reports on file with CCJP describe women detainees being herded into such a cage, spattered with blood and faeces from previous detainees, and being given lice-infested blankets.[298] Eight nearby security cells held other detainees, and the interrogation and torture occurred in an adjacent set of offices.

Beating and other forms of physical torture were very common in the 1980s. It was unusual to be detained and not to be beaten; with truncheons, rhinoceros-hide whips, rubber hoses or sticks, often on the soles of the feet.[299] Other forms of torture were also used, including electric shocks, burning, suspending people by their ankles or arms for hours, and stretching people to breaking point with hands tied to one object and ankles to another. Interrogating people while they were completely naked, and immersing their heads in water until the point of unconsciousness were also commonly reported forms of torture from those years.[300] Hanging victims upside down and then beating them, with their heads in buckets of water, was also reported.[301]

Although not all detainees were beaten, torture victims would be returned in their traumatized state to the joint holding cages, causing acute distress to other detainees, who were unable to assist the injured adequately, and were left in terror of undergoing the same ordeals themselves.[302]

The widespread incidence of torture was against the State's own interests: time and again accused persons had cases against them dismissed, as the Courts decided their evidence had been extracted from them under duress. Yet individual members of the CIO escaped prosecution for this, and even had the tacit approval, or sympathy, of the Government. In 1983 Prime Minister Mugabe excused torture in custody on the grounds that police work long hours and therefore tend to "do their work over-enthusiastically." On 18 August 1982 *The Chronicle* claimed that the Government was "more than justified in pinching the checks of the friends of dissidents."[303]

Trials relating to torture

In mid-1983, the public trial of six white Air Force officers accused of sabotaging aircraft at the Thornhill Airbase near Gweru first brought the issue of torture to public attention. Air-Vice-Marshall Hugh Slatter gave convincing testimony of having been given electric shock treatment, and all six defendants were acquitted when their confessions were ruled inadmissible on grounds of having been coerced.[304]

Another trial, which was held *in camera* for "security reasons", involved the bringing of a civil action for damages against the Government by Wally Stuttaford, an elderly white Member of Parliament. He was arrested in December 1981 and held incommunicado for a month. During this time he was tortured in an attempt to get him to admit to conspiring with Nkomo to overthrow the Government. Papers released only recently from the *in camera* proceedings relate how Stuttaford was subjected to hours of kicking and punching, forced exercise, and had his arms, hands and ankles crushed until he screamed with pain and begged for mercy.[305] While it was unclear at the time what the outcome of the case had been, it is now on record that Mr Justice Waddington awarded the equivalent of US$4 500 in damages to Stuttaford. However, Prime Minister Mugabe refused to pay, saying it was "a waste of the nation's money."[306] Stuttaford recently revived his efforts to be compensated, and papers put before Mr Justice Sandura in July 1996 claimed US$6 000, covering the original award plus interest. Stuttaford had the tractor of one of the CIO agents seized as surety against the amount owed him, and an out of court settlement was finally reached in November 1996.[307]

There were also charges of torture laid against the Government by some ZAPU officials.[308] However, some ZAPU detainees were unaware of their rights in terms of the law, and others who knew their rights were too afraid of further repercussions if they pressed charges. This situation echoed that of state torture victims of the 1970s. All the same, many cases were dismissed from magistrates' courts on the grounds of the defendants having been tortured.[309]

E) POLICE INTERNAL SECURITY INTELLIGENCE UNIT: PISI

PISI was "an elite and secretive division within the Home Affairs ministry."[310] Its function was similar to that of the CIO, and in addition to intelligence collection, they had powers of arrest. The unit had functioned under the name Zipolis,[311] but had been in disuse for some years before Enos Nkala was made Minister of Home Affairs in August 1985. PISI had a reputation for being even more ruthless and brutal than CIO, and at times would arrest people in the guise of CIO, a fact which annoyed CIO intensely.[312] It also makes it hard to allocate blame to one or other of these agencies now: people tended to assume CIO was making arrests, but as both PISI and CIO were plainclothes units, it was easy to confuse them.

PISI was used by Enos Nkala almost as his own personal agency while he was Minister for Home Affairs. Nkala was an Ndebele-speaker with a long-standing vendetta against Joshua Nkomo, dating back to the split between ZANU and ZAPU in 1963. Nkala's inflammatory remarks at a rally in November 1980 had helped spark off the first Entumbane disturbances, and Lord Soames had forbidden Nkala to stand in the first General Election in 1980, because of his aggressive stance.[313]

In the General Election of 1985, Nkala campaigned in Filabusi in Matabeleland South, and received less than 10 per cent of the vote, as ZAPU retained all 15 seats in Matabeleland. However six weeks after the election, in September 1985, Nkala filled a Parliamentary vacancy which had arisen in the Karoi district, north of Harare. Prime Minister Mugabe promptly appointed him Minister of Home Affairs. This appointment was "a deliberate affront to the Ndebele... there could not have been a more irresponsible person in whose hands to place the sweeping authority of the Emergency Powers Regulations."[314]

Minister Nkala immediately made militant speeches, in which he told the nation:

"We want to wipe out the ZAPU leadership. You've only seen the warning lights. We haven't yet reached full blast... the murderous organisation and its murderous leadership must be hit so hard that it doesn't feel obliged to do the things it has been doing."[315]

ZANU-PF had expected to have a clean sweep in the General Elections, and ZAPU's success in Matabeleland led to a change in strategy on the part of the ruling party. The appointment of Nkala was an important aspect of the ruling party's new strategy to crush ZAPU, together with a new wave of detentions, and finally the banning of ZAPU rallies and the closure of ZAPU offices early in 1987.

F) DISSIDENT VIOLENCE IN 1984-85

The LCFHR reports that in the latter part of 1984, through to the election, dissident activity dwindled to almost nothing. However, immediately after the election there was a surge of dissident activity, with the Government reporting 45 civilian deaths at the hands of dissidents in October 1985.[316] LCFHR reflects the Government rationale that this up-swing "may have reflected a disappointment in ZAPU's snowing in the election." However, having expected a clean sweep, ZANU-PF was probably more disappointed in the election results than ZAPU, who retained all of its 15 seats.

One of the worst cases of dissident violence took place immediately after the election in August 1985, in the Mwenezi District of southern Zimbabwe.[317] Here 17 Shona-speaking villagers, including small children, were murdered by dissidents, allegedly for voting for ZANU-PF in the elections. Thirty-five people were herded into a hut and the Ndebele speakers were then allowed to leave. The rest of the people were shot at and the hut was set on fire. As survivors tried to escape, they were shot, including two 2-year-olds. The dissidents then went on to loot a nearby store and killed a further five people, bringing the total number murdered that day to 22.

The harsh attack on civilians in this area has been explained by dissidents as part of a dissident strategy to try to force the Government to extend the curfews to Shona-speaking parts of the country, so that Shona-speaking civilians would suffer hardships as those in Matabeleland had done. Some dissidents claim this massacre was a direct response to what they saw as the tribalist targeting of Ndebele-speakers by the Government in the 1980s.[318] (The tragedy of such "ethnic" rationales for the violence has been previously discussed in this report.)

Photo 9: Remains of Sweetwater Ranch, Mwenezi, after dissidents shot and burnt 17 people to death

CCJP was among the many who expressed deep shock and condemned unreservedly "the abhorrent and cowardly violence" of the Mwenezi attack. The commission lamented the purposeless killing which was destroying "peace and stability", and called on all those "with real or imagined political grievances to forsake violence and to address their grievances to Government in a peaceful and responsible manner."[319]

G) MORE DETENTIONS AND THREATENED TREASON TRIALS
Within a week of Enos Nkala's appointment in 1985, Joshua Nkomo's house had been raided, and his personnel arrested. More detentions followed for ZAPU, including the detention of five ZAPU Members of Parliament and eight high-ranking National Army officers, all ex-ZIPRAs. The MPs were Sydney Malunga, Edward Ndlovu, Welshman Mabhena, Stephen Nkomo and Kembo Mohadi. Four of the army officers, namely Kindness Ndlovu, Charles Gray, Tshile Nleya and Lt Col Eddie Sigoge were accused in their detention orders of conspiracy to overthrow the

Government, as was William Henry Kona, Chairman of ZAPU.[320] All were held in custody for several months while the Government considered formalising the charges of conspiracy to overthrow the Government against them. Edward Ndlovu was never formally charged with an offence, although his detention order accused him of treasonous activities: he was released from jail in May 1986, because of serious health problems.[321]

The trial of Sydney Malunga

It is worth looking briefly at Malunga's trial, in order to evaluate what evidence the State had in 1985 of ZAPU leaders being involved in supporting dissidents, a charge repeatedly laid at ZAPU's door between 1982 and 1987.

Malunga was first detained when he was ZAPU MP for Victoria Falls, in November 1980. He was held at Chikurubi for 60 days without charge, and then released. He was then redetained in March 1983, and released after 31 days, having been told there was no case against him.

Malunga, then ZAPU's chief whip, was detained yet again on 31 July 1985 but was not charged for some time. He was frequently transferred from one prison to another, making communication with his lawyer extremely difficult. Malunga was also tortured during his detention, suffering severe beatings to his feet.

Malunga's ZAPU colleagues were detained during late September 1985, but they were also not immediately charged. In terms of the Emergency Powers Regulations, detainees had to be served with a written order after 30 days. In all cases, the detainees' written orders accused them thus:[322]

1. You are a member of PF (ZAPU) war council tasked to overthrow the constitutional Government of Zimbabwe.
2. You and others attended meetings on several occasions and agreed to overthrow the Government of Zimbabwe by force of arms.
3. You and others had agreed to assassinate the leadership of the present Government.
4. You incited some ex-ZIPRA combatants to take up arms and fight the Government of Zimbabwe.
5. You are a threat to public safety and state security.

Malunga was finally formally charged with aiding and abetting dissidents.[323] The precise nature of the charge against him was that on two occasions in November 1982, he had met with two different men outside a beerhall in Bulawayo, and given them the equivalent of US$3 and US$6 respectively, to buy canvas shoes "for dissidents in Lupane". The trial began in Bulawayo, but the State requested the trial's transfer to Gweru, out of concern for the safety of State witnesses.

The only witnesses for the State were the two who had supposedly received this money from Malunga. Interestingly, the witnesses appeared to be in police custody: they arrived at the trial in the back of a caged and guarded police van. The trial resumed on 6 January 1986 in Gweru, and evidence was presented *in camera*. It was soon established that both the State witnesses were in fact accomplices, and their evidence was contradictory on several counts. Malunga was also proven to be in Harare on at least one of the days on which the offences supposedly occurred. Malunga claimed he had seen the witnesses for the first time when they were all three in detention in 1983. Malunga also said they had tried to persuade him to make a false, self-incriminatory statement at that time, which he had refused to do.

The State could produce no other evidence against Malunga, who argued the charges against him were a political frame up, as he was an outspoken critic of the Government who had condemned 5 Brigade activities among other things. Malunga was acquitted in July 1986.

However, he was retained in detention, while the State decided whether it had enough evidence to proceed with a charge of treason against the other ZAPU officials still in detention. Their sole further piece of incriminating evidence against any of them was a statement made by Welshman Mabhena accusing the men of conspiring to overthrow the government. However, when brought before the Court, Mabhena made it clear that his evidence was false, and that his statement had been coerced through the use of torture. He withdrew his accusation, and the State finally had to admit it had no further grounds for detaining the men, and in September 1986, after a year in detention, they were all released.

In addition to those already mentioned in this report, the following ZAPU Members of Parliament were also targeted during the 1980s: Sikhuili Moyo was badly beaten and left for dead, Isaac Nyathi was detained, and Aikin Ndlovu, MP for Beitbridge and an ex-ZIPRA Commander, fled the country for Norway in fear of his life.[324] By the end of 1986 there were very few ZAPU officials, ranging from ZAPU's national leadership down to the least significant office bearers in remote rural areas, who had not been detained, harrassed, beaten, killed, or forced into exile.

H) OTHER EVENTS DURING 1986 AND 1987

i) Dissident activity in 1986-87

1986 had remarkably little press coverage relating to dissident atrocities. There were only nine reported dissident murders, 21 losses of property and 16 assaults by dissidents in *The Chronicle* during this year.[325] However, in the Parliamentary debate on renewing the State of Emergency in January 1987 the Government claimed 116 civilians had been killed by dissidents in 1986. As all information pertaining to the dissident situation was state-controlled, there is no way of explaining this disparity in numbers.[326]

During 1987, there was a noticeable increase in press-reported dissident atrocities. 66 murders, 44 property losses and 17 assaults by dissidents were reported. Several of the murdered were white farmers and their families. There was substantial press coverage of several major dissident attacks. These included a May attack on a commercial farmers' club in a rural area near Gweru, which resulted in the deaths of four farmers and the wounding of the barman. In June, two German tourists were murdered in Nyamandlovu, on the main road to Victoria Falls.

Six clinic staff were murdered in September 1987 on a remote road in Nkayi: while *The Chronicle* attributed these murders to dissidents, strong circumstancial evidence from those first on the scene suggested this was more likely a CIO ambush.[327] Some of the evidence cited includes the fact that while six Ndebele-speakers were killed, the two Shona-speakers in the vehicle were not killed. These two survivors gave implausible and mutually contradictory accounts of how they came to survive while the others died, and how having survived the initial ambush, they then managed to leave the vehicle undetected before it was set alight by the ambushers.

The killing of Gwesela, a notorious dissident responsible for many deaths, was announced in the press on the same day as it was announced that ZAPU was backing unity.[328] But a few days later, on 28 November 1987, the murder of four men, seven women and five children on a Christian mission farm in Matobo made headlines around the world. The 16 were murdered when local squatters, who were angry over their threatened eviction, called in dissidents under the command of the pseudo-dissident "Gayigusu" to murder all those living in two adjacent farmhouses. The victims were axed to death one by one, including a six-week-old baby.[329]

ii) Moves towards unity

Once the General Election year of 1985 was over, the ZANU-PF

Government had an apparent change in strategy. On the one hand it continued to target ZAPU (see previous section), while on the other there was clearly a move afoot to unite the two parties. Judging from media coverage, the Government had assumed that ZANU-PF would win seats in Matabeleland in 1985: having failed to do so, the dissolving of ZAPU into ZANU-PF remained an option. ZANU-PF was clearly in a strong position at this stage, with ZAPU effectively unable to operate, and its followers thoroughly demoralised in the wake of 5 Brigade activity.

Events reported in *The Chronicle* in 1986 give some indication of the slow progress towards unity that took place during these years. In March 1986, the ZAPU official, Vote Moyo, and Commander Lookout Masuku were released from years of detention, and Masuku died shortly after this, in April.[330] In October, first Nkala and then Shamuyarira announced that unity talks were going well, and that the dissident activity was now so low as to be "not worth bothering about."[331] In December 1986, Dumiso Dabengwa was released from indefinite detention, after nearly five years in Chikurubi Prison. His release and that of four others was announced by Enos Nkala to have been occasioned to facilitate unity talks.[332]

The progress towards unity continued in 1987, although there were clearly times during this year when a negotiated settlement seemed remote. In February 1987, Joshua Nkomo held a big rally in Bulawayo, and talked of unity being imminent: the problem of what to name the new united party was given as the sole remaining issue to be settled, although a day later, Minister Nyagumbo said that the name of the new party had been agreed.[333] In April, Joshua Nkomo announced a breakdown of unity talks that was a temporary set back. And in May, Prime Minister Mugabe said that the talks had failed because ZANU-PF refused to put two bulls, as symbols of ZAPU, on to the flag of the new united party, although it would consider other symbols.[334]

However, the entire process of negotiation faltered in mid-year, with Enos Nkala once more launching a full assault against ZAPU. On 20 June, Minister Nkala banned all ZAPU rallies and meetings, and further announced that he was considering banning ZAPU altogether. He also stated that dissidents now numbered "less than 100". In September, Minister Nkala said the ban on ZAPU meetings would continue "ad infinitum". He further said: "ZANU-PF rules this country and anyone who disputes that is a dissident and should be dealt with."

A week later, ZAPU offices in Bulawayo were raided and 12 ZAPU officials were detained in Gweru and Kwekwe.[335]

On 22 September, ZAPU was effectively banned: Minister Nkala had all ZAPU offices closed and directed that "all ZAPU structures be set aside... From now on ZAPU would be viewed in the same manner as the MNR bandits in Mozambique."[336]

In October, all six district councils in Matabeleland North, which were ZAPU-dominated, were dissolved by the Government. On 10 October, Minister Nyagumbo announced that unity talks were dead, but on 30 October, just when the chances of unity seemed once more to have vanished, it was announced that a group of four top ZAPU officials wanted to re-open talks.

The CCJP considered the resumption of talks to be essential for any hope of peace in Zimbabwe, and CCJP officials met privately with the Minister of Home Affairs, Enos Nkala, to appeal for talks to resume.[337] Minister Nkala claimed Joshua Nkomo did not want unity, so the CCJP approached Nkomo, who promptly denied this charge. CCJP went back to Nkala, who agreed to resume talks on the premise that Nkomo would accept unity of ZAPU and ZANU-PF. Talks resumed shortly after this, and on 18 November, it was announced that ZAPU had backed unity.[338]

On 1 December the press reported the re-opening of ZAPU offices in Harare and Bulawayo.

ii) The Unity Accord: Amnesty

On 27 December 1987, Prime Minister Mugabe and ZAPU leader Joshua Nkomo signed the Unity Accord. ZANU-PF and ZAPU were once more united, for the first time since the collapse of the Patriotic Front prior to the election of 1980, but this time the two parties were united under the single title ZANU-PF.

On 18 April 1988, the prime minister announced an amnesty for all dissidents, and Nkomo called on dissidents to lay down their arms. On 28 April 1988, Clemency Order No. 1 of 1988 was signed by Acting President Simon Muzenda and Minister of Justice Emmerson Mnangagwa. [339] This stated that all those who were dissidents and who reported to the police between 19 April and 31 May 1988, would be offered a full pardon for any crimes committed. The pardon included those who had aided dissidents and also ZAPU "political fugitives from justice". The pardon specifically excluded agents of foreign states.

Pardon was also granted to those already serving jail sentences for a multitude of crimes, on condition they had already served at least one third of their term and had less than a year left to serve. This clause excluded habitual criminals. Offences pardoned included murder, rape, robbery, fraud, bribery and drug-related offences, meaning that many jailed criminals apart from those serving for dissident-related crimes were subject to pardon.

Over the next few weeks, 122 dissidents handed themselves over to the authorities.[340]

The speed with which dissidents surrendered has been cited as evidence suggesting that they had been under Joshua Nkomo's control, after all. However, the dissidents themselves explain the orderly surrender as the product of the fact they had continued to maintain ZIPRA-style discipline, and once they had reached the shared decision to obey Nkomo's call, they acted in unison. The dissidents had remained loyal to ZAPU, even while being abandoned by the ZAPU leaders who were actively denouncing them. When they could see that unity was a reality – Dabengwa was out of prison and Nkomo was reinstated as part of a government of national unity – there was no incentive for them to remain as outcasts.

In June 1988 the Amnesty was extended to include all members of the Security Forces who had committed human rights violations: all army personnel who were serving prison sentences for crimes committed in the 1980s were released from jails. The 1980s disturbances were finally at an end, leaving in their wake both relief and, in some parts of the country, a legacy of health and practical problems, material impoverishment and a mistrust of the authorities.

NOTES – PART ONE

Part One, I

1 See the Historical Overview, pp 50-59, 40ff, for sources and detailed discussion of this and other issues raised in the following two paragraphs.
2 Such disturbances also occurred in the east — see Historical Overview, p 65.
3 This assertion is supported in the historical overview that follows, and also in the two case studies.
4 In this we are not alone: it is the belief that a nation's history should be transparent that currently motivates Truth Commissions in South Africa, Rwanda and the former Yugoslavia, among others.
5 For example, in recent years a few members of 5 Brigade went back to a village in Matobo where they had killed some people and begged forgiveness. See p 93 for more details.
6 Academic accounts of events in the 1970s are listed in the history following, p 42.
7 D Martin and P Johnson, *The Struggle For Zimbabwe,* ZPH, Harare, 1981, and D Caute, *Under the Skin,* Allen Lane, London, 1983 provide merely two examples of accounts of these massacres.
8 For a listing of some academic accounts of the 1980s, see pp 13 and 29.
9 *The Financial Gazette,* 30 Oct 1992: "No Apologies says Mugabe", *Zimbabwe News, Editorial,* Dec 1992.
10 This report does not claim to be, nor does it recommend, a Truth Commission. At the same time, the report committee acknowledges that the precedent set recently in other parts of Africa, including South Africa, Rwanda and Malawi, of holding governments accountable for their human rights violations, has added impetus to the perceived need for this report.
11 *In Search of Truth and Reconciliation,* SAPEM, June 1996. This perception was confirmed in interviews with representatives of the Truth and Reconciliation Committee, Johannesburg, August 1996.
12 R Werbner, *Tears of the Dead,* Baobab Books, Harare, 1992, makes this claim: it is examined in greater detail in the Historical Overview.
13 For more detail on the data collection procedure, see following section, pp 18-20.
14 Interviews, also with CCJP official, Sept 1996.
15 Restoring dignity, honour and victims' good names is a major objective of the South African Truth and Reconciliation Commission, as outlined by the ANC, in their statement on 16 August 1996.
16 See "Discussion of Data Sources" for comprehensive discussion of source material for this report.
17 Joshua Nkomo, *The Story of My Life,* Methuen, London, 1984.
18 For a full discussion of all data, see section following.
19 For figures, see Part Two in its entirety.
20 It is acknowledged that the forensic evidence to support claims of current physical and psychological damage to survivors is not readily to hand at this time, although there are extant medical records for many hundreds

of victims, and many hundreds of victims complain of backaches, etc. which date from mass beatings as inhibiting their ability to function well. However, compensation for two "missing persons" has now been paid out by government, so some legal precedents have been set (the issue of legal damages is discussed at greater length in Part Three of this report). Known psychological consequences of witnessing or experiencing violence is discussed in general terms also in Part Three, I, in the chapter on Organised Violence.

21 Legislation used in the 1980s is discussed in more detail in Part One, III.

22 "Mugabe Says NO — Compensation Ruled Out For Fifth Brigade Victims", *Financial Gazette,* 7 October 1992.

23 See Part Four for Recommendations.

Part One, II

1 Lawyers' Committee for Human Rights, *Zimbabwe: Wages of War,* New York, 1986, p 27.

2 St Luke's medical records for 1983 are attached as Appendix B I.

3 Three of these Commission of Inquiry statements have been included in Part Three, I.

4 This medical record, with names of victims removed, is attached as Appendix B I. It is not the only such medical listing on file, although it is more comprehensive than some others.

5 One such letter is attached as Appendix B II.

6 Estimates by the Lawyers' Committee For Human Rights are included in the Historical Overview in Part One, III in this report, p 103. See also p 299.

7 HR Database is the name of the main database for this project: see Methodology.

8 The law in Zimbabwe requires either the presence of the father at the birth registry office, or presentation of his death certificate, before a birth certificate can be issued for a child. It is also typical in rural areas for parents to delay seeking birth certificates until the time their children are ready to start school, when proof of age is required for school registration. So large numbers of children who were aged five or under at the time their fathers were killed have faced this dilemma. The CCJP form, Appendix A I, is typical of the requests for birth certificates that still come in.

9 Paralegals use the "Missing Persons" form devised in 1993, attached as Appendix A II, to record events relating to the 1980s, although these events do not always relate specifically to missing persons, as in fact the attached form does not: it relates to several murders and one gunshot wound, sustained at Silwane, Lupane, in February 1983.

10 It is not part of the archival CCJP data referred to under "CCJP" above: for example of the interview form used by CCJP, see Appendix A I.

11 See Appendix A III for the BLPC Human Rights Fact Sheet, devised for the 1995-96 interviewing procedure.

12 The Matobo Case Study looks in more detail at the interviewing experience in this district.

13 This is a valuable source that researchers have agreed to keep confidential. File H consists of 18 closely written pages summarising events, villages and names of victims from the Pumula Mission area, compiled by an independent source in 1992.

14 See "village by village" summary for examples of how different sources were used together.

15 See Appendix A III. Form devised in 1994.

16 Some civilians nonetheless expressed resentment towards the dissidents for their incessant demands for food, and meat in particular – hence their Ndebele name, "Silambe Over", meaning "We are very hungry".

17 LCFHR pp 27-28 refers to this practice of using disguise in both the 1970s and 1980s. The confusion caused by this, and the impossibility of arriving at a final truth in such cases, is also raised by them.

18 LCFHR, *Zimbabwe: Wages of War,* LCFHR, New York, 1986, pp i-ii.

19 See "Historical Overview", p 112 for more on these events.

20 See Appendix A IV for an example of the Media Report format used to compile *The Chronicle* database.

21 *The Chronicle,* 12 Feb 1983.

22 LCFHR, *Zimbabwe: Wages of War,* pp 8, 51 and others.

23 *The Chronicle,* 19 Aug 1982. These murders were widely attributed to 5 Brigade, and even the local newspaper reports never attributed these deaths to "dissidents", only commenting that it "was not clear" whether the national army had been responsible for the shootings. Relatives of the victims believed 5 Brigade was responsible.

24 LCFHR, *Zimbabwe: Wages of War,* also refers to this shoot-out in detail and also concludes the murders were most likely at the hands of Government agents.

25 See pp 48-50 for details on South African involvement.

26 Interviews with doctors and mission personnel, 1996, for all information in this paragraph. See Appendix B I for an example of one hospital listing compiled in 1983.

27 Confirmed in an interview with the specialist concerned, who now lives outside Zimbabwe. The relevant medical records are on file with NOVIB, a non-governmental organisation based in the Netherlands.

28 All these instances are looked at in greater detail in the following history.

29 The sensitive issue of what to do with these sites was raised as a concern by those interviewed: see Part Three, III, and Part Four.

30 The chapter on "Organised Violence" looks at this issue in more depth, and establishes definitions of various types of torture.

31 While CCJP numbered victims were seldom used on the HR Database, they were used in the case study areas – see section following.

32 LCFHR, *Zimbabwe: Wages of War,* p 136.

33 LCFHR, *Zimbabwe: Wages of War,* pp 74-5.

34 While the term "village" has been used to designate the areas in which people live, rural civilians tend to refer to their "villages" as "lines": homesteads were laid out in long lines when people were forcibly resettled in the 1960s. It was felt that to refer to "line by line summaries" in a written document would be confusing, hence the use of "village" instead.

PART ONE, III

1 D Martin and P Johnson, *The Struggle For Zimbabwe*, ZPH, Harare, 1981, provides a comprehensive account of ZANU's contribution to liberation; N Bhebe and T Ranger (eds), *Soldiers (vol 1)* and *Society (vol 2) in Zimbabwe's Liberation War*, UZP, Harare, 1995, provide a wide-ranging background to events during the 1970s; R Werbner, *Tears of the Dead*, Baobab, Harare, 1992 and Lawyers' Committee For Human Rights, *Zimbabwe: Wages of War*, New York, 1986, draw connections between events in the 1970s and the Matabeleland crisis years, to mention just four of many contributions on the topic.

2 As indeed some did: see, for example, the case of *S v Hartlebury and Evans* 1985 (1) ZLR 1 (H).

3 Abuses were committed by both white and black personnel in the Rhodesian Army, and ZIPRA and ZANLA had their share of human rights abusers too.

4 David Caute, *Under the Skin*, Allen Lane, London, 1983, p 29.

5 Ronald Weitzer, "In Search of Regime Security: Zimbabwe Since Independence", *Journal of Modern African Studies*, 22, 4, 1984, pp 529-55; also John Hatchard, *Individual Freedoms and State Security in the African Context: The Case of Zimbabwe*, London, 1993.

6 LCFHR, *Zimbabwe: Wages of War*, p 143.

7 LCFHR, *Zimbabwe: Wages of War*, pp 148-62 deals in length on these and other legal issues.

8 The October 1989 Africa Watch Report on Zimbabwe and LCFHR both refer to this.

9 All these documents are fully referenced in Part One, II. The CCJP Confidential Report on Torture was presented to the Bishops' Conference in January 1987, and then to the prime minister.

10 Richard Carver's two documents, op cit, and LCFHR in particular, all make a strong case for particular personnel being responsible for abuses across two decades.

11 See "Historical Overview" for more details.

12 R Carver, "Africa Watch", p 8.

13 N Bhebe and T Ranger (eds), "Introduction", *Soldiers (vol 1)*, argue for downplaying these aspects.

14 See section following on Enos Nkala, pp 110-111.

15 T Ranger, *The Invention of Tribalism in Zimbabwe*, Gweru, Mambo, 1985; "The Invention of Tradition Revisited" in T Ranger and O Vaughan (eds), *Legitimacy and the State in Twentieth Century Africa*, London, Macmillan, 1993; "African Identities: Ethnicity, Nationality and History: The Case of Matabeleland 1893-1993", in J Heidrich (ed). *Changing Identities*, Berlin, Centre for Modern Oriental Studies, 1994; T Ranger, "Missionaries, Migrants and the Manyika: The Invention of Ethnicity in Zimbabwe", in Leroy Vail (ed), *The Creation of Tribalism in Southern Africa*, James Currey, London and University of California Press, Berkeley, 1989. Richard Werbner, *Tears of the Dead*, op cit, p 159, also refers to the debate surrounding the apparent invention by white settlers of two hostile "tribes".

16   Such claims were made by 5 Brigade. However, more recent conflicts, such as that at Entumbane, were more commonly used as justification for human rights abuses in the 1980s.

17   For a cross-section of essays looking at some aspects of this debate, see N Bhebe and T Ranger (eds), op cit.

18   The Entumbane Uprising is looked at in more detail in the section, "The Dissident Problem".

19   See sections following for justification of these claims.

20   Baobab Books, Harare, 1991.

21   R Werbner, *Tears of the Dead*, p 159.

22   R Werbner, *Tears of the Dead*, p 159.

23   R Werbner, *Tears of the Dead*, p 159 for this definition of "Gukurahundi".

24   J Hanlon, *Apartheid Power in Southern Africa*, Indiana University Press, 1986; also D Martin and P Johnson (eds), *Destructive Engagement: Southern Africa at War*, ZPH, Harare, 1986.

25   J Hanlon, *Beggar your Neighbours*, p 177; also LCFHR, op cit, and Africa Watch, op cit. It must be added that not every ex-Rhodesian became a saboteur: many have remained loyal to the government of the day.

26   J Hanlon, *Beggar your Neighbours*, p 175.

27   J Hanlon, *Beggar your Neighbours*, p 177: Hanlon comments also that South African reconnaissance planes had been seen over Thornhill six weeks prior to the blast. People interviewed in South Africa in September 1996 also believe this attack was the work of South Africans.

28   J Hanlon, *Beggar your Neighbours*, p 176.

29   Interview, South Africa, Sept 1996.

30   J Hanlon, *Beggar your Neighbours*, p 183.

31   *Moto*, October 1996, p 7, for all information in this paragraph.

32   In November 1996, this new theory was brought to the attention of the TRC in Johannesburg, for their consideration. For more on the kidnappings, see p 71.

33   Interviews, Johannesburg, September 1996 for all information on Operation Drama.

34   For more on Super ZAPU, see "The Dissident Problem" pp 57-58.

35   J Hanlon suggests numbers of Super ZAPU could be counted in "tens".

36   For example, the Mozambique operation was partially entrusted to SADF personnel doing their compulsory National Service, who had no proven loyalty to the SADF. These servicemen knew about Operation Drama, but were not entrusted with details – interview, Johannesburg, September 1996.

37   See, *inter alia*, speeches by Government Ministers in *The Chronicle*, 21 & 23 May 1980; 30 June 1980; 7 July 1980; 10 Nov 1980; and 13 Feb 1981, implying or asserting ZAPU allegiance to dissidents; also LCFHR op cit and D Martin and P Johnson (eds), 1986, op cit.

38   J Nkomo, op cit; also numerous interviews in the 1990s and statements on file in CCJP Archives.

39   D Martin and P Johnson (eds), 1986, op cit, see South Africa as partially responsible.

40   J Alexander, *Dissident Perspectives on Zimbabwe's Civil War*, Seminar, St Antony's College, Oxford, 1996.

41　See p 113 for details of Sydney Malunga's trial in 1986.

42　J Alexander, op cit, p 25.

43　LCFHR, op cit, p 26: also see Part Two of this report for discussion and Tables referring to dissident atrocities.

44　These assertions are all supported in the text following.

45　This statement is borne out by countless interviews and documents on record, many of which will be referred to in the village by village summaries.

46　Abiodun Alao, "The Metamorphosis of the 'Unorthodox': The Integration and Early Development of the Zimbabwean National Army" in N Bhebe and T Ranger (eds), *Soldiers in Zimbabwe's Liberation War, Volume One,* UZP, Harare, 1995, pp 104-17.

47　J Alexander, op cit, p 4, for information in this paragraph.

48　The areas specified here include the first case study area, Part Two, I.

49　*The Chronicle,* 1 Feb 1980; 8, 12, 16 July 1980; 26, 28, 30 Aug 1980; 2 Sept 1980, 1 Nov 1980 – all these reports are about ZANLA guerrillas causing problems in Mtoko, Mount Darwin and Gutu.

50　J Alexander, op cit, p 3.

51　A Alao, op cit, p 109, and *The Chronicle,* 11 Sept 1980.

52　*The Chronicle,* 10 Nov 1980. Nkala told assembled crowds: "ZAPU has declared itself the enemy of ZANU-PF... if it means a few blows, we will deliver them."

53　See, *inter alia,* LCFHR, op cit, p 19; A Alao, op cit, p *109; The Chronicle,* 6, 7, 14 May 1981, and numerous other sources for events surrounding Entumbane.

54　*The Chronicle,* 2 September 1982.

55　J Alexander, op cit., p 2 ff. Research recently conducted by J Alexander in northern Matabeleland is unique in that she relies on the testimonies of more than twenty ex-ZIPRA dissidents – more than one-sixth the total number that surrendered in 1988 – as well as the statements of those who lived in rural Matabeleland and experienced the dissidents first hand. This research, being based on the accounts of those most directly involved (i.e. the dissidents and the rural communities in which they lived), is in keeping with most of the data used throughout this report, which consists almost entirely of first-hand testimonies of events.

56　See, *inter alia,* A Alao, op cit, p 110, LCFHR, *The Chronicle* and others.

57　Quoted in LCFHR, op cit, p 87.

58　For more on the arms caches, see section following.

59　LCFHR, op cit, p 32 estimates approximately 1 000, while R Hodder-Williams estimates 4 000 in "Conflict in Zimbabwe: The Matabele problem", *Conflict Studies,* No. 151, Institute for the Study of Conflict, London, 1983, p 15.

60　J Alexander, op cit, p 14.

61　J Alexander, op cit, pp 20-21 for all information on Super Zapu and dissident activity and numbers.

62　For example, see comments by Prime Minister Mugabe in *The Chronicle,* 8 February and 22 March 1982, and by Minister Zvobgo, 16 July 1982. Some comments in 1980-81 have been footnoted above.

63　Interview, November 1996.

64 J Alexander, op cit, p 9.
65 J Alexander, op cit, p 14.
66 K Yapp, *Voices From the Conflict: Perceptions on Violence, Ethnicity, and the Disruption of National Unity,* paper presented at The Britain Zimbabwe Research Day, St Antony's College, Oxford University, 8 June 1996. All quotes following are from this paper.
67 K Yapp, *Voices*, pp 6-8.
68 J Alexander, op cit, p 14 and p 27.
69 Ibid, pp 21-22 for all information following on the zones.
70 Ibid, p 22.
71 Ibid, pp 20 and 27.
72 See previous section p 50.
73 J Hanlon, op cit, p 180. For more on South African destabilisation in Zimbabwe, see previous section.
74 Ibid, p 180. However, another source interviewed in Johannesburg in September 1996 reported that Calloway had (in a telephone conversation) denied any involvement in recruiting for Super ZAPU; interestingly, he did not deny the other charges commonly laid against him.
75 J Hanlon, op cit, pp 180-81, also D Martin and P Johnson (eds), 1986, op cit. Ammunition and weapons clearly dated as having been manufactured after Independence, and therefore not part of ZIPRA caches is cited.
76 D Martin and P Johnson (eds) 1986, op cit, p 61. This policy has been explained as an awareness on the part of South Africa that killing whites gained more international and Zimbabwean media coverage, and also caused alarm and despondency among Zimbabwean whites who were economically important to Zimbabwe.
77 J Alexander, op cit, pp 18-20; J Hanlon, op cit, p 181 acknowledges "strong antagonism by organised ex-ZIPRA dissidents to South Africa" as a reason for Super ZAPU's demise.
78 J Hanlon, op cit, p 182.
79 J Hanlon, op cit, p 182.
80 D Martin and P Johnson (eds), 1986, op cit, p 62, suggest this mainly because of an increase in the killing of white farmers at this time, which was in keeping with known Super ZAPU activity.
81 J Alexander, op cit, p 11, draws a distinction between those unruly and disgruntled elements who caused trouble around APs in 1980, and the thousands who deserted the army after February 1982, whose primary motive was fear, and who made up most of the group who finally became the "dissidents".
82 LCFHR, op cit; Minister Mubako, *The Chronicle,* 5 Oct 1983; and other Government ministers also acknowledge from time to time that some so-called dissident crimes could be the work of ordinary criminals. The dissidents themselves also complain of the problem that some who wished to join them were criminals, with no proper training or discipline. J Alexander cites this attitude, op cit, p 22.
83 Interview, October 1996.
84 Interview with lawyer of the accused, July 1996.
85 All information here on dissident numbers is based on what dissidents themselves reported to Alexander; however, their statements are borne

out by others, including that of Minister for State (Security) Emmerson
Mnangagwa, who said dissident numbers were never much over 300
– see LCFHR, p 16. While official references to dissidents quoted in *The
Chronicle* would cumulatively put dissident figures at around 800 (see Part
Two, III, Table 9 of this report), this figure is surely dramatically inflated.

86 J Alexander, op cit, p 23.

87 J Alexander and J McGregor, *Democracy, Development and Political
Conflict: Rural Institutions in Matabeleland North After Independence,*
paper presented at the International Conference on the Historical
Dimensions of Democracy and Human Rights in Zimbabwe, Harare,
September 1996, p 9.

88 J Alexander, op cit, p 23.

89 Ibid, p 24.

90 HR Database interview numbers 1371, 189, 712, among others.

91 This issue has already been raised in this report.

92 All this information is from interviews with commercial farmers in
Nyamandlovu.

93 J Alexander, op cit.

94 Interviews with commercial farmers, also *The Chronicle.*

95 Martin and Johnson (eds), 1986, op cit.

96 There are comparatively few dissident murders in communal areas – see
Part One, II and Part Two, III, Table 2, for more detail.

97 LCFHR quotes a figure of 500–600 murders, given to them by a
government official in 1985: two years of dissident activity followed this
statement, and the government claimed 116 deaths in 1986 and the press
reported 66 murders in 1987.

98 See Part Two, III of this report for more details.

99 Interviews, October 1996.

100 Many reports in *The Chronicle* testify to this, also CCJP and BLPC
interviews – see village by village summaries.

101 J Alexander, op cit, p 25.

102 Ibid, p 25.

103 See sections following on 5 Brigade, and village by village summaries.

104 The failure of the Government to prove ZAPU–dissident collusion is
discussed elsewhere. The two case study areas refer further to dissident
activities in their regions, and comparative tables, quantifying dissident
and other atrocities can be found in the tables and graphs in Part Two.

105 *The Chronicle,* 27 June 1980.

106 *The Chronicle,* 29 April; 26 June; and 26 August 1982 quotes Nkomo
condemning dissidents.

107 *The Chronicle,* 4 May 1981.

108 See comments by Mugabe, Nkala and Zvobgo, among others: *The
Chronicle,* 26 October 1981; 5, 10, 22 November 1981; 16 July 1982.

109 *The Chronicle,* 8 February 1982.

110 *The Chronicle,* 12 February 1982. There is more comment on these caches
in the previous section.

111 *The Chronicle,* 17 February 1982.

112 *A Place For Everybody: Twenty Years of CCJPZ: 1972-1992,* Edwina
Spicer Productions, 1992. J Hanlon, op cit, p 183, argues strongly in

favour of this theory. Calloway was already acting on behalf of South Africa at this time, and framing ZAPU with arms caches would have been in keeping with South Africa's policy of destabilising all independent countries in the region.

113 Interview, October 1996.
114 See Part Two, III, Table 6.
115 *The Chronicle,* 22 March & 30 July 1982.
116 As mentioned above, this kidnapping may not have been a dissident act. Some of the robberies were also very likely not committed by "dissidents": the problem with allocating blame in such instances is raised above.
117 Also referred to as "Specific Reports" – see Part One, II.
118 *The Chronicle,* 4 October 1982.
119 Interview, September 1996.
120 See previous section for more on Super ZAPU.
121 Helicopters or aeroplanes flew over target areas giving instructions and information over loudspeakers.
122 *The Chronicle,* 6 & 16 July 1982.
123 *The Chronicle,* 22 July 1982.
124 Interview with specialist concerned, December 1996, for all information in this paragraph.
125 See map of Eastern Nyamandlovu, village by village summary following.
126 *Africa Confidential,* 11 April 1984.
127 J Alexander, op cit, p 10.
128 *The Chronicle* quotes Nkomo on 29 April, 26 June and 30 August, as condemning dissidents.
129 *The Chronicle,* 6 July 1982. Sekeramayi said this. See also 26 June and 26 & 30 July.
130 Nkala, quoted in *The Chronicle,* 14 June 1982: see also section following.
131 *The Chronicle,* 4 August 1982.
132 See speeches by Government leaders cited above in *The Chronicle*; also 18 August 1982.
133 *The Chronicle,* 8 March 1985.
134 LCFHR, op cit, p 21.
135 *The Chronicle,* 31 January 1984.
136 *The Chronicle,* 18 January 1986.
137 *The Chronicle,* 23 and 25 June 1987.
138 *Moto,* October 1996, p 7.
139 CCJP Press Statement, released 25 July 1982.
140 LCFHR, op cit, p 38.
141 For more discussion of this allegation, see pp 85-87, 95, 100-101 and 116 of this report.
142 *The Chronicle,* 12 Feb 1983.
143 See village by village summaries for interview details supporting this.
144 See LCFHR, p 155 ff and elsewhere, and also CCJP *Report on Torture,* January 1987. Those acquitted of crimes by the Courts could also be re-detained indefinitely, as were Dabengwa and Masuku.
145 *The Chronicle,* 8 May 1982, for example.
146 *The Chronicle,* 4 February 1983.
147 CCJP Press Release, 5 November 1982.

148 See the rest of this report for an expansion on this.

149 *Gukurahundi – Ten Years Later,* Zimbabwe Defence Forces Magazine, Vol 7, No 1.

150 *The Chronicle,* 12 August 1980.

151 *Gukurahund" – Ten Years Later,* Zimbabwe Defence Forces Magazine, Vol 7, No 1.

152 *The Chronicle,* 14 & 21 August 1981.

153 *The Chronicle,* 22 August 1981.

154 *The Chronicle,* 25 August 1981.

155 *The Chronicle,* 27 August, 1981: for definition of "Gukurahundi", see R Werbner, op cit.

156 *The Chronicle,* 14 September 1981.

157 *The Chronicle,* 9 September 1982.

158 Many interviews report such statements by 5 Brigade, including archival CCJP records.

159 Zimbabwe Defence Forces Magazine 1992, op cit. This comment is the only oblique reference in this lengthy article on 5 Brigade to the thousands of atrocities committed by its members. How this "disciplinary machine" worked, or how many soldiers were disciplined by it, is not mentioned. Certainly very few 5 Brigade soldiers ever faced prosecution within the normal judicial system.

160 Ibid: apparently no spare parts or maintenance were provided by the Koreans.

161 J Alexander, op cit, p 11.

162 Comments along these lines are frequently made by civilians who encountered the 5 Brigade. Alexander, op cit, p 12, speculates they were from Tanzania or Mozambique.

163 *The Chronicle,* 16 July 1982.

164 J Alexander, op cit, p 10. Also in July 1982, three British tourists, a woman and two men, were shot dead in Nyanga, which was the area where 5 Brigade was based. These murders have been widely attributed to 5 Brigade.

165 'Gukurahundi' – Ten Years Later.

166 R Werbner, op cit, pp 152 ff.

167 See Section in the report on "The Dissident Problem", for sources of figures. Government troop figures are based on interviews with CCJP personnel, and are conservative: *"Africa Confidential",* 11 April 1984, estimates 15 000 Government troops in Matabeleland South in 1984.

168 See Part Two in its entirety for a justification of these figures. These figures are a conservative estimate – in Tsholotsho, the only area in Matabeleland North that was extensively studied for this report, approximately 1 000 people are now assumed to have been killed in this period.

169 One of more than two dozen personal accounts of events in Silwane on 6 February is included in this report as Appendix A ii.

170 See village by village summaries, Part Two, I, especially Pumula Mission Area.

171 See Map of Zimbabwe showing curfew zones.

172 See Part Two, II for more on the food curfew.

173 This justification is cited in LCFHR, op cit, p 32, and is also offered as

an explanation in A Alao, "The Metamorphosis of the Unorthodox: The Integration and Early Development of the Zimbabwean National Army", in N Bhebe and T Ranger (eds), *Soldiers in Zimbabwe's Liberation War, Volume One* (UZP, Harare, 1995), p 114.

174 See Part Two, I and II of this report for evidence of this.

175 J Alexander, op cit, p 12, also for quote following.

176 See Part Two, I and II of this report.

177 J Alexander, op cit, p 12; R Werbner, op cit, also argues this.

178 See Part Three, I of this report for a graphic and lengthy first hand account of such a "pungwe."

179 J Alexander, op cit, p 23.

180 Interviews with commercial farmers, 1995.

181 5 Brigade soldiers were here referring to the outbreaks of violence between ZIPRA and ZANLA in Matabeleland and the Midlands, in February 1981: see previous section of this report, p 53.

182 The burning to death of people in huts was also reported in Lupane, and two such cases are currently on record.

183 See Part Two of this report, pp 149, 166, 176, 202, 206.

184 R Carver, *Amnesty*, op cit, describes some events in Silobela, as do CCJP archival materials.

185 *The Chronicle*, 27 January 1983.

186 On 12 February the Catholic Bishop of Bulawayo sent a letter and statements to Prime Minister Mugabe, and a few days later a private citizen met with Nhongo, Brigadier Aggripah Mutambara and Justin Nyoka, Director of Information. She related what she had heard about atrocities from people in affected areas, and arranged for copies of Bishop Karlen's submissions to Mugabe to be shown to Nhongo. Interview, 1996.

187 *The Chronicle*, 26 February 1983.

188 *The Chronicle*, 28 February 1983

189 *The Chronicle*, 3 February 1983.

190 *The Chronicle*, 8 March 1983.

191 *The Chronicle*, 7 March 1983.

192 *The Chronicle*, 10 March 1983.

193 *The Chronicle*, 10 March 1983.

194 See Part One, II of this report for an outline of their evidence: also village by village summaries, Part Two, I and II.

195 CCJP has this dossier on record.

196 *The Chronicle*, 30 March 1983.

197 *The Chronicle*, 6 April 1983.

198 *The Chronicle*, 9 April 1983.

199 *The Chronicle*, 15 April 1983.

200 This term is used by Sekeramayi: *The Chronicle*, February 1983.

201 *The Chronicle*, 18 April 1983.

202 *The Chronicle*, 5 March 1983.

203 Forced attendance at weekend-long pungwes was a notable feature in Matabeleland North in March, April and May of 1983: see Part Two for more detail.

204 *The Chronicle*, 5 April 1983.

205 *The Chronicle*, 26 April 1983.

206 *The Chronicle,* 14 September 1983.

207 See p 97, following, for more on this Commission.

208 See village by village summary, Part Two, I.

209 See village by village summaries, Part Two, I and II of this report.

210 This was a tactic used by some elements of the Rhodesian forces too: see p 27, for more on this, and the problems of proving or disproving such allegations now.

211 See Part Two, I of this report, Pumula Mission Area.

212 CCJP Archives.

213 See Part Two, I and II of this report for specific cases.

214 R Werbner, op cit, p 152.

215 Several interviews on record report people shot specifically for mourning. See Part Two, I.

216 These claims are more fully explored in Part Three, I.

217 LCFHR, op cit, p 61 quotes this figure, and says approximately 80 cases of abductions at this time are well documented: interviews in Tsholotsho have turned up some names of men who vanished in 1985, but also fewer than 120. Some who were detained could have been subsequently released.

218 See Case Study II for more on this curfew.

219 *Africa Confidential,* 11 April 1984.

220 LCFHR, op cit, p 20.

221 See Part One; II p 26, for definition of "Specific Reports"; and Part Two, III, Table 5.

222 *The Chronicle,* June 1983.

223 LCFHR, op cit, p 26.

224 J Alexander, op cit, p 21.

225 Ibid, p 21.

226 LCFHR, op cit, pp 135-141.

227 Part Two, II deals with the curfew in more depth.

228 CCJP has extensive information on Bhalagwe – see Part Two, II.

229 BLPC interviews, see Part Two, II for more detail on all claims here. Interviews referring to Bhalagwe portray a very consistent pattern in this regard and others.

230 LCFHR, op cit, p 135, mentions a figure of 5 000. See Case Study 2 for more on Bhalagwe and a rationale for figures.

231 *The Observer,* April 1984. Peter Godwin also personally visited Antelope Mine in 1984 and smelled this stench of rotting flesh: *Mukiwa,* Macmillan, 1996, chapter 21.

232 Zimbabwe Defence Forces Magazine, op cit, p 36.

233 See village by village summary, Part Two, I, Interview 206. Post-election abuses were widespread in late 1985, but CIO, ZANU-PF Youth and the ZANU-PF Women's League are far more commonly the perpetrators of offences at this time.

234 The ZNA does still have a "5 Brigade", but this is very different in nature from the 5 Brigade of the 1980s: it is subject to normal army command structures, and has no history of atrocities.

235 Zimbabwe Defence Force, op cit, p 36.

236 File H: see Part Two, I, village by village summary.

237 J Alexander, op cit, p 12.

238 This is a CCJP documented event: the 5 children were all aged between 7 and 12.

239 Interviews, CCJP officials 1996.

240 An ex-5 Brigade member made a statement to BLPC to this effect in December 1996, claiming ongoing psychiatric problems, and psychologists also report being approached by ex-5 Brigade members for help.

241 Statements by Dyke to K Yapp, and cited in her paper presented at the Britain–Zimbabwe Society's Research Day, June 8 1996.

242 Desire for revenge among dissidents has been raised in the section on "The Dissident Problem".

243 J Hanlon, op cit, p 180, discusses recruitment of refugees for Super ZAPU: dissidents brought to trial also refer to this.

244 It must be added that there is little independent corroboratory evidence for the Government's claims that these crimes, in particular the murders, were committed by dissidents; but as it is those who support the state who justify 5 Brigade activity, it is interesting to look at their own statistics in this regard. For reliability of *The Chronicle,* see Part One, II.

245 J Alexander and J McGregor, op cit, pp 14 to 16 for this and following quotes in this section.

246 Ibid, p 16.

247 Ibid, p 16. A multitude of interviews conducted in the 1990s, as well as archival 1980s files, claim these justifications were given by 5 Brigade, not only in Matabeleland North in 1983 but in Matabeleland South in 1984. People in 1996 had still not forgotten these messages.

248 The speech made at a rally by one such "Black Jesus" is quoted in full in this report, Part Three, I.

249 J Alexander and J McGregor, op cit, p 16.

250 J Alexander and J McGregor, op cit, p 19 deal with this issue in depth, pp 17-20.

251 Ibid, p 25.

252 Ibid, p 25: quoting councillors and headmen in 1995 in Lupane. Similar comments were made to personnel involved in the current project in Tsholotsho and Matobo. R Werbner, op cit, also quotes civilians who consider the 5 Brigade as the worst war ever.

253 Interviews with CCJP personnel, 1995-96.

254 *The Chronicle,* 14 January 1984.

255 Interview; also existing archival interview. Fifty-five people died in this massacre and seven survived with serious injuries.

256 See pp 313-316, 321-322.

257 It must be borne in mind that, even as this Committee was collecting evidence of the previous year's atrocities, the Government was in the middle of a further calculated process of brutalising civilians: Bhalagwe Camp was in full swing as the Committee sat.

258 Interviews with CCJP personnel, 1995-96.

259 Interview with Bulawayo lawyer, July 1996.

260 LCFHR, op cit, p 140-41.

261 CCJP archives have this statement in full.

262 *The Chronicle,* 10 April 1984.

263 *The Chronicle,* 16 April 1984.

264 *The Chronicle,* 28 April 1984.

265 *The Chronicle,* 27 & 30 April 1984.

266 *A Place For Everybody: CCJP 1972-1992,* op cit. This video covers the trip in depth. P Godwin, op cit, also refers in detail to this trip, during which the army commander, General Mujuru, publicly threatened to shoot Godwin dead.

267 LCFHR, op cit, p 40.

268 For a thorough overview of these events, see LCFHR, op cit, pp 115-29: their report was compiled contemporaneously to events in 1985 and much of the detail following in the current section relies on their account.

269 See paragraphs on the Beitbridge violence in 1984, and the Silobela violence in 1985.

270 LCFHR, op cit, pp 54-57, for all information following on ZANU-Youth, unless otherwise indicated.

271 Summary of damage described by LCFHR, op cit, pp 115-132.

272 *The Chronicle,* December 1984, confirms this.

273 LCFHR, op cit, p 113.

274 Many statements in *The Herald,* Harare's daily paper, and *The Chronicle* suggest ZANU-PF was confident of an almost clean sweep.

275 This speech was broadcast by ZBC within a day or two of the election results: interview, July 1996.

276 LCFHR, op cit, p l27.

277 Police Internal Security and Intelligence unit: see section E following.

278 LCFHR, op cit, p l33.

279 PISI is discussed in section E following.

280 LCFHR, op cit, p 67.

281 CCJP documentation; also *The Guardian,* 9 June 1985.

282 LCFHR, op cit, p 122: CCJP has this full report in their records.

283 On the basis of current research, this figure seems very conservative: detentions almost certainly ran to several hundred in rural Matabeleland. For example, a police document sent to CCJP in response to an inquiry from them about a missing person, acknowledges that police detained 80 people in Nkayi alone on a single day, but says most were later released, and claims they have no record of the missing man.

284 LCFHR, op cit, p 111.

285 The CIO official was Robert Masikini, who was found guilty of murder, and immediately pardoned under a presidential amnesty. *Africa Watch Report,* October 1989.

286 Torture at Esigodini is referred to by *Africa Watch,* op cit, 1989; as well as CCJP documents and other interviews on file. The "wrack" method was also used by the Rhodesians.

287 *Africa Watch Report,* October 1989, pp 33-42.

288 See Case Study II for more on CIO practices at Bhalagwe.

289 LCFHR, op cit, p 148 ff, refers to this illegal practice; reference to it is also made in *The Guardian,* June 9 1985.

290 Many interviews on record testify to official indifference or denial after people were detained.

291 See Part Three, II, Legal Damages, for more on these two cases.

292 The widows of these abductees speak at length in *A Place For Everybody,*

CCJP, op cit. Their case has also been legally documented.

293 Ibid.
294 CCJP documentation.
295 *The Chronicle,* 1992 and September 1995.
296 Interviews, 1995-96.
297 That the coins were Zimbabwean was clear from ZTV's own footage of the body recovery exercise.
298 LCFHR, p 73 also refers to this.
299 See LCFHR, op cit, p 89-111; also CCJP *Report on Torture 1987,* and numerous interviews on file for detention conditions.
300 See sources cited above: also Part Three, I of this report for more on torture.
301 Amnesty International, op cit, reports all these methods, as does CCJP.
302 CCJP, Amnesty International, LCFHR, all op cit. See Part 5 for more on psychological torture.
303 In *The Chronicle,* July 1983, LCFHR also discusses the issue of torture in custody at length, pp 89-111.
304 LCFHR, op cit, pp 98-99.
305 *Zimbabwe Independent,* 19 July 1996.
306 Ibid.
307 *The Weekly Mail & Guardian,* Johannesburg, November 1996.
308 ZAPU MP Kembo Mahadi, for example, was tortured in 1985, and was awarded damages by the court: these were never paid.
309 LCFHR, op cit, pp 101-04, cites *S v Abednico Sibindi,* where serious charges were dismissed on the grounds that the defendant had been treated "quite outrageously". Nor was this an isolated case.
310 Ibid, pp 50-54 for much of the information following.
311 Herbert Ushewokunze had used Zipolis to keep an internal "eye" on ex-Rhodesians still in the force.
312 LCFHR, op cit, p 50.
313 Ibid.
314 Ibid, p 51.
315 Ibid, p 52.
316 Ibid, p 27. Mnangagwa gave this analysis of dissident activity. *The Chronicle* reported 17 of these murders and also the destruction of property worth $100 000 by dissidents.
317 This incident is well covered in *The Chronicle,* and also in LCFHR, op cit, p 29.
318 J Alexander, op cit, p 26 quotes dissidents who offer the "tribal" explanation for this attack.
319 CCJP telegram to ZBC, on file.
320 LCFHR, pp 75-79 also documents these events.
321 Far from conspiring against Zimbabwe, Ndlovu was already actively engaged in negotiating the "dissolving of ZAPU into ZANU" in the interests of national unity: documents on record support this contention.
322 Original CIO detention order for Edward Ndlovu, signed by Enos Nkala, 17 October 1985.
323 Information on Malunga's trial is all on record with his lawyer, who

allowed its use for this report.

324 Interview, November 1996.

325 See Part Two, III, Tables 5 and 7, pp 298 and 299.

326 LCFHR comments on the unreliability of statistics in Zimbabwe. The lack of truly impartial press reporting confounds the problem. See Part One, II.

327 There is further evidence of this attack on file, but it cannot be cited in detail in order to protect informants who would be easily identifiable.

328 *The Chronicle,* 18 November 1987.

329 *The Chronicle,* 28 November 1987.

330 *The Chronicle,* 12 March 1986.

331 *The Chronicle,* 1 & 20 October 1986.

332 *The Chronicle,* 5 December 1996.

333 *The Chronicle* 2 & 3 February 1987.

334 *The Chronicle,* 20 April & 15 May, 1987.

335 *The Chronicle,* 20 & 23 June, 10 & 16 September 1987.

336 *The Chronicle,* 22 September 1987.

337 *A Place For Everybody,* op cit.

338 *The Chronicle,* 18 November 1987.

339 *Zimbabwean Government Gazette Extraordinary,* 3 May 1988: all details of the Amnesty are from this.

340 For more information on where the handful of dissidents had been operating when the Amnesty was declared, see the previous section, p 57.

PART TWO
FINDINGS

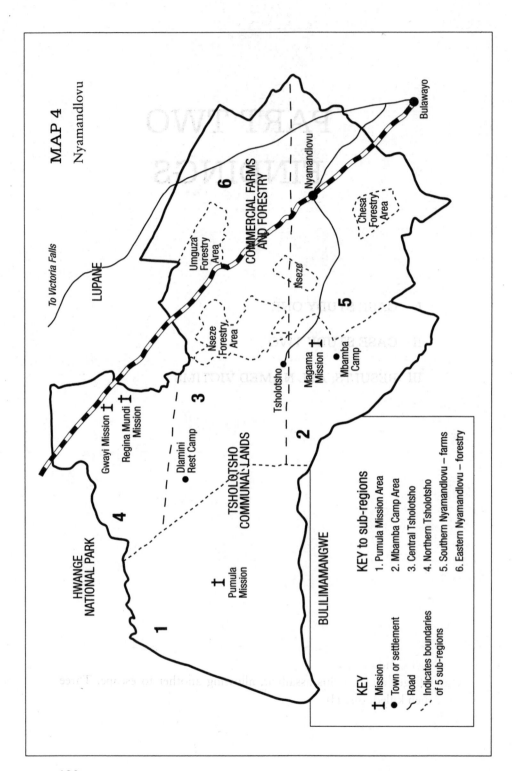

MAP 4
Nyamandlovu

KEY
✝ Mission
● Town or settlement
  Road
∙∙∙ Indicates boundaries
    of 5 sub-regions

KEY to sub-regions
1. Pumula Mission Area
2. Mbamba Camp Area
3. Central Tsholotsho
4. Northern Tsholotsho
5. Southern Nyamandlovu – farms
6. Eastern Nyamandlovu – forestry

HWANGE
NATIONAL PARK

To Victoria Falls

LUPANE

Gwayi Mission ✝
Regina Mundi ✝
Mission

Dlamini ●
Rest Camp

Pumula ✝
Mission

TSHOLOTSHO
COMMUNAL LANDS

Nseze
Forestry
Area

Umguza
Forestry
Area

COMMERCIAL FARMS
AND FORESTRY

Nseze

Nseze

Chesa
Forestry
Area

Tsholotsho ●

Magama ✝
Mission

Mbamba ●
Camp

Nyamandlovu ●

Bulawayo ●

BULILIMAMANGWE

1

4

3

2

5

6

I

CASE STUDY ONE

NYAMANDLOVU, INCLUSIVE OF TSHOLOTSHO:

THE VILLAGE BY VILLAGE[1] SUMMARY:

INTEGRATION OF NAMED AND UNNAMED VICTIMS

Data Sources and Methodology in Part One deals in detail with the data collection and collation process in the two case study areas. To summarise, data used consists of archival CCJP material, information extracted from the media, academic studies, and interviews conducted in the 1990s. All of these sources are archival, apart from the interviews: these latter serve to illustrate not only the past, but current perceptions of the past and current consequences of past events.

1. ARCHIVAL DATA – *THE CHRONICLE*

A summary of events specifically in Nyamandlovu/Tsholotsho, as revealed by *The Chronicle,* Bulawayo's daily newspaper, is given here. This tends to highlight dissident activity, and is a useful counterpoint to data from other sources.

1981

FEBRUARY   The second outburst of fighting between ZIPRA and ZANLA forces spills over into Nyamandlovu, where army units loyal to the Government intercept columns of ZIPRA troops heading for Bulawayo from Gwayi in the north.

APRIL   Two people are shot dead near Khami, and a third is injured, by "armed men."

1982

17 MAY   A Nyamandlovu farmer is ambushed by dissidents and sustains a gunshot wound. Two days later a lorry driver

	is shot and killed near Godzo, in Tsholotsho. In the same month, a farmer's wife drives through a dissident ambush but is not injured.
JUNE	Dissidents rob a bus, a beer garden and four stores in Nyamandlovu. They also burn out two resettled villages in Nyamandlovu, leaving 75 families homeless. "One woman" is also killed.
4 JULY	The manager of Grant's Sawmills, Nyamandlovu, is shot at by dissidents – no injury.
13 JULY	A police auxiliary constable is shot and injured at Hillmiles store.
23 JULY	A local farmer drives through an ambush at the 76km peg on the Victoria Falls road (in Nyamandlovu), does not stop and sustains no injury – perpetrators, dissidents.
23 JULY	Six foreign tourists stop when ambushed at the 76km peg on the Bulawayo–Victoria Falls road, in Nyamandlovu, and are abducted.
AUGUST	Two mineworkers are shot dead 20km north of Bulawayo. Seven off-duty soldiers are lined up against a wall in Ngoma beerhall, Nyamandlovu, and are bayoneted: five die and eight are wounded – by dissidents. Three buses are robbed, and so are "stores", all in Nyamandlovu.
4 SEPTEMBER	Two Swiss tourists witness a shoot out between security forces and dissidents, 90km north of Bulawayo. A curfew is imposed on northern Matabeleland, banning buses and private vehicles in the communal areas, and banning reporters.
OCTOBER	Dissidents rob a bus in Nyamndlovu.
DECEMBER	There are several incidents involving dissidents. In Tsholotsho, Z$2 million of Government equipment is destroyed. In Nyamandlovu, six people including two children are shot dead in a farm ambush, on 31 December. One unnamed villager and two named villagers are also reported murdered by dissidents in Nyamandlovu.

1983

6 JANUARY	The Government agrees to allow farmers to re-arm, to protect themselves against dissidents. They had all surrendered their weapons at Independence.
26 JANUARY	Stringent curfew regulations are introduced: at the same time, 5 Brigade is deployed into the region, and begins

	to work its way northwards, through Tsholotsho, into Lupane and Nkayi.
MARCH	An elderly commercial farming couple and their two young granddaughters are brutally beaten and then shot by dissidents on their farm in Nyamandlovu.
5 APRIL	The curfew is lifted. There are repeated ZANU-PF rallies in Matabeleland in February, March and April at which people are warned not to support ZAPU, and dissidents are paraded, declaring their PF-ZAPU allegiance. More than 20 000 ZAPU supporters surrender their cards and join ZANU-PF.
MAY	A forestry commission ranger is murdered and another abducted by dissidents in Chesa Forest Area, Nyamandlovu.
JUNE	30 youths in Nyamandlovu are reported abducted by dissidents, and are rescued.
NOVEMBER	Two men are reported murdered by dissidents in Nyamandlovu.

1984

JUNE	20 dissidents kill one person and beat others, in Tsholotsho.
SEPEMBER	An unnamed boy is reported as being killed by dissidents, another as kidnapped, while unnamed, unnumbered "workers" are beaten and property burnt, in Nyamandlovu.
OCTOBER	Inquest into the murder in February 1983 of two men and two women, whose car was stopped on the Bulawayo–Victoria Falls road by four 5 Brigade soldiers. The inquest finds them responsible for "exceedingly cruel" murder. (LCFHR p 40)
NOVEMBER	Jini Ntuta, ZAPU MP, is reported murdered by dissidents. Other sources later attribute his murder to CIO (LCFHR, BLPC interview).

1985

MARCH	One woman is reported murdered and nine injured, by dissidents.
JULY	Dissidents burn a bus in Nyamandlovu.
SEPTEMBER	Dissidents burn out a school complex, and kill one person, in Nyamandlovu.

OCTOBER   A commercial farming couple and their foreman are shot
                and killed by dissidents. Dissidents also kill three villagers
                and four Zanu-PF party officials in Tsholotsho.

1986

                There are no press reported incidents involving dissidents/
                armed men/bandits designated as occurring anywhere
                in Matabeleland North, including Nyamandlovu, in
                1986.

1987

JUNE   Two German tourists are shot and killed in Nyamandlovu
                by dissidents.

AUGUST   A Nyamandlovu farmer on his way to a cattle sale is
                shot dead with his militia man, by dissidents.

DECEMBER   Unity Accord.

1988

EARLY   Amnesty is announced for dissidents, and then for
                security forces. A total of 122 dissidents surrender.

Quantifying dissident offences

According to *The Chronicle,* dissidents murdered a total of 50 people
in the Nyamandlovu/Tsholotsho region. These totals are fairly similar
to BLPC interview tallies, which indicate a total of 39 murders either
by dissidents or "armed men". BLPC data also refers to five crossfire
incidents in which four villagers are killed and three sustain gunshot
wounds in shoot-outs between dissidents and security forces; whether
dissident or ZNA bullets are responsible is not clear.

   The Chronicle specifies a total of 30 assaults by dissidents in
Nyamandlovu/Tsholotsho.

   Specific news reports also identify as taking place in Nyamandlovu/
Tsholotsho the following: two rapes; 31 abductions; the theft or
destruction of 94 properties. Seventy-five of the property offences
involve the burning of homesteads on a mine in Nyamandlovu, and the
destruction of US$200 000 worth of government equipment, being used
to build dams in the area.[2]

   BLPC and CCJP data refer to 32 assaults by dissidents on civilians in
Tsholotsho, invariably related to people being accused of being "sell-outs".
They also record three gunshot wounds and three incidents involving
mutilations. These totals are again very similar to *The Chronicle,* which

suggests civilians are not inclined at this stage to protect dissidents, and reported their offences to project personnel.[3]

Other BLPC interviews make reference to dissidents, often in passing, when villagers are beaten by 5 Brigade after being forced at gunpoint to feed dissidents the day before.

2. DATA INTEGRATION – CCJP ARCHIVES AND INTERVIEWS IN 1995 – 1996

There is a vast amount of information in CCJP files on events in Tsholotsho. For a complete outline of what forms such information takes, see CCJP as a data source in Part One. CCJP data remains invaluable and is more reliable than most other sources where dates are concerned. Details given in the archives have frequently served to confirm accounts given in interviews in 1995-96.

A total of 910 *named* victims in Tsholotsho was collected through interviews, many of who suffered more than one human rights violation. For an outline of the interviewing procedure in Tsholotsho, see Part One, II.

Data from both CCJP archives and recent interviews were integrated in a village by village summary, with village as the common parameter allowing for the integration of named and numbered victims, without their being counted twice, once with and once without a name.

The "village by village" summary of events proved to be a very productive strategy when analysing data on Tsholotsho, and helped reveal the broad patterns of events. In addition to facilitating the quantification of atrocities and their perpetrators, this method also revealed the location of army units at different times, in particular 5 Brigade. Tsholotsho was therefore divided up into approximately four parts, to correspond with the concentration of 5 Brigade in the various parts of the area. In fact, as is clear from the summaries, 5 Brigade reached most villages in the area, and camped in small groups in many different locations: the four rough divisions indicate locations of larger units and interrogation centres, from which patrols appear to have set out. In addition, the rest of Nyamandlovu was divided into two sections, one consisting largely of commercial farms in the south, and the other of the forestry areas in the east.

The sub-regions of Nyamandlovu are:
1. Western Tsholotsho, around Pumula Mission.
2. Southern Tsholotsho, around Mbamba Camp.

3. Central Tsholotsho, including Tsholotshi Town and Dhlamini Rest Camp to the west.

4. Northern Tsholotsho, around Gwayi and Sipepa.

5. Commercial farms in the south.

6. Forestry, resettlement and commercial farmland in the east.

Maps

On page 136 there is a map of Nyamandlovu, inclusive of Tsholotsho Communal Lands, which shows the areas into which the entire region has been divided for the purposes of this summary, and which indicates the major centres.

Five larger scale maps of Nyamandlovu, corresponding to the divisions in the text, have been included in the body of the village by village summary. These indicate not only the villages but also the general type and number of offences experienced in the vicinity of each village. Approximate numbers killed, beaten or having homesteads burnt is thus visually represented on the maps.

Three of these maps show Tsholotsho Communal Land and its rough divisions into four parts. The other two maps show commercial farmland, and the forestry and resettlement areas in Nyamandlovu.

3. SUMMARY OF 5 BRIGADE IMPACT IN MATABELELAND NORTH

The commissioning, training and deployment of 5 Brigade has already been dealt with in detail in Part One of this report. To summarise, 5 Brigade was deployed in Matabeleland North in January 1983, coinciding with the imposition of a severe curfew in the region. Thousands of atrocities, including murders, mass physical torture and the burnings of property occurred in the ensuing six weeks. 5 Brigade was withdrawn for a month in the middle of the year, then redeployed. Disappearances and detentions became more common than other offences. Mbamba Camp in the south of Tsholotsho is frequently referred to as a detention centre. 5 Brigade was mainly deployed in Matabeleland South in early 1984, although a platoon of 5 Brigade was in Matabeleland North at this time too. However, there was no curfew in force in Matabeleland North in 1984, and 5 Brigade activities were centred on the southern half of the country.

The presence of the 5 Brigade in an area in 1983 meant an inital outburst of intense brutality, usually lasting a few days, followed by random incidents of beatings, burnings and murders in the ensuing weeks, months and years. It meant that any community which had once experienced 5 Brigade lived in a state of intense anxiety and fear, unsure where and when it might strike again, or who its next victims might be.

The terror and insecurity throughout the region also led to many hundreds of people, especially young men, fleeing to urban centres such as Bulawayo, or to Botswana. To stay in the area if you were a young man meant almost certain victimisation by 5 Brigade, who assumed that all such people were ex-ZIPRA and therefore dissidents.

Many communities suffered massive material loss in the initial onslaught, losing huts and granaries. They also lost village members who had been killed or abducted, and were frequently forced to watch others close to them dying slowly from injuries sustained from beating, burning, shooting or bayoneting. Villagers were warned not to seek medical help, and risked being shot for curfew breaking if they did seek help.

Many who were beaten were left with permanent disabilities, ranging from paralysis, blindness, deafness, recurrent miscarriage, impotence, infertility and kidney damage, to partial lameness and recurring backaches and headaches. These injuries have left victims with impaired ability to work in their fields or do any of the heavy labour, such as carrying water, on which survival in the rural areas depends. Inability to work in the fields is a recurring theme in interviews.

In addition to the physical injuries, it is clear from interviews that large numbers of people in Tsholotsho suffered some degree of psychological trauma, leading in extreme cases to insanity, and in many cases to recurring depression, dizzy spells, anxiety, anger or a permanent fear and distrust of Government officials.

Families were left without breadwinners. Children were left without one or both parents, and with the trauma of having witnessed appalling violence against those they loved. Families were left without the consolation of truly knowing the fate of their kin, or their burial places. Communities were left to deal with the trauma of having seen their parents, husbands and community leaders harmed and humiliated. Many families have had to face practical problems arising from the number of dead for whom death certificates were never issued. This has meant problems gaining birth certificates for children, or drawing money from bank books in the name of the deceased. Other people who fled employment in the area, in order to protect their lives, have been denied pensions for having broken their service without notice.

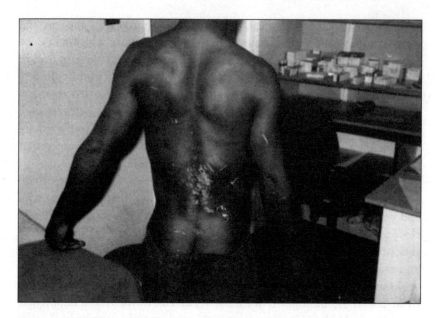

Photo 10: A Tsholotsho resident showing scars from burning plastic, February 1983

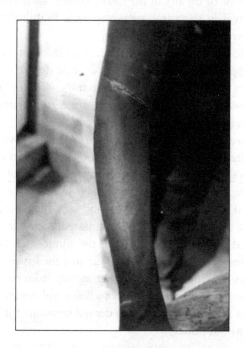

Photo 11: This Tsholotsho 5 Brigade victim suffered permanent paralysis in both forearms as a result of being tied up with wire, February 1983

Photo 12: A 5 Brigade victim buried where he died, near a school gate in Tsholotsho

Photo 13: A mass grave in Tsholotsho, western area: Thirteen 5 Brigade victims were buried here, February 1983

4. OVERVIEW OF HUMAN RIGHTS ABUSES – NYAMANDLOVU / TSHOLOTSHO

A) DEATHS AND DISAPPEARANCES

Deaths have been assessed in terms of both sex and age of victims, with three age categories being used for each sex:

MALE: 83% of all deaths
FEMALE: 17% of all deaths

MALE
Under 20 yrs: 4% of all deaths
Aged 20-60 yrs: 70% of all deaths
Aged over 60 yrs: 9% of all deaths

FEMALE
Under 20 yrs: 4% of all deaths
Aged 20-60 yrs: 9% of all deaths
Aged over 60 yrs: 4% of all deaths

Men aged between 20 and 60 years are of "bread-winning age" (i.e. 70 per cent of all dead). However, approximately 30-40 per cent of them can be assumed to have had no dependants, as many had just returned from the war and had not yet married. Many others, at the top end of this age group, had fully grown children.

This means between 42 per cent and 50 per cent of all those killed can be assumed to have had dependants. In addition, a few of the women killed were widows with dependants, whose children were henceforth orphans. Around two per cent fall in this category.

Total breadwinners killed is likely to be around 45% of total deaths.

In terms of current figures on Nyamandlovu/ Tsholotsho:

Total deaths: approx 900+
Breadwinners dead: approx 400

The vast majority of these were self-employed farmers, who supported themselves from their fields and occasional labour on surrounding farms and in nearby towns.

B) PROPERTY LOSSES: HOMESTEADS BURNT

This constitutes the largest category of property loss reported.

Reported burnt: 345 homesteads, with others implied. (Involves burning of 26 villages either entirely or substantially.)

C) BEATINGS

This is the largest category of offence, involving both isolated beating incidents and also at least 70 incidents in which most or all villagers in a village were beaten. Both men and women were beaten, with no obvious preference for beating men in the mass beatings. Preference was sometimes shown to the elderly, who would be beaten less severely or not at all.

Individual or small group assaults: 314
Mass village beatings: 70 villages
Mass railway siding beatings: 4

If approximately 50 villagers is assumed per mass beating, 4 000 villagers can be estimated to have been beaten. The most common beating technique was that the victim(s) would be forced to lie face down on the ground, and then would be repeatedly beaten, often for several hours, with thick sticks or gun butts. The most common complaints include:
• Permanent back / arm / leg / neck / hand aches, inhibiting any heavy work.
• Fractured fingers / arms and other bones.
• Permanent scarring of buttocks and back.
• Recurring headaches, dizziness and high blood pressure.
• Permanent eye damage and hearing disorders.
• Jaw damage including loss of teeth.
• Permanent uterine disorders.
• Permanent kidney damage, also male impotence.

For a region by region breakdown on all offences, see the Summary following the village by village summaries.

5. THE VILLAGE BY VILLAGE SUMMARY – DETAILING INCIDENTS ACCORDING TO TIME AND PLACE

NOTE:
Numbers in brackets indicate source numbers of BLPC interviews from which information was derived.
** indicates source document is in a CCJP file.

> **** indicates an incident involving dissidents.
> For all other incidents, the perpetrators are identified as army units or other Government agencies such as the Central Intelligence Organisation (CIO), or Police Support Unit (SU).

5 Brigade (written as 5B in the accounts) may be assumed as the perpetrator unless another unit is mentioned.

Tsholotsho has been roughly divided up into four regions for this section, each one being an area within the vicinity of known 5 Brigade base camps. In practice some villages were affected by more than one of these units, and in early 1983 the far south of Tsholotsho was probably affected by the unit based in Tsholotsho, as the one at Mbamba Camp appears to have been established later in 1983. The four regions are:

1. Pumula Mission, covering the whole western area and much of the south.
2. Mbamba/Nanda, in the extreme south and east.
3. Tsholotsho town and the central part of Tsholotsho, west towards Dhlamini Rest Camp.
4. Gwayi/Sipepa region, in northern Tsholotsho.

The spellings of names of "villages" or "lines" have been standardised in accordance with the 1975 Surveyor General's map of the Nyamandlovu region (Sheet SE-35-15).

5.1. PUMULA MISSION AREA (WEST TSHOLOTSHO)

In general, this seems to have been very badly affected by 5 Brigade, who set up camp close to the Mission from late January 1983. From interviews, it is clear that many settlements within a very wide radius of the mission experienced mass beatings, or were burnt to the ground because villagers had fled the area.

A few parts of this area, to the west of the Mission (e.g. Korodziba, Soloboni), have been entirely resettled since the early 1980s, so reports on 5 Brigade activities here trickle in from other locations in Tsholotsho, wherever people have been resettled to. Fortunately, events around Pumula Mission were well documented by CCJP, and File H[4] also has comprehensive accounts of events in some villages. It has therefore been possible to place those few interviews that lack detail in context within the broader data framework.

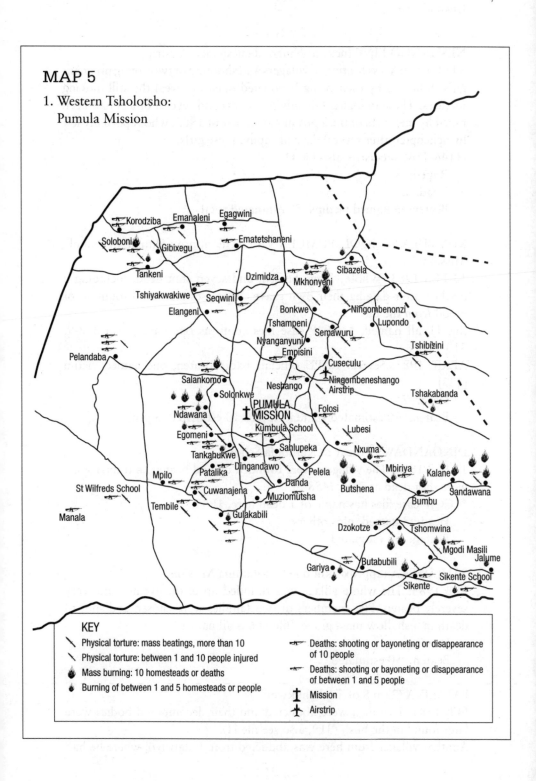

MAP 5

1. Western Tsholotsho:
   Pumula Mission

KEY

\ Physical torture: mass beatings, more than 10

\ Physical torture: between 1 and 10 people injured

🔥 Mass burning: 10 homesteads or deaths

🔥 Burning of between 1 and 5 homesteads or people

—∧— Deaths: shooting or bayoneting or disappearance of 10 people

—∧— Deaths: shooting or bayoneting or disappearance of between 1 and 5 people

✝ Mission

✈ Airstrip

NESHANGO LINE (next to Ningombeneshango Airstrip)
3 FEB 1983: Mass beating of villagers and shooting of two young pregnant girls, followed by their being bayoneted open to reveal the still-moving foetuses. These two girls (already pregnant) and several others had been raped by members of the ZNA in November of 1982, who reportedly left by helicopter after several days of raping these girls.
(1146-1168 inclusive, also file H).

    Raped: 8
    Dead: 2
    Beaten: 6 named victims, 50 estimated total

KUMBULA SCHOOL, PUMULA VILLAGE (approx 5km SE of Pumula Mission)
13 FEB 1983: Whole village beaten, and seven shot dead, including a teacher, after digging their own grave. Witnesses refer to a fountain of blood from the pit.
(file H, all named, **CCJP case files confirms one name, also 298-9, 310-11)
APRIL 1983: Several ZAPU officials badly beaten, one named victim (323)

    Dead: 7
    Beaten: 50 estimated (January), plus 10 estimated (April).

DINGANDAWO: (near to Kumbula School)
11 FEB 1983: The villagers were rounded up and beaten, and then some were shot dead at 7pm. (458-9)
**CCJP case files has name of 1 dead here, 1983

    Dead: 3 named, plus others
    Beaten: 50 estimated

SAHLUPEKA (approx 7km due S of Pumula Mission)
FEB 1983: The whole village was rounded up in the evening and very severely beaten. Five members of two families were chosen and shot to death in a shallow mass grave. (file H has all names.)

    Dead: 5
    Beaten: 50 estimated

PATALIKA (2km S of Tankahukwe)
FEB 1983: Two men were abducted and their decomposed bodies were later found in the bush (319, also see file H).
Another villager from here was abducted from Bulawayo, where he had

gone for safety, and was later shot dead at Tshitatshawa in Tsholotsho. (482)

Dead: 3

PELELA (approx 8km due S of Pumula Mission)
FEB 1983: Man killed coming home from a beer drink. A stranger to the village was also tortured and left for dead. He managed to crawl almost to the village and died – nobody knows who he was. (file H, 303)
FEB 1983: Man accused of supporting dissidents and killed. (320)
FEB 1983: A villager from here fled to Plumtree, where he was killed by 5B. (294)
APRIL 1983: Villagers who were in church were forced to leave by 5B and made to sing and dance all day. 5B also killed and ate three goats. (3257)

Dead: 4

DANDA (approx 9km due S of Pumula Mission)
FEB 1983: Three ex-ZIPRAs from Mkubazi were among many taken to the pan here and shot. One escaped with gunshot wounds to Botswana and one was killed. The other went missing. (3246-8)

Missing: 1
Dead: 1
GSW: 1

MUZIOMUTSHA (10km S of Pumula Mission)
14 FEB 1983: Four villagers were badly beaten, then three were taken to Pumula Mission. One was tied to a tree and was later shot. The other two had to bury him. (257, 2259-60)

Dead: 1
Beaten: 3

CAWUNAJENA (10km SW of Pumula Mission)
8 FEB 1983: Entire village rounded up, and many were beaten very severely. Twelve men and women, including two school teachers, were shot dead. This happened during the night. 5B camped nearby and the dead were not buried until a year later, by which time many bones were scattered around (file H has all names, also 479). Two other men abducted and killed here in February (315, 318)
A woman was also abducted into the bush and shot with her baby on her back. (314)
Another woman was also abducted in February and shot. (481)

Dead: 17
Beaten: 50 estimated

TEMBILI (adjacent to Cawunajena)
FEB 1983: People here were beaten by 5B after church and made to cook daily for the soldiers, who killed and ate some of their livestock. (3258-60)
APRIL 1983: A man visiting from Patalika was shot by 5B. (3256)
Dead: 1
Beaten: 20
Property: livestock eaten

GULAKABILI (approx 20km SSW of Pumula Mission)
12 FEB 1983: Whole village abducted from nearby to the Pumula Mission area, where they were beaten. Some were then forced to dig a mass grave, made to climb in, and were shot. They were buried while still moving, and villagers were made to dance on the grave and sing songs in praise of ZANU-PF. Number of dead given as 12. (file H has all names, also BLPC 300, 305-9 incl.)
One victim locked in a hut and burned to death. (296)
MARCH 1983: 5B burnt five homesteads one morning. (3246-48)
ZNA soldier killed while trying to visit his mother, on leave. (304)
Two others from this area also killed by 5B, circumstances unclear. (478, 484)
A woman was accused of cooking for dissidents and was shot dead. (293)
A woman and her child were taken from here to Pumula Mission and killed (292, also file H)
Seven others from this area met individual deaths – one was detained trying to get to Plumtree and was never seen again, another went missing from a house in Bulawayo, and his wife and child were apparently killed by 5B, while trying to flee to Botswana. Another man had his throat cut and bled to death. (file H)
Dead: 25 named victims
Beaten: 50 estimated
Destroyed: 7 known homesteads

MPILO (due W of Tankahukwe)
OCT 1982: ZNA took the store-keeper and killed him and assaulted his wife. (3264/5)

JAN 1983: Two men from here were killed by 5B because they ran away when they saw 5B coming. (3262-3)

> Dead: 3
> Beaten: 1

TANKAHUKWE (7km SW of Pumula Mission)
FEB 1983: All the villagers were rounded up and severely beaten. Twelve were selected and shot after being forced into two mass graves. One of the chosen managed to run away, so his younger brother was killed instead. 5B came back in 1984 and stabbed the escapee to death, also severely beating another brother at this time. Another villager who was badly beaten ran away but died later of his injuries. (file H has all names; also 295, 297, 312, 324, 455, 3264-6)

> Dead: 14
> Beaten: 50 estimated

EGOMENI (5 km almost due W of Pumula Mission)
FEB 1983: Villagers were rounded up and beaten. Five were then shot and buried in one grave. (301-2, 321)
A villager was shot dead in February and then had his hut burnt down. (461)
One villager killed trying to return to work in Harare. (314)
Another villager was abducted in a truck as a dissident and shot at a nearby farm. (483)
Another villager was killed in the Sonqinyana area. (463)
13 FEB 1983: One villager shot at dawn at his home. (460)
FEB 1983: Woman shot dead by 5B who also burnt the homestead. (461)
**CCJP case files report one named death here, could be first incident. A man was also detained and never seen again here. (319)

> Missing: 1
> Dead: 10
> Beaten: 50 estimated

MAZHOU (near Egomeni)
FEB 1983: Four villagers were abducted to the bush, and were tortured with sticks and knives.
One villager attacked his assailant, allowing another to escape. Three were then killed. (file H)

> Dead: 3
> Beaten: 1

ST WILFRED'S SCHOOL (Pumula Mission area)
2 FEB 1983: Some of the ex-ZIPRAS in this area ran away in January. The mothers of two were tortured for "parenting dissidents", and were then shown five men including their sons. These five were taken to Tsholotsho town, and two weeks later one returned, with serious gunshot wounds. He had climbed out of a mass grave in which he had been shot with many others, and had made his way home. He died a day later. (609-11)
    Dead: 5, plus possibly others
    Beaten: 2, plus possibly others

MANALA (W of Pumula Mission, resettled)
29 MARCH 1983: One man beaten, bayoneted, finally killed the next day, and his body burnt by 5B. (1230)
    Dead: 1

SALANKOMO (approximately 5km NW of Mission)
**28 JAN 1983: Twenty 5B soldiers came in the morning and killed the village ZAPU chairman and two schoolboys, one aged 14. They were beaten in front of the villagers first, and all the adults present were also beaten. (Commission of Inquiry Statement, also file H).
**28 FEB 1983: Same soldiers rounded up people in the village and put two men, seven women, two with babies, and three children into one hut. They set fire to the hut, and the men inside forced the door open. As the twelve ran out, six were shot and killed including a baby and a girl, and one was shot and left for dead.
**CCJP has on record the Medical Cards and Comm. of Inquiry statement of the victim who suffered a gunshot wound to the stomach in February 1983 incident – records start from May 1983, by which time wound is very infected. (file A, also file H)
Two more homesteads were burnt at a later date. (BLPC 338-9, 457, 3274-5)
    Dead: 9
    GSW: 1
    Beaten: 5, plus possibly others
    Homes burnt: 3 known

NDAWANA (6km W of Pumula Mission)
FEB 1983: Two villagers from here were curfew-breaking and their tracks were reported by villagers from Egomeni nearby, who did not know who they were. 5B prepared to beat and destroy all at Egomeni, and had already dug mass graves. However, the two from Ndawana were caught

before this happened, and they were killed instead (file H, also 3273-6). The soldiers then moved to Ndawana, where the commander ordered the whole village into a hut and set fire to it. Once the commander left, another 5B soldier let the villagers out of the hut, so they were spared. (file H)

MARCH 1983: An old man from here was taken to Pumula Mission, tied to a tree and forced to make animal sounds. 5B also killed his ox. (3272)

>Dead: 2
>
>Tortured: 1
>
>Burnt: 2 homesteads

SOLONKWE (4km NW of Pumula Mission, now resettled)
**JUNE 1983: CCJP Commission of Inquiry report of 22 villagers including women and children burnt to death in a hut, after being brutally beaten first. The owner of the hut begged for the lives of his four youngest children to be spared, and this was allowed, although the life of an older daughter was not spared. (file A, file H also refers; also 316-17, 322, 462)

>Dead: 22
>
>Burnt: 1 hut

PELANDABA (W of Pumula Mission)
29 JAN 1983: 5B rounded up many men from the area, tortured them until they couldn't walk and shot them. File H names eight victims, **CCJP case files also reports 11 other named deaths here in 1983, probably same day, and one death in 1984. BLPC names two more victims from January incident. (342-346)

Three others killed, including a married couple who went to report dissidents in the area. (345, 348)

>Dead: 25 named victims
>
>Beaten: 50 estimated

SEQWINI (approx 15km due N of Pumula Mission)
15 APRIL 1983: One person killed by 5B, bayoneted to death. (1232)

>Dead: 1

TANKENI (NW of Pumula Mission)
1983?: A villager from here was one of six men beaten and then machine gunned by 5B at Mzimwatuga. 5B also burnt homesteads in the village and destroyed crops and livestock. (403)

Dead: 6
Burnt: several homesteads

KORODZIBA (W of Pumula Mission, now resettled)
FEB 1983: 5 Brigade came to the school and took about 60 pupils aged over 14 years. They were all beaten and asked about dissidents. 20-30 girls were raped and then ordered to have sex with some of the boys while the soldiers watched. They were beaten for 3 hours. (3311)
4 MARCH 1983: Five villagers were murdered at night for being PF-ZAPU members. (1223-27 incl)
MARCH 1983: Two children out of a group of children died of starvation trying to run away from 5B in this area. They were trying to reach Ngamo railway siding, which is about 100km NE of Korodziba. The dead were aged 9 and 14, the survivor was 15. (1234-5)

Dead: 5, plus 2
Raped: 25 estimated
Beaten: 60

SOLOBONI (W of Pumula Mission, now resettled)
23 FEB 1983: 5 Brigade rounded up entire village to the borehole. Six people were chosen at random and were bayoneted to death, and buried in one grave. Everyone was then beaten. Five people were beaten to death, and one person died years later, partly as a result of injuries from this beating. Another man who wept to see his brother killed, was severely beaten and died a few weeks later from his injuries. One old lady who was found in her hut was raped, and 5B then set fire to a plastic bag and burned the old lady with it, setting fire to her blanket. She died 3 weeks later from the burns. (3313) 1 hut was burnt. (1238-42 incl, 1282-87)

Dead: 14
Raped: 1
Beaten: 50 estimated
Burnt: 1 hut

GIBIXEGU (NW of Pumula Mission, now resettled)
2 FEB 1983: 5 Brigade entered the village in a truck and rounded all the villagers up. Two women were tortured and a man taken away was never seen again. Six people were beaten to death, including four women. (275, 697-703)

Dead: 6
Missing: 1
Beaten: 2 known, plus others

EMANALENI (7km NW of Ematetshaneni)
On the same day that 5B beat and killed people at Gibixegu, they "did the same" at Emanaleni. (698)
A villager was taken by the army and killed with bayonets, because he had asked "World Vision" to film atrocities in their area. (613)
MARCH 1983: 5 Brigade killed a headman from Filabusi and chopped off a woman's head. (1228-9)
   Dead: 4, plus others

EGAGWINI (approx 25km due N of Pumula Mission)
MARCH 1983: One young man was taken by 5B, badly beaten, returned, and while his parents were washing his wounds, 5B came back and shot him. (1236)
   Dead: 1

EMATETSHANENI (approx 24km due north of Pumula Mission)
FEB 1983: School treasurer beaten and then shot for not handing over funds, 500m from his home. (1237)
   Dead: 1

SIHAZELA (30km NNE of Pumula Mission)
FEB 1983: An old man was shot 500m from his home by 5B. They came back three days later and killed the old man's wife and daughter, and burned down the homestead. They also kicked a year-old child and broke his back. (599-603)
   Dead: 3
   Injured: 1
   Burnt: 1 homestead

MKHONYENI (Between Dzimidza-Sihazela, approx 20km NNE of Pumula Mission)
END JAN 1983: The first woman to die in this area was accused of feeding dissidents. She was pregnant and was bayoneted open to kill the baby. She died later. (350)
FEB 1983: All the villagers were forced to witness the burning to death of 26 villagers, in the three huts of Dhlamini. (326-37 incl, 347-49, 605-7). Women and children died. There was only one survivor. File H lists all names of victims. The same report says that a few days before the hut burning, many men were killed in punishment for having failed to catch a local thief the 5B wanted. (five names in file H, 7 more in **CCJP case files)

**CCJP case files also name nine who died here, probably same incident as above. Just before the hut burning, at least one woman was beaten to death. (334)

MARCH 1983: Many men were shot dead at Mzimwatuga Pan. This was in punishment for having failed to catch a local thief 5B wanted. This report also mentions the hut burning. (file H, also 604)

Another villager was stabbed to death at Tshiyakwakiwe, near the pan. Another villager also died in this area. (332,353)

**CCJP also report 1 missing here in 1983.

   Missing: 1

   Dead: 1 (pregnant), 26 in the hut, 12 named victims at the pan; 3
       others = 42

****JULY 1984: Dissidents killed the ZANU chairman as he was addressing a meeting. (1231)

   Dead: 1

SEMAWURU/CUSECULU/NINGOMBENONZI (10km NE of Pumula Mission)

FEB 1983: All the people from these villages were rounded up and beaten and some were killed.

Name of one dead victim. (600, 1125)

JUNE 1983: 5 Brigade shot two cows who ate their washing off the line. (3211)

**** JULY 1983: As dissidents passed through the village of Semawuru, the army arrived and started shooting. The villagers ran away and a woman was shot in the foot. Her husband took her to hospital and in their absence army vandalised the house. (1248) *Crossfire*

OCT 1983: A villager was asked about dissidents by "Nai Ka" and then hit in the mouth, losing all his teeth.

A villager found milking and the headman of his village were taken to Pumula Mission by the Commander whose nickname was "Nai Ka", and the villager was killed. (658, 590)

An old man from the neighbouring kraal of EMPISINI was hit with rifle butts. (608)

A villager was assaulted when he asked a soldier to pay for goods taken from a child. (1120)

   Dead: 1 known victim

   Beaten: 150 estimated

BONKWE/NYANGANYUNI (15km NE of Pumula Mission)
FEB 1983: A young woman from Bonkwe going to buy mealie meal was
beaten for wearing her husband's watch. Her husband was summoned to
Nyanganyuni and beaten to death. Every bone in his body was broken
– he is referred to as being "like a cloth". (612)
Another local was abducted to Pumula Mission and killed there. (file H)
   Dead: 2
   Beaten: 1

FOLOSI (7km due E of Pumula Mission)
3 FEB 1983: Whole village beaten with sticks. Boys were made to fight
each other, while other villagers were forced to dig a mass grave. Four
men were made to lie face down in the grave and were then shot. (1169-
1174 incl)
Two other men were abducted and tortured to death and buried in
shallow graves. (file H)
   Dead: 6
   Beaten: 50 estimated

LUBESI (10km SE of Pumula Mission)
7 FEB 1983: The entire village was rounded up, was forced to sing songs
and then beaten.
Three men were made to dig a grave (two were "curfew-breakers" from
neighbouring Nxuma). They were made to jump into the grave, and were
then shot. They were buried while still moving.
Five Brigade also killed and ate a cow and some goats around this time,
while camped at Lubesi Dam. (1135-7 incl, 1139, file H also refers to
two of these dead)
   Dead: 3
   Beaten: 50 estimated

MBIRIYA and NXUMA (15km SE of Pumula Mission)
END JAN 1983: All villagers in these two neighbouring settlements were
assembled in Mbiriya. They were accused of cooking for dissidents and
everyone was beaten, after being placed in small groups. Ten people were
shot dead at the dam (nine names). Four were beaten to death, while
others were badly beaten, including a four-month-old baby. Some of
the injured went to Pumula hospital. After the beating, the villagers of
Mbiriya deserted the village for a while, and 5B came back and burnt 15
homesteads to the ground.

Ten others were killed at Nxuma, and buried in one grave (all names, file H). In another incident in February 1983, two teachers at Mbiriya School were badly assaulted, one was killed, and a house was burnt down. (1182-4,1199, 1186-92 incl, 1257, 1262-1268 incl, 1292-93, 2016ff)

APRIL 1983: An army Puma carrying villagers after a rally where Mugabe spoke, was fired at and people were injured near Nxuma. (3273)

Dead: 25

Beaten: 100 estimated

Burnt: 15 homesteads

BUMBU (just E of Mbiriya)

END JAN 1983: A councillor and a man back from working in South Africa were shot dead. Eleven homesteads were torched to the ground. When other villagers saw the fires, they ran away, but 5B fetched them back. One man was made to bury the dead and another was taken away and never seen again. (628, 634, 1116-18 incl, 1128-32 incl, 3261)

JAN 1983: A man trying to return to work in Harare from here has never been seen again. (1272)

**CCJP case files names another man who went missing in 1983.

Dead: 2

Missing: 3

Burnt: 11 homesteads

BUTSHENA (just W of Mbiriya)

11 FEB 1983: The villagers moved out of their houses after witnessing what had happened in neighbouring villages. On 11 Feb they saw 5B burning all their homesteads. (1143)

Burnt: 22 homesteads, 9 granaries

SANDAWANA (approx 10km E of Mbiriya)

4 FEB 1983: A man accused of telling others to bury their property to save it was taken to Pumula Mission and killed. (1279)

10 FEB 1983: All the villagers assembled and some were selected and beaten. At least one was taken away and killed. (1275)

After this, the villagers deserted the village, and 5B found it empty and burnt down 30 homesteads – names of 28 owners given. (Exact date not clear – reports say variously Jan, Feb, April – Feb seems most likely, as the curfew was still in force).

On this same day, a girl found near the homesteads was severely beaten. She was hidden by her parents and then smuggled by scotch cart 30km southwards to Ndolwane clinic. (1179, 1254-58 incl, 1288-91 incl, 1300-17 incl, 1261)

Two men killed after being tortured at a borehole in this area. (file H)

MAY 1984: A villager from here was among five taken from a bus for having no ID, and was apparently tortured and killed at Bhalagwe Camp in Kezi (see Part Two, II for Bhalagwe Camp). (1278)

NOV 1984: A man from here had his house burnt down, ran away and was never seen again, although rumour had it that he was buried at Empandeni Mission, in Bulilimamangwe. (1280)

   Dead: 5 known

   Beaten: 1 named, plus others

   Burnt: 30 homesteads

KALANE (near Sandawana)

18 FEB 1983: The day the villagers saw neighbouring Sandawana go up in flames they ran away. One villager came back to let his cattle out and was badly beaten. Eleven kraals were burnt down that day. (1261)

SEPT 1983: A villager was beaten to death and 3 homesteads were burnt. (1273-4)

   Dead: 1

   Beaten: 1

   Burnt: 14 homesteads

TSHOMWINA and DZOKOTZE (5km due S of Mbiriya)

JAN-FEB 1983: All the villagers of Tshomwina were forced/marched to Dzokotze nearby. They were beaten, and five were killed. One man died after terrible mutilations that included having his jaw broken and his tongue cut out. This man ran away and was found by his family in a neighbouring village. He took eight days to die, without medical care. (1186-98)

Twenty homesteads in Tshomina were burnt down. (1186-98)

A ZNA member home on leave was taken to Pumula, tortured, taken from there in a car and never seen again. (1144)

Another interview refers to six villagers from TSHOMWINA detained in January 1983, taken to Pumula Mission, where they were beaten and released after 6 weeks. (1140-41)

   Dead: 5

   Missing: 1

   Beaten: 100 estimated

   Burnt: 20 homesteads.

   Detained: 6

DZOKOTZE

OCT 1983: **** Dissidents shot dead four and injured a fifth, accused of conniving with the Army. (1295-99 incl)
> Dead: 4
> GSW: 1

GARIYA – near BUTABUBILI (12km due S of Mbiriya)

5 Brigade referred to as raping all the women in the village, and forcing them to cook for them. (Time not given, but probably early 1983). They are then said to have returned some months later, posing as dissidents and beating people. (569)

Another interview refers to 3 killed by 5B, including the kraal head, in 1983. (569-70)

JUNE 1983: A few villagers found at a nearby dam were beaten and nine villagers were killed. (1292-4)

SEPT 1983: 5B came at night and took away four men in the village, who were then shot at a nearby kraal. One survived. (575)

OCT 1983: Six homesteads are burnt, and three villagers are beaten. The woman who was ZAPU chairwoman for the area was burnt to death in her hut. (1270-71, 1279)

DEC 1984: 5 Brigade interrogated villagers about dissidents. They injured one man, and woman had her leg broken. They then burnt one villager to death in his hut. (576-7, 670)
> Dead: 17
> Raped: several
> GSW: 1
> Beaten: 6 known, plus others
> Burnt: 6 homesteads

MGODI MASILI (5km E of Butabubili)

2 FEB 1983: Villagers heard 5B coming and ran away. Two who stayed behind were bayoneted and beaten to death. An old woman was also killed, and seven huts and two granaries were burnt. (555, 557, 581)

Young men were taken from the villages in the area to train as "youth patrol" to look out for dissidents. Some youths were shot dead by 5B during the training exercise. (1259-60)

15 FEB 1983: An ex-ZIPRA was picked up and never seen again. (1253)

FEB 1984: A man was picked up and stabbed 32 times with bayonets by 5B, and thrown in a pit – he survived. (554)

1984: A man and his wife were picked up at the shopping centre and beaten, then were taken to an army camp in Plumtree for a week, before

being hospitalised. (1723-24)
One other man was also killed. (546)
One other man was beaten. (574)

    Dead: 6 known victims, plus others
    Missing: 1
    Stabbed: 1
    Beaten: 3 known
    Burnt: 7 huts, 2 granaries

SIKENTE (approx 10km due S of Sandawana)
END JAN 1983: The whole village was marched to Sekatawu Pan. Many were beaten and some were accused of being dissidents and were shot and buried in one grave. Number of dead not given, one named victim. (562)
Early 1983(?): Villagers were gathered at Sikente School and beaten. Some were shot dead, others were shot and injured. Details including time are vague. (558)
**2 FEB 1983: CCJP reports store keeper and one other shot dead, also one woman with a gunshot wound.
Three teachers were also robbed and told to leave the area, and all the homesteads along the Nata River were burned down. (file B – this sounds as if it was the same day as 558)
LATE 1983: One man detained at night and never seen again. (560)
JUNE 1984: A man was taken off a bus in this area, was never seen again. (573)

    Missing: 2
    Dead: 3 known, plus several others from Jan incident
    GSW: 1
    Beaten: 100 est (incl 2 incidents)
    Burned: Most homesteads – more than 10 estimated

Another incident, SIKENTE area, time not clear, but probably not during early 1983, but later. 5 Brigade are accused of posing as dissidents, collecting a group of men and women, taking them into the bush and chopping them with axes. Interviewee suffered serious injuries – unclear how many others died or were injured. (568)
Another incident, SIKENTE area, time not clear – or perpetrator – this might have been dissidents although it sounds more like an early 5B incident. An unspecified number of villagers is referred to as having been "killed while worshipping" in the bush. 5 Brigade could well have killed people here as curfew-breakers – the dissidents almost without exception

kill only sell-outs and usually make their motive clear. This could be the same incident as the one above or it could be same as a church shooting incident among the Plumtree reports. (567) (Plumtree is 544)

> Dead: 2 named victims, plus others
> Injured: 2 named, plus others

JALUME (5km NE of Sikente)

1983: A man was killed on his way back from a cattle sale. He was tortured with burning plastic and then shot. (580)

6 NOV 1985: 5B in plainclothes badly beat a woman, and axed her husband. They then burnt him to death in a hut along with his eldest child. Their footprints led back to the army camp nearby. (571, 572)

> Dead: 3
> Beaten: 1

TSHIBIZINA (between Nengombenshango and Dhlamini airstrips)

3 FEB 1983: Mass beating of the village, by 5B from Dhlamini Camp, and the headman was shot dead. Two women who were beaten too badly to walk were also shot dead. At least one homestead was burnt. (1122-3, 1126, 1142)

****FEB 1983: Six *dissidents* are referred to as beating two villagers in Tshibizina. (1133-4)

1983: 5B shot dead a man in the village, and then next day the commander apologized. (1180)

**CCJP reports closure of school here after the headmaster was beaten up in front of the pupils, after which he fled the area. (file B)

SEPT 1983: Three taken to Pumula Mission for interrogation, one then killed. (1121)

**** NOV 1985: Dissidents pulled a man out of bed and shot him dead. (1115)

> Dead: 5
> Beaten: 50 estimated

TSHAKABANDA (approx 20km due E of Pumula Mission)

7 FEB 1983: The whole village was beaten by 5B, and two were shot dead.

Another interview refers to two people found chopping wood, who were accused of being dissidents and were bayoneted to death in front of the other villagers – it is not clear when this was. (497)

SEPT 1983(?): Three homesteads in Tshakabanda were burnt, villagers were beaten, and one victim was beaten to death. (1273-74)

Dead: 5
Beaten: 50 estimated
Burnt: 3 homesteads

BEMBA (10km due N of Tshibizina)
6 FEB 1983: 5B marched villagers from Bemba to the school, where there were some from Pumula Mission. They were beaten for the whole day (Seven named victims plus others). They also broke windowpanes and killed chickens and a goat.
Beaten: 50 estimated
Property: 2 chickens, 1 goat

5.2. SOUTH AND SOUTH EASTERN TSHOLOTSHO

Parts of this very southern end of Tsholotsho seem to have been in the path of the early 5B onslaught, while others escaped until later in 1983. In mid to late 1983, 5B set up an interrogation centre at MBAMBA – there are numerous reports of selected people being beaten and killed at Mbamba Camp from mid-1983 onwards.

(**** It is also interesting to note that interviewees from this very southern end of Tsholotsho seem to report a higher incidence of dissident presence and atrocities than any other area. (816, 824, 823, 826, 846ff) 5 Brigade atrocities still by far outnumber those of dissidents.)

NANDA AREA (approx 15km due W of Mbamba)
BHANTI KRAAL
29 JAN 1983: Whole village rounded up and beaten and then several selected and shot. It is not clear how many were involved, names of five deceased and two assaulted. (378, 379, 359, 377, 382-3-5)
FEB 1983: Two girls collecting water beaten by 5B. One victim beaten again in March with her husband. (1719-20)
1983: A man from here ran away to Plumtree where he was bayoneted to death by 5B. (381)
**CCJP case files also reports name of 1 dead here in 1983.
Dead: 6 known victims
Beaten: 50 est.

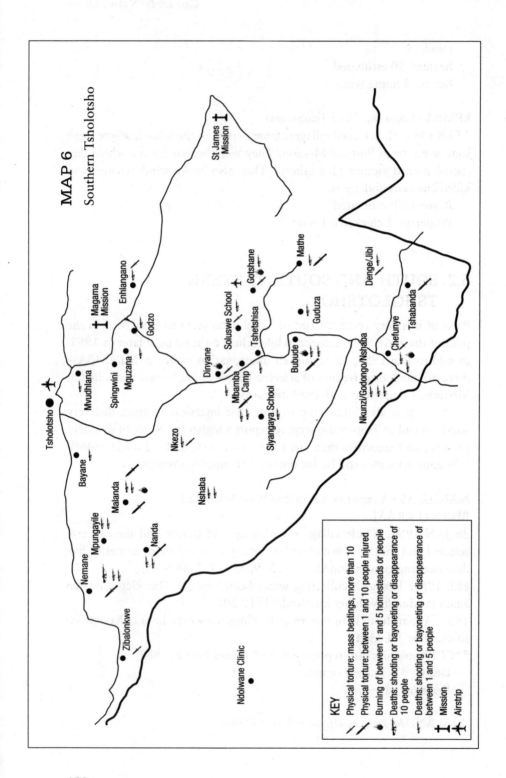

MAP 6
Southern Tsholotsho

KEY

Physical torture: mass beatings, more than 10

Physical torture: between 1 and 10 people injured

Burning of between 1 and 5 homesteads or people

Deaths: shooting or bayoneting or disappearance of 10 people

Deaths: shooting or bayoneting or disappearance of between 1 and 5 people

Mission

Airstrip

Tsholotsho

Bayane

Mvudhlana

Spingwini

Mguzana

Godzo

Magama Mission

Enhlangano

St James Mission

Nemane

Mpungayile

Malanda

Nanda

Nkezo

Dinyane

Soluswe School

Mbamba Camp

Siyangaya School

Tshetshisa

Gotshane

Mathe

Zibalonkwe

Nshaba

Bubude

Guduza

Nkunzi/Godongo/Nshaba

Chefunye

Tshabanda

Denge/Jibi

Ndolwane Clinic

NANDA, NEMANE SCHOOL

JAN 1983: A man found with goods stored in his house was taken to the school, made to say goodbye to his children and was then shot in the toilet. His family were told to celebrate his death, to "make umpululu". His wife was then abducted and taken to "be a wife" for 5B. (578-632)

**EARLY 1983: CCJP report tells of whole village being taken to Nemane School. A roll-call was called and those on it were shot dead, totalling 12. Mistresses (no number) were raped. (file B, also 384)

**9 FEB: A few days after the above killings a man was shot dead near the local store. (file B)

EARLY 1983: A villager trying to get to Tsholotsho to get an ID card was taken to the school where people were being killed. He was killed, along with others. (559 – this sounds as if it was the same day as the CCJP report.)

MARCH 1983: People were rounded up and taken to Nemane School, and were never seen again. Names of four victims, two women, two men. (371, 373, 375, 376)

17 AUG 1983: Seventeen Puma trucks took all young men in the greater area to Nanda air strip where they were beaten and tortured for seven days. "Many" died and others were crippled for life. (1340, 1357, 1366)

> Dead: 16 known, plus others from 3 different incidents
> Missing: 4
> Raped: 3, plus others
> Beaten: 50 estimated

NANDA AREA

Time not clear, but after early 1983. 5 Brigade posing as dissidents locked people in their huts and then shot several. One named victim. (374)

NOV 1983: Two men were burnt to death in a hut, by 5B – one was a herbalist accused of using his powers to help dissidents. (1276-77)

DEC 1983: Two men were taken away for interrogation, also one from Denge, also a woman from Ngubomlilo, and were never seen again. (357, 358, 372, 1341)

NOV 1984: A solitary 5B soldier in uniform shot a man after the victim had given him food. (380)

> Dead: 4
> Missing: 3

MALANDA (approx 20km NW of Mbamba)

JUNE 1982: (This may be 83, as 5B is accused, or it may be another ZNA unit). Man assaulted for failure to report dissidents. (1364)

14 JAN 1983: Villagers were told to assemble at Malanda Stores, where they were beaten. (1362-63)

**21 JAN 1983: A doctor based at Tsholotsho hospital reports a man shot dead here by 5B and his wife severely beaten by 5B. This man's brother was shot a few days later, while home on leave from Bulawayo. (file E)

24 JAN 1983: A small group of 5B went from house to house on this day, and shot any young men they found, including two ZNA soldiers home on leave. They also severely beat up a pregnant woman, so that her baby was later born in pieces. (444, 466-7, 476-7, 1358) *See page 83 for full statement.*

1983: Several individual assaults. (1338, 1355, 134)

APRIL 1983: A couple badly beaten, man taken to Nanda and returned. They also shot up a neighbour's granary. (1368-69,1370)

A man was detained and beaten after he went to report dissidents. (1371)

MAY 1983: A villager was taken in a truck and never seen again. (475)

JUNE 1983: A man found milking was shot and seriously injured. (1281)

JUNE 1983: Young men were gathered at Malanda School and were beaten and forced to fight each other. Others were assaulted in their homes on this day; all 5B as perpetrator. (1359-61)

Man badly assaulted and then taken away some days later, missing – by 5B. (1365)

Two girls were raped in their home in front of their family, and then were force-marched with others to Malanda School where they were beaten. Could be same day as above – by 5B. (1373-74)

JULY 1983: ZAPU official beaten with burning logs – by 5B. (1354)

AUG 1983: Man beaten and tortured with burning plastic – by 5B. (1337)

A woman horsewhipped – by 5B. (1367)

OCT 1983: A villager was beaten, detained and had his house burnt down – by 5B (1269)

MAY 1985: Local herbalist beaten to death – by 5B. (1352)

    Dead: 8
    Missing: 2
    Raped: 2
    Beaten: 23 known, plus others
    GSW: 1
    Burnt: 1 homestead

MPUNGAYILE (near Nemane School)
1983: 5B shot dead a mentally retarded boy, and then shot three other men. Because the women wept, four of them were also shot. (547-52 incl, 561, 566)
   Dead: 8

ZIBALONKWE SCHOOL (8km SW of Nemani School)
FEB 1983: Villagers were rounded up in the store and spent the night there. In the morning the teachers were released. It is unclear whether widespread beating took place during the night, but the interviewee was beaten with gun butts and had property stolen. (545)
   Beaten: 1, plus probably others

BAYANE (approx 13km W of Tsholotsho town)
DATE UNKNOWN: Man abducted from here and never seen again. (352)
FEB 1985: Man abducted from here, by CIO, never seen again. (367)
   Missing: 2

MBAMBA AREA (far S Tsholotsho)
Numerous reports of incidents in this area, from early 1983 – but more towards the end of 1983 and parts of 1984.
**EARLY 1983: CCJP reports seven young men in Mbamba region gunned down. (file B)
MAY 1983: A villager from near here was taken and never seen again. (840)
AUGUST 1983: A teacher was detained and tortured for five days. (791)
AUGUST 1984: Sixteen teachers from this area were badly tortured at Mbamba army camp. (792)
****One of the teachers in the above incident was also stabbed by a dissident in 1982, for refusing him money. (792)
JULY 1983: An ex-ZIPRA demobbed man was taken off the bus at Mbamba shopping centre and never seen again, although his family were asked by the police to forward his ID card, demob information, etc. (1325)
SEPT 1985: A man and his wife were beaten by CIO and the man was taken away to Mbamba where he was killed. (189,712)
   Dead: 8
   Missing: 2
   Tortured: 17
   Injured: 2

DINYANE (1km N of Mbamba)
DEC 1983: Woman made to cook for plainclothed armed men speaking Shona (i.e. not dissidents), then is beaten the next day by 5B for feeding dissidents. Her entire household was burnt down. (822)
1983: A villager was killed by 5B at neighbouring Matole.
FEB 1983: Several villagers in nearby SILANDE were beaten by 5B. (818)
  Dead: 1
  Beaten: 5 estimated
  Burnt: 1 homestead

SOLUSWE SCHOOL AREA (3km E of Mbamba)
1982(?): A villager was shot by ZNA for curfew breaking. (837)
NO DATE: Two soldiers from SU harassed and beat two women before shooting their husbands dead. (832-34)
JAN 1983: 5B shot a man in the back and injured his father. (829-30)
?****SEPT 1985: Seven "armed men" shot the local ZANU chairman. (836)
?****SEPT 1985: One woman was killed and another bayoneted by "armed men". (851-2)
?****SEPT 1986?: Five "armed men" beat five women from TSHETSHISA for "being in love with soldiers". (846-50)
  Dead: 2 (diss) 3 (army)
  Beaten: 7
  Injured: 2

SIYANGAYA AREA (5km SSW of Mbamba)
14 JAN 1983: Two schoolboys were shot dead at the school by 5B. (813-4)
A ZNA soldier home on leave was also shot dead here.
?****Five "armed men" killed a villager after he had cooked them a chicken at their request. (831)
  Dead: 4

TSHETSHISA (4km south of Mbamba Camp)
18 JAN 1983: Two young men were shot dead by 5B. (819-20)
  Dead: 2

BUBUDE (10km S of Mbamba)
?****1 JAN 1982: Two villagers were badly beaten by "five armed men". (802-3)

MARCH 1983: A man on his way to Tsholotsho CBD was detained, badly beaten and taken to Mbamba Camp before release. (801)

JULY 1983: Two brothers were taken by plain clothes CIO and were never seen again. (1321-22)

AUG 1983: A man from here was detained, tortured at Tsholotsho, then at Stops Camp, then put in Chikurubi until 1987. (797)

DEC 1983: A three-year-old child was run over and killed by an Army Puma truck. (800).

DEC 1983: Villagers were force-marched, tortured and beaten. Two dead are named, also one badly tortured. (799)

FEB 1985: Two young men taken by CIO and never seen again, although blood was seen on the road. (1323)

    Dead: 3
    Missing: 4
    Tortured: 3 known
    Beaten: 10 estimated
    Detained: 3

BUBUDE

****JULY 1982: Death in crossfire (1319-20,1322).
While dissidents were asking for water from the villagers, a ZNA unit entered the village and shot up a hut, killing a dissident and also seriously injuring two villagers, one of whom died.

    Dead: 1 villager, 1 dissident
    Injured: 1 villager

GUDUZA (SE of Mbamba Camp)

DEC 1983: A man was shot while trying to collect his ID from a bus he had just left, at the request of 5B. (1372)

    Dead: 1

GOTSHANE – LUZE (8km SE of Mbamba Camp, Mbalibali school area?)

MARCH 1983: At Dibha line, a homestead was burnt down by 5B. (827).

DATE UNKNOWN: Five villagers were taken to the school and badly beaten, over several days. One victim went insane from this, ran away from hospital and has never been found. (841-5)

MARCH 1984(?): A villager found watering goats was taken to Mbamba and badly beaten, suffering broken hand and kidney damage. (828)

1984: Two villagers were tortured by 5B, beaten and semi-drowned. (810)

****JULY 1984: Two villagers were killed by dissidents for joining ZANU, and one house burnt. (823- 4)
   Dead: 2
   Missing: 1 (insane)
   Beaten: 9
   Tortured: 5
   Burnt: 2 homesteads

MATHE (SE of Mbamba)
FEB 1983: The whole village was called to the primary school and was beaten by 5B. ZAPU chairman, and others (at least 4) were taken and tortured overnight. (1334-36) 1983: Ex-ZIPRA man beaten and then shot dead, by 5B. (1327)
SEPT 1986: Two men hanged by wire, by the "army", one then burnt to ashes in his hut. (1331-32, 1938)
   Dead: 3
   Beaten: 50 estimated
   Detained: 4

MBALIBALI SCHOOL AREA (S of Gotshane)
1983: Several villagers from this area were beaten by 5B on different occasions. (807-8)
AUG 1983: A woman and her 12-year-old son were detained, taken to Tsholotsho and beaten severely. The woman woke up in Mpilo hospital. (804-5)
A ZNA soldier from this area went missing. (806).
JAN 1985: A man from here was detained. (202).
   Missing: 1
   Beaten: 4 named
   Detained: 1

TSH AB ANDA AREA (approx 20km S of Mbamba)
4 JAN 1983: The whole village was rounded up to the local school by 5B and was beaten, some very badly, including the local ZAPU treasurer. One victim was beaten again very severely in AUG 1983. (1326, 1342-43)
JUNE 1984: A man was assaulted with rifle butts at the store, by 5B. (1089)
APRIL 1985: Three villagers badly beaten for not reporting dissidents. (1100-2)
   Beaten: 50 estimated

DENGE – JIBI (near Tshabanda and Nkunze)
FEB 1983: Four villagers watering cattle were severely tortured and beaten by 5B. (1088)
1983: Three villagers were severely beaten by 5B. (1077-79)
APRIL 1983: An ex-ZIPRA man was taken by 5B and never seen again. (1083)
****APRIL 1983: A man and his wife and others were beaten by dissidents for preparing a meal too slowly. (1084-5)
MAY 1983: A villager was beaten by 5B with an axe and a gun. (1082)
JUNE 1983: A schoolgirl was killed and two others injured in a truck accident on the way back from a "pungwe". (1086-7)
MARCH 1984: 5B came at night and tortured a man and wife, pulling her ear off with pliers. They then raped the two daughters aged 12 and 15. The same month they also abducted an ex-ZIPRA man who was never seen again. They beat him and his mother. (1094-5)
　Dead: 1
　Missing: 1
　Raped: 2
　Beaten: 10
　Tortured: 2
　Injured: 2

CHEFUNYE (South)
MARCH 1983: 5B took away a ZAPU chairman, who was never seen again. (1098)
1985: Two villagers were taken away at night. The one was first forced to drink insecticide, and was beaten. The other was blind, and his wife found his ID paper torn up in the road, next to blood stains. (1097, 1099) *See Part Three, I, page 326, for full statement.*
MARCH 1985: The ZAPU vice-chairman from Matshadula area was taken by 5B, who beat his wife and burnt the house down. In August they were shown his grave. (825)
　Missing: 3
　Dead: 1
　Beaten: 1
　Burnt: 1 homestead

NKUNZI–GODONGO–NSHABA (south)
GODONGO–NSUKAMINI
FEB 1983: The whole village was marched to an open space near a river, and was beaten by 5B. At least two died and many others were badly

injured. One interviewee comments that this was the only time 5B came to Godongo itself. (1348-49-50, 1375-87 incl, 2262)

FEB 1983: A villager was abducted at night and never seen again. (1347)

JULY 1985: A villager was seriously beaten. (1328)

5B detained 15 people at the Nkunzi business centre and sjamboked them. They were then shot at by 5B, who missed. (1103)

One man was detained by 5B and went missing. (1347)

The owner of a big trading store in Nkunzi had all his stock stolen by 5B. (280)

The store owner was badly beaten in 1983 (1344).

Man detained, missing 1983. (1351)

> Missing: 3
> Dead: 2 known, plus others
> Beaten: 50
> Detained: 18

NSHABA SCHOOL
FEB 1983: Seven ex-ZIPRA men were killed, after the whole village was gathered at the school for the day. Not clear whether any beatings took place. (1346)

> Dead: 7

GODZO (approx 2km S of Magama Mission)
7 FEB 1983: Two villagers beaten, taken from their homes and killed. (1206-7)

4 MARCH 1983: Man taken and never seen again. (1205)

JAN 1985: A villager was detained from here. (201)

> Dead: 2
> Missing: 1
> Detained: 1

MGUZANA (approx 2km SE of Magama Mission)
5 FEB 1983: Two taken and never seen again, one man, one woman. (1208-9)

> Missing: 2

ENHLANGANO (20km SE of Tsholotsho town)
FEB 1983: Two villagers from here were force-marched to Mananzwa line on the other side of Magama Mission, and then beaten before being shot dead. (1206-7)

FEB 1983: An old man mistaken for ZAPU chairman was very badly beaten. (1210)
  Dead: 2
  Beaten: 1

MATSHADULA (15km S of Tsholotsho town)
FEB 1983: One Botswanan refugee taken and never seen again. (1676)
  Missing: 1

MVUDHLANA (5km S of Tsholotsho town)
FEB 1983: A man from here went missing after visiting his mother further south. (1676)
  Missing: 1

NKEZO (near Tshanda)
****SEPT 1985: Several villagers beaten by dissidents, looking for a ZNA soldier. (1104-8,1110-11)
  Dead: 4
  Beaten: 4 named victims, plus others
  Burnt: 3 homesteads

SOLUSI MISSION
**EARLY 1983: CCJP report of five schoolmistresses raped by the ZNA, and also a 16-year-old schoolgirl. (file B)
OCT 1983: Man tortured by the army and beaten for having raised ZIPRA combatants. (1732)
  Raped: 6
  Tortured: 1

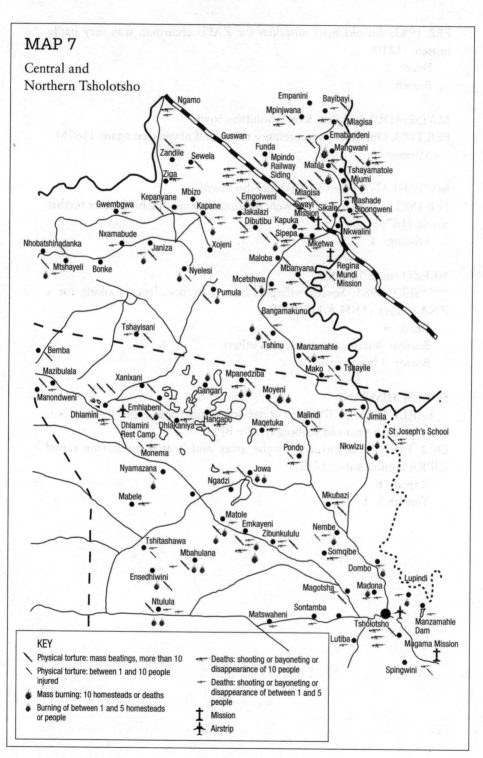

MAP 7

Central and
Northern Tsholotsho

Ngamo
Empanini
Bayibayi
Mpinjwana
Mlagisa
Emabandeni
Guswan
Mangwani
Zandile
Funda
Sewela
Mpindo
Railway
Mahla
Tshayamatole
Siding
Ziga
Mjumi
Mbizo
Emgolweni
Mlagisa
Mashade
Kepanyane
Gwayi
Sikale
Sipongweni
Gwembgwa
Kapane
Jakalazi
Mission
Dibutibu
Kapuka
Nkwalini
Nxamabude
Sipepa
Nhobatshinadanka
Janiza
Xojeni
Mketwa
Mtshayeli
Bonke
Maloba
Mbanyana
Regina
Nyelesi
Mundi
Mcetshwa
Mission
Pumula
Bangamakunu
Tshayisani
Bemba
Tshinu
Manzamahle
Mazibulala
Mako
Tshayile
Xanixani
Mpanedziba
Gangari
Moyeni
Manondweni
Emhlabeni
Malindi
Jimila
Dhlamini
Dhlakaniya
Hangapu
St Joseph's School
Dhlamini
Maqetuka
Rest Camp
Pondo
Nkwizu
Monema
Nyamazana
Jowa
Ngadzi
Mkubazi
Mabele
Matole
Emkayeni
Nembe
Zibunkululu
Tshitashawa
Somqibe
Mbahulana
Dombo
Ensedhlwini
Magotsha
Madona
Lupindi
Ntulula
Sontamba
Manzamahle
Matswaheni
Dam
Tsholotsho
Lutiba
Magama Mission
Spingwini

KEY

\ Physical torture: mass beatings, more than 10
\ Physical torture: between 1 and 10 people injured
🔥 Mass burning: 10 homesteads or deaths
🔥 Burning of between 1 and 5 homesteads or people
↠ Deaths: shooting or bayoneting or disappearance of 10 people
↠ Deaths: shooting or bayoneting or disappearance of between 1 and 5 people
† Mission
✈ Airstrip

176

5.3. CENTRAL TSHOLOTSHO

TSHOLOTSHO TOWN AREA

From eyewitness accounts it is clear that Tsholotsho Business Centre showed obvious signs of the disturbance being caused by 5B in Tsholotsho as a whole. There are references to about 400 refugees camped permanently near the council offices, because their houses had been burnt down or because they thought they might be safer in a bigger centre. Many hundreds spent days queueing for Identity Cards, and also for ZANU-PF cards, without which they were likely to be shot. The safety many sought in Tsholotsho town proved elusive: there are reports of young men in the town being rounded up, beaten or executed at the nearby 5B camp. A variety of interviews and CCJP documents testify to this. (609-11, 189, 1672-4, CCJP files B and E, all ff)

JAN 1983: Man taken from his workplace and never seen again. (444)

FEB 1983: Mass beating and deaths at "the borehole" – this could be the same incident as the deaths referred to at the "hospital tap"? (522 – CCJP refers to similar incident)

FEB 1983: Many young men shot in a grave they had been made to dig themselves. Some of these were from other parts of Tsholotsho – this incident has already been recorded in the Pumula Mission section. (609-11)

> Dead: Several
> Missing: 1
> Beaten: 50 estimated

Another interviewee refers to being beaten for buying food, and says "they" were forced to dig their own grave, but she manages to escape before being killed. Number of people involved not clear, could be part of above incident. (1353)

MARCH 1983: A man was assaulted by SU, just east of the centre. (3249)

**14 MARCH: CCJP reports between 600-700 women and children being loaded onto trucks and being taken away, and the same thing the next day. No men were around, destination remains unclear.

JUNE 1983: Three store employees were taken from the CBD in a Puma to Mbamba Camp and were tortured, allegedly for phoning the store owners in Bulawayo and warning them 5B were still in the area. (1679-80-81)

1983: Member of ZNA taken and never seen again. (1200)

**4 FEB 1984: A Botswanan refugee was detained by 5B and was believed to have been shot. (file '84)

FEB 1985: Seven bodies were found on Tsholotsho football field, after the dead had been collected by Land Rover from their homes at night. This murder was a reprisal for murder of ZANU officials. (204)

SEPT 1985: A man abducted from Matola was tortured at Tsholotsho police camp and then drowned in the well. His wife was also badly assaulted. (189)

NOV 1985: A woman disappeared after release from detention. (185)

    Dead: 9 known plus others

    Missing: 2

    Tortured: 3

    Beaten: 2 known

TSHOLOTSHO DISTRICT COUNCIL OFFICES

FEB 1983: Several council employees taken by truck, were seen being beaten and killed. Seven named victims. (469-70, 1251-2, 1675)

FEB 1985: Two employees were abducted by CIO and never seen again. (114, 474)

**CCJP also refers. (file B)

    Dead: 7 known, plus others

    Missing: 2

TSHOLOTSHO HOSPITAL

**FEB 1983: CCJP document reporting dramatic increase in casualties who have been beaten or suffered gunshot wounds at the hands of the army. One victim is a survivor of a mass shooting at Madona (see below), and the CIO arrive at the hospital and remove this man "for interrogation". Same witness reports massive influx of refugees into the town. Three named victims are reported as being severely beaten while walking to Tsholotsho from Madona. (file E)

    Beaten: 3 named, many others indicated

    GSW: 1, man then detained

MADONA–LUPINDI–DOMBO VILLAGES (1-7km N of Tsholotsho town)

FEB 1983: 5 Brigade referred to as "burning huts and killing people" in these three villages on 1 and 2 February. At least one named victim was also killed at Manzamahle Dam to the east of Tsholotsho town on this day.

Seven named villagers taken and never seen again, two killed in their houses, two homes burnt, homes of four other villagers plundered – Madona (1672-4, 1743-51 incl)

EARLY 1983: CCJP reports deaths of ten people in Madona, eight were shot and two were burnt to death in a hut. (file B; file E also refers)
At least two homes burnt and one person killed – Dombo (1670-71, 1672-73-74)
Homes burnt and people killed – Lupindi.
FEB 1985: Two villagers taken the same day two Council employees disappeared (see above), never seen again. (1670-71)

    Dead: 14 victims, plus others
    Missing: 9 named
    Burnt: 4 known homesteads, plus others
    Plundered: 4 homes

MUSIKAWA (near Tsholotsho town)
30 JAN 1983: CCJP document reports 12 shot dead here on this Sunday. Many others were beaten here on the same day. (file E)

    Dead: 12
    Beaten: 20 estimated

Apart from 5B units based at Tsholotsho town, there seems to have been an interrogation centre at Dhlamini Rest Camp to the west, and villages between Dhlamini and Tsholotsho town were repeatedly involved in 5B incidents.

MAGOTSHA (between Tsholotsho town 7km away, and Emkayeni)
FEB 1983: Interviewee reports being involved in a mass beating here, on his way between the two centres. At least one shot dead. He talks of escaping from this after being beaten, to the hospital, where he witnesses 5B killing people at the "water tap" at the hospital. (522)
3 FEB 1983: CCJP also report a mass beating here, during which a man found driving a scotch cart is accused of buying cigarettes for dissidents and is shot dead. (file E)

    Dead: 2 known, plus several others, exact number unclear
    Beaten: 50 est.

EMKAYENI (approx 25km NW of Tsholotsho town)
Very badly hit by 5B in early Feb 1983.
EARLY FEB: Seven teachers killed and thrown into a pit latrine (CCJP file E).
Man sitting outside his house shot dead. (493)
7 FEB: Mass beatings, burning of all homesteads, and five young men shot dead. (514, 529)

Some also died later from beating injuries. (521)

This same group of 5B, numbering possibly 200, also hit Zibunkululu on this day, and several villagers from Emkayeni were later shot at Zibunkululu. (530-1)

12 FEB 1983: A man was accused of running away from 5B and was beaten to death and robbed. (527)

MARCH 1983: Many rounded up and beaten, then taken to Dhlamini Rest Camp, from where they never returned. One was a man on leave from SA. (501, 516-17, 524, 525)

**MAY 1983: CCJP report of 10 schoolgirls being forced by 5B to have sex daily after school in the vicinity of Dhlamini Rest Camp. Exact villages of origin not on the document, to safeguard girls concerned.

****AUG 1984: Man beaten by eight dissidents with sticks and a hammer for being a sellout. He died later. (504)

Another man, date not clear, beaten until his ears bled, by 5B, for not revealing whereabouts of dissidents. (506).

Villager, time not clear, beaten by 5B at night, then was shot through the back of the head. (515)

Villagers, time not clear, beaten while herding cattle and tilling the land. (518)

Another taken by 5B while tilling, never seen again. (523)

Dead: 20
Missing: 5
Beaten: 100 estimated
Raped: 10
Burnt: 15 huts

ZIBINKULULU (near Emkayeni, 20km NW of Tsholotsho Town)

11 FEB 1983: Mass beating, shooting, and burning of huts, by huge group of 5B. Six named victims. Some interviews estimate as many as 200 5B present, and say they were moved to Emkayeni before the beating. Some of the dead were picked up at Tsholotsho Beer Garden because their names were on a list. (360, 362, 366, 444, 530-531, 526, 1185)

FEB 1983: The day after the beating, they detained a boy who had run away, and killed him. (363)

APRIL 1983: Another villager was detained, and never seen again. (365)

JULY 1983: A man was taken with a neighbour to Tsholotsho Town and detained at Mkwazini. They were tortured and beaten, then released. (364)

Missing: 1
Dead: 9

Beaten: 50 estimated
Burnt: Unknown

MATOLE (3km NW of Emkayeni)
FEB 1983: Villagers from here were also rounded up to Emkayeni on 7 February and beaten, and their houses were also burnt down. A man ferrying mealie-meal in a scotch cart was badly beaten. Another villager, who passed 5B dressed as dissidents on the path, and then failed to report their presence, was killed by the same 5B men. (498, 528, 532, 536, 1244)
FEB 1983: Several villagers from Tuli line were grouped in the bush and beaten with bayonets (3219-20)
MARCH 1984: Two villagers were taken by a truck at night and never seen again. (533-4)
MARCH 1984: A man was beaten in front of his family, and then made to run away. He was shot in the back. (535)
   Dead: 2
   Missing: 2
   Beaten: 50 estimated
   Burnt: Several homesteads – 4 named

NYAMAZANA and MBUHULANA (approx 7-10km SW of Matole)
FEB 1983: Villagers from these two lines were marched to Matole School. Dissidents shot at 5B and some villagers escaped. All the others were made to lie down and were beaten with logs (five named, plus others). After the beating, homesteads were burnt (seven names). A man from here was detained. (3200-7)
   Dead: 1
   Beaten: 100 estimated
   Burnt: 9 homesteads
   Detained: 1

NGADZI and JOWA (approx 30km NW of Tsholotsho town, on a pan)
JAN 1983: People rounded up from fields by 5B and beaten, first the women and then the men.
References to "all" the houses being burned, some taken to Dhlamini Rest Camp, and never seen again. (499, 500-1-3, 505, 507-8, 520, 1726, 3283)
OCT 19(??): Another villager taken by 5B, brought back and shot at his kraal. (442)
   Dead: 1

181

Missing: 3 known
Beaten: 50 estimated
Burnt: 6 named homesteads, plus others

MANONDWENI and MAZIBULALA (10km NW of Dhlamini Rest Camp)

FEB 1983: Whole village of Manondweni force-marched to Mazibulala and beaten all morning. At 2pm two men were killed, one for being the father of a ZAPU official. (1175-99 incl)

Dead: 2
Beaten: 100 estimated

DHLAMINI REST CAMP

1983: In the village of Emhlabeni, one homestead was burnt. (3283)

NOV 1985: Mass beating of all the young men from the villages of DLAKANIYA, BAYANI, TSHAYI-SANI (Mabhanda), EMHLABENI, XANIXANI, VAGASINI and DHLAMINI. They were rounded up in groups of 30 or more and beaten, by 5B, first at the rest camp and then in Tsholotsho. They were released after several days. (206)

Beaten: 210 estimated
Burnt: 1 homestead

MONEMA (6km E of Dhlamini)

APRIL 1984: The army beat a man and smashed his radio. There is reference to several "fellow workers" being taken and never returning. (3215)

Missing: 1+
Beaten: 1

DLAKANIYA KRAAL (approx 10km E of Dhlamini Rest Camp)

END JAN 1983: A mass beating of several kraals, with at least one death. (675-678)

**CCJP has a Commission of Inquiry statement on this incident, in which villagers were forced to beat each other as well as being beaten by 5B. One villager was beaten to death. (file A)

FEB 1983: A ZNA man on leave was taken and never seen again. (659) Another villager, time not clear, possibly 1985 (see Hangapu) was picked up in a truck at night and never seen again. (660)

****MARCH 1985: *Dissidents* came to a homestead and demanded food. SU arrived and two villagers were *killed in crossfire,* and one injured. (694-6)

Dead: 3 known, possibly others
Missing: 2
GSW: 1
Beaten: 30 estimated

HANGAPU (just E of Dlakaniya)
MARCH 1985: Four men were picked up on the same night from different kraals, and were never seen again. (662, 664, 695, 3306)
Missing: 4

GARIGARI (3km N of Hangapu)
****MARCH 1986: Dissidents burnt down three homesteads completely. (3277-9)
Burnt: 3 homesteads

MPANEDZIBA (approx 20km NE of Dhlamini Rest Camp)
FEB 1983: 5 Brigade were camped at their borehole at this time. It seems there were several incidents in a short time here.
EARLY FEB 1983: Several homesteads (11 known) were burnt, one killed, others beaten. (668, 3280-1, 3284-8)
11 FEB 1983: A woman was tortured and her house was burnt with her in it, although she survived. (1201)
25 FEB 1983: Villagers were all gathered together and beaten in the morning by one group of 5B. Then later the same day, another unit beat them again. This is different to the above incident, as interviewee refers to it as happening "after the huts were burnt". (661, 663, 668)
MARCH 1983: A young woman coming from the fields was asked to take her baby off her back and was then beaten until unconscious, by 5B. (665)
MARCH 1983: A ZNA soldier on leave was picked up by 5B and never seen again. (370)
EARLY 1983: An ex-ZIPRA from here was detained in Bulawayo where he was hiding, and was never seen again. (669)
APRIL 1984(?): This happened after victim had rebuilt his burnt hut. He was beaten, shot at, and then managed to stab 5B soldier with a knife. (666) Another villager was taken off the bus at a month-end (pay day) and was never seen again. His wife was beaten. (667)
FEB 1985: Three villagers were abducted by vehicle, and never seen again. (354, 368, 369)
1986: Two villagers, one of them a small child, injured by 5B. (543)
Dead: 1, plus others

Missing: 6
Beaten: 50 estimated
Burnt: 11 known homesteads

MOYENI (5km SE of Mpanedziba)
**FEB 1983: 11 kraals were burnt – CCJP Comm. of Inquiry statement.
(file A, also 3289-3305)
On the same day, all the villagers from Moyeni and Maqetuka were taken
to Moyeni and beaten. (3282)
   Beaten: 100 estimated
   Burnt: 11 homesteads

MAQETUKA (due W of St Joseph's)
FEB 1983: One homestead was burnt here on the same day as Moyeni
burning. (3282)
FEB 1985: 5 Brigade drove up and down the line knocking on every door,
taking certain people, who were never seen again. (1097-98-99)
   Missing: 3 plus others
   Burnt: 1 homestead

MALINDI (12km SE of Mpanedziba)
** APRIL 1983: CCJP has copies of medical records of victim who
was first beaten near Tshabangu store and then taken with other men
to Tsholotsho airstrip. Here he was tied to a tree and beaten, suffering
permanent damage to his arms. He was also given electric shocks to
his testicles. He mentions 20 others (not all from his town) receiving
similar treatment. Dated from May '83 – beating apparently in April '83.
(Commission of Inquiry)
JULY 1985: Two men were picked up by CIO and never seen again.
(193-4)
   Missing: 2
   Tortured: 20

MAKALALE LINE (Chief Mswigana's area)
OCT 1984: A woman was raped and abducted by "soldiers", while her
husband was a refugee in Botswana. She later died. (1729-30)
   Dead: 1
   Raped: 1

NEMBE (15km NNW of Tsholotsho town)
MAY 1985: Four beaten, and a homestead burnt, by 5B. (1217)

FEB 1983: Two boys taken by 5B to Dhlamini Rest Camp and beaten. One never returned, and was rumoured to have been killed and buried there. (1668-69)

Missing: 1
Beaten: 6
Burnt: 1 homestead

MKUBAZI (20km NNW of Tsholotsho town)
FEB 1983: Villagers heard 5B vehicles coming to the dam and many ran away. Those that stayed were beaten, and two were killed, shot dead after the beatings. (3222-4)
MARCH 1983: One villager was beaten by 5B.
APRIL 1983: An old woman was accused of harbouring dissidents and beaten. Two others died this same day. (3226, c-r 3231)
MAY 1983: Villagers brewed beer to appease their ancestors, and were accused of brewing for dissidents and beaten. (3227-8)
JULY 1983: A villager at a beer drink was assaulted by 5B. (3229)
****JULY 1983: *Dissidents* shot one villager dead and beat his wife. (537)
1983: A villager going to buy cigarettes at the store was shot dead by 5B (3230). Another villager disappeared, last seen running away from 5B. (3231, c-r 3226)
1987: A man who owned his own grinding mill was assaulted for "feeding dissidents", by ZNA. His grinding mill was destroyed, and he was badly injured in the groin.

Dead: 5
Beaten: 50 estimated

PONDO (6km N of Mkubazi)
JUNE 1983: An old man was detained by 5B and tied to a tree all night. He was assaulted, a rib was broken, taken to various camps and then to Tsholotsho CBD where he was kept in a pit for seven days. He was assaulted throughout this time, then released. (3242)
JULY 1983: Another old man from here was accused of growing fat on cattle originally stolen from Mashonaland (a reference to Ndebele plundering in the 19th century). He was taken by a Puma and never seen again, along with another man from Malindi line.

Missing: 2
Beaten: 1
Detained: 3

SOMQIBE (13km NNW of Tsholotsho town)
FEB 1983: A ZNA soldier was beaten by 5B and then taken to Dugwe school and killed. (464)
APRIL 1983: An old woman was woken and bayoneted by 5B, and her son was dragged out of bed and shot dead. (3240-1)
> Dead: 2
> Bayoneted: 1

LUTIBA (7km SW of Tsholotsho town)
MARCH 1983: Villager taken by 5B and never seen again. (471)
> Missing: 1

SONTAMBA (15km W of Tsholotsho town)
MARCH 1983: A man who saw 5B coming ran home and warned his family to flee. He stayed behind to buy them time, and was killed. (351)
FEB 1984: CIO took away an old man and he was never seen again. (468)
> Dead: 1
> Missing: 1

MATSWAHENI (18km due W of Tsholotsho town)
NOV 1985: Five people killed by CIO disguised (?) (538)
> Dead: 5

NTULULA (approx 30km due W of Tsholotsho Town)
1 FEB 1983: A woman fetching water was shot dead and so was her baby, by 5B. They beat her father who came looking for her. Then they came back to the village and bayoneted the father and his nephew to death, as well as burning huts. (563-4-5)
4 FEB 1983: All the villagers were rounded up and beaten by 5B, some beaten to death – two named deaths. Huts were also burnt. (546,556)
JUNE 1983: Villager reports 5B beating villagers and burning several homesteads – could be above incident, with wrong date? (2440)
****MARCH 1984: Two *dissidents* killed a ZNA member by cutting off his testicles and his head. They also killed his mother and brother, as sell-outs. (355)
> Dead: 9 known, plus others
> Beaten: 50 estimated
> Burned: 4 homesteads plus others

MABELE (4km NNW of Tshitashawa)
EARLY 1983: 5B took two men away. One returned and reported the other had been killed and buried. 5B stole property. (3221)
Dead: 1

TSHITASHAWA (approx 10km N of Ntulula)
FEB 1983: Teacher assaulted and property stolen. Three others, one aged 14, gunned down in this area and buried separately. (file H)
SEPT 1986: Dissidents passed through this area and the next day 5B came and stole some property and hit one villager on the side of his head. (1124, 1250)
Dead: 3
Beaten: 2

ENSEDHLWINI (4km ESE of Tshitashawa)
JUNE 1983: 5B beat the whole line for several hours, allegedly for failing to report dissidents. At least one homestead was burnt. (3216-17)
Beaten: 50 estimated
Burnt: 1 homestead

ST JOSEPH'S SCHOOL (East Central, 30km S of Tsholotsho town)
2 FEB 1983: Everyone was marched by 5B to a nearby pool, two women "tortured", six shot dead, others beaten.
MARCH 1983: One villager went missing. (809)
Missing: 1
Dead: 6
Beaten: 50 estimated

NKWIZHU (2km SW of St Joseph's School)
APRIL 1983: Man beaten and tortured, and house burnt down for failing to inform 5B of dissident presence. (1735)
Beaten: 1
Burnt: 1

MANAWENI (near St Joseph's school)
MARCH 1983: Two killed, one woman had her head chopped off, and her homestead burnt, by 5B. (1228-29)
Dead: 2
Burnt: 1 homestead

JIMILA (5km W of St Joseph's)
JAN 1983: 5 Brigade burnt down many houses here. In Jan and Feb they also shot eight men, several in one incident and others in separate incidents. (2415-2435)
JUNE 1983: A villager was taken away by 5B and shot. (2421)
**21 JUNE 1983: Builders ran away from 5B and one was killed. CCJP case files name nine dead here in 1983, ten property losses, and one assault.
  Dead: 9
  Beaten: 1
  Burnt: 10

NTULANI (? Amnesty refers)
JAN 1985: Two men were detained from here. (1196-7)
  Detained: 2

MGUZANA (? Amnesty refers)
JAN 1985: Two men were detained from here. (199-200)
  Detained: 2

SPINGWINI–MAGAMA (15km SE of Tsholotsho town)
MARCH 1983: 5 Brigade abducted several men, after severely beating several villagers and destroying property. They chopped off one man's arms and legs and came back the next day and shot him. At least one other was killed, and several taken were never seen again. (472-473)
JAN 1985: A villager was detained here. (198)
  Dead: 2 known
  Missing: Several, one named
  Beaten: 5 estimated
  Detained: 1

TSHAYISANI (15km due S of Janiza)
****AUG 1982: Six villagers reported the presence of dissidents. The army attacked the dissidents, who returned and beat them, killing one villager, and cutting off the ear of one. (3214)
  Dead: 1
  Mutilated: 1
  Beaten: 5

5.4. NORTHERN TSHOLOTSHO

Along the railway line. Many incidents at the railway sidings near Gwayi, including Mpindo and Mlagisa, involving mass beatings and shootings. Villagers from surrounding areas were sometimes taken to the railway line and then beaten and killed. (640, 448) (617, 635, 644, 647-9, 653, 582, 623, 624, 640)

**CCJP case files (MCF) reports names of two dead and one assaulted here in 1983.

Deaths: 6 known, plus others
Beaten: 10 named victims
Mass beatings: 4 mass beatings referred to

EGCENI (N of Sipepa, between Mlagisa and Mpindo sidings)
**1 FEB 1983: CCJP reports that 50 people were estimated killed here, and the rest severely beaten. This may be a mass killing at Mlagisa railway siding, as this is very close by. (file B)
SEPT 1983: Three young men were taken by 5B, first beaten in their village and then taken to Dhlamini Rest Camp, where they were allegedly killed. (446, 453, 492)

Dead: 50 estimated
Missing: 3
Beaten: 50 estimated

MPINDO LINE (approx 15km NW of Regina Mundi, on the railway line)
FEB 1983: All the villagers were called together and were beaten. Seven were selected and shot dead. One escaped with a gunshot wound, and 5B came back and burnt down his very large homestead of 25 huts. (2469-72)

Dead: 6
GSW: 1
Beaten: 50 estimated
Burnt: 1 homestead

FUNDA (3km due N of Mpindo Siding)
FEB 1983: Villagers heard firing and ran away. 5B came and burnt their houses down. (410, 454)

Burnt: Several homesteads

MPINJWANA LINE (approx 20km N of Mlagisa)
2 FEB 1983: All the young and old men were assembled and beaten. Eight were shot, all named. (589-597, 687) St Lukes hospital records also refer.

2 MARCH 1983: At nearby Stezi line, a girl was beaten and her boyfriend was shot dead. (598)
    Dead: 9
    Beaten: 50 estimated

BAYIBAYI (N of Mlagisa town)
JULY 1984 (?): All the men in the village were rounded into a swamp and beaten, and the kraal head killed by 5B. (646-579)
Another villager was badly beaten on another occasion. (654)
    Dead: 1
    Beaten: 30 estimated

MLAGISA TOWN (approx 20km N of Gwayi Mission)
3 FEB 1983: Seven people, including women, badly beaten. (619-642)
One of the interviews refers to beatings on 8 FEB; this may be another incident, or the same as the above. (643)
FEB 1983: A villager was taken away by 5B and shot dead. (645)
FEB 1983: A villager ran away when he saw 5B coming, so his wife was shot to punish him. (674)
    Dead: 2
    Beaten: 7, plus possibly others

XABAMUDE LINE (at Mataphula, near Mlagisa town)
MARCH 1983: Men beaten. (620,1731)
?****APRIL 1983: One villager taken away by "plainclothed armed men" after a beating and then shot dead. (621)
    Dead: 1
    Beaten: 10 estimated

EMABANDENI KRAAL (approx 20km N of Gwayi Mission)
15 FEB 1983: 5 Brigade burnt homes. Some villagers ran away, but most were rounded up and beaten and then 10 men and women were shot one by one. (679-687)
**CCJP also reports names of two killed here (file B).
    Dead: 10
    Beaten: 40 estimated

MANGWATU (approx 15km N of Gwayi Mission)
9 FEB 1983: The villagers heard screaming and shooting in the neighbouring village and ran away. They saw 5B come and burn all the houses. 5B returned some days later and said they burnt the homes

because the villagers supported dissidents. (411,414)
    Burnt: Many homesteads

MALILA (approx 13km N of Gwayi Mission)
2 FEB 1983: The soldiers found two women preparing lunch and accused them of cooking for dissidents. They shot one dead. They took the daughter into the bush and raped her all night. The other, who was pregnant, was beaten with all the other villagers. (650-51-52, 2460)
    Dead: 1
    Raped: 1
    Beaten: 20 estimated

TSHAYAMATOLE (Just E of Malila and Mangwatu)
**CCJP case files name 11 dead here in 1983.
FEB 1983: A big group of 5B moved through the area, forcing people from their homes into the road, where many were beaten. Some were forced to strip naked before beating, and one was burnt with plastic. One was shot and left for dead. Some villagers managed to run away and many homesteads were burnt down. (406-9 incl, 415)
12 FEB 1983: 5B went to several individual kraals beating and shooting people. At one kraal, four adults and three small children aged 11, 2 and 1 were shot dead. (2473-80 incl). Two other children aged 4 and 2 were shot dead at another kraal. (2482-3) At least two homesteads were burnt down, and everyone in the line deserted the area. (2481)
MARCH 1983: 30 5B returned and beat villagers for the whole day. At night they fitted lights to their heads, chose six men and shot them. Three were killed. (682, 2484-5)
AUG 1983: Two men and a woman were very badly beaten by 5B, looking for dissidents. (2205-7 incl)
    Dead: 13
    Tortured: 1
    Beaten: 50
    GSW: 1
    Burnt: Many homesteads, more than 8

MJUMI (approx 12km NE of Gwayi Mission)
FEB 1983: Villagers saw 5B coming and ran away and caught the train to Bulawayo. When they returned they found houses burnt down. (412)
AUG 1983: A small group of 5B came on foot and beat many villagers. They also raped a girl, leaving her pregnant. (405)
    Raped: 1

Beaten: 15 estimated
Burnt: At least 1 homestead

MASHADE (1km N of Sipongweni)

**FEB 1983: A villager was accused of being a dissident and shot.
    Dead: 1

SIPONGWENI (approx 12km NE of Gwayi Mission)

**31 JAN 1983: CCJP: Three brothers found together were shot and killed. A fourth was wounded. A man herding cattle in this area in FEB 1983 was also killed. Two boys from this village were among those pulled from the trains and shot in FEB. (file B)

**CCJP case files names four dead – could be some of the above.

MARCH 1983: 5B arrived in the village one morning and ordered everyone to the school, where they were stripped naked and were beaten. Three 5B returned some nights later, and one stole property while the other two raped the young girls (no number). They were all then also beaten very badly. (416)

MARCH 1983: A villager caught coming back from the store was marched away and then bayoneted to death. (655)

APRIL 1984: One villager taken away by soldiers, remains of body returned three years later. (2458)

FEB 1985: The kraal head was shot dead by 10 soldiers. (2459)
    Dead: 7
    Beaten: 40 estimated, some twice
    Raped: more than 2
    Property: stolen

SIKALE (approx 10km NE of Gwayi Mission)

**1 FEB 1983: CCJP reports "more than 5 shot dead" here between 31 Jan and 1 Feb 1983. (file B)

20 FEB 1983: Six 5B arrived in the village and asked for someone by name. They then shot him in cold blood, and killed two other villagers, and seriously injured a third. (421-2,625-28) On the same day they detained a villager they met walking in the area, and his bones were found in the bush in 1984, recognisable because of his shoes. (436) Another villager was also shot in this area on this day. (440) Another young man who ran away at this time was never seen again. (633)
    Dead: 10
    Missing: 1

NKWALINI (just E of Gwayi Mission)
FEB 1983: A man from here, trying to take his wife away to Bulawayo, was shot dead at MLAGISA siding, and so was his wife because she cried when she saw him shot. (641-2)
**CCJP report on events between 31 Jan and 8 Feb 1983 refers to four killed here, and two thoroughly beaten. (file B)
   Dead: 4
   Beaten: 2

GWAYI (just E of Gwayi Mission, near Regina Mundi Mission)
**FEB 1983: CCJP reports four primary girls, average age 13, raped in front of their parents. Next day 18 families left the area. There is also reference again to mass beatings of all getting off the train at the siding here, and to the deaths of 50, recorded above under EGCENI. Another report, same file (B), refers to women being forced to have sex with soldiers before being allowed to board the trains.
FEB 1983: A man detained here ultimately disappeared. (107)
   Missing: 1
   Raped: 4 known, plus others.
   Beaten: 50 estimated
   Detained: 1

SIPEPA AREA (10km W of Gwayi Mission)
**31 JAN 1983: CCJP refers to all villagers being gathered and told of the curfew. One person carrying mealie-meal was shot on sight and injured. Two curfew breakers were shot dead on sight. 5B told them they would come looking for any ex-combatants, ZAPU officials or refugees in every kraal. The same day, school children on their way home from Sipepa and Gwayi were beaten and so were teachers. One teacher was shot and injured. (file B)
**3 FEB 1983: CCJP reports one policeman shot dead and another wounded and smuggled away by colleagues to Bulawayo – they were ex-combatants. (file B)
**Different list, same file, (B) refers to six dead, one boy beaten and wounded with a bullet, and a headman beaten.
Six schoolgirls from Sipepa were raped and not allowed to go to hospital. Soldiers referred to as going door to door and raping any women found alone at night. (file B)
FEB 1983: Whole village forced to dig roots, some were then beaten, and two schoolboys who looked too old for their class were shot dead. (629-631). One woman raped, had money stolen, she went to Bulawayo to join

her husband, and their home was destroyed in their absence. (1684-5)

10 FEB 1983: Villagers ran away when they heard 5B, and one failed to return. (633) There is also a report of a homestead burnt in Feb 1983. (2468)

MARCH 1983: Nine men from surrounding villages were badly beaten at the police station, by 5B. (616)

    Missing: 1
    Dead: 6
    Raped : 7, plus others
    GSW: 4
    Beaten: 100 estimated
    Burnt: 1 homestead

SIPEPA CLINIC

FEB 1983: Two 5B soldiers entered the clinic in the morning, and shot dead a hospital clerk who was an ex-combatant. (445: CCJP also refers – file B) Also in 1983, a ZRP member was beaten and gagged with sand by 5B, was unconscious for 3 months. (241)

**FEB 1983: A whole family of seven was killed behind the clinic. (file B)

OCT 1983: Man shot dead in the back in cold blood. (1718)

DEC 1983: Three women very badly beaten in front of whole village. (1736-37)

**FEB 1984: CCJP report detentions of many by the CIO, and the shooting of one girl in the leg. 5B was also knocking at doors at 1am announcing their intention to kill people.

    Dead: 9
    Detained: Unknown number
    Beaten: 4
    GSW: 1

KAPUKA (1km E of Sipepa)

A 75-year-old man was shot in his fields by 5B, time not clear. (486)

**CCJP report 31 Jan to 8 Feb 1983 refers to five people killed here.

    Dead: 5

MKETWA (near Sipepa)

JAN 1983: A man from here was beaten, taken to the fields and shot dead by 5B. (1686) A couple were badly beaten, one killed, in their kraal, in front of family who then ran away. (1686-7)

** CCJP refer to what seems to be the above incident, and also add that a student who was an ex-Botswanan refugee was taken from school and

also shot with the man killed above (file B). At another kraal, one villager was badly beaten, then they returned and beat his wife, wanted to rape her but she ran away while they were shooting another villager. (1689-90)
FEB 1983: A man was shot in his doorway while trying to hand over his ID card to 5B. (447)
  Dead: 4
  Beaten: 3

DIBUTIBU (Near Mpindo-Sipepa)
LATE JAN: A villager was beaten unconscious by 5B because he was cutting wood. (656)
2 FEB 1983: Several families beaten, seven shot dead, one injured, by 5B. (596, 240, 643, 3245)
  Dead: 7
  GSW: 1
  Beaten: 50 estimated

JAKALASI (near Sipepa)
FEB 1983: Whole village rounded up and beaten, at least two shot dead. (487, 491, 512, 1682) A man was shot while working in his fields. (494) Another villager was shot dead in his room in Gwayi. (513)
  Dead: 4
  Beaten: 50 estimated
****JAN 1983: Dissidents beat four villagers as sell-outs. One died. (488-89-90)
A relative came to visit one of the injured, and was killed at EMGOLWENI, on her way to Mpindo Siding. (489)
  Dead: 1 (diss) 1 (army)
  Beaten: 3 (diss)

EMGOLWENI (10km NW of Sipepa)
FEB 1983: Interviewee refers to two shot dead "with others", everyone being beaten and their homestead being burnt. (510-11)
**FEB 1983: CCJP refers to five killed here – presume same case as above. (file B)
  Dead: 5
  Beaten: 10 estimated
  Burnt: 1 homestead

KAPANE (approx 20km W of Gwayi Mission)
**CCJP case files name six dead here and one loss of property here in 1983

FEB 1983: Three ex-ZIPRAS were shot by 5B, one name. (639)

MARCH 1983: 5B assaulted all the big pupils in the school. The girls were then taken for raping, more than 50 of them. They were raped repeatedly over the next few months, until the army left the area. Some fell pregnant and others ran away and never went back to school. (Three named rape victims: 3314-17)

1983: After a pungwe, four people, including one very elderly woman, were badly beaten by 5B because their surname was the same as that of a man 5B had killed. (622).

1983: Several families were very badly beaten by 5B. At least two men were shot dead and their wives ordered to laugh and then bury their "dogs". (2442-5 incl)

    Dead: 7
    Raped: 50 estimated
    Beaten: 100 estimated
    Property: 1

KEPANYANE (approx 5km W of Kepane)
FEB 1983: Villagers were rounded up by 5B and all beaten, men and women. One woman was raped. The older people were then ordered to go home, and the younger adults were shot. Shooting was heard for some time. Names of four dead. (2436-37, 2446,3329-30)

    Dead: 4
    Raped: 1
    Beaten: 50 estimated

ZIGA (approx 7km NW of Kepane)
**CCJP case files names one dead here in 1983.
    Dead: 1

ZANDILE (approx 15km NNW of Kepane)
FEB 1983: All the villagers were rounded up by 5B and badly beaten. One was then chosen and 5B told others to look at him die. They shot him dead. (2438-39)
    Dead: 1
    Beaten: 50 estimated

NGAMO (approx 40km NW of Gwayi, on the railway line)
FEB 1983: Four villagers were shot by 5B. Two were beaten first, one was shot in his yard and his brother was taken away for shooting the next day. (2462-5)

**CCJP case files reports names of same four dead here in 1983 and one dead in 1984.
SEPT 1983: A villager from another village was shot dead for curfew breaking. (637)
    Dead: 6

SEWELA (approx 10km S of Ngamo)
3 FEB 1983: All the villagers were rounded up to the borehole and were beaten. Three men were selected and shot dead. 5B soldiers continued to beat the dead men and to laugh at them. Two houses were also burnt down.
    Dead: 3
    Beaten: 30 plus
    Burned: 2 homesteads

JANIZA (approx 25km due W of Gwayi Mission)
5 FEB 1983: Mass assembling of villagers for beating by 5B. One interviewee shot and injured. (618) One interview refers to a mass beating by 5B at Janiza Hall in early March – could be same as above. (671)
MARCH 1983: A villager was taken away to Nyamandlovu and given electric shock treatment. When he was released he found his home burnt down. (673)
MARCH 1983: The ZAPU chairman was taken by 5B; as he left, he told his family he was already a dead man. He has not been seen again. (638)
APRIL: 5B soldiers slaughtered and ate a cock and goat in the area. (449)
DATE UNCLEAR: A villager was accused of giving dissidents a "charm", and was thrown alive into a fire, at Kepane, and then shot while burning. (672) A man from Janiza was shot dead in Plumtree, where he was working. (636).
NOV 1983: Ten men and women were beaten by 5B with hoe handles, at the borehole. Interviewee complains of loose teeth and poor vision. They also killed a goat and ate it. (3323, 3327)
    Dead: 2
    Beaten: 10
    Missing: 1
    Tortured: 1
    Beaten: 50 estimated
    Burnt: 1 homestead

GWEMBGWA (near Janiza)
****APRIL 1983: *Dissidents* ordered the villagers to feed them, and then 5B arrived and fired at them. The villagers ran away, but one was killed: *Crossfire.* (657)
Dead: 1

NHOBATSHINADANKA and MTSHAYELI (30km W of Gwayi Mission)
APRIL 1983: Villagers from Nhobatshinadanka were rounded up and marched to Mtsheyeli, after at least one homestead was burnt. At Mtsheyeli they were all severely beaten. The son of one of the victims on his way home from school for the holidays was taken from a bus and shot because he had no ID card. They do not know where he was buried. (451-2)
Dead: 1
Beaten: 40 estimated
Burnt: 1 homestead

BONKE (near Mtshayeli)
APRIL 1983: A woman was beaten and her husband taken away and killed at neighbouring Nxamabude line. (2461)
Dead: 1
Beaten: 1

REGINA MUNDI MISSION
(**JULY 1982: CCJP reports the rape of four girls, one teacher and one domestic worker, by army personnel, (yellow ZNA file))
**3 FEB 1983: CCJP report from priest, of army in the area refusing him permission to collect and bury the dead. A man he is giving a lift to is made to get out of the priest's car, and he finds this man beaten very severely a few hours later.
**10 FEB 1983: CCJP report from priest in charge of mission, on mission staff being brutalised by 10 armed, drunk 5B soldiers. About 30 people were beaten, the priest was threatened, and he refers to 5B as out of control, and contradicting one another. Many civilians who had come to the mission for protection then ran away into the bush, including the sick and wounded. People are referred to as starving, and food shortage is critical. (file B)
**16 FEB 1983: CCJP priest in charge reports further beating of mission workers, but this time some of 5B stationed at the mission intervene to stop it. (file B)

**25 FEB 1983: CCJP reports the raping of two more girls – the youngest one haemorrhaged for five days. (file B)
    Raped: 4 (1982) plus 2 (1983)
    Beaten: 40

ST MARK'S (2km from Regina Mundi)
**FEB 1983: CCJP report refers to people being beaten up and one teacher having a broken arm. (file B)
    Beaten: several

MALOBA (approx 10km SW of Gwayi Mission)
JAN 1983: Many villagers were gathered together and beaten for saying they did not know where the dissidents were. (1693-94)
    Beaten: 50 estimated

MCETSHWA (approx 15km SSW of Gwayi Mission)
JAN 1983: 5B forced whole village to one kraal, where they had to sing songs all night. They returned the next day and destroyed property, burning several homesteads. (1688, 2449-50)
**1 FEB 1983: CCJP: three people were beaten, young lady teachers were raped and then beaten (no number of victims given). (file B)
10 FEB 1983: Many 5B soldiers rounded up all villagers to a nearby dam, where many were beaten. One woman miscarried as a result. Some men were chosen and beaten, and were then made to run before they were shot dead. Many villagers fled the area afterwards. (423-25, 2447-8)
**CCJP case files list names of three dead, two assaulted and three property losses here in 1983.
    Dead: 5
    Raped: several
    Beaten: 10 named, 50 estimated
    Burnt: 3 homesteads

PUMULA LINE (7km W of Mcetshwa)
AUG 1983: 5B followed footprints from Tabagwa nearby to this line. They beat nine villagers, including women, and burnt one hut. (3319)
****APRIL 1985: A man here reported dissidents and so the dissidents came looking for him. In his absence they beat his wife and burnt his hut. (3320)
    Beaten: 10
    Burnt: 2 huts

NYELESI (beyond Pumula Line)
AUG 1983: Same incident as August 1983 above: 5B came through the
line looking for dissidents and badly beat one person and burnt one
homestead.
    Beaten: 1
    Burnt: 1 homestead

MBANYANA (approx 12km S of Gwayi Mission)
**1 FEB 1983: CCJP reports the whole village was rounded up and two
were shot dead and another received gunshot wounds. All the villagers
present, aged between 20 and 40 were forced to strip completely naked,
both men and women. They were then beaten savagely. Then all the older
people were also beaten, but not quite so badly.
    Dead: 2
    GSW: 1
    Beaten: 50 estimated

MAHLABA (approx 13km S of Gwayi Mission)
** 9-11 FEB 1983: CCJP reports three girls raped and then later shot
dead. (file B) There is also reference to one villager thoroughly beaten
but still alive.
    Dead: 3
    Raped: 3
    Beaten: 1

TSHINU and BANGAMAKUNI (approx 15km S of Gwayi Mission)
5 FEB 1983: Villagers were taken to the borehole and were badly beaten.
Three women had to be carried home and all three later died after days
in agony. (2451, 2455-56) At Hlabekisa Line nearby a villager was badly
beaten and at least two homesteads burnt down. (2453-4)
11 FEB 1983: Villagers were taken by five Puma vehicles to the school
yard, where they were beaten, men and women – nine homesteads were
burnt, and one villager was burnt in his house and died three months later.
5B came back the next day to make sure all the houses were completely
destroyed. (1211-12, 1698-1711 incl, 1714-15-16, 1727-28, 1738)
MARCH 1984: A dip tank assistant was beaten. (1725)

**CCJP case files name 3 dead here in 1983.
>Dead: 4
>Beaten: 50 estimated, some twice
>Burnt: 11 homesteads

MANZAMAHLE (approx 3km S of Tshinu)
FEB 1983: Villagers force-marched to Tshinu, where 5B made.them lie down and beat them. This might have been the same day as above, and involved all the women as well as the men. One named victim shot dead, plus others referred to. One house burnt, others plundered. (1739-41, 1721-22)
****Victims refer to being beaten by dissidents in 1985. (1739)
FEB 1983: Two villagers killed by 5B, one in her hut, and one caught in the fields milking, who was shot. (1717)
>Dead: 3
>Beaten: 50 estimated
>Burnt: 1 homestead, others robbed

MAKO (approx 12km SSE of Tshinu)
FEB 1983: One villager badly beaten and another shot dead. (1733)
>Dead: 1
>Beaten: 1

TSHAYILE (approx 30km due S of Gwayi Mission)
1983: The headmaster of the school was badly assaulted, and other staff members were beaten. A week later, their house in nearby TSHINU was raided, property destroyed. Victims ran away to Bulawayo and when they returned in 1986 all the furniture was missing. (1712-13)
>Beaten: 5
>Property: furniture destroyed

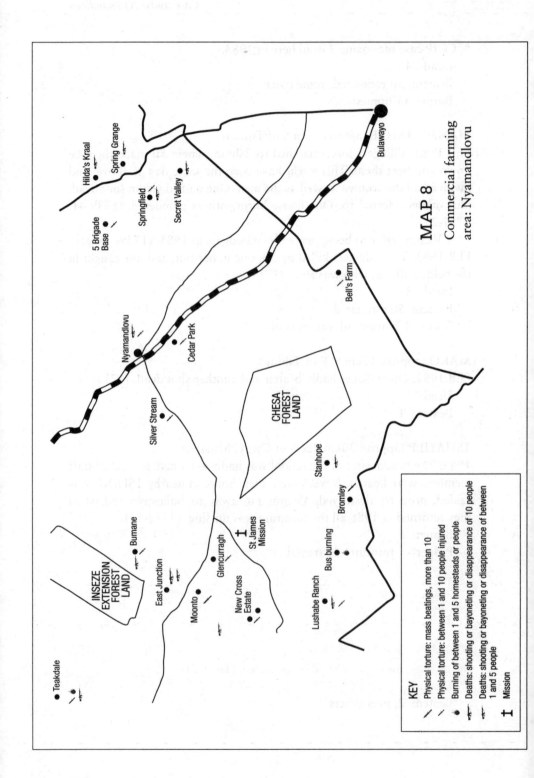

KEY

/ Physical torture: mass beatings, more than 10

/ / Physical torture: between 1 and 10 people injured

● Burning of between 1 and 5 homesteads or people

⚔ Deaths: shooting or bayoneting or disappearance of 10 people

⚔ Deaths: shooting or bayoneting or disappearance of between 1 and 5 people

✝ Mission

MAP 8

Commercial farming area: Nyamandlovu

5.5. COMMERCIAL FARMING AREA – SOUTHERN NYAMANDLOVU

Some of the following incidents were recounted in interviews with commercial farmers, and therefore have no case number as reference.

LUSHABE RANCH
1983: Several farm employees were beaten and detained by 5B after feeding dissidents. (858)
****JUNE 1983: A farmer and his foreman and two other workers were shot and killed, and two others were injured, by dissidents.
****APRIL 1986: This report accuses 5B of posing as dissidents and then holding up a bus at gunpoint. The bus was burnt and a widow with six children was shot dead. (1329) Commercial farmers remember this bus burning, but can shed no light on who the perpetrators were. (This report does not correspond clearly with any bus burning reported in *The Chronicle* – there were no buses burnt in 1986 according to CH, and none in April of any year. However there were often buses held up in this area, and they were always attributed to dissidents.)
    Dead: 1
    Beaten: 3 estimated

BROMLEY (NYAKATHA) FARM
Time unclear – many women who had been cutting thatching grass were beaten for six hours by 5B from two Pumas. (859)
    Beaten: 20 estimated

PETERSEN'S FARM
NOV 1983: Several farm workers beaten and one homestead burnt down by 5B, accused of keeping dissidents. (1734)
    Beaten: several
    Burnt: 1 homestead

BELL'S FARM
1983: 5 Brigade came to the farm and accused workers of feeding dissidents. They beat them until one died. A woman went insane from the beating, and others were hospitalized. (1691-2)
    Dead: 1
    Beaten: 2, plus others

NEW CROSS FARM
SEPT 1983: Labourers assaulted by 5B.
   Beaten: 5 estimated

GLENCURRAGH FARM
1983: Elderly farm labourer beaten by 5B.
   Beaten: 1

MOONTO FARM
****Dissidents crushed a farm worker's head, killing him. They also shot dead two other workers, and injured two. They then went on to "kill the master."
   Dead: 4
   GSW: 2

EAST JUNCTION FARM
1984-5: Time not clearly remembered, but the rancher here found 15 human skeletons in a remote area: this sounds like 5B.

BUMANE FARM
****JULY 1983: A farm worker who reported a dissident presence was in turn reported by others to the dissidents, who beat him and then shot him dead.
   Dead: 1

TEAK DALE FARM
FEB 1983: Dissidents spent the night on the farm, and the next day 5B arrived and beat those living there, and burnt their house. (1249)
APRIL 1983: An ex-ZIPRA now in ZNA came to visit his family here and was assaulted by 5B, who broke his collarbone. (3251)
1987: An employee from Teak Dale was forcibly resettled by the army, who destroyed his granary. (3307)
   Beaten: 6
   Burnt: 1 homestead, 1 granary

ROSIN FARM
FEB 1983: 5 Brigade badly beat the foreman for denying knowing any dissidents. The farm manager arrived and took him to hospital.
   Beaten: 1

SILVER STREAM FARM
SEPT 1983: Labourers assaulted by 5B, on the same day as labourers on New Cross Farm and Cedar Park.
Beaten: 5 estimated

CEDAR PARK
SEPT 1983: Labourers assaulted by 5B.
Beaten: 5

SPRINGFIELD FARM
NOV 1984: The owner who was an MP was murdered, allegedly by the army. His son was detained with six others for two weeks. (340-1)
Dead: 1
Detained: 6
OCT 1985: A farmer and his wife were shot and killed and so was their foreman – perpetrator dissidents.
Dead: 3
AUG 1987: A farmer on his way to a cattle sale was shot dead and so was his militia man.
Dead: 2
OCT 1987: A farmer and his wife were ambushed and sustained serious injiuries, the wife sustaining permanent brain damage. Their militia man was killed.
Dead: 1
Injured: 2

NGOMA BOTTLE STORE (Nyamandlovu town)
****AUG 1982: Man killed by dissidents. (2248)
Dead: 1 (diss)

NGOMA TOWNSHIP (Nyamandlovu Town)
MARCH 1983: A man was beaten until his ears bled by 5B for saying he had no daughters at home. (1233)
Beaten: 1

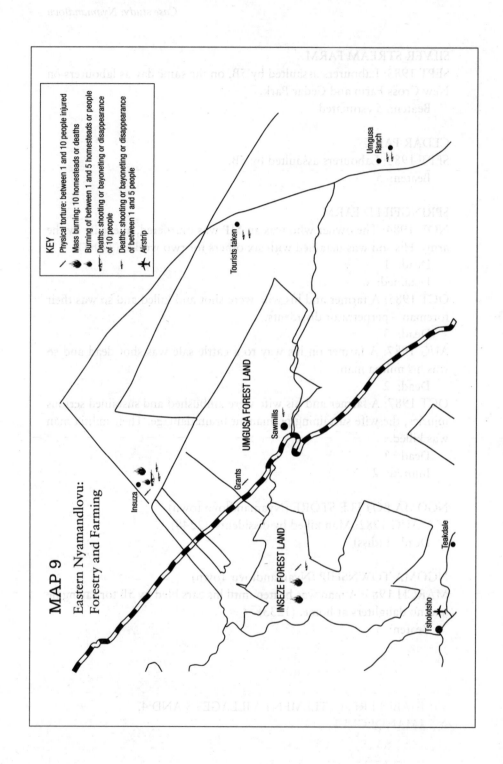

MAP 9

Eastern Nyamandlovu:
Forestry and Farming

KEY

／ Physical torture: between 1 and 10 people injured
⚫🔥 Mass burning: 10 homesteads or deaths
🔥 Burning of between 1 and 5 homesteads or people
⚫ Deaths: shooting or bayoneting or disappearance of 10 people
⚡ Deaths: shooting or bayoneting or disappearance of between 1 and 5 people
✈ Airstrip

Insuza

Tourists taken

Umgusa
Ranch

Grants

Sawmills

UMGUSA FOREST LAND

INSEZE FOREST LAND

Teakdale

Tsholotsho

5.6. EASTERN NYAMANDLOVU – FORESTRY AND FARMING

The resettlement areas to the east of Tsholotsho were affected by both dissidents and by 5 Brigade. Most deaths here were at the hands of 5 Brigade, but dissidents destroyed property. The dissidents were opposed to the Government resettlement policy, and burned down resettled villages to make a political statement. Villagers were often caught in the middle of this conflict: dissidents would burnt down their homes and then flee, and then army forces would arrive and arrest and "interrogate" the locals for information. Several interviews on file testify to this pattern. In addition to this, resettled villagers were also subjected to 5B brutality in early 1983, as were most parts of Northern Matableland.

Eastern Nyamandlovu is also where the dissidents ambushed and abducted six foreign tourists, in 1982, and it was later established that they were murdered and buried close to their place of abduction, although their grave is in Lupane and not Nyamandlovu.

Abducted: 6

ZIMDABULI RESETTLEMENT AREA – NSEZI
FEB 1983: One man shot by 5B and his neighbour's homestead of 10 huts burnt down. The neighbour escaped death by directing 5B in opposite direction, when they asked for him by name.
AUG 1985: The son of this man was picked up by CIO and badly tortured. (1696-7)
FEB 1983: A boy found milking was accused of being ZIPRA, was asked to bend down and was shot in the head. (441)
FEB 1983: 5B called a pungwe, and one soldier fired off his gun, killing a woman. (631)
**FEB 1983: CCJP files report five children aged between 7 and 12 who were shot dead by 5B while sitting in front of their hut by themselves eating sadza. (file A)
****OCT 1984: A man was assaulted twice by groups of *dissidents*, and fled to Bulawayo. He was detained by police for 21 days and released. (287)

Dead: 8, including 5 children (5B)
Tortured: 1
Beaten: 1 (dissident)

ZIMDABULI RESETTLEMENT VILLAGES 3 AND 4, NYAMANDLOVU
****These villages were burnt out by *dissidents*. Homes and the local school were razed, and villagers were also beaten.

[Exact date of when this happened is conflicting. Some reports say June 1983 and some June 1985. As incident is identically reported in all cases, it is fair to assume one, not two, incidents took place. *The Chronicle* reports mass burning of houses at a mine in July 1983 in Nyamandlovu (141) – this does not seem to be the same affair. There is also, on 26 Sept 1985, a *Chronicle* report of dissidents setting ablaze a schoolblock, four teachers' houses and several villagers' huts in the Nyamandlovu area – this sounds like it could well be the same incident. CCJP also refers to dissidents destroying resettled villages in 1983, but this is most likely Lupane, where villages in 1983 were destroyed by dissidents in the Mbembesi Forestry Area. (417- 420 incl, 427-434 incl)

The army arrived on the scene of the above and the dissidents fled. The army then picked up several villagers, whom they took to their camp and beat. They were made to dig a grave, and one villager was killed. Rain then stopped the proceedings. (435)

  Dead: 1 (killed by army)
  Beaten: 8 named victims (by dissidents), and several others (by army)
  Burnt: 12 known homesteads

JAN 1983: 5B arrived in the area and shot one villager in the fields who said he worked in South Africa. They also burnt his house. (437-8)

FEB 1983: Four soldiers came into the village and took one man and shot him dead. (439)

  Dead: 2
  Burnt: 1 homestead

SAWMILLS – EASTERN NYAMANDLOVU

JUNE 1983: 5B took men from their homes into the bush, where they beat them severely and then buried them while still alive. Name of one dead. (2408) One man who worked for the forestry commission was taken by the army. They first took him to say goodbye to his family and he was never seen again. (426)

**FEB 1983: CCJP reports raping of three, one a young schoolgirl, after they were taken off the train here by 5B. (file B)

  Dead: 1, plus others
  Missing: 1
  Raped: 3

GRANTS FARM – NYAMANDLOVU

3 FEB 1983: A family of eight were beaten by 5B. They did not burn the huts because it was raining. (413)

  Beaten: 8

UMGUSA RANCH
JUNE 1985: Two tourists killed, by dissidents.
   Dead: 2

6. SUMMARY OF TSHOLOTSHO ATROCITIES BY REGION

Note: Beatings are counted separately from other forms of physical torture
to highlight their prevalence: numbers in "mass beatings" are estimated
separately from incidents in which a few, specifically numbered/named
victims were beaten, hence the two totals for beatings in each listing.
A conservative estimate of 50 per mass beating was decided on.[5] In the
summary following GSW stands for gunshot wound.

PUMULA MISSION AREA
   Dead: 333 known, plus others implied[6]
   Missing: 10
   Beaten: 45+ named victims
   Mass beatings: 22 villages experienced this – estimated 1 100
                    villagers involved.
   Raped: 11
   GSW: 4
   Burnings: 148 homesteads – involves 11 villages where many
                    or all homes were burnt
Seven of the above burnings involved the burning to death of people,
ranging in number from one to thirty per incident.

NANDA-MBAMBA AREA: SOUTH-SOUTH-EAST
   Dead: 94 known, plus others implied
   Missing: 31
   Tortured: 33
   Beaten: 86+ named victims
   Mass beatings: 5 villages experienced this – estimated 250 villagers
                    involved
   Raped: 13+
   GSW: 4
   Bayoneted: 3
   Burnings: 10 homesteads – No reports of entire villages burnt.
                    No reports of people burned in huts.

TSHOLOTSHO TOWN AND CENTRAL AREA
Dead: 124 known, plus others implied
Missing: 43
Tortured: 23
Beaten: 43+ named victims
Mass beatings: 18 villages experienced this – estimated 900 villagers involved
Raped: 12+
GSW: 3
Burnings: 55 homesteads – involves 9 villages where many or all homes were burnt. Two reports of people burnt in huts, 1 in each case

NORTHERN TSHOLOTSHO
Dead: 206 known, plus others implied
Missing: 6
Tortured: 1
Beaten: 74+ named
Mass beatings: 25 villages experienced this – estimated 1 250 villagers involved (3 of these incidents involved everyone stripping naked first). Four railway siding beatings – estimated 200 involved
Raped: 28
GSW: 9
Burnings: 54 homesteads – involves 4 villages where many or all homes were burnt. One report of person in a hut, which was burnt

OTHER PARTS OF NYAMANDLOVU – COMMERCIAL FARMS, RESETTLEMENTS AND FORESTRY AREAS
Dead: 45
Missing: 1
Tortured: 1
Beaten: 66
Raped: 3
Burnings: 15 homesteads – also burning of clinic and school

DETENTIONS – ALL AREAS
Western Tsholotsho   42+
Southern Tsholotsho 131+
Central Tsholotsho   300+
Northern Tsholotsho 15+

These figures exclude people forcibly removed from one village to another venue close by, such as an adjacent village or school or river plain. They also exclude general figures for detentions available from other sources, such as LCFHR.

TOTALS

Dead:	802 known, plus others implied
Missing:	91
Tortured:	58
Beaten:	314
Mass beatings:	70 villages – estimated 3 500 villagers involved
	4 railway sidings – estimated 200 villagers involved
Raped:	67
GSW:	20
Bayoneted:	3
Burnings:	345 homesteads – involves 26 villages in which many or all homes were burnt. Nine reports of people burnt inside huts

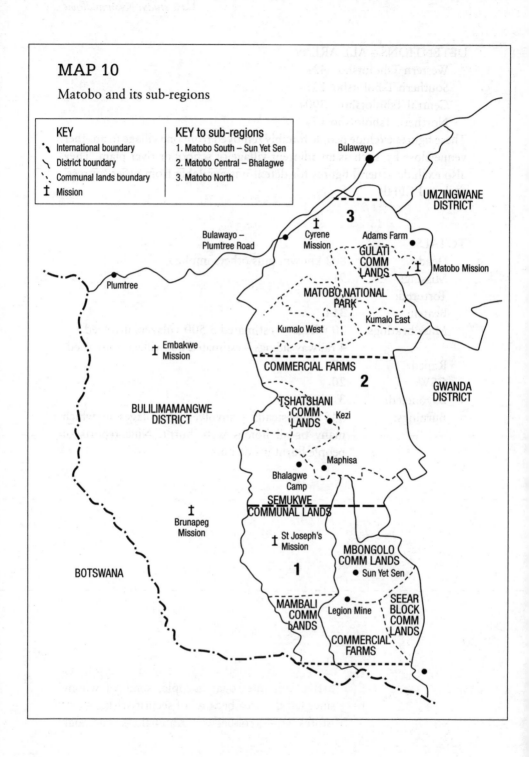

MAP 10

Matobo and its sub-regions

KEY
- ⌐ International boundary
- ＼ District boundary
- ⌐ Communal lands boundary
- ✝ Mission

KEY to sub-regions
1. Matobo South – Sun Yet Sen
2. Matobo Central – Bhalagwe
3. Matobo North

Bulawayo

UMZINGWANE DISTRICT

3

Bulawayo – Plumtree Road

✝ Cyrene Mission

Adams Farm

GULATI COMM LANDS

✝ Matobo Mission

Plumtree

MATOBO NATIONAL PARK

Kumalo West

Kumalo East

✝ Embakwe Mission

COMMERCIAL FARMS

2

GWANDA DISTRICT

BULILIMAMANGWE DISTRICT

TSHATSHANI COMM LANDS

Kezi

Maphisa

Bhalagwe Camp

SEMUKWE COMMUNAL LANDS

✝ Brunapeg Mission

✝ St Joseph's Mission

MBONGOLO COMM LANDS

● Sun Yet Sen

BOTSWANA

1

MAMBALI COMM LANDS

Legion Mine

SEEAR BLOCK COMM LANDS

COMMERCIAL FARMS

II

CASE STUDY TWO

MATOBO (KEZI)

The *Discussion of Data Sources* in Part One deals in detail with the data collection and collation process in the two case study areas. To summarise, data used consists both of archival material, information extracted from the media, academic studies, and interviews conducted in the 1990s.

1. ARCHIVAL DATA – *THE CHRONICLE*

A summary of events specifically in Matobo (Kezi) District, as revealed by *The Chronicle* newspaper, is given here. There are other reports of dissident activity in Matabeleland South, particularly in the Gwanda and Bulilimamangwe districts on either side, but these are not included here. In these surrounding areas there were dissident killings of civilians in the communal lands, a train driver, a Catholic missionary, a headmaster and his wife[1] and several commercial farmers and their families.

1982

APRIL 23	A CSC cattle sale raided by dissidents, 50km south of Kezi. One person is killed and four are injured, and $40 000 is stolen. A further sale has police protection.
MAY 31	An off-duty constable in Kezi beaten to death by three members of National Army.
JUNE 8	Store robbery near Kezi, perpetrators not mentioned.
JUNE 9	Three bandits armed with a hand grenade rob a store near Sun Yet Sen. Three bandits with rifles rob a store in Semukwe Communal Area.
JUNE 10	Two dissidents, one with a hand grenade, rob headmaster at Matobo Mission, Gulati Area.
JUNE 16	Dissidents demand food at Homestead. Army units then arrive and interrogate people, some of whom have since left the area because of security risk.
JUNE 17	Two storekeepers robbed in Khumalo Communal Lands, by man with rifle. Four armed men rob store near Kezi.

213

JUNE 19	Man stops a bus on Matobo–Byo road, but flees when he sees police on board.
	Owner of Bidi store robbed by two men with rifles.
JUNE 21	Two men with rifles rob store in Matobo commercial farming area.
	Same two men rob a businessman in Gulati Communal Lands. They also rob a store in Khumalo Communal Lands.
JULY (?)	"Some builders" killed and others attacked by dissidents in Kezi area while working on Government projects.
AUGUST 21	One policeman killed in a dissident ambush near Mbembeswana.
AUGUST 26	Police involved in a gun battle with dissidents on Lucydale Farm in Matobo – no casualties.
NOVEMBER	A bus robbed by dissidents and three passengers assaulted, in Matobo.
NOVEMBER 28	Nkomo addresses a rally in Matobo and tells people to keep their children away from dissidents.
DECEMBER 19	Two dissidents set up a roadblock just north of Kezi and stop seven buses and a Mercedes-Benz. They burn four buses and the car, before shooting breaks out and the dissidents (one wounded) escape in a hijacked car. They later kill the car owner.

1983

JANUARY 17	A lone bandit in Tshatshane area fires at random at a bus, killing a passenger.
FEBRUARY 10	A corporal in the ZNA ambushes a car near Antelope Mine; a four-year-old child is killed and his mother shot in the arm.
FEBRUARY 26	Captured dissidents strengthen evidence that Kezi is a "core area" for Super Zapu, according to police sources in Kezi.
	Director of Information, Justin Nyoka, conducts a press tour of Kezi to prove no army atrocities are taking place. (5 Brigade is in Matabeleland North, 100km away).
FEBRUARY 27	Seven armed dissidents beat a man and destroy construction equipment at Legion Mine.
MARCH 1	Enos Nkala addresses a rally in Sun Yet Sen area.

MARCH 3	Twenty schoolchildren abducted by dissidents and taken to Botswana.
AUGUST 30	An empty bus is hijacked by five bandits and burnt.
OCTOBER	Four members of one family shot on a commercial farm, by dissidents. Initially one man and two women in the family are attacked in their farmhouse, and another family member who rushes to the scene to help is subsequently killed.
NOVEMBER	A commercial farmer killed by 25 dissidents in Matobo, when he went to check his cattle.
DECEMBER 24	Two girls aged 13 and 16 had their noses and ears cut off by dissidents, in Matobo village.

1984

No incidents involving dissidents/bandits/armed men specifically designated as occurring in Matobo (Kezi) District were reported in *The Chronicle*. (Incidents in surrounding areas are reported.)

FEBRUARY	Members of ZNA stand trial, accused of murdering six civilians in February 1984.

1985

JUNE 6	Three dissidents killed by security forces in Semukwe area of Matobo.
JUNE 11	Bandits rob and destroy property on three commercial farms in the Matobo area, and order farm workers to leave.

1986

JANUARY 29	Dissidents destroy and burn property at five schools and also burn two stores in Matobo.
FEB 21	$65 000 damage caused when dissidents burn buildings and shoot 38 cattle on a commercial farm in Kezi.
APRIL 26	A lone bandit is shot in Whitewaters area of Matobo.
JUNE 19	Three employees of Matopos Research Station are killed by dissidents. They also rob others and set a store room and office ablaze.
OCTOBER 2	Dissidents burn a clinic, two houses and a pump house in Matobo.
OCTOBER 8	One man killed and three others assaulted, by dissidents in the Kezi area.

215

1987

JANUARY 29	Dissident killed in Bezha area of Matobo.
FEBRUARY 19	A bandit forces seven others to burn a beerhall at Bidi in Matobo.
MARCH 30	Dissidents destroy a commercial farm homestead in Matobo, valued at $49 000.
JULY 7	A militia man is shot dead by dissidents on a commercial farm near Figtree.
AUGUST 18	A commercial farming couple is shot dead and their car burnt by dissidents in the Figtree farming area.
NOVEMBER	Sixteen missionaries in two adjacent farm houses in north eastern Matobo are murdered by dissidents. The dead include women and children.
DECEMBER 23	Unity.

1988

MARCH 28	"Gunmen" kill 34 animals on a commercial farm, and burn a house in Matobo.
	This is the last recorded act of terror in western Zimbabwe.

2. CCJP ARCHIVAL DATA AND BLPC INTERVIEWS IN 1995–1996

A) ARCHIVES

The CCJP archives for events in 1984 are far better organised than those for 1983: the first arrival of 5 Brigade in Matabeleland North had caught everyone by surprise. By 1984, mission staff in Matabeleland South were prepared for what might ensue. Mission personnel kept in regular touch with personnel in Bulawayo, who made typed records of telephone conversations, which were on occasion conducted in German to foil whoever might be listening in.[2] There are also detailed minutes of meetings between personnel in Bulawayo with outlying mission staff during the curfew. In addition, the CCJP was preparing to present evidence to the Committee of Inquiry by early 1984, and systematic, formal typed statements were taken from witnesses from Matabeleland South, and several were sworn and signed in front of a Commissioner of Oaths.

B) BLPC INTERVIEWS

The Matobo Case Study is an extended pilot study rather than a comprehensive report on Matobo District. The process of interviewing was far less complete than in Tsholotsho, largely as a result of time and funding constraints, but also owing to other factors. While the Tsholotsho interviewing began in earnest in mid-1995 and was completed by a back-up session in mid-1996, in Matobo the procedure was condensed into approximately ten weeks, from July 1996 to mid-September 1996.

July was spent trying to establish contact with the local councillors, who were not previously known to project personnel, and to gain their co-operation in publicising the project among their ward residents. The Tsholotsho councillors had been well known to project personnel and had proved very co-operative, but this was not the case in Matobo. In spite of support for the project from the Provincial Governor and from certain chiefs in the region, certain ward councillors remained wary of getting involved in the project. They were hesitant to encourage the people in their wards to give evidence. In some cases, councillors actively undermined the project, by ordering those in their wards not to attend pre-arranged interview sessions. Other councillors expressed fear of what the ZANU-PF Central Committee might say if it were known they had supported the data collection process.

In addition, the CIO attended certain interview sessions, remaining visible but at a distance of about 30 metres. In one instance, they returned a few days after interviewing in a region, and questioned a man who had been involved. It was the belief of project personnel that the CIO became involved at the instigation of certain councillors. Their behaviour was intimidatory, and indicative of the desire of some government officials to prevent the facts of those years from being discussed or acknowledged. The behaviour of CIO in Matobo was partially successful in preventing people from coming forward to testify: project personnel had approached priests at all missions in Matabeleland South to help in data collection, but after news of the CIO interest spread, many decided they would rather not get involved with the project.

If there is truly nothing to hide about events in the 1980s, then government resistance to establishing the facts makes no sense.

In spite of the difficulties experienced, a total of nine interview sessions were conducted, at six different venues. All these sessions were conducted in the southern parts of Matobo. No interviews were conducted in areas north of Kezi, such as in Gulati Communal Lands or in Khumalo Communal Lands, as time ran out. A few selective interviews took place in Khumalo after mid-September, in order to try and establish a general sense of how affected this region had been, but there is clearly scope for further investigation of events in this northern region of Matobo.

At the interview sessions in southern Matobo, many people came forward to give their testimonies. A total of 350 named victims were identified, and thousands of others were implied by witnesses. Some witnesses who were in wards where their councillors were discouraging involvement in the project, actually walked to neighbouring wards to give testimony, or gave testimony through the local missions. People were turning up in large numbers to give witness in the last few sessions, indicating that if time had allowed and the interviewing procedure could have been extended, the database would have been substantially added to.

While fewer interviews were collected in Matobo than in Tsholotsho, a consistent picture emerged from those who gave testimony. As in Tsholotsho, corroboratory evidence of State strategy was given by witnesses from areas very distant from one another, and data collected in 1996 bore out data collected by CCJP in the 1980s.

3. OVERVIEW OF EVENTS REVEALED BY DATA

A) A BRIEF CHRONOLOGY

In February 1983, the northernmost areas of Matabeleland South felt the effects of the first 5 Brigade onslaught, which primarily affected Matabeleland North. Civilians using the main Bulawayo–Plumtree road were particularly vulnerable, with several recorded instances of people being taken from buses at road blocks, and never being seen again.

The 5 Brigade was first reported in Matabeleland South in July 1983, at Brunapeg Mission in Bulilimamangwe. By late 1983, there were several major 5 Brigade incidents on record, including some deaths, beatings and the burning of 24 homesteads in Mbembeswana in Matobo.

However, it was in February 1984 that the 5 Brigade launched a systematic campaign of mass beatings and mass detentions in Matabeleland South, lasting several months. These tailed off after May 1984, after which the 5 Brigade was withdrawn for retraining. Sporadic reports of violations by both the army and dissidents continued until the Amnesty in 1988.

Apart from abuses at the hands of 5 Brigade, there was a far higher incidence of CIO as perpetrator than in Matabeleland North, mainly because of their involvement at Bhalagwe Camp and Sun Yet Sen. In addition, there were several reports of "Grey's Scouts", or a mounted unit, abusing people while on follow-up operations. There were no complaints filed against mounted ZNA units in Tsholotsho.

B) THE FOOD EMBARGO[3]

The food embargo was a major factor in events in Matabeleland South in 1984. Throughout the early months of 1984, residents of Matabeleland South were suffering from starvation caused in the first place, by three consecutive years of drought and in the second place, by Government restrictions preventing all movement of food into and around the region. Drought relief was stopped and stores were closed. Almost no people were allowed into and out of the region to buy food, and private food supplies were destroyed.

The psychological impact of the food embargo was profound. While the "village by village" summary which follows does not make continuous reference to the food embargo, many of those interviewed mentioned its effects. All events which occurred did so against the background of a seriously weakened and demoralised populace, who were having to watch the children cry and beg for food their parents were unable to provide on a daily basis. State officials, largely in the form of the 5 Brigade, also actively punished those villagers who shared food with starving neighbours. The speeches of 5 Brigade commanders at rallies repeatedly stated the desire of the Government to starve all the Ndebele to death, as punishment for their being dissidents. In the most cruel speeches, people in the region were told they would be starved until they ate each other, including their own wives and children. (One such speech is included in this report in full: see Part Three, I.)

Those interviewed recount how they struggled to stay alive during the embargo, by eating the roots and fruits of wild plants. However, in some areas the 5 Brigade tried to prevent even this, and punished people for eating wild marula fruit. Even water was severely rationed. People also talk of risking their lives and breaking the curfew to share food with neighbours after dark, and their disbelief at seeing bags of maize ripped open and destroyed wherever 5 Brigade found them – on buses or in homes.

CCJP archives reveal grave concern at the food situation, which missions in Matabeleland South monitored on a continuous basis. Their requests to be allowed to administer food in rationed amounts to their parishioners and employees were denied by the authorities, although St Joseph's Mission was allowed to feed 300 under-fives on a daily basis. Other feeding schemes that had been operating collapsed as mealie-meal stocks ran out.

CCJP also kept track of which stores were open, and on which days. From March onwards, the total ban on stores was slightly modified. Three stores in Matobo were opened for only two days a week, at Bidi,

Kezi and Maphisa (Antelope). This meant that people near St Joseph's Mission were 60km away from the nearest store, too far to walk in a day under curfew conditions. Other settlements were even further away.

People were banned from the use of any form of transport under the curfew. This not only affected access to operating stores, but also access to clinics. All the hospitals and clinics in Matabeleland South reported falling attendances, and a concern at the fact that sick people were unable to walk the often-extensive distances to reach help, and could die as a result. In addition, those being beaten by 5 Brigade were expressly forbidden to seek medical help, even if they were within the vicinity of a clinic.

There is mention that even operating stores were not allowed to sell mealie-meal. On some occasions the stores were opened purely for propaganda purposes. There is a reference in mission correspondence to Col Simpson of the Paratroopers opening a store for three hours to coincide with a tour by the local press on 10 March 1984. On 21 March 84 people gathered at Bidi Store and waited all day only to be told that no mealie-meal was to be sold. This was the pattern at other stores too, where people gathered, having walked 30 km or more, and would wait for hours only to be told they could not buy anything.

Stores were not allowed to restock any products during the curfews, and those that occasionally opened soon had no food of any kind to sell. The army took control of the regional National Foods depot to ensure mealie-meal was not distributed to stores. Anyone wishing to buy food in Bulawayo, to send to relatives in curfew zones, needed a permit from the police or army, and these were rarely granted. There are also in interviews many accounts of people being brutally tortured when found waiting at shopping centres, the accusation being that they were trying to break the food curfew.

Schoolteachers were among the few who were allowed food, as the government expressly intended schools to remain open, but the teachers were severely restricted in terms of how much they could request, to prevent them from feeding others in the region. Mechanisms of how teachers received food depended on the orders of local army commanders: some teachers were allowed transport into Bulawayo to buy food for themselves, others were only allowed to place a food order with the army who then purchased the food on their behalf. This placed teachers in an awkward position: while teachers may have had some food, their pupils had none.

CCJP records indicate that a request for supplementary feeding through the schools was denied, and that school attendance declined as pupils became faint with hunger and as others fled the area hoping to find a place in schools in Bulawayo. At some mission schools, pupils would be given a drink of "mawehu", made from a local grain by mission staff, during lessons – but staff commented that this was not enough to sustain the children's growing bodies. Pupils also had to face being picked up and beaten up by the army – mission staff were aware that this was happening, but were powerless to protect the schoolchildren.

In addition to preventing food from coming into the area, 5 Brigade also broke down fences to allow cattle to graze whatever few hardy crops might have survived the drought, thus ensuring that starvation was absolute.

Catholic Mission staff in affected areas expressed increasing alarm and by the end of March 1984 they began to fear for the lives of the sick, the elderly and the very young. As people became more desperate, there were even those who wished to be detained, in the hope that in custody they might at least receive food. In fact, those in custody were kept in appalling conditions and received little food. Hunger and the problem of getting food to those nearing starvation became a dominant theme in CCJP correspondence during the curfew months.

The food embargo alone was thus a significant and effective strategy which proved, to 400 000 ordinary people in Matabeleland South, the power of the State to cause extreme hardship.

C) 5 BRIGADE AND CIO

In Matabeleland South in 1984, the pattern of 5 Brigade behaviour differed notably from their behaviour in 1983. Killings were less likely to occur in the villages. However, mass beatings remained very widespread, with many variations on a theme. While the most common pattern still involved making people lie face down in rows, after which they were beaten with thick sticks, there are a large number of interviews referring to sadistic refinements in mass physical torture. People were on occasion made to lie on thorny branches first, after which 5 Brigade ran along their backs to embed the thorns before the beatings. People were made to roll in and out of water while being beaten, sometimes naked. They were made to push government vehicles with their heads only, and were then beaten for bleeding on government property. Women were made to climb up trees and open their legs, so 5 Brigade could insult their genitals, while simultaneously beating them. Men and women were made to run round in circles with their index fingers on the ground, and were beaten for falling over.

These mass beatings invariably ended with at least some victims so badly injured that they were unable to move, so that they had to be carried away by others the following day. As in Matabeleland North, people were threatened with death if they reported to hospitals or clinics, and the majority of injuries remained untreated. Victims mention fractured limbs that set themselves crookedly, perforated ear drums which became infected, and other injuries (which might have been easily treated) resulting in long-term health problems.

Genital mutilation is more commonly reported in Matobo than in Matabeleland North. The practice of forcing sharp sticks into women's vaginas is independently reported by several witnesses. This phenomenon was apparently common at Bhalagwe, and witnesses refer to women at Bhalagwe adopting a characteristic, painful, wide-legged gait after receiving such torture.

In addition, men were also subjected to beatings that focused on their genitalia. The testicles would be bound in rubber strips and then beaten with a truncheon. Some men complain of permanent problems with erections and urinating as a result of such beatings. At least one man is reported as dying after his scrotum was burst during a beating. Several witnesses also report being told to have sex with donkeys while at Bhalagwe, and being beaten when they failed to do so. The practice of widespread rape and of young women being "given as wives" to 5 Brigade at Bhalagwe is also referred to by several independent sources.

The CIO seemed to work very closely with the 5 Brigade in Matabeleland South, and gained a reputation for being even more lethal in their methods of torture than 5 Brigade. The CIO conducted most of the "interrogation" at Bhalagwe and Sun Yet Sen: they would ask questions, while 5 Brigade, who could not speak or understand Ndebele, beat the victim regardless of what he/she responded. CIO used electric shocks to torture people. They attached wires to the backs, ears and mouths of witnesses before shocking them. Witnesses frequently refer to being tortured by 5 Brigade and then CIO consecutively, or being passed from the custody of one to the other and back again. In Bhalagwe, there are repeated references to a particularly cruel woman CIO officer who used to sexually torment her male victims.

Water torture was also apparently widespread under both CIO and 5 Brigade. This commonly involved either holding a person's head under water, or forcing a shirt into somebody's mouth, then pouring water onto the shirt until the victim choked and lost consciousness. The perpetrator would then jump on the victim's stomach until s/he vomited up the water. This practice commonly stopped once the victim was vomiting blood.

While killing by 5 Brigade was less widespread than in Matabeleland North in 1983, there are still many horrific atrocities on record, including the following, all perpetrated by 5 Brigade. A four-month-old infant was axed three times, and the mother forced to eat the flesh of her dead child. An eighteen-year-old girl was raped by six soldiers and then killed. An eleven-year-old child had her vagina burnt with plastic and was later shot. Twin infants were buried alive.[4]

D) MASS DETENTION

Mass beatings and rallies invariably ended in mass detentions in 1984. Those detained included all ex-ZIPRAs, all ZAPU officials, and other men and women selected on a seemingly random basis. Those detained could include the elderly, and also schoolchildren. Trucks seemed to patrol, picking up anyone they met and taking them to detention camps.

It was usual for detainees to be taken first to the nearest 5 Brigade base, for one or more days, before being transferred to Bhalagwe. Interviewees report being held in small 5 Brigade camps, until there were enough of them to fill an army vehicle to Bhalagwe. A truck-load seems to have been around 100 people. In southern Matobo, the main "holding camp" was at Sun Yet Sen, where both the CIO and the 5 Brigade were based. This camp reportedly held up to 800 detainees at one time, and people were sometimes held here for a week or longer. There were smaller bases in the west and north.

Detainees in southern Matobo were commonly beaten before their detention, tortured at Sun Yet Sen, and then transferred to Bhalagwe for further torture and detention. In addition to detentions after rallies or mass beatings, 5 Brigade also went through some areas on foot, hauling out villagers from the homesteads as they passed, and then herding them ahead on foot, while beating them. Some interviewees report covering extensive distances in this way, as 5 Brigade made a sweep through many villages in an area, gathering a growing number of detainees as they went.

E) BHALAGWE

The most notorious detention centre of all was Bhalagwe Camp, situated just west of Antelope Mine. From information gathered from interviews it appears that Bhalagwe operated at full capacity from the beginning of February until the end of May 1984, a period of four months. It continued to operate after May 1984, but the phenomenon of mass detentions had dissipated by then, and there were fewer new inmates.

On 15 May 1982 aerial photographs of the Bhalagwe area were taken for the purposes of updating maps of the area. An enlarged section of one such photograph (see page 227) shows that at this date, Bhalagwe was an operational military camp: military vehicles are visible, as are soldiers on parade. It would appear that 1:7 Battalion was based here in 1982, consisting mainly of ex-ZIPRAs incorporated into the Zimbabwe National Army. At some point in 1982, the ZIPRAs here were allegedly accused of being dissidents, and Bhalagwe Camp was surrounded by elite Paratroop and Commando units and was shut down.[5] However, a military presence was maintained here, as there are references to Bhalagwe being used as a detention centre for ex-ZIPRAs and others from mid 1982 onwards, when the anti-ZIPRA sweep in the wake of the tourist kidnapping gained momentum.

Visible at Bhalagwe in May 1982, are 180 large, round roofed asbestos "holding sheds", each measuring approximately 12 x 6 metres, and 36 half-sized ones, measuring 6 x 6 metres. According to testimonies on record since March 1984, which have been confirmed in interviews in 1996, these asbestos structures were where detainees were kept. It is also clear from the aerial photography that these structures were arranged, apparently within fences, in groups of a dozen – eleven 12 x 6 metre structures and one smaller one. What is not clear is how many of these structures were used in 1984 to house detainees, and how many were used to house military personnel, or served storage or interrogation purposes. Perhaps many were out of use. There is also reference by some detainees to some of the asbestos sheds having suffered wind and storm damage, so by February 1984 the camp may have been less intact than it appears in the May 1982 photograph.

Detainees confirm that 136 people were routinely kept in each 12 x 6 metre shed.[6] There were no beds, and the floor space was so limited people had to sleep squeezed together on their sides, in three rows. There were no blankets or toilet facilities. An assumption, based on affidavits, of 136 per shed would allow for the detention of at least 1 500 people within each fenced enclosure of a dozen sheds. Bhalagwe camp has been variously estimated by ex-detainees to have had 1 800, 2 000, 3 000 or up to 5 000 people detained at one time. On 7 February 1984, the number of detainees was 1 856, consisting of 1 000 men and 856 women. This figure was given to CCJP in 1984 by a detainee who was ordered by 5 Brigade to help others count the number of detainees. As the curfew had only been in effect a few days at this stage, and the phase of mass detentions was just beginning, it is very likely the number rose over the following weeks.

It is quite clear from the aerial photograph that Bhalagwe's holding capacity was vast, and easily capable of absorbing at one time the highest figure currently claimed, that of 5 000. However, the exact number detained at Bhalagwe's peak remains unconfirmed. The first records of detentions in the Bhalagwe area date from the middle of 1982, coinciding with the detention exercises going on in Matabeleland North at that time. Reported detentions in 1982 and 1983 are few, however: it is in February 1984 that Bhalagwe becomes the centre of detentions throughout Matabeleland.

The remains of Bhalagwe Camp were still visible in November 1996 (see photos pp 226-229). The camp is ideally situated in terms of combining maximum space with maximum privacy. There are natural barriers on three sides: Bhalagwe hill lies to the south, and Zamanyone hill demarcates its western edge. The eastern perimeter lies in the direction of Antelope Dam, and there are no villages between the camp and the dam. Water was piped in from Antelope Dam nearby, into water storage tanks. Although the camp is scarcely a kilometre from the main road running south of Bhalagwe hill, it is invisible to passersby.

People were trucked in from all over Matabeleland South to Bhalagwe, not just from Matobo. Women and men were separated. Different zones within the camp were designated to detainees who had been brought in from the different bases at Bulilimamangwe, Plumtree, Gwanda, Mberengwa, Sun Yet Sen and northern Matobo. There is even reference to detainees from Chipinge – these could have been potential MNR dissidents, although who they were exactly is not clear. As well as being sorted by district, Bhalagwe survivors refer to new arrivals being sorted and designated holding rooms on the basis of their usual line of work and their employers, such as whether they worked in town or were communal farmers. At times schoolchildren were also sorted and kept separately. Detainees also refer to identity documents and letters related to employment being taken by 5 Brigade, and the latter destroyed. Interviewees also refer to the fact that ex-ZIPRAs and ZAPU officials were kept separately from the ordinary civilians.

As detainees at any one time at Bhalagwe had been selected from a wide area, people in detention together seldom knew more than a handful of the other detainees. As most travel in the rural areas is on foot, people then (and now) did not know those who lived even a few villages away from their usual footpaths. One of the consequences was that when a person died in detention, possibly only one or two other inmates from the same village, and possibly nobody at all, would know that person's name.

Photo 14: Remains of a sentry box, October 1996, showing Bhalagwe hill on the far right: Point A in photos 16 and 17

Photo 15: Remains of officers' mess October 1996 (point B in photos 16 and 17) showing Zamanyone hill in the background, and the ruins of an asbestos holding shed in the foreground

Photo 16: Bhalagwe Camp: Surveyor-General's aerial photograph, 15 May 1982. Soldiers can be seen on parade at point D

Photo 17: Bhalagwe Camp: Surveyor-General's aerial photograph, May
1990

Photo 18: Remains of officers' mess, north side, October 1996

Photo 19: Remains of a mass grave (point C in photos 16 and 17), believed to have held three victims, Bhalagwe Camp, October 1996

Inmates of Bhalagwe speak of daily deaths in the camp, but they are seldom able to name victims. They will merely comment how they witnessed people being beaten or shot, or how on certain mornings there would be people in their barracks who had died in the course of the night, as a result of the previous day's beatings. The digging of graves is mentioned as a daily chore by some in early February. However, according to witnesses, at a certain point although the date is not clear, these graves were dug up and the bodies taken away on the trucks. The empty grave sites were still clearly visible in November 1996. Other accounts refer to the nightly departure of army trucks, carrying away the dead and dying to an unknown destination. It is now believed that these people were disposed of in local mine shafts, and in 1992, human remains were found in Antelope Mine, adjacent to Bhalagwe. Other people speak of their belief that Legion Mine, near Sun Yet Sen, also contains human remains from the 1980s.

The ex-ZIPRAs and ZAPU officials were singled out and kept in a separate area, in small buildings with low roofs and no windows, although there were ventilation slats. They were also kept shackled throughout their detention, unlike the other detainees, and were subjected to the most brutal torture.

Turnover at Bhalagwe was high. The length of detentions varied greatly. Most people recount having spent a few days or weeks in Bhalagwe. Approximately one to two weeks seemed to be a common detention period. Some interviewees claim to have spent as long as six to nine months in detention here, but these tend to be the ex-ZIPRAs and ZAPU officials. Women were commonly held a few days, unless selected as "wives" for the soldiers, in which case their detention might stretch to a few weeks. If two weeks was assumed as an average stay, and a conservative turnover of 1 000 every two weeks was assumed, it could be estimated that around 8 000 people passed through Bhalagwe in the four months it operated at its peak. The turnover could have been nearer double this figure.

Whatever the length of detention, those detained were subjected to at least one brutal interrogation experience. The majority were beaten on more than one occasion. There is reference to electric shocks being administered by the CIO. Some witnesses report making false confessions under torture, naming invented people as dissidents, only to be caught out the next day when they failed to remember their previous day's testimony. Interrogations always involved accusing people of being dissidents or feeding dissidents or of failing to report dissidents. This was routine, with no evidence being cited. The sexual focus of much of the torture has already been mentioned, with widespread rape, genital mutilation and forced sex with animals.[7]

Bhalagwe survivors have referred to a wide variety of physical tortures. One pastime for 5 Brigade was to force large numbers of detained men and women to climb on to branches of trees, until the weight of human bodies snapped the branch, sending everyone crashing to earth. People broke limbs as a result of this. Several interviewees comment on the way 5 Brigade laughed to see them suffer.

Another form of torture was to force three men to climb into a 2m asbestos drainage pipe. The men on each end would be told to come out, and as they started to leave the pipe, 5 Brigade would begin to beat them fiercely, causing the men to spontaneously pull back into the pipe, crushing the third man who would be crowded in the middle. On occasion, this resulted in the man in the middle being crushed and kicked to death by his two panicking companions.

Detainees were fed only once every second day, when mealie-meal would be dished up on dustbin lids, with between 10 and 20 people per lid. Sometimes people would be forced to eat without using their hands for the amusement of 5 Brigade. People were given half a cup of water a day each. Detainees had to dig toilets, wash army clothes and pots, and chop firewood in between their interrogation sessions. Interrogations used to begin at 5.30am every day.

Bhalagwe Camp was operating at its full potential at the very time that the Chihambabwe Committee was collecting data on the previous year's atrocities.

4. SUMMARY OF MATOBO INCIDENTS BY REGION

ABBREVIATIONS
GSW Gunshot Wound
MASSDETN Mass Detention (50 villagers estimated)

SOUTHERN MOTOBO
    Dead: 16 plus others implied
    Missing: 10
    Torture: 70
    Assault: 342, includes 104 from accident
    Mass beatings: 12, estimated 600 villagers beaten
    Raped: 13, plus others implied

GSW: 3
Detained: 136
Massdetn: 8, estimated 400 villagers
Property burnt: 3 homesteads

CENTRAL MATOBO
Dead: 102, plus others implied
Missing: 20
Torture: 1, plus others implied
Assault: 141
Mass beatings: 13, estimated 650 villagers beaten
Raped: 2, plus others implied
GSW: 1, plus others implied
Detained: 28
Massdetn: 10 estimated, 500 villagers detained
Property burnt: 31 homesteads

NORTHERN MATOBO
Dead: 55
Missing: 9
Assault: 57
Mass beatings: 2
Raped: 2
Detained: 60
Property burnt: 1

TOTALS
Dead: 183, plus others implied
Missing: 39, plus others implied
Torture: 71, plus hundreds implied
Assault: 540
Mass beatings: 27, estimated 1350 villagers beaten
Raped: 17, plus hundreds implied
Detained: 224
Massdetn: 18, estimated 900 villagers detained
Property burnt: 35

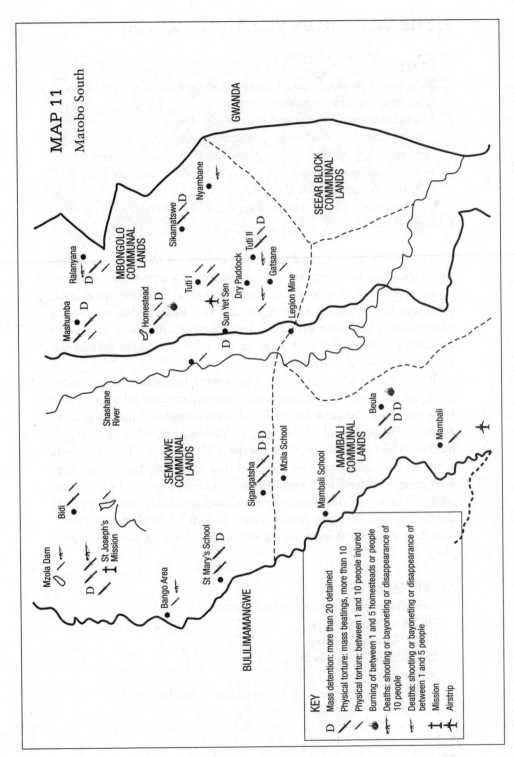

MAP 11
Matobo South

KEY

D   Mass detention: more than 20 detained

Physical torture: mass beatings, more than 10

Physical torture: between 1 and 10 people injured

Burning of between 1 and 5 homesteads or people

Deaths: shooting or bayoneting or disappearance of 10 people

Deaths: shooting or bayoneting or disappearance of between 1 and 5 people

Mission

Airstrip

5. THE VILLAGE BY VILLAGE SUMMARY

NOTE:
Numbers in brackets indicate source numbers of BLPC interviews from which information was derived.
** indicates source document is in a CCJP file.
**** indicates an incident involving dissidents.
For all other offences, the perpetrators are army units, or Government agencies such as the Central Intelligence Organisation (CIO), or Police Support Unit (SU).
5 Brigade (5B) may be assumed as perpetrator unless another unit is mentioned.

Matobo has been divided into three regions for the purposes of this summary. While there appear to be some discernible patterns of difference in the experience of one region from another in this case study area, this could be the consequence of the fact that interviewing was not as widespread as in the first cast study area. Current differences, such as the apparently large number of dead in the central region, might balance out with more thorough interviewing.

It was noteworthy that before interviewing took place in September 1996, all the archival and academic information from all sources had been placed on the database, and had revealed only 47 named dead in Matobo. The process of interviewing and assessing in terms of "village", increased this figure to over 220 in the space of four weeks. This represents a five-fold increase: many of the dead that were included at this stage were numbered dead, indicated with full details of where and when, from the CCJP archives. This is perhaps an indication of what might happen to the current figures for the dead in other districts where there is currently little data available, if interviewing and village by village assessment took place.

ABBREVIATIONS
    ASS: Assaulted (physical torture/beatings)
    DETN: Detention
    GSW: Gunshot Wound
    MASS BEAT: Mass Beating
    MISS: Missing
    TORT: Tortured (physical methods other than beatings)

All names of "villages" or "lines" have been standardised in accordance with Surveyor-General's Maps of Matobo District, which on a scale of 1:250 000 encompasses parts of four separate maps. The maps used are: Plumtree (edition 2) SF-35-3 (1990); Bulawayo (edition 2) SF-35-4 (1990); Mphoengs (edition 2) EF-35-7 (1975); West Nicholson Sheet SF-35-8 (1975). The exception to this is Bhalagwe, which is found spelled in various documents and maps as Bhalagwe, Belagwe, Balaqwe, Belabgwe and Balagwe. "Bhalagwe" is the preferred spelling in this document.

5.1 SUN YET SEN AREA – SOUTHERN MATOBO

Sun Yet Sen was used as a 5 Brigade Army Camp during late 1983 and in 1984. It was used as an interrogation centre and also as a holding camp for detainees en route for Bhalagwe, and there are also reports of CIO interrogating people here. Numerous interviews from people in southern Matobo refer to being rounded up in vehicles or marched on foot to Sun Yet Sen, where they were tortured for one or more days before being transferred by vehicle to Bhalagwe. Some villagers in the northern part of this area were taken directly to Bhalagwe on their detention. This is particularly the case for those who lived in the vicinity of St Joseph's Mission. There was a small 5 Brigade base near to the mission, at Bidi, and people were often rounded up to this base, and from there to Bhalagwe.

ST JOSEPH'S MISSION (approx 30km SW of Kezi)
(For the purposes of this report, the designation "St Joseph's Mission" refers to an area of approximately 10km in radius around the mission, inclusive of many settlements which are not always clearly indicated by name on topographical maps of the region.)
****NOV 1982: Bango Area. Unknown people came at night and shot dead two men, an ex-ZIPRA and his uncle. (3451-2)
****NOV 1982: Dissidents tied up a woman and abducted her daughter and two other young girls, whom they raped and released in the morning. (3477-5)
**END FEB 1983 (CCJP report): Enos Nkala addressed a rally at Kafusi Dam and people were trucked there from all over Matabeleland South. The Provincial ZAPU treasurer was detained for two months after this meeting, was given electric shock treatment, and severely beaten. He was detained because he challenged Nkala who said people willingly supported dissidents. The ZAPU official asked Nkala when in history people without guns had been able to arrest those with guns. He also

asked if the 5 Brigade really intended to kill all the Ndebele, as they kept saying. This same man had been badly beaten by the army a month earlier. (3456 also reports the incident). *The Chronicle* also reports on this rally (on 1 March), and on the first comment made by this man, although it neglects to mention the man's subsequent detention and torture for this comment.

DEC 1983: Mgulatshani area. Eight named men and women plus "many others" were detained by a ZNA unit (not 5 Brigade). Some were demobbed ZIPRAs. All were severely beaten. They were tortured by CIO and given electric shocks to the testicles at Kezi Air Strip. One of those detained in 1983 was detained again in May 1984 at Bhalagwe. He was with other ex-ZIPRAs, held for four months and regularly tortured. Many of the ZIPRAs just disappeared during this time, and others were threatened with ending up "down mine shafts". Five named. (3459-68)

JAN 1984: ZANU-PF officials addressed a rally at Mbembcswana in central Matobo. People were forced to attend and were trucked in from all over the region, including St Joseph's. ** (CCJP formal report) On the way home from this rally, an army Puma crashed, killing six schoolchildren from St Joseph's Mission and injuring 104 others, some very seriously. The CCJP report comments that *The Chronicle* reports the incident, but gets the location of the accident wrong. (3469-76 also refer, giving all names of dead).

FEB 1984: Villagers in the area were rounded up first to the 5 Brigade camp near St Joseph's and then to Bhalagwe. (Tshipisane village mentioned, among other unnamed villages). Victims, both men and women, refer to being beaten with logs and also thorn branches. People talk of being tortured into making false confessions. There is also reference to women having sharp sticks pushed into their vaginas. (3418-3424, 3448-50)

A man found herding donkeys west of the mission was beaten by 5 Brigade for "curfew breaking", taken to Bhalagwe where he was tortured and detained for three months. (3447)

FEB 1984: An elderly woman who ran a grinding mill was severely beaten by 5 Brigade at Bidi Store for breaking the curfew and the food embargo. The next day her female co-workers were also beaten, and forced to open the store so 5 Brigade could drink beer. (3481)

Two villagers (ZAPU branch secretary and one other) were severely beaten by 5 Brigade in the bush, and were hospitalised for 3 months. (3482-3) Two villagers, a man and a woman, were severely beaten in their home by 5 Brigade one morning. (3484-5) Two women, one with a baby, badly beaten by 5 Brigade, one of them on two occasions. (3486-7) A husband and wife found on the road were badly beaten, the wife stripped naked

first. Another was beaten with them and taken to Bhalagwe. (3488-90)
A woman, her brother and two others were removed from their homes,
beaten, and taken to Bhalagwe; the woman had sharp objects forced into
her vagina, along with further beatings. (3491/3)

FEB 1984: An old man and one other were severely beaten for "parenting
dissidents", and were taken to Bhalagwe for several months. (3494-7)

FEB 1984: Mzola Dam area. A group of at least eight elderly men
(named) were severely beaten by Brigade for eating at 11 in the morning.
They were forced to do strenuous exercise while being beaten throughout
the day. One was then released, while the others were kept overnight,
transferred to Guardian Angel and then Mabisi Dip. Torture continued
and several of the men collapsed completely and one was finally beaten
to death (named). (3497-3504 incl)

FEB 1984: Near St Joseph's dam. 5 Brigade summoned an old man
across a field and beat him for not running. He fell over and was beaten
with sticks until his nose and mouth bled. His family took him home by
wheelbarrow. (3505)

APRIL 1984: A man found driving a car at Bidi Shopping Centre was
accused of being senior ZAPU and beaten. His wife and child were beaten
and his car was shot full of holes. He was then detained at Bhalagwe for
three months and was tortured by CIO. (3453-55)

NOV 1984: Mtsuli village. Nine members of 5 Brigade severely beat a
man in front of others and kicked him in the diaphragm until he vomited
blood. (3446)

**11 FEB 1985 (CCJP formal report): A man from Bidi was among
many abducted throughout Matabeleland in nightly raids by CIO. By
Nov 1985 he had not been located. Two other named men went missing
in this area in Feb 1985 (3339-40)

****MAY 1987: Dissidents accused people in Mtsuli village of being
sell-outs. They severely beat two men. The incident was reported to ZRP
and the two dissidents were later shot. (3457-8)

    MISS: 3 named, plus others implied
    DEAD: 9
    TORT: 16
    RAPE: 3, plus others implied
    ASS: 41
    MASS BEAT: 1, 104 injured in accident
    DETN: 16

MASHUMBA AREA (20km SSE of Kezi)
1984: All the villagers in the area were herded to the school by 5 Brigade.

Some were called by name and were forced to lie on thorn bushes. Soldiers then walked on them to push the thorns in, while other soldiers beat the victims with thick sticks. (Two named victims, one male, one female: 3675-6)

1984: A woman and her mentally retarded son were severely beaten by 5 Brigade. (3693-4)

FEB 1984: A woman found trying to buy mealie-meal at Mashumba stores was accused of feeding dissidents and detained for five days at Bhalagwe. (3695)

FEB 1984: Two men cycling from home near Mashumba to Maphisa, to buy ZANU-PF cards, were badly beaten by 5 Brigade for breaking curfew regulations by cycling. One victim suffered permanent damage to his testicles. (3616)

APRIL 1984: Dissidents burnt some tractors near Homestead, and ZNA units on horseback went through adjacent areas rounding up and beating men. At Mashumba, 13 named men found at a beer drink were beaten, given water torture (i.e. semi-drowned after which soldiers would jump on their stomachs to force the water out), then detained at Kezi. Three other named men in the area suffered similarly. The CIO took over and they were further tortured and held for 30 days in Gwanda before release. (3616-18, 3711-22)

APRIL 1984: A young woman teacher was accused with others of hiding dissidents. They were severely beaten over two consecutive days, taken to the 5 Brigade base at Bidi overnight, then forced to walk home. (3677).

NOV 1984: 5 Brigade rounded up many people, beat them, and forced them to roll in a pool of water while being beaten, for several hours. (3615).

   TORT: 16
   ASS: 24
   MASS BEAT: 2
   DETN: 20

RATANYANA (10km E of Mashumba)

FEB 1984: All the men in the area were rounded up from their homes by 5 Brigade, who marched them to Sun Yet Sen. Here they were beaten and kept until there were enough people to fill a Puma truck. Then they were transferred to Bhalagwe where they were tortured severely and held for varying lengths of time, from weeks to months. Six named victims. (3579-82, 3595-7)

****AUG 1986: Six dissidents beat a young woman for being a sell-out. (3707)

AUG 1986: Five ZNA soldiers accused two women, found at home washing, of failing to report dissidents. They were severely beaten and warned that if they reported the incident, the army would return and burn their home. One suffered permanent ear and eye damage. (3575-6) Five ZNA soldiers beat another woman for failing to report dissidents. They then asked her for water, but she was too weak to carry the bucket. (3708)

AUG 1986: Five ZNA soldiers accused a man of failing to report dissidents. A scuffle ensued as the man tried to avoid a beating. He was shot at and wounded as he fled. The soldiers pursued him through the neighbouring kraal, where they beat the neighbour to death. (3577-8)

****OCT 1986: Three dissidents accused a man of being a sell-out and threatened to kill him. He managed to escape, but was shot in the wrist as he fled. (236)

    DEAD: 1
    TORT: 6 named, others implied
    ASS: 11
    MASS BEAT: 1
    GSW: 2
    DETN: 6 named, 1 mass detention

HOMESTEAD (7km due S of Mashumba)
****SEPT 1983: Dissidents passed through the area, apparently shooting a member of the security forces dead. The ZNA then moved through the area interrogating people. Five named people were assaulted, including one man in his seventies, who collapsed after being detained at Sun Yet Sen. Another man reports permanent ear damage. (3610-14 incl)

FEB 1984: A man found herding cattle was accused by 5 Brigade of being a dissident. He was beaten, knocked down and jumped on, resulting in a broken hip. (3565)

MARCH 1984: Two villagers were picked up by 5 Brigade near their homes, were tied together to a tree, beaten, then detained in Gwanda for six days. (3696)

APRIL 1984: Many people were driven out of their houses at night and taken to Sun Yet Sen where they were beaten. Those detained included women. They were then transferred to Bhalagwe Camp, where the CIO tortured them. The women were given to 5 Brigade soldiers to "be their wives". The repeated raping led to uterine disorders, including permanent inablity to have children in at least one case. (3672-4)

APRIL 1984: ZAPU branch secretary was severely beaten by 5 Brigade at his home, resulting in eye and ear damage. Three days later he was detained and tortured at the army camp, along with others accused of going to the shops. (3606)

JUNE 1984: A woman was taken from her home by 5 Brigade, and transported to a camp near Lingwe mountains. She was accused of feeding dissidents, then released, then immediately re-detained by CIO at Sun Yet Sen, where she was badly tortured for one week. (3697)

1984: Two men collecting their cattle were accused of breaking the curfew. They were beaten and subjected to strenuous physical exercise. They were soaked with water and made to roll over while being beaten, until long after dark. (3566-7)

1984: Two men found fishing in the Shashane River were accused of being dissidents, were severely beaten, taken to Bhalagwe, beaten again and detained there for three months. 5B accused the Ndebele of growing fat on stolen Shona cattle. (3602/3)

1984: At least four villagers (one man, three women named) were severely beaten until unable to move by 5B asking them about dissidents. One woman who ran away during the beatings was shot at, and then her homestead was burnt down to punish her. (3679-82)

1984: The ZAPU district chairman was taken by 5B and CIO to Kezi police station where he was given electric shocks to his testicles and beaten until his collar bone broke. He was held for three weeks and tortured regularly. His wife was also beaten, resulting in semi-paralysis of one leg. (3604-5)

    TORT: 2, plus others implied
    RAPE: 3 named, others implied
    ASS: 23
    MASS BEAT: 1
    GSW: 1
    DETN: 15, 1 mass detention
    PROP: 1 homestead burnt

SIKAMATSWE AREA (12km ENE of Sun Yet Sen)
FEB 1984: Everybody was called to the local school. People were rounded up from nearby fields. A man carrying water was accused of helping dissidents. People were severely beaten (ten named victims, including two women). They were handcuffed with their hands behind their knees, hooked onto sticks, and whipped with tyre strips. They were then transferred first to Sun Yet Sen, then Bhalagwe, where they were further tortured, for varying lengths of time, resulting in permanent disabilites. (3506-10, 3539-43)

MAY 1984: A teacher and one other person were accused of speaking to 5 Brigade victims in hospital in order to report on the 5 Brigade, and were beaten for four hours with logs. (3518-9)

**11 FEB 1985 (CCJP report): Two men from here were among many others abducted from all over Matabeleland in nightly raids by CIO. By Nov 1985 they had not been located.

    MISS: 2

    TORT: 12 named, others implied

    ASS: 14

    MASS BEAT: 1

    DETN: 12, 1 mass detention

NYAMBANE AREA (4km SE of Sikamatswe)

**11 FEB 1984 (CCJP report): A man from here was among many abducted from all over Matabeleland in nightly raids by CIO. By Nov 1985, he had not been located.

    MISS: 1

TUTI – I (3km NE of Sun Yet Sen)

DEC 1983: 5 Brigade beat a villager who said he did not know where dissidents were. (3533).

1983(?): A couple was approached by people purporting to be dissidents, demanding food. They were fed, and the same three people then returned a week later as army personnel. All the villagers were assembled and made to watch the man and his wife being beaten for over two hours. They were then detained at Sun Yet Sen and beaten by the CIO, for three days. (3589-90)

FEB 1984: 5 Brigade are reported as beating people daily once the curfew was in force. After a beating, some people ran away, and when they returned some years later, they found their house vandalised and property missing. (3598-99) Another couple was severely beaten in their home by 5 Brigade, resulting in many lost teeth and permanent back and hip damage. (3529-30) Three other men were accused of feeding dissidents and were beaten by 5 Brigade, and then tortured by CIO at Sun Yet Sen. (3561-3)

MARCH 1984: A woman found sharing tea with two neighbouring women was hit on the head by 5 Brigade, suffering permanent damage and partial loss of vision. (3600)

APRIL 1984: 5 Brigade rounded people up, took them to the school and beat them. (3517, 3564)

APRIL 1984 (see Mashumba, April 1984): After dissidents burnt tractors near Homestead, 5 Brigade picked up three men from Tuti, detained them and beat them for a week. Other young men ran away in time. (3544-6)

****AUG 1984: Dissidents accused a man of being a sell-out, hit him, then gave him a warning and left. (3521).

SEPT 1984: A man and wife were beaten by 5 Brigade for not knowing where their son was. The woman was told to dig her grave with her bare hands in her bedroom floor. Her eye and back suffered permanent damage. (3537-8).

> ASS: 18, plus others
> MASS BEAT: 1
> DETN: 8
> PROP: 1 homestead vandalised

TUTI – II (6km SE of Sun Yet Sen)

FEB 1984: 5 Brigade went through the area choosing people to take to Bhalagwe. They badly beat and then repeatedly raped a woman in her home, while beating and then detaining her husband. She suffered permanent kidney and uterine damage. (3568-9). They rounded up other young men (13 named, plus others), and made them carry army supplies as the 5 Brigade went through the area collecting others from all the settlements in the area. The young men were repeatedly beaten and made to push the Puma with their heads. If they bled on the vehicle, they were beaten for damaging government property. They were made to fight each other, were subjected to water torture at Sun Yet Sen, then transferred to Bhalagwe. Here they were tortured, and also forced to simulate sex with a donkey. A regular form of torture at Bhalagwe was the tying up of a man's testicles with rubber, after which they were repeatedly hit with a truncheon. (3547-57 incl, 3591-3)

**1l FEB 1985 (CCJP report): Two men from this area were among the many who were abducted during night raids by the CIO. In Nov 1985 they had still not been located.

> MISS: 2
> TORT: 13, plus others
> RAPE: 1
> ASS\S: 15
> DETN: 14, 1 mass detention

DRY PADDOCK AREA (between Tuti II and Sun Yet Sen)

FEB 1984: A young woman and her father-in-law were asked about dissidents and beaten. They were then stripped naked and told to have sex with each other. The father-in-law said he would die first. A shot was fired, missing them, and the two were then severely beaten and left for dead. (3558-9)

MAY 1984: The husband of the ZAPU chairlady was severely beaten by 5 Brigade, damaging his teeth, ear and back. His wife was taken into the bush by them for an hour (rape implied). They also shot two dogs, and took a ram. (3527-8)

JUNE 1984: A man found watering his donkeys was detained, beaten and taken to Gwanda. He and many other inmates were tortured daily. He claims he saw approximately 50 people killed there during his month of detention. (3534)

198?: A young girl in her 20s disappeared one night without trace. Army boot marks were seen outside the door, and army was nearby at Sun Yet Sen. (3535)

> MISS: 1
> DEAD: (50?) [this figure is not included in totals at end of this summary: too unsubstantiated]
> TORT: 1 named, many others implied
> RAPE: 1
> ASS: 4
> DETN: 1 named, others implied

SIGANGATSHA (15km WSW of Sun Yet Sen)
FEB 1984: Everyone was called to a morning rally at the business centre. They were forced to sing songs, were accused of being dissidents and were beaten with mopane logs, resulting in some losing consciousness and suffering permanent disability. The old people were then allowed home, and the younger were detained and taken to Bhalagwe. The old people were told to attend further meetings in surrounding villages, where they saw other young men being taken away. (3343, 3346, 3352-3360)

FEB 1984: About 20 people were rounded up one evening and were tortured throughout the night for not revealing dissidents. One victim complains of permanent disability, meaning he could no longer work. (3345)

FEB 1984: A woman was beaten for not revealing her son's whereabouts, taken to the 5 Brigade base nearby and then to Sun Yet Sen for a week. (3479-80)

MARCH 1984: Many people found drinking at the Business Centre were marched by 5 Brigade to their base 500m away, where they were beaten with logs for half an hour. They were told never to come to the shopping centre unless to report dissidents. (3342)

1984: Three villagers, one a woman, were taken from their homes to the 5 Brigade base, and were beaten. (3347-8)

****JUNE 1986: Dissidents had been in the area in 1985, and one dissident had been found and killed by CIO. The others came back and beat two men as sell-outs. One victim needed a skin graft on his leg. (3350)

APRIL 1986: The new headmistress to the school heard the CIO were coming for her and tried to flee on a bicycle. She was detained on reaching Kezi, and was beaten before being taken to Sun Yet Sen. She was asked if she knew how many people the CIO had killed, and where they buried them. She was detained for a further week. (3654)

ASS: 27
MASS BEAT: 2
DETN: 3 named others implied; 2 mass detentions

ST MARY'S SCHOOL AREA (27km due W of Sun Yet Sen)
1984 (probably same day as Sigangatsha rally mentioned above): Villagers were rounded up from all over to Sigangatsha and were tortured. One young woman from St Mary's was so badly injured she could not walk. She had no medical care at the time, and has never recovered the use of her right foot. (3349)

FEB 1984: People were rounded up, taken to New Mine at Sun Yet Sen, and beaten. Some were detained for several months, first here and then at Bhalagwe, suffering permanent disabilities including damaged scrotums, loss of teeth, blindness and damaged limbs. (3344, 3351)

**OCT 1986: (CCJP lawyer's file) Dissidents passed through this area and the next day locals reported this to the ZNA. In March 1987, the dissidents came back and accused them of being sell-outs. They severely beat seven villagers, including five women, with rubber strips, after forcing them to strip naked. The villagers feared for their lives if they reported this incident. Six women and a man were subsequently arrested and found guilty of failing to report dissidents and were jailed for 15 months.

ASS: 7 named
MASS BEAT: 2
DETN: 7, 1 mass detention

BEULA AREA (bottom SW corner of map, on Botswana Border)
MARCH 1983: 33 people, including children, were found at a beer drink and were all taken to the 5 Brigade camp at Gatsane. Many were here subjected to water torture. Three were then taken from here to Gwanda for a further month's detention, while the others were released. (3425, 3435-43 incl)

1984: A man was beaten for knowing nothing about dissidents. He and his wives were taken to the army base, where he was beaten and his wives raped. (3433/4)

1984: A woman was beaten for not answering when questioned in Shona, permanently disabling her. (3430)

1984: A man on leave from the ZNA was taken to Bhalagwe for six months, after which he was sick for three months. (3429)

1984: A ZAPU youth chairman was accused of being a dissident when out looking for cattle, was beaten, taken to Bhalagwe where he was tortured and held for six months. (3432)

FEB 1984: Ntabasimbi village. The vice branch chairman for ZAPU was taken by 5 Brigade to their base, where he was seriously beaten. He was then taken to Bhalagwe for six months, where he was further tortured. His legs still have lumps. (3431)

APRIL 1984: Villagers from Ntabasimbi village were beaten for going to the local shops. (3428) Another man was assaulted by 5 Brigade at his home. (3427)

AUG 1984: The ZAPU district commissar was accused of not reporting dissidents, was beaten and detained in Gwanda for a month. (3428)

****JUNE 1986: A man was unable to find food for two dissidents who came demanding it. They came back two days later, and burnt down his entire homestead, destroying all the property of himself, his two wives and eleven children. (3444)

****?1987: An unknown man shot a headman, and made his wife cut off his head and throw it in the dam. (3426)

    DEAD: 1
    TORT: 2 named, many implied
    RAPE: 2
    ASS: 46
    DETN: 43
    PROP: 1 large homestead burnt

MAMBALI AREA (bottom SW corner of map, on Botswana border)
FEB 1984: People were rounded up and taken to Mambali Clinic and beaten (five named, including a woman). An elderly ZIPRA was made to dance while being beaten, then made to sing for Joshua Nkomo. He was taken to Mayobodo ZRP station (in Plumtree), beaten again, then released. He left for South Africa when the pain was better. (3361-65)

    ASS: 6
    MASS BEAT: 1
    DETN: 1

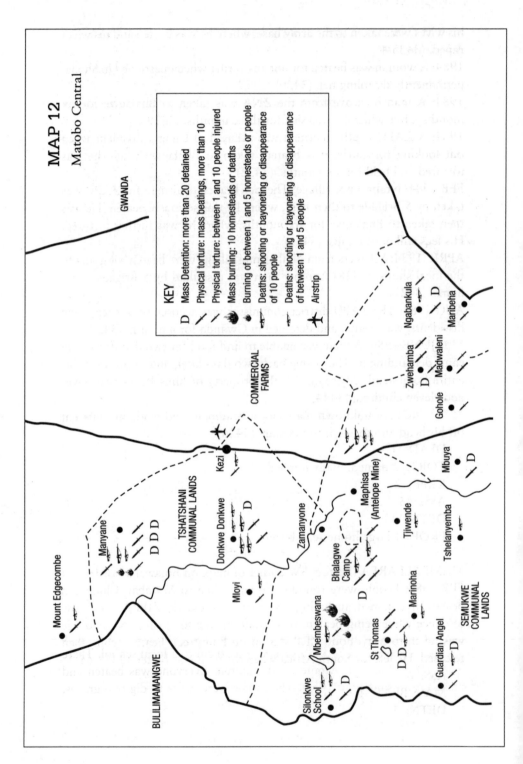

MAP 12
Matobo Central

GWANDA

KEY

D — Mass Detention: more than 20 detained

⚡ — Physical torture: mass beatings, more than 10

⚡ — Physical torture: between 1 and 10 people injured

🔥 — Mass burning: 10 homesteads or deaths

🔥 — Burning of between 1 and 5 homesteads or people

† — Deaths: shooting or bayoneting or disappearance of 10 people

† — Deaths: shooting or bayoneting or disappearance of between 1 and 5 people

✈ — Airstrip

COMMERCIAL FARMS

Kezi

TSHATSHANI COMMUNAL LANDS

Mount Edgecombe

Manyane   D D D

Donkwe Donkwe   D

Zamanyone

Mloyi

Maphisa (Antelope Mine)

Mbuya   D

Zwehamba   D

Ngabankula   D

Gohole

Madwaleni

Maribeha

Tjiwende

Tshelanyemba

Bhalagwe Camp   D

St Thomas   D D

Marinoha

Guardian Angel   D

SEMUKWE COMMUNAL LANDS

Mbembeswana

Silonkwe School   D

BULILIMAMANGWE

246

MATEMANI AREA (near Sun Yet Sen)
APRIL 1985: Dissidents passed through a village, and then security forces
arrived. A villager talking to the dissidents was wounded in crossfire, and
then shot dead afterwards by ZNA soldiers, who shot him in the head as
he lay wounded. Two other men, one in his sixties, were beaten by the
soldiers. (154-5)
DEAD: 1
ASS: 2

5.2 CENTRAL MATOBO – BHALAGWE CAMP

KEZI AREA
1983: An ex-ZIPRA who was integrated into the National Army and
based at Maphisa disappeared without trace some time in 1983. (1345)
**1984 (MCF – CCJP): Case Files name four dead, killed by the army
in Kezi area.
FEB 1984: The Support Unit were pursuing dissidents from near Minda
Mission area, and beat a man and his sister for not knowing where the
dissidents were. They were beaten for several hours. (3515-6)
**MARCH 1984 (CCJP formal report): A man who telephoned in a
list of four people killed by 5 Brigade was subsequently arrested, and in
March nobody knew where he was detained (no follow up given).
MISS: 1
DEAD: 4
ASS: 2
DETN: 1

SONTALA AREA
**1984 MCF – CCJP: Three named dead in 1984. A man from Sontala
was similarly abducted without trace.
MISS: 1
DEAD: 3

DONKWE DONKWE AREA (7km due W of Kezi)
**FEB 1984 (CCJP Commission of Inquiry sworn statement): 5 Brigade
rounded up everyone in the area and took them to a local school. There
were about 200 men, women and children. Everyone was beaten and
kicked from sunrise to 10am. Then some were made to dig two graves,
while others were made to fight each other. Six men were chosen at
random and placed in two groups of three. They were then shot dead.

Everyone else was told to sing songs praising Mugabe and condemning Nkomo. While some sang and danced, others were beaten. Some of the villagers were made to bury the six dead, three to a grave, and then had to join the singing while being beaten. At 4pm about 19 young men were taken away, and another man was shot as they departed.

**FEB 1984 (CCJP formal statement): A witness reports the murders of six men in a field by 5 Brigade: the witness escaped when he was sent to collect a pick. This witness also reports seeing men, women and children being beaten at Kezi business centre.

**5 FEB 1984 (CCJP formal statement): Eight people were reported murdered by 5 Brigade after first digging their own grave. **On the same day, villagers found drinking at Shashane River Store were shot by 5 Brigade. Some, including the store owner, were killed and many others were injured. (One named dead, no precise numbers.)

**On the same day, 13 people were severely beaten, then thrown down a disused well shaft. Grenades were thrown in after them, and all were killed. Among the dead were three primary-school teachers.

**MARCH 1984 (CCJP sworn statement): A villager from Bonkweni fled from this area to Bulawayo, out of fear of either starving to death or being killed by soldiers if he stayed. He reports forced attendance of everyone, including schoolchildren, at rallies every Saturday. 5 Brigade would harangue them at these meetings, and threaten them with death, saying they wanted them to suffer. He reports people collapsing at these rallies due to lack of food.

**1984 (MCF – CCJP): Case Files name 10 dead from Donkwe Donkwe – could be individuals from any of the above incidents.

**11 FEB 1985 (CCJP report): Three men from here were among the many abducted from all over Matabeleland in night raids by the CIO. By November 1985 they had not been located.

    MISS: 3
    DEAD: 35
    ASS : 2 mass beatings
    GSW: several implied
    DETN: 19

MLOYI AREA (W of the Shashane River, near Donkwe Donkwe)
FEB 1984: Approximately 100 adults and schoolchildren were rounded up after school and taken back to the school. They were told they were in for a treat. They were made to sing songs, including a song containing the words: "You are in trouble now, for your ancestors have deserted you." People were then beaten, including a 12-year-old girl, her sister and their

father. The two girls were so badly beaten they were later hospitalised. Their father was then shot dead in front of everyone, and his children were made to search his pockets to see if they could find any evidence that he was a dissident. Apart from this family, it is unclear how many others were beaten. (3737-8)

    DEAD: 1

    ASS: 2 known

ZAMANYONE AREA (just NW of Antelope Mine)

**MARCH 1985 (CCJP report): Five dissidents badly beat a woman for failing to cook properly for them. She managed to escape before they burnt her alive in her hut. They then raped her two daughters, aged 12 and 16.

    RAPE: 2

    ASS: 1

ANTELOPE MINE AREA (now MAPHISA) (20km due S of Kezi)

This is the Bhalagwe Camp area, and the mine where bodies were allegedly dumped nightly by 5 Brigade from Bhalagwe. This is dealt with in detail elsewhere: most people at Bhalagwe came from other parts of Matabeleland South.

**1983 (MCF- CCJP): Case Files report two children dead near Minda Mission. Also name one adult dead in 1983 – perpetrator army in all cases.

**1983: (MCF – CCJP): Case Files report assault of school matron at Antelope Mine, by army.

**1984: (MCF–CCJP): Case Files report the army killing 22 villagers near Minda Mission, and assaulting 27 women in two separate incidents.

**11 FEB 1985: Two other men from this area were among the many abducted all over Matabeleland by the CIO. By Nov 1985 they had not been located.

    MISS: 2

    DEAD: 25

    ASS: 28

TSHELANYEMBA (SW of Maphisa, in direction of St Joseph's)

FEB 1985 (**CCJP also refers): The man who owned the butchery in the Tshelanyemba business centre tipped off a teacher after the CIO came looking for him. The CIO then returned at night and others heard the butchery owner screaming as he was assaulted in his store. The following morning, this man, his wife and their 18-month-old child were missing and have never been seen since. (1245-7)

    MISS: 3

TJIWENDE AREA (just S of Bhalagwe)
AUG 1984: A teacher from the local school was aroused at night and asked for directions to Bhalagwe. The people insisted he go with them, and he has never been seen again. (3366)
    MISS: 1

MANYANE AREA (15km NW of Kezi)
NOV 1983: Three young men were detained at Mt Edgecombe shopping centre by a person in ZNA uniform on horseback. They were beaten with a bicycle chain. They were forced to run ahead of the horses to their homes, while being beaten. (3371-74)
DEC 1983: A group of about 30 dissidents forced villagers to cook for them at gunpoint. The next day 5 Brigade came, and were shown which way the dissidents went. Everyone was rounded up and was beaten. 5 Brigade went through the area beating everyone they found, including school teachers and school children. They made no effort to pursue the dissidents. People were forced to dig with their heads while being beaten. Women were made to climb trees so the soldiers could look up and insult their private parts. This continued all day until it rained after dark. Seven homesteads were burnt to the ground, leaving at least eight families destitute; soldiers commented that it was a pity they had not burnt the people in the huts, as they had done in Tsholotsho. Twenty-seven names of assault victims. (3367-8, 3370, 3393-3417)
FEB 1984: Some of the people in the above incident were beaten again, after being taken off a bus near Donkwe Donkwe. Some were on their way to hospital, and were beaten with logs and forced to board a bus back to their homes. One woman was five months pregnant and later miscarried. (3402, 3407)
FEB 1984: Everyone in the area was called to see some people die. A young man was told to lie down and then stand up. As he stood he was shot dead. The 5 Brigade asked for an ex-ZIPRA by name, and when he wasn't there, they decided to kill his mother instead. They shot her twice, but she was still alive, so they shot her again to kill her. (3387-8)
FEB 1984: In a nearby village, another woman was also shot dead in place of her ZIPRA son. (3386)
FEB 1984: The same men from the November 1983 incident and many others were rounded up to the army base near Mt Edgecombe school. All ex-ZIPRAs and refugees were called by name and were publicly beaten with logs. One man, who was ZAPU District Chairman and an ex-ZIPRA, was made to climb a tree. 5 Brigade then threw stones at him till he fell out, unconscious. He was further beaten. Others were beaten almost to

death, and had to lie there overnight. The next day, those who could move carried the others away. The man who was stoned was in a coma for some time, and never recovered his hearing or his powers of speech. His spine was damaged, and he died a few years later. (3374-6 incl)

FEB 1984: Others were rounded to a rally at the school, and taken from there to Bhalagwe, where they were beaten by logs, and detained for up to four months. (3377)

**FEB 1984 (CCJP Commission of Inquiry sworn statement): Three young men were arrested by police, taken to their station in Matopos village and held overnight. These three men were among thirty men and women. These people were all beaten with ropes and truncheons while lying face down in small groups. The next day they were taken to Bhalagwe. This witness gives a full account of Bhalagwe, including numbers of detainees and treatment – see Part Three, I, pp 313-315 for his full statement.

**5 FEB 1984 (CCJP formal report): Teachers here were beaten by 5 Brigade.

MARCH 1984: Villagers in the area were rounded up after dark and taken to a nearby homestead, where 5 Brigade soldiers took turns beating them for five hours. 5 Brigade set up camp on the banks of the Shashane River the following month (April) and again beat and intimidated people in the area. (3389-91)

AUG 1984: A group of villagers who had been digging manure in return for beer were rounded up by 5 Brigade. They were asked about dissidents, and six were then shot dead (all names given). Two others suffered gunshot wounds and were taken to hospital by a white farmer. (3379-85 incl)

**1983 (MCF – CCJP): Case Files name eight dead in Manyane – all new names.

**11 FEB 1985 (CCJP report): A man from here was among many abducted from all over Matabeleland in night raids by the CIO. He had not been located by November 1985.

MARCH 1985: Dissidents passed through the area, and ZNA came looking for them. Villagers showed ZNA which way the dissidents had gone, but were accused of feeding them, and four villagers were severely beaten, including an old man and a pregnant girl. Men were detained and beaten overnight at Kezi. (3369)

FEB 1986: A married couple and a girl were beaten by ZNA while collecting water from the Shashane River. (3378)

    MISS: 1
    DEAD: 17

ASS: 58 named, 4 mass beatings
DETN: 3 mass detentions
PROP: 7

MBEMBESWANA AREA (18km due W of Antelope Mine)
FEB 1983(?): A man originally from here was sought out by 5 Brigade: they beat his children, then went to Bulawayo to find him. They accused him of having a gun, took him to Bubi and shot him dead in front of his family. (3632-3)
JAN 1984: Twenty-four homesteads in this area were burned out after a battle in which dissidents were shot. Two villagers received gunshot wounds in the crossfire. Everything was destroyed, leaving approximately 50 family units destitute. One ex-ZIPRA also went missing on this day. (286, 3649-52, 3656-69 incl)
**CCJP also reports this incident: they supplied food and clothing to those affected.
18 JAN 1984: There was a compulsory rally in the area, at which Government officials spoke. People were trucked in from all over the area (see St Joseph's Mission).
**FEB 1984 (CCJP formal report): A man and his wife are reported shot by 5 Brigade. Two chiefs and another man were also shot by 5 Brigade on 3 February (all named).
FEB 1984: An ex-ZIPRA was taken from his home in nearby Silonkwe to Mbembeswana. He was badly beaten, then his family were summoned to fetch him. He had both arms broken and no teeth. He refused to leave, saying he was dead already. 5 Brigade then shot him in the head. (344)
**1984 (MCF-CCJP): Case Files name three other dead here, and confirm two of above named dead, army as perpetrator in all cases.
    DEAD: 10
    MISS: 1
    ASS: 3
    PROP: 24 homesteads burnt

SILONKWE AREA (just W of Mbembeswana)
**FEB 1984 (CCJP formal statement): The army rounded up all the villagers in the area and took them to Bembeswana school, where everyone, including women, was beaten. Three men were assaulted to the point of death – one had his testicles burst. These and about 100 other men were put on a truck to Bhalagwe. One body, with every bone smashed, was returned the next day, but the other two were never returned. The other men returned after a week, some seriously injured.

11 FEB 1985 (CCJP report): Three men from neighbouring Tailor's Block were among the many who were abducted from all over Matabeleland in night raids by the CIO. They had not been located by Nov 1985.

    MISS: 5

    DEAD: 1

    ASS : 1 mass beating (200)

    DETN: 1 mass detention (100)

ST THOMAS AREA (5km due S of Mbembeswana)

MARCH 1983: A man from here was accused of having a gun, was taken by 5 Brigade and later seen at Mbembeswana looking in very bad shape. He was never seen again. (3653)

FEB 1984: Dissidents shot at ZNA in this area, who then came and rounded people up for beating and interrogation. They were taken by 5 Brigade to Kezi, where they were beaten, then to Bhalagwe, where they were further beaten. The 5 Brigade used to jump on people's limbs to break them, and beat men's testicles, causing urinary and sexual problems. (3671)

APRIL 1984: People were gathered at the school and were beaten. A herbalist became possessed by his "healing spirits" and ran away in a trance. 5 Brigade shot him dead. (3670)

    MISS: 1

    DEAD: 1

    ASS: 1, 2 mass beatings

    DETN: 2 mass detentions

MARINOHA AREA (5km SE of St Thomas)

FEB 1984: A big lorry came through the area, and most people ran away. A man was taken away by 5 Brigade and was later seen at Bhalagwe. He never came home. (3704)

    MISS: 1

GUARDIAN ANGEL SCHOOL – SIHAYI AREA (10km SSW of Mbembeswana)

MARCH 1983: Nine ZNA soldiers (four white, five black) came looking for dissidents. They beat three villagers very severely, one so badly he died in 1986, partly from his injuries. They also ate three chickens. (3642-4)

SEPT 1983: ZNA assembled the villagers and then beat an old woman whose daughter had gone to town. They used a spiked truncheon, causing serious injury. (3639)

1983: A woman asked about dissidents was kicked in her private parts and beaten with a gun butt. (3641)

OCT 1983?: A man who was found eating goat meat at home was accused of feeding dissidents and severely beaten. He was taken to Bhalagwe for 10 days and returned very ill. (3645)

APRIL 1984: A young man visiting his aunt to tell her somebody was ill, was beaten for five hours as a curfew breaker. His aunt was also beaten, and then the man was beaten to death publicly in the schoolyard. (3638-40)

JUNE 1984: Three men caught buying tobacco from a neighbour were badly beaten with knobkerries by 5 Brigade, who left them for dead, and drove off in the direction of Bhalagwe with a Puma full of other villagers. (3646-8)

**1984 (MCF – CCJP): Case Files name three dead from Sihayi, perpetrator 5 Brigade.

   DEAD: 4
   ASS : 9 named
   DETN: 1, 1 mass detention

MBUYA AREA (25km S of Kezi)
1984: Everyone was called to the school, and made to sit in lines. Some people were then called out and loaded into a Puma. The rest were told to lie down and were beaten with sticks, causing permanent injuries. Those in the truck were then taken to Bhalagwe. (3620-24 incl)

   ASS: 1 mass beating
   DETN: 1 mass detention

GOHOLE AREA (3km E of Mbuya)
FEB 1983: A man walking to the bridge being built at the time in this area, was caught in crossfire between dissidents and ZNA. He was shot badly in the left leg, paralysing it. (3625)

1984: A woman told to bring chicken to the local Brigade army base was beaten because she did not. (3627).

1984: A woman was beaten at her home by 5 Brigade and left for dead. (3626).

   ASS/S: 2
   GSW: 1

MHLONHLWENI / MADWALENI AREA (3km E of Gohole)
FEB 1984: Villagers in the area were all rounded up by 5 Brigade and taken to a nearby dam where they were punished for not knowing about

dissidents. They were made to roll in and out of the water while being beaten. They were forced to run in circles with one finger on the ground and were beaten if they fell. They were made to dig the earth with their hands, and to push a truck with their heads. This continued all day. (3520-26)

****1985: Two dissidents beat a woman whom they said was a sell-out. (3703)

ASS: 7 named, 1 mass beating

ZWEHAMBA AREA (4km NE of Gohole)

FEB 1984: All the people in this area, both men and women, were forced out of their beds at 4am and force-marched to the 5 Brigade base at Zwehamba mountains. They were divided into two groups and were brutally beaten with sticks and gun butts. 5 Brigade also ran up and down on victims' backs. This lasted till 3pm. Many people suffered serious injury and broken bones, but were told not to seek medical attention. After this, the children were sometimes forced to collect water and firewood for the soldiers. (3683-7 incl)

FEB 1984: Men were rounded up late one afternoon – this appears to be the day following the incident above, as there is mention of some victims from the "previous night's beating" still lying around the base, seriously injured. Some men were tied together and all were severely beaten after being divided into four groups at the Zwehamba base. Some were then taken to Bhalagwe where they were held for six months. Senior ZAPU officials were picked out and sent to Whawha for detention. (3570-74, 3587-8, 3698-9)

FEB 1984: A man was taken from his home by 5 Brigade and forced to walk while being beaten. He was beaten so severely that after a while he could no longer move, and was left behind. (3583)

1984: A woman and her elderly mother were taken with others by Puma to Bhalagwe, where they were beaten and detained for three months. Another woman walking in the area was also detained and beaten at Bhalagwe. (3700-2 incl)

FEB 1984: The ZAPU branch treasurer was detained and when his mother tried to object, she was beaten and had her arm smashed. Her son returned after three weeks, badly injured. (3705-6)

ASS: 19 named, 2 mass beatings
DETN: 5 named, 1 mass detention

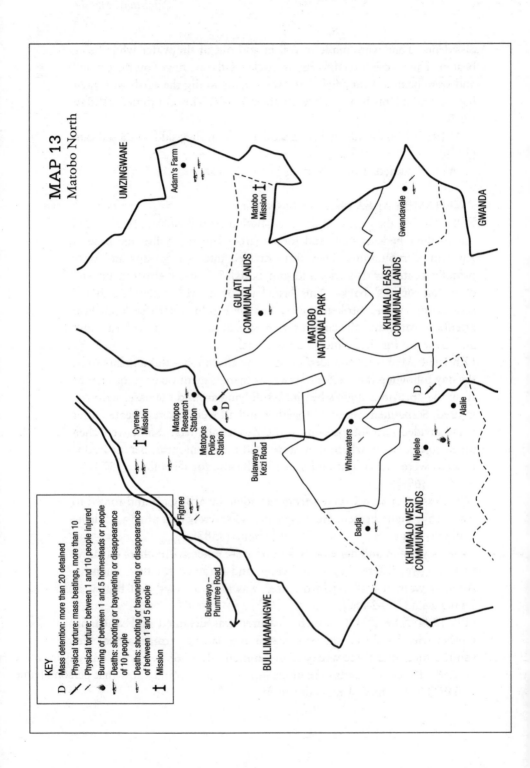

MAP 13
Matobo North

KEY

D   Mass detention: more than 20 detained

⟋   Physical torture: mass beatings, more than 10

⟋   Physical torture: between 1 and 10 people injured

●   Burning of between 1 and 5 homesteads or people

⤚   Deaths: shooting or bayoneting or disappearance of 10 people

⤚   Deaths: shooting or bayoneting or disappearance of between 1 and 5 people

✝   Mission

UMZINGWANE

Adam's Farm

Matobo Mission

GULATI COMMUNAL LANDS

MATOBO NATIONAL PARK

KHUMALO EAST COMMUNAL LANDS

Gwandavale

GWANDA

Cyrene Mission

Matopos Research Station

Matopos Police Station

D

Bulawayo – Kezi Road

Figtree

Bulawayo – Plumtree Road

BULILIMAMANGWE

Badja

Whitewaters

Njelele

D

Alalie

KHUMALO WEST COMMUNAL LANDS

MARIBEHA / NGABANKULA AREA (5km E of Zwehamba, on Gwanda border)

FEB 1984: Villagers were all rounded up in the early morning and taken to the local dip, where they were beaten brutally until midday, by a large group of 5 Brigade soldiers. Several of the men were then taken to Bhalagwe, where one was beaten to death. (3689-92 incl)

**FEB 1984 (CCJP formal report): A truck with six soldiers shot out the tyres on a scotch cart and badly beat the driver. Three other villagers were also severely beaten, one of them a woman. This witness also refers to widespread starvation, and children crying from hunger as their parents begged without success for permits to buy food.

MARCH 1984: A man and his wife were beaten almost to death. When a family member asked 5 Brigade for permission to take the woman to hospital, she was beaten and then detained for a month. (3689)

APRIL 1984: A man in this area told the others to mark their shoes with an X to tell their prints apart from dissidents, but when the 5 Brigade found out they detained him and took him to Bhalagwe where he was tortured. (3688)

DEAD: 1
TORT: 1
ASS: 8, 1 mass beating
DETN: 2 named, many others implied

5.3 NORTHERN MATOBO – FIGTREE, GULATI, KHUMALO

Extensive interviewing was not carried out in this area. The following information is, therefore, far less complete than that for the other two areas of Matobo. However, from a few in-depth interviews with selected residents in Khumalo West Communal Lands, it is clear that this area was not as badly hit by 5 Brigade as areas further south, but was worse affected by dissidents.

The names of eight people killed by dissidents were given, this being the total number of known dead in Khumalo as a result of the 1980s disturbances. (Only one of these deaths was in Khumalo East – there may be other deaths in Khumalo East not yet reported). There were some CIO-related disappearances after the imposition of the curfew, but no clear number could be given. Information on Khumalo East and Gulati was not available from these informants.

The dissidents travelled regularly through Khumalo West, and were greatly hated and feared by the civilians, who particularly resented their continual demands to feed them. The notorious dissidents "Fidel Castro", "Gayigusu", "Danger" and "Idi Amin" were among those who regularly traversed this region. "Fidel Castro" and "Danger" were killed in Khumalo. The mountainous terrain and lush vegetation of this part of Matobo provided ideal cover for the dissidents, who could hide easily and escape quickly from army personnel. Residents of Khumalo had never heard of Super ZAPU, or of South African trained dissidents: all dissidents were the same from their point of view – dangerous and resented. Gayigusu remains infamous for his role in overseeing the massacre of 16 missionaries, including women and children, in an area just east of Gulati Communal Lands.

The 5 Brigade made regular excursions through this region during the curfew months of 1984, and there were mass beatings and many young men and women were taken away to Bhalagwe. However, the impact of 5 Brigade seems less intense than that further south. Interviewees recall 5 Brigade actually saying that people in Khumalo should consider themselves lucky and that those living further south (such as in Kafusi) were receiving worse treatment. Perhaps it was the proximity of this area to the Matobo National Park and to commercial farms that dampened 5 Brigade's activities in this region, or perhaps the mountainous nature of Khumalo also helped. 5 Brigade would have found it impossible to drive trucks through much of this region, and it is hard work to walk through the bush.

GULATI COMMUNAL LANDS
FEB 1985: A man was abducted from his home near Tokwe School by CIO. People in an official vehicle had been there earlier in the day asking who ZAPU officials were. The man's wife, who was eight months pregnant, was raped. The man was never seen again. (2251/2)
    MISS: 1
    RAPED: 1

ADAMS FARM (NE of Gulati Communal Lands)
****NOV 1987: Dissidents summoned by local squatters hacked to death 16 people, including women, children and a six-week-old baby with axes. *(The Chronicle)*
    DEAD: 16

BADJA SCHOOL AREA (25km S of Figtree)
****APRIL 1986: A man here was murdered by dissidents for failing to give them clothes. (3468)
    DEAD: 1

CYRENE MISSION (Northern Matobo, near the main Bulawayo–Plumtree road)
**FEB 1983: The bodies of 12 men taken from buses by 5 Brigade and shot, were later found buried in two graves in the vicinity of Cyrene Mission. The skull of one victim was presented to the Commission of Inquiry in 1984.
    DEAD: 12

FIGTREE AREA
1983(?): A young man was taken from the Figtree bus stop with many others by 5 Brigade. They were taken away in a Puma, and he has never been seen again. (1081)
FEB 1983: An ex-ZIPRA who went to Bulawayo to get his demob pay was taken off the bus at a Figtree road-block by 5 Brigade. (Could be same day as above.) He was never seen again. (227)
FEB 1983: An ex-ZIPRA who had been demobilized was taken off the bus at the Figtree road block and was taken home four days later, and his home was searched. Then he was taken away and never seen again. His mother was told when she asked the police later that all who had been detained that day were killed. (269)
FEB 1983: Four Posts and Telecommunications Corporation employees were taken away by Support Unit and 5 Brigade one morning from the compound where they lived. They were never seen again. (272, 276)
**1983 (MCF – CCJP): Case Files name five others dead in Figtree area: perpetrator, army.
1984: An ex-ZIPRA who had integrated into the army and was stationed at Kariba came home on leave. He was taken off the bus at Figtree, was seen being beaten, and then never seen again. (273)
    MISS: 8
    DEAD: 8
    ASS: 1
    DETN: 8

MATOBO NATIONAL PARK
**1984 (MCF – CCJP): Whitewaters School. Case Files name one person assaulted here by army.
    ASS: 1

KHUMALO COMMUNAL LANDS – WESTERN PART

****1982: A man was accused of being a sell-out and was killed by dissidents. (3728)

****1984: A man who lived near Njelele was accused of being a sell-out and was killed. (3729)

****198?: The names of four men and one woman were given – all killed by dissidents between 1982 and 1987, although exact years of their deaths could no longer be remembered. (3730-34) Informants mention with bitterness the way in which the army failed to respond to reports of dissidents in their area.

FEB 1984: An old woman was among others from a village in the area rounded up from their homesteads by 5 Brigade and severely beaten. Seven of her neighbours, including women, were taken away to Bhalagwe for some weeks. This woman also reports 5 Brigade behaving in a similar way in many villages in the area. (3725)

FEB 1984: A man who was 16 in 1984 was among 70 people in his village who were beaten by 5 Brigade the day the curfew began. Twelve of them were then selected and taken to Bhalagwe, four women and eight men: seven were schoolchildren. At Bhalagwe he was subjected to "submarino" on three occasions, was beaten, and saw the murder of nine men, whom he then had to help bury. (3737)

****NOV 1984: Six dissidents stole two raincoats from a man who refused to give them blankets. (3740)

****1986: A woman living near Alalie Hill was assaulted by dissidents for failing to cook good quality food for them. Next day the dissidents assaulted the woman next door for the same reason. They then returned a few days later, and threatened the first woman's husband with death if their presence was reported. The couple feared for their lives and abandoned their home, moving to Bulawayo until after the amnesty. The husband had been detained by CIO in late 1983 when the couple lived at Kafusi. He was among the more than 20 detained at the same time in Kafusi, taken to Sun Yet Sen and regularly beaten by 5 Brigade. The army and the dissidents were so bad in Kafusi that the couple had moved to Khumalo, hoping things would be better there. (3723/4)

****1984: Dissidents abducted a 16-year-old girl for the night, after accusing her of sleeping with soldiers – rape implied. (3728)

APRIL 1987: A woman in Alalie had four huts burnt down, resulting in the total loss of her property, when the army engaged dissidents in a battle. Bullets in the crossfire set her thatch alight. The same complainant had been beaten by 5 Brigade in Kafusi in 1984: the soldiers had paraded as dissidents and demanded food, then the same men returned and beat people for failing to report dissidents. (3739)

DEAD: 17
ASS : 120 (approximately 25 of these were Kafusi beatings)
DETN: 52 (approximately 20 in Kafusi)
RAPE: 1
PROP: 1 homestead destroyed
(NOTE – Kafusi is in the far south of Zimbabwe, on the border with Botswana.)

KHUMALO COMMUNAL LANDS – EASTERN PART

****1982: In Gwandavale, which is on the Matobo side of the dividing line between Matobo and Gwanda, a woman in her thirties was accused by dissidents of being a witch and was thrown into a cattle dip. She was then shot dead. Other members of her family were beaten. (3735-6)

DEAD: 1
ASS: 5

III

RESULTS: PRESENTATION AND DISCUSSION OF HUMAN RIGHTS OFFENCES ON NAMED VICTIMS

1. HUMAN RIGHTS DATABASE – NAMED VICTIMS

Methodology has already been covered in some depth in Part One, II. To summarise, named victims were extracted from multiple sources, including CCJP archival material, interviews conducted in the 1990s, paralegal clients, and previously published human rights and academic documents. These named victims were entered into the HR Database. Each name was allocated a number, a set of letters indicating offence/s, and district and perpetrator were also tabulated. The following totals were arrived at:

TOTAL VICTIMS: 3 534 entries in combined HR Databases

OFFENCES: 7 246 (Most victims suffered two or even three offences. Occasionally one entry clearly indicates more than one victim. See Part One, II for examples.)

Approximately 1 000 victims were validated from more than one source, and more than 300 were validated by three or more sources.

2. *THE CHRONICLE* DATABASE

Data from *The Chronicle,* Bulawayo's daily newspaper, were entered into an identical, but separate database, for reasons discussed in Part One, II. *The Chronicle* listed victims in two ways, defined for the purposes of this report as "General" and "Specific" reports. General Reports are the six-monthly statements in Parliament, giving total numbers of dissident offences without any clear indication of where they occurred. Specific Reports are the day-by-day reports of dissident activities, which tended to give the district where offences took place and the number of victims or value of property lost, but not usually the exact names of victims. Only Specific Reports were entered into *The Chronicle* database.

The Chronicle database consisted of 562 entries, and covered the months from June 1982 to March 1988.

3. METHODOLOGY

Victim data were computer-sorted along various parameters for assessment. It was sorted alphabetically by:
1. District
2. Year and month (numerical sorting)
3. Type of offence
4. Surname and then first names of victim

A process of counting rows, once this sorting was complete, made it possible for the computer to quantify offences in required ways. Data were sorted by district and offence (Table 1) and resorted by perpetrator, offence and year (Table 2). Total numbers of offences exceeded total number of named victims, as the majority of victims suffered multiple injuries, such as loss of property and death, or detention and torture. If victims suffered injuries from more than one agency (i.e. 5 Brigade and CIO), then only the primary agency is counted as the perpetrator.

As mentioned previously, data from *The Chronicle* were kept separately, but were sorted and counted in the same way as other data.

4. GRAPHS AND DISCUSSION OF RESULTS

The following graphs are based on figures that can be found in the Tables on pp 289-300. Tables have been graphed to show distribution of offences by district, by perpetrator, and by district and perpetrator together. The different categories of offence have also been extracted and graphed over time. "Perpetrator" is always as recorded in archival data, or as alleged by interviewees.

Figures currently in the HR Database must be viewed as the known minimum number of victims in listed districts. These numbers of victims can only grow as more evidence comes to light. While the Database is far from comprehensive, it will be noted from the graphs that certain trends are nonetheless clearly apparent. The offences on file, their alleged perpetrators, and the years in which certain offences lie grouped, confirm the general claims made in the earlier parts of this report.

In addition, there is now the evidence from the case study areas, showing how dramatically figures rise when data is actively sought. In all other areas, data is archival, and not comprehensive even in the assessment of archival sources, in that numbers of victims indicated by archival material were not included on the HR Database, in order to prevent counting victims twice, once with and once without a name. The numbers of offences listed in the HR Database are therefore the most conservative figures possible to consider at this stage. For a brief examination of how it might be possible to use our knowledge from the case study areas, together with HR Database figures and our general knowledge at this stage, to arrive at a truer picture of the scale of the disturbances, see the final section of this discussion.

Report compilers discussed the possibility of including at the back of this report a list of NAMED DEAD. Human rights reports have opted to do this in recent years. The permission of surviving family members would ethically be needed in order to list the dead. However, many names on file are archival with no clear postal address for surviving family members now known. The interview form used in the 1990s also did not have on it a request for permission to publish names. While postal addresses for those interviewed in the 1990s are available, the logistics of sending out a request to publish names, and waiting for responses would be enormous. In some cases, where four or more sources confirm the name of a certain dead or missing person, several variations of how precisely the name is spelt may be given. Authenticating correct spelling is another problem that would have been faced if seeking family permission had been decided on as a course of action.

The compilers of this report also believe that it is still necessary to protect their sources in every way possible. There is therefore no list of the dead, nor are any victims named in this report, apart from those who held high political office. Victims are referred to by their HR Database number or CCJP archival file only.

A) MATABELELAND SOUTH

When results for clearly indicated victims in Matabeleland South are graphed, the impact of the second case study is evident. There is no archival or other general evidence to suggest that civilians in Matobo suffered more than those in adjacent regions, particularly in Bulilimamangwe and Gwanda. Any apparent difference is a consequence of the fact that the case study in Matobo allowed for the identification of a substantial number of victims. The impact of Bhalagwe is also evident when the Matobo results are graphed: the largest number of offences in any group was under "Detention". It must be noted that the figure graphed here for detainees is based on the Commission of Inquiry sworn statement made in February 1984 which claimed 1 856 detainees in the first week of February. The remainder of Matobo detainees includes those named or clearly numbered civilians detained at other centres, such as Sun Yet Sen. It must also be noted that this number is very conservative: possibly 8 000 or even double this number passed through Bhalagwe in the first four months of 1984, but this included civilians detained from all parts of Matabeleland South and also a few from Matabeleland North. Similarly, up to 800 detainees could be held at one time at Sun Yet Sen, and again, this number is not represented on the graph above. While detainees' accounts of Bhalagwe claim all inmates were systematically beaten during detention, this has not been assumed: figures for assault/injury are therefore also extremely conservative. Only named or clearly indicated eye witnessed assaults have been included under "Injury".

It is also noteworthy that prior to the Matobo Case Study, which was more of a pilot survey than a comprehensive study, the number of named dead for Matobo was 47. These names had been extracted from all existing archival sources. Once the "village by village" summary was undertaken, the number of clearly identifiable dead and missing rose to over 220, a five-fold increase. This was after only nine interview sessions, restricted mostly to central and southern Matobo. The figure for the dead would undoubtedly increase still further with more comprehensive investigations. (See Part Two, II for details). Only the named dead, a figure of 87, have been included in this graph: for a table showing full results of integrated named and numbered victims in Matobo, see Part Two, II.

This dramatic increase in identifiable victims once a pilot study took place in Matobo gives an indication of how the figures for the dead and all other offences might rise if similar pilot studies were carried out in adjacent regions. However, this report is not prepared to undertake such extrapolations in a dogmatic way.

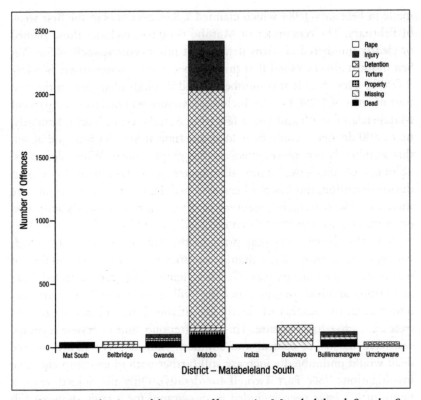

Graph 1: Distribution of known offences in Matabeleland South. See Table 1, pp 289-290. District – Matabeleland South

B) MATABELELAND NORTH

As in Matabeleland South, the impact of recent research in the Matabeleland North case study area, Tsholotsho, is apparent when HR Database information on Matabeleland North is graphed. (See Graph 2 on page 267.) Tsholotsho towers above all other districts in all offence categories, with 770 named dead and missing. The "village by village" summary allowed the clear identification of a further 130+ dead and missing in this region, but only named dead are graphed here. (See Part Two, I).

Lupane and Nkayi were also badly affected by events in 1983. Independent researchers in these two regions have conservatively estimated that 1 500 were killed in 1983 in these two districts combined, excluding those who went missing.[1] The HR Database currently has around 450 named dead and missing for these two districts combined. The HR Database has better archival information on Lupane in particular, than on other non-case study regions. This is owing in large part to the very thorough medical records kept by mission staff in Lupane in 1983. Figures on Nkayi are also higher than in some other regions, also as a result of mission staff in adjacent regions keeping records, and also because of interviewing carried out in this region in 1992, by CCJP.

Other regions in Matabeleland North were known to have been less affected by 5 Brigade in 1983 than the three regions of Tsholotsho, Lupane and Nkayi, but records of abuses in these other parts of Matabeleland North are almost certainly also incomplete at this stage.

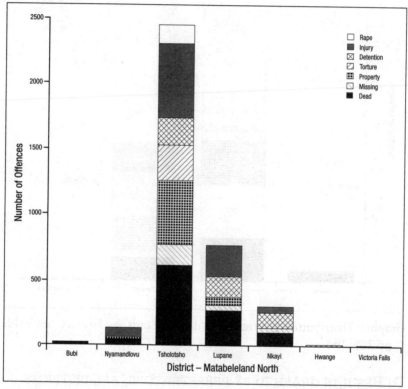

Graph 2: Distribution of known offences in Matabeleland North. See Table 1, pp 289-290. District – Matabeleland North

C) THE MIDLANDS

The graph of HR Database victims for the Midlands shows that this region was less affected than Matabeleland. However, data for this region are far from complete: offences graphed include only offences where victims' names are known, and other sources such as LCFHR, suggest far more property damage in Gweru and Kwekwe than the above figures indicate. Detentions were also widespread at certain points in time, but few named detainees from the Midlands are on HR Database files. The Midlands data, nonetheless, indicate approximately 100 missing or dead and around 60 burnt homesteads, in addition to more than 100 assault victims.

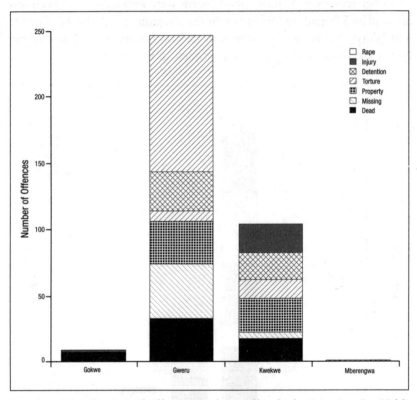

Graph 3: Distribution of offences in the Midlands, by District. See Table 1, pp 289-290

D) RESULTS GRAPHED BY PERPETRATORS, ALL DISTRICTS

Approximately 80 per cent of all offences were committed by 5 Brigade. They are implicated in 1 300+ deaths and disappearances, where names of victims are known. In addition, they destroyed 523 homesteads, detained well over 2 000 people (a conservative estimate) and assaulted approximately 1 300 (also very conservative – see case studies for more details). 5 Brigade was responsible for ten times as many deaths as any other party.

CIO committed 6.5 per cent of offences. This figure is a dramatic underestimate because of CIO involvement at Bhalagwe Camp in 1984.

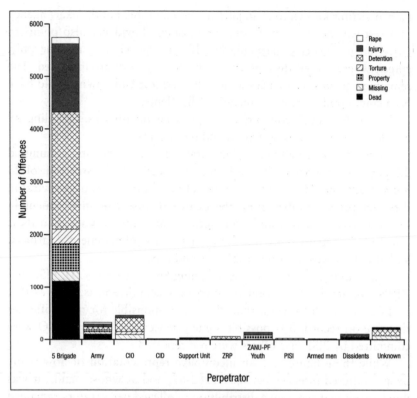

Graph 4: Perpetrator and Offences, 1982-87. See Table 2, p 291

People at Bhalagwe were almost invariably detained by 5 Brigade, and only the primary agent committing offences against a victim was recorded on the data base, to prevent apparent inflating of numbers of victims. Yet CIO was heavily involved with the interrogation of thousands of victims at Bhalagwe. (See case study, Part Two, II). CIO are directly implicated in over 100 named deaths and disappearances, and are also the most likely perpetrator for certain offences, recorded currently under "Perpetrator Unknown", including another 40 named disappearances – see below.

"The Army" committed 4.5 per cent of offences. Some of these could be 5 Brigade offences. These offences included 155 deaths and disappearances, the second largest total of deaths by perpetrator. A very few offences were identified as being committed by specific units such as Grey's Scouts, or as definitely not being 5 Brigade, although the actual unit was not known to the victim.

"Perpetrator Unknown" committed 3.5 per cent of offences. The largest group of offences in this category is detention. These detentions were certainly committed by Government agencies, as they represent named victims known to be in jails at a certain time, but the exact agency of arrest was not known. Strong circumstantial evidence also points to Government agencies (particularly CIO) as the main, if not the only, culprit where the 40 disappearances in this category are indicated. The remaining groups of offences under "Perpetrator Unknown" could have been committed by anyone, including dissidents.

ZANU-PF Youth committed 2.3 per cent of offences, including 29 murders, 73 properties destroyed and 63 assaults.

Dissidents, or armed men (here assumed to mean dissidents), committed 2.2 per cent of offences. These include 64 deaths, the destruction of 23 homesteads and 44 assaults. As with all other categories of perpetrator, these figures are understating the degree of dissident involvement in offences. Dissidents certainly committed many more crimes than these few, including many more murders, in particular of commercial farmers, and also hundreds of armed robberies and rapes.

Police units of various kinds, including Support Unit, CID, PISI, and ZRP committed 1.5 per cent of offences. General reports, such as that by LCFHR, would suggest that PISI was responsible for more offences than are on record: it is possible some offences attributed to CIO were committed by PISI, and others were not reported.

While these figures are an incomplete representation of how many people suffered offences between 1982-87, and at whose hands, it was noteworthy that the above distribution of alleged perpetrators remained fairly constant throughout the data collection process. At various points during the collation process, data were assessed for perpetrator distribution, and 5 Brigade as perpetrator ran at between 80 per cent and 95 per cent of all offences at all times. If numbers were to be included for those involved in known mass beatings, and those forced to witness violence at mass rallies – neither of which are currently included in the database – 5 Brigade as perpetrator becomes well over 90 per cent of all offences.

E) RESULTS: DISTRIBUTION OF OFFENCES BY EACH PERPETRATOR

Note: The scales on all the following graphs vary greatly, although some effort has been made to make them representative: the variation is necessary as certain perpetrators committed very small numbers of overall offences – see Graph 4 for true proportions. All graphs include an indication of numbers of offence on the vertical axis.

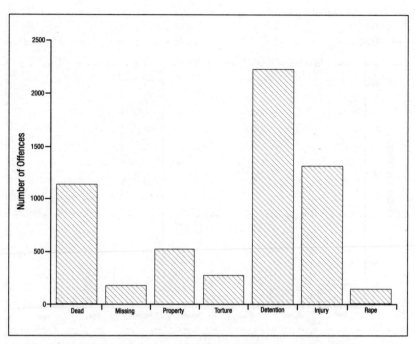

Graph 5: 5 Brigade offences, 1983-85. See Table 3, pp 293-295

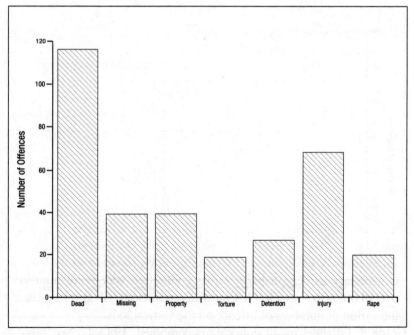

Graph 6: Army offences, 1982-87. See Table 2, p 291

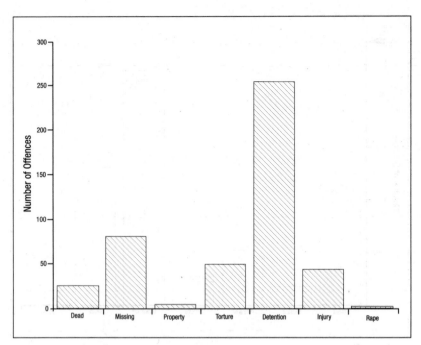

Graph 7: CIO offences. See Table 2, p 291

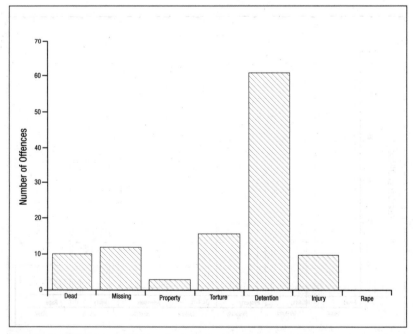

Graph 8: Offences by all police units combined, 1982-87. See Table 2, p 291

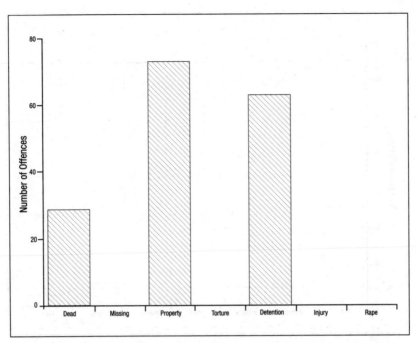

Graph 9: Offences by ZANU-PF Youth, 1984-85. See Table 2, p 291

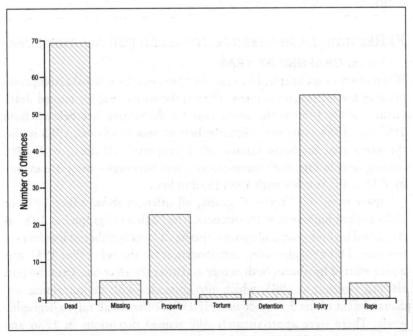

Graph 10: Dissident offences, 1982-87. See Table 2, p 291

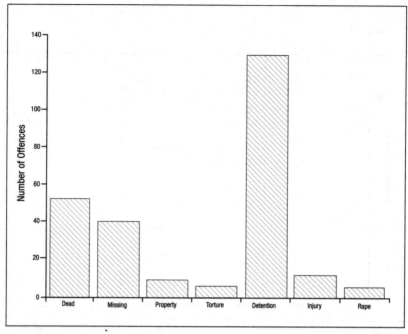

Graph 11: Offences by unknown perpetrators, 1982-87. See Table 2, p 291

F) RESULTS: EACH OFFENCE TOTALLED FOR ALL PERPETRA-TORS, GRAPHED BY YEAR

When offences are graphed by year, they bear out the general assumptions made in the historical overview. 1983 is the worst year for named death victims, while 1984 is the worst year for detentions (see below). Both 1983 and 1984 show very high numbers of assault victims. 1983 is also the worst year for burnt homesteads ("Property" offences), with 1985 coming next in line, with significantly fewer burnings – these are mainly by ZANU-PF Youth – with 1984 third in line.

Apart from the "Torture" graph, all offences show either 1983 or 1984 as their highest year for offences. The "Missing" graph has 1985 as its second highest year, and torture also has a large number of incidents in this year. This provides some corroboration for the belief that 1985 was a year marred by abuses both before and after the election. After the post election violence in 1985, which also coincides with the retraining and disbandment of the 5 Brigade in early 1986, offences all fall to negligible levels. There were approximately 100 named detentions in 1986 and some more in 1987, but all other offences, in terms of named victims, are low.

G) RESULTS – HR DATABASE COMPARED WITH THE CHRONICLE "SPECIFIC REPORTS"

This graph (see Graph 18 on page 280) illustrates neatly the impossibility of ever reconciling the "official view" of the 1980s disturbances with that held by the civilians who experienced these disturbances at first hand. The graphic representation of HR Database figures alongside those of *The Chronicle* highlights the way in which the main offenders become reversed, with civilians attributing over 90 per cent of offences to government agencies, and *The Chronicle* attributing 90 per cent to dissidents.

The graphed results also highlight the fact that far more offences were being committed during those years than one would have assumed, if one had merely been reading *The Chronicle* on a daily basis. The HR Database has NAMED offences that exceed *The Chronicle* named and clearly numbered offences by approximately 7 to 1. And, as repeatedly stated, the HR Database is very conservative.

The graph of Table 8 (Graph 19, page 280) compares the daily news records of dissident offences with the numbers of offences claimed in Parliament every six months, in order to justify the renewal of the Emergency Powers. This illustrates a dramatic disparity in all offence categories, as previously discussed in this report. "General Reports" claim between two and four times as many offences as "Specific Reports", in all categories except assault, where "Specific Reports" outnumber the "General Reports".

The Chronicle data and the HR data were then further compared. The highest available total for offences in each category was arrived at for *The Chronicle* data, for the years 1982-87. For example, where "General Reports" for a year exist, these totals were used, and for 1982 and 1986-87, when there were no "General Reports", "Specific Report" totals were used.

In the case of assaults, the "Specific Report" totals for assaults were higher than those of "General Reports": The higher figure was then used.

The total number of offences which *The Chronicle* attributes to Government agencies were then also added in to the totals for dissident offences. These "highest available totals" were then graphed against the HR Database totals. It must be pointed out that while *The Chronicle* totals include generalised information for which no known victims were clearly indicated, the HR Database figures are for clearly identifiable victims only. For example, general estimates of civilians involved in known mass beatings in the case study areas were NOT included in the

275

HR Database figures. Neither were the clearly identified numbered, but not named dead from the Case Study Areas. For example, the figure of 87 named, dead and missing for Matobo was used, not the 220 identified dead from the case study figure.

In other words, the HR Database used its most conservative figures, while the least conservative figure was used from *The Chronicle* database. This was done to try and establish whether the difference in figures given by the HR Database and *The Chronicle* would begin to approach each other in this way, perhaps pointing to a difference merely in how *perpetrators* were assessed by the two sources, rather than in how the scale of the disturbances were assessed.

As the graph illustrates (see Graph 20), the figures remained very different. The HR Database remains far higher in all categories, except for Property Offences. The HR Database only includes burnt homesteads under property, while *The Chronicle* Database includes every petty theft for a few dollars as a separate property offence.

When highest totals for *The Chronicle* are used instead of "Specific Reports" (see Graph 19), the gap between the two sets of offence totals does close, but glaring disparities remain.

The Chronicle data, being archival, is also finite at this point, whereas the HR Database, being based on victims' accounts both past and present, will continue to grow: this disparity in the two databases can only increase in the future.

The disparities in the two databases, now clearly apparent, only serves to confirm the claims made by this report that most people in this country can currently have no idea of the true scale of the nature of the disturbances in the 1980s, apart from those immediately affected. Certainly, reading the newspaper every day would not have given Zimbabweans in unaffected regions any realistic notion of what was happening in the rest of Zimbabwe, or who was perpetrating the crimes.

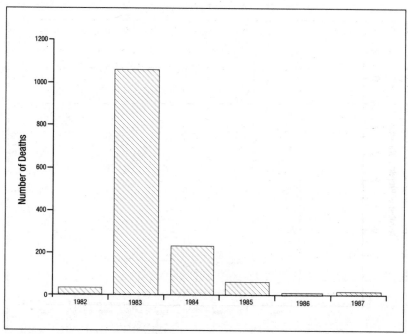

Graph 12: Number of deaths by year. See Table 3, pp 293-295

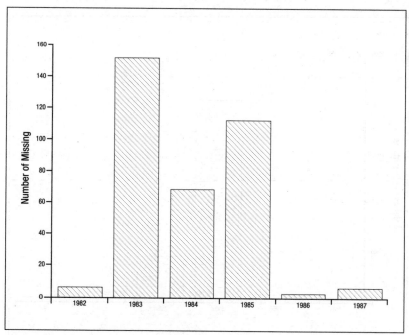

Graph 13: Number of missing by year. See Table 3, pp 293-295

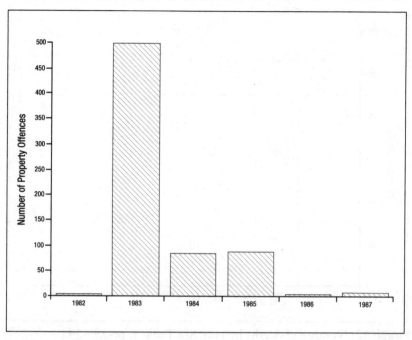

Graph 14: Number of property offences by year. See Table 3, pp 293-295

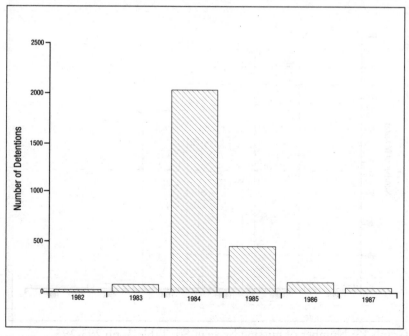

Graph 15: Number of detentions by year. See Table 3, pp 293-295

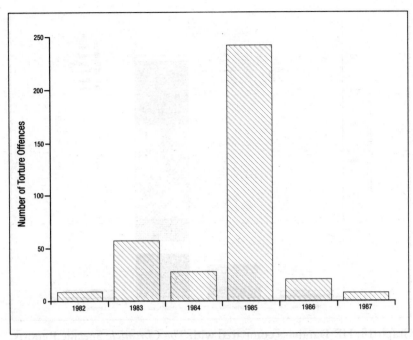

Graph 16: Number of torture offences by year. See Table 3, pp 293-295

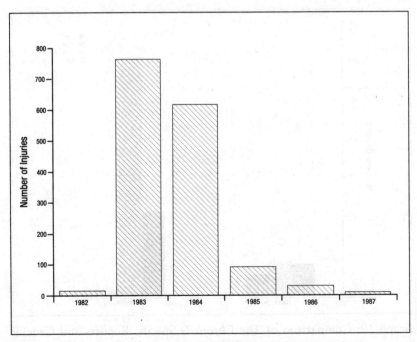

Graph 17: Number of injuries by year. See Table 3, pp 293-295

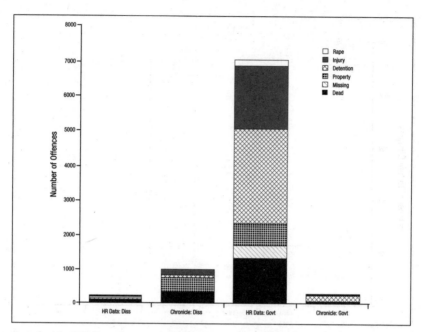

Graph 18: HR Database compared with *The Chronicle* Specific Reports.
See Table 2, compared with Tables 5 and 6, p 298

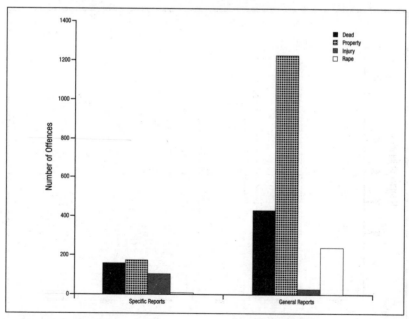

Graph 19: Comparison of *The Chronicle* Specific Reports and General
Reports totals for dissident offences. Tables 5 and 7 compared, pp 298
and 299

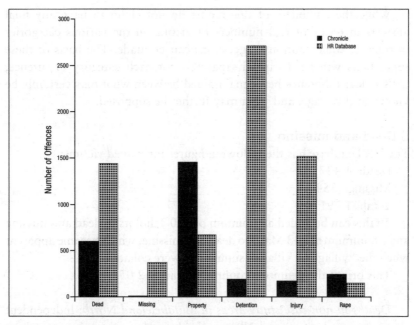

Graph 20: HR Database compared with *The Chronicle* database, selectively combined to give *The Chronicle* the highest numbers of offences available from its own records. Table 2 compared with Tables 5, 6 and 7, pp 291, 298 and 299

H) ASSESSING THE IMPACT OF THE 1980S DISTURBANCES

The figures in the HR Database are clearly a baseline set of figures which can only grow in the future. Only one district in Zimbabwe was fairly comprehensively researched for this report – namely Tsholotsho. In addition, a pilot study was conducted in Matobo. Both of these studies resulted in a dramatic increase in existing knowledge of how events unfolded in these two regions in the 1980s, and both extended the named database considerably, and allowed the incorporation of numbered victims. Numbered victims are generally excluded from all other districts.

What was also noticeable in Tsholotsho was how the gap between numbered and named victims closed as interviewing progressed, and a larger proportion of named as opposed to numbered victims began to be reported.

The lower levels of offences evident in the other districts in Zimbabwe reflect the fact that extensive research has not been done in these regions, rather than reflecting that these districts were not severely affected by events.

While the compilers of this report do not claim to have any final answers in terms of real numbers of victims in the various categories of offence, some cautious suggestions can be made. The basis of these suggestions will be discussed separately for each category of offence, with a clear difference being maintained between what may certainly be known at this stage, and what may further be supposed.

i) Dead and missing

The HR Database has the following figures for *named* victims:

Dead: 1 437
Missing: 354
Total: 1 791

To this can be added a minimum of 130 Tsholotsho dead and missing and a minimum of 133 Matobo dead and missing, which became apparent when the "village by village" summaries were collated.

This brings the definitely confirmed dead to 2 052.

Deaths in non-case study areas in Matabeleland North: Independent researchers in Lupane and Nkayi, who have done extensive interviews for a different purpose in these regions in recent years, suggested that approximately 1 300 dead would be a fair estimate for these two regions combined.[1] Their intention was not specifically to "count the dead" in these regions, and they have not collected names. Their estimates are based on ward-by-ward estimates given to them by councillors in the general course of their interviews on other topics, but they feel these estimates are, if anything, conservative, and exclude the missing.

As this estimate was put forward by researchers of proven integrity with a known understanding of events in these districts, and no possible motive for exaggeration or misrepresentation, it seems fair to consider including it in an estimate: this would add another 1 000 to the figure for the dead, bringing it to about 3 000.

There is little known about deaths in other regions in Matabeleland North, although indications are that they were considerably less affected by 5 Brigade than Tsholotsho, Lupane and Nkayi. No comment or estimate will therefore be made about these regions.

Deaths in Matabeleland South: It has already been commented that the pilot study in Matobo, which was far from comprehensive, resulted in a five-fold increase in the numbers of dead and missing. Yet prior to the case study, the *named* dead for Gwanda, Matobo and Bulilimamangwe were *all* in the range of 40-50. Judging from the CCJP archives and paralegal information, which is the only current source of data on Gwanda and Bulilimamangwe, these two districts were as severely hit in 1984 as Matobo. There is in archival file evidence of mass murders, mass graves, mass beatings and mass detentions in these two districts. We can also assume that the figure of 220 dead in Matobo is conservative, as interviewing here was limited.

In addition, there are the many eye witness accounts of Bhalagwe on file. These include both archival accounts and those recorded in the last few months. All are very consistent in referring to daily deaths at Bhalagwe. From mid-February, villagers adja ent to Antelope Mine also refer to nightly trips by trucks to the mine shaft, followed by the disposal of bodies and the throwing of grenades in afterwards.

There was a change in strategy on the part of 5 Brigade in 1984. They had apparently realised in 1983 that it was not possible to kill hundreds of well-known people in front of hundreds of witnesses in their home villages, and expect the fact to remain hidden. In 1984, the new strategy of translocating many thousands of civilians and grouping them at Bhalagwe, where everyone effectively became strangers, has made it much harder now to identify either exact numbers or names of the dead. Most detainees did not know the names of those they were detained with. Also, people cannot remember exact dates on which they witnessed a certain number of people beaten to death or shot, so it is not possible to sort out eyewitness accounts in a way that prevents double counting of deaths.

One solution for those who wish to arrive at some idea of how many might have died at Bhalagwe, is to estimate five deaths a day, multiplied by 100 days (February to May) and to decide that approximately 500 died at Bhalagwe. Five deaths a day might well be too conservative, however. The real number could be anything between 300 and 1 000. The inability to arrive at more accurate figures at this stage is a testimony to the effectiveness of the 1984 strategy in keeping deaths anonymous. For example, one person interviewed, who was 16 years old when incarcerated at Bhalagwe, recounted how he personally helped dig the graves and helped carry and bury the corpses of nine men, seven of whom had been beaten to death and two of whom had been shot. He did not know the name of a single one of these nine victims, nor could he say exactly how many others had died during the ten days he was there, except to say that they were "very many". These dead were from all over Matabeleland South, and some were from Matabeleland North: only extensive interviewing in all districts will help resolve the issue of how many died at Bhalagwe.

Other evidence on the archives for Gwanda and 56 Bulilimamangwe states that there are mass graves in both districts, mainly from 1984, but in the case of Bulilimamangwe, also from 1983, when parts of this district were adjacent to the curfew zone and affected by 5 Brigade in Matabeleland North. Judging by the pilot study in Matobo, it seems fair to estimate at least several hundred deaths in each district. Only extensive further research will come up with more accurate figures.

In the rest of Matabeleland South, including Beitbridge, deaths also occurred, although in smaller numbers. No comment or estimate will be made on these.

Those who are concerned about putting a precise figure on the dead in Matabeleland South could choose a number between 500 and 1 000, and be certain that they are not exaggerating.

Deaths in the Midlands: Named and numbered dead and missing for the Midlands suggest Gweru was worst hit with around 70-80 deaths, with deaths and missing for the whole province currently standing at a conservative 100. Archival figures for unnamed victims suggest several hundred more deaths and disappearances – no more accurate suggestion can be made than this, without extensive further research.

Deaths according to The Chronicle: While it seems reasonable in the face of conflicting reports to disregard the "General Report" claims in respect of dissident offences, the "Specific Report" figures have been borne out in part. Even this statement is not made without qualification: there were several occasions where recent interview data convincingly attributed offences to the army or CIO when *The Chronicle* attributed these offences to dissidents. However, in Tsholotsho, while the route to the final number may have differed, figures arrived at in interview data and in *The Chronicle* were fairly close in terms of how many people were specifically killed by dissidents. In addition, there are some murders that can be uncontentiously attributed to dissidents in the non-case study districts, and which have not been taken into estimate yet, including the deaths of commercial farmers. *The Chronicle* may therefore be conservatively assumed to provide support for the deaths of at least 100 to 150 people at the hands of dissidents, which have not been factored in elsewhere.

FINAL ESTIMATE: The figure for the dead and missing is not less than 3 000. This statement is now beyond reasonable doubt. Adding up the conservative suggestions made above, the figure is reasonably certainly 3 750 dead. More than that it is still not possible to say, except to allow that the real figure for the dead could be possibly double 3 000, or even higher. Only further research will resolve the issue.

The number of dead is always the issue in which there is the most interest, wherever in the world human rights offences are perpetrated. While such a focus is understandable, it should not be considered the only category of offence to give an indication of the scale of a period of disturbance. From the point of view of this report, compilers are concerned with the plight of those still alive. Of course, the loss of a breadwinner compounds the plight for his/her survivors, and in this way the number of dead from the 1980s indicates the number of families having to survive without financial assistance from able-bodied husbands, wives and children. But many other families who perhaps suffered no deaths were left with permanent health or emotional problems that, a decade later, have seriously compounded on their families in monetary and social terms.

ii) Property loss

The HR Database currently has on record 680 homesteads destroyed. A reading of the "village by village" summary of Tsholotsho will confirm that this figure is conservative. Researchers in Lupane and Nkayi have also referred to hut burnings, and the burnings of entire villages, particularly in Lupane. What this means in terms of final figures is hard to say, therefore no estimate will be made.

Properties were also destroyed in Matabeleland South which are not yet formally recorded, and the ZANU-PF Youth riots affecting the Midlands in 1985, and the property destruction resulting from this has been documented, for example in LCFHR. Readers of the report should therefore bear in mind that the figure of 680 homesteads destroyed is far from complete.

In addition, there was the damage caused by dissidents. *The Chronicle* reports a multitude of bus burnings and the destruction of dam and road building equipment. Cooperative ventures were also destroyed on occasion, and commercial farmers had livestock shot and property destroyed. Again, to try to assess this now in precise monetary terms would be a complicated and somewhat arbitrary procedure. The section following (Part Three, II) on legal damages attempts to make this sort of assessment on ten specific cases only, to illustrate how such damage might be assessed.

Perhaps the most significant type of "property loss" to those in affected regions, is the fact that throughout the 1980s, when the government was investing in development projects in other parts of the country, Matabeleland was losing out, on the true premise that the disturbances made development difficult.

iii) Detention

Possible numbers of detainees are also very difficult to assess at this stage. Some attempt was made in the case study on Matobo to estimate a figure for those detained at Bhalagwe. Based on an average stay of two weeks, and an average holding capacity of 2 000, it was assumed that any number of civilians between 8 000 and double this figure could have passed through Bhalagwe. As some reports put the holding capacity at considerably higher than 2 000 at its peak, this assumption does not seem unreasonable, but it is an assumption nonetheless.

Apart from Bhalagwe, both documents on file and lists of named victims in Chikurubi in 1985 suggest certainly hundreds and likely thousands of detainees over the period from 1982 to 1987. The detention centres at St Paul's in Lupane and in Tsholotsho operated from mid 1982, and certainly hundreds were detained in 1982 alone. *Africa Confidential* refers to 700 detained at Tsholotsho in 1982, and St Paul's detention centre was also large. There is also reference to 1 000 detained in Bulawayo in March 1983. In 1985 and 1986 there were further detentions, both before and after the general elections. Elected ZAPU officials were picked up in rural areas, and hundreds were detained in urban centres too. LCFHR refers to 1 300 detained in Bulawayo in early 1985 and 400+ detained in Bulawayo in August 1985. There are official documents signed by police confirming large numbers of detainees. For example, CCJP wrote to Nkayi police station inquiring the whereabouts of a certain man who had been detained. The police wrote back saying they had detained 80 people that day in Nkayi, and most had been subsequently released. They had no record of this particular man.[2]

Again, there is no easy formula for arriving at a figure for detainees. It seems reasonable to assume at least 10 000 were detained, some for a few days and some for far longer, between 1982 and 1987. This is an assumption based on what is known now of the general unfolding of events, and the holding capacities of various detention centres.

iv) Tortured/wounded

Named torture victims, inclusive of those assaulted, stand at around 2 000.

In addition to these named victims, the Tsholotsho case study identified 70 villages involved in mass beatings, and four mass beatings at railway sidings. The Matobo case study identified another 25 mass beatings. This is a total of 99 known mass beatings. A figure of 50 per mass beating was decided on as reasonable (see Part One, II), which would mean 4 950 further assault victims. This puts the total number of those fairly definitely known to have been physically tortured at about 7 000.

Mass beatings were also a definite phenomenon of 5 Brigade behaviour in Lupane and Nkayi in Matabeleland North, and Silobela in the Midlands, as well as in Bulilimamangwe and Gwanda in Matabeleland South, but no estimate will be placed on how many people this may have affected. In addition, reports of Bhalagwe make it clear that detention here was synonymous with beatings, usually daily. Physical torture of one kind or another was almost mandatory, not only at Bhalagwe but in all detention centres and jails.

Several thousand more beating victims could therefore safely be assumed, but precisely how many remains to be established.

v) Conclusion
The above estimates are offered merely as precisely that: estimates. A careful reading of the Historical Overview will make it clear that the evidence on record supports the general claims being made here in terms of likely numbers of victims, and will in fact suggest that these claims are conservative. But only further comprehensive research will establish more accurate numbers for all categories of offence.

5. TABLES

Table 1   HR Database: Summary of Offences by District and Type of Offence
Table 2   HR Database: Summary of Perpetrators and Type of Offence Totalled for Years 1982-87
Table 3   HR Database: Summary of Perpetrators and Type of Offence Each Year 1982-87
Table 4   *The Chronicle:* "Specific Reports" Summary of all Offences by District and Type of Offence
Table 5   *The Chronicle:* "Specific Reports" Dissident Offences
Table 6   *The Chronicle:* "Specific Reports" Government Agencies Offences
Table 7   *The Chronicle:* "General Reports"
Table 8   *The Chronicle* – Total Numbers of Offences: "General Report" Totals Compared to "Specific Report" Totals for the Same Time Spans

Table 9   *The Chronicle* Database – Official References to Dissidents

KEY TO OFFENCES
X   Death
M   Missing, presumed dead
P   Property loss – destruction or theft
T   Physical torture – includes all torture not covered by other categories, such as electrical shock, tying up of victim, submarino, etc.
D   Detention (by Government agencies)
K   Kidnapping or abduction (by dissidents)
AS   Physical torture: Assault with sticks or other blunt weapon
AB   Physical torture: Assault with burning object, or enclosure of victim in burning building
ABy Physical torture: Assault with bayonet, or other sharp weapon
AG   Physical injury; gunshot wound
R   Rape

Psychological torture: Forced witnessing of violence, in particular against those you love and respect, is a very effective and devastating form of torture: thousands of Zimbabweans were victims of this experience. Being forced to watch your family starve as the result of food embargos, or being subjected to verbal threats, are other forms of psychological torture that whole populations endured. As this was so widespread, no attempt has been made to quantify psychological torture. Definitions and implications of psychological torture are dealt with in Part Three, I of the report.

Table 1

HR Database – Summary of Offences by District and Type of Offence

District/ Province	Death X	Missing M	Property P	Torture T	Detention D	Assault AS/B/G/By	Rape R	TOTAL
MAT SOUTH	35							35
Beitbridge	1	2	2	12	21			38
Gwanda	45	8	1	3	15	(S) 26 (G) 1		99
Matobo	87	5	30	25	1872 (214)	(S) 384 (B) 1 (G) 5	10	2419
Insiza	3			1	5	(S) 3		12
Bulawayo	6	28	4	10	106	(S) 8		162
Bulilimamangwe	51	16	4	3	6	(S) 22 (G) 2	5	109
Umzimgwane		2		8	17	(S) 3		30
MAT NORTH								
Bubi (Inyathi)	21		2					23
Nyamndlovu	46	4	18			(S) 61 (G) 6		135
Tsholotsho	621	148	494	298	211	(S) 530 (B) 4 (G) 23 (By) 9	138	2446
Lupane	275	41	58	2	158	(S) 189 (B) 10 (G) 37 (By) 1	6	774

Table 1
continued

District/Province	Death X	Missing M	Property P	Torture T	Detention D	Assault AS/B/G/By	Rape R	TOTAL
Nkayi	117	24	5		116	(S) 39 (G) 8		309
Hwange	5	1			7	(S) 3		16
Vic Falls 6	5				1			
MIDLANDS								
Gokwe	7					(S) 1		8
Gweru	33	40	33	7	30	(S) 103		246
Kwekwe	18	4	26	14	20	(S) 22		104
Mberengwa 1					1			
UNKNOWN	46	27		5	63	(S) 34 (G) 1		176
MASHONALAND								
Chegutu		1	1					2
Makondi	2							2
Gutu		1						1
Harare	10		2	1	7	(By) 3		23
Kadoma				5	24			29
Masvina	2				23			25
MANICALAND								
Mutare		2						2
Botswana								
TOTALS	1 437	354	680	366	2713	1537	159	7 246

Total of HR Database offences in country: 7 246

Table 2

HR Database: Summary of Perpetrators and Type of Offence, Totalled for Years 1982-1987

(For Year-by-Year Breakdown, See Table 3 Following)

All Years Perpetrator	Dead X	Missing M	Property P	Torture T	Detention D	Assault ASB\G\By	Rape R	Total
5 Brigade	1 134	169	523	273	2 232	1 284	128	5 743
Army	116	39	39	18	26	67	19	324
CIO	24	81	5	51	256	46	2	465
CID	3	4		1	6			14
Supp Unit	4	4	5		2	3		18
ZRP	6	11	3	12	39	3		74
Zanu-PF Youth	29		73			63		165
PISI		1		4	20	4		29
Armed Men	5	1				11		17
Dissidents	64	4	23	1	2	44	4	142
Perpetrator Unknown	52	40	9	6	130	12	6	255
TOTALS	1 437	354	680	366	2 713	1 537	15 907	7 246

Total of HR Database offences in country: 7 246

NOTES:

i) Perpetrators are recorded as perceived by interviewees: many could not clarify or did not mention which unit in the "Army" had committed a certain act.

ii) When perpetrator is perceived as "Police" or "ZRP" this could also mean one of several units, such as Special Constabulary, CID, Police Support Unit, PISI, or regular ZRP members.

iii) In the vast majority of "Detentions – Perpetrator Unknown", Government agencies can be assumed. In 1985 in particular, many men were taken from their beds at night by men from Government vehicles. Also included in "Detentions – perpetrator Unknown" were many named detainees from Chikurubi, who were obviously detained by Government agencies, but which precise agency is not on record.

iv) CIO often acted in conjunction with other agencies, such as PISI, and such cases have been recorded only under CIO, in order not to inflate apparent numbers of offences. This means other agencies were in fact more commonly implicated than would appear from the Table alone. The number of offences by the CIO is also dramatically underestimated in the table, because of the role CIO played at Bhalagwe Camp; both 5 Brigade and CIO tortured people here, but offences in Bhalagwe have been attributed to 5 Brigade only, again in order not to inflate apparent numbers of people tortured – those tortured at Bhalagwe by CIO run to hundreds if not thousands. See Matobo case study and Part Three, III.

v) "Armed Men" could be either dissidents or Government agencies.

Table 3

Perpetrators and Type of Offence, Totalled for each Year, 1982-87

Year	Perpetrator	X	M	P	T	D	A	R	Total
1982	Army	13	4	3	2		S: 5 By: 1	7	35
	CIO				6	9			15
	Armed Men						2		2
	Dissidents	16	1				8	3	28
	Unknown	3	1						4
1982	TOTALS	32	6	3	8	9	16	10	84
1983	5 Brigade	970	122	464	42	33	S: 667 By: 5 B 8 G: 41	107	2 459
	Army	39	8	16	8	14	S: 23 G: 1	1	110
	CIO	2	8		3	12	4		29
	CID	1	3						4
	Supp unit	1	3	3		1			8
	Armed Men	3							3
	Dissidents	11		10	1	1	8		31
	Unknown	33	8	3	3		4	6	57
1983	TOTALS	1 060	152	496	57	61	761	114	2 701

Table 3
continued

Year	Perpetrator	X	M	P	T	D	A	R	Total
1984	5 Brigade	157	39	59	21	1 989	556	10	2 831
	Army	32	10	8	5	7	14		76
	CIO	6	9	1	1	18	3		38
	Supp unit	1	1	2		1	2		7
	ZRP	2	2			1	1		6
	Zanu-PF youth	15		10			31		56
	Armed Men						2		2
	Dissidents	15		2		1	4	1	23
	Unknown	1	7			7	3		18
1985	5 Brigade	5	7		210	210	7	11	450
	Army	9	11	7		4	10	11	52
	CIO	9	64	1	18	104	20	1	217
	CID	2	1		1	6			10
	Supp unit	2						1	3
	ZRP	4	5	3	11	20	2		45
	Zanu-PF youth	14		63			32		109
	PISI				2	13	4		19
	Armed Men	2					1		3
	Dissidents	11	3	7			15		36
	Unknown	5	21	6		96	1		129
1985	TOTALS	63	112	87	242	453	93	23	1 073

Table 3
continued

Year	Perpetrator	X	M	P	T	D	A	R	Total
1986	Army	1	1		1	1	S:4 By:1 G:1		10
	CIO	1			18	89	17	1	126
	ZRP				1	1			2
	PISI					2			2
	Armed Men		1				4		5
	Dissidents	3		4			S:3 G:1		11
1986	TOTALS	5	2	4	20	93	31	1	156
1987	Army	1	1	2			2		6
	CIO	6		3	5	21	2		37
	ZRP		4			17			21
	PISI		1		2	5			8
	Dissidents	4					5		9
	Unknown	1					1		2
1987	Totals	12	6	5	7	43	10		83
Year not known	5 Brigade	2	1						3
	Army	21	4	3	2		5		35
	CIO					3			3
	Armed Men						2		2
	Dissidents	4							4
	Unknown	9	3		3	27	3		45
	TOTALS	36	8	3	5	30	10		92

Matabeleland and Midlands

Table 4
The Chronicle – June 1982 to March 1988: "Specific Reports"
Summary of all Offences by District and Type of Offence

Offence District/Provinces	Death X	Missing M	Property P	Kidnapping/ Detention	Assault Bs	Rape R	TOTAL
MAT SOUTH	18						18
Beitbridge	12		7		2		21
Gwanda	23		64	1 (K) 1 (D)	32	5	126
Insiza	3		6				9
Matobo	39		38	20 (K)	5		102
Bulilimamangwe	26		49	4 (K)	36		115
Bulawayo	5	3	9	83 (D) 2 (K)	4	1	107
Umzingwane	3		5		1		9
MAT NORTH	23			77 (D)			100
Nyamandlovu	37		87	31 (K)	16		171
Tsholotsho	27	1	7	1 (D) 8 (K)	14	2	60
Inyathi (Bubu)	11		11		1		23
Nyaki	34		16	1 (K)	4	2	57
Lupane	20		76	1 (D)	2	6	105
Hwange	8		3		4	4	19
Binga	1						1
TOTALS NORTH & SOUTH	290	4	378	163 (D) 67 (K)	121	20	1043
MILANDS							
Gokwe	5		5		2		12
Kwekwe	2		5		1		8
Gweru	25		7	3 (D)	22		57
Mberngwa	8		2		3		13
TOTALS	40		19	3 (D)	28		90

Other Locations including
Unknown

Table 4
continued

Offence	Death X	Missing M	Property P	Kidnapping/ Detention	Assault Bs	Rape R	TOTAL
MANICALAND							
Chipinge	2		9	9	7		27
Chimanimani				2	2		4
Nyanga	3						3
MASVINGO	2						2
MASHONALAND	1						1
Centenary	4				1		5
Chegutu	1						1
Harare (Seke)	1		1	6 (D)	16		24
Mazowe	4				1		5
Marondera	1		1				2
Mudzi	1						1
Sundry Villages	11		4		5	1	21
UNKNOWN	3		1	5			9
TOTALS	34		16	16 (K) 6 (D)	32	1	105

Total offences (all perpetrators) in country = 1 238

Table 5

The Chronicle, June 1982 to March 1988: "Specific Reports": Dissident Offences by Year

Year	Dead X	Property P	Kidnapping K	Assault As	Rape R	TOTAL
1981	3	3		1	1	8
1982	60	185	1	67	2	315
1983	61	107	52	26	1	247
1984	29	4	8	16	6	63
1985	91	48		23		162
1986	9	21		15		45
1987	70	44	10	17	1	142
1988		1	12	1		14
TOTAL	323	413	83	166	11	996

Table 6

The Chronicle, June 1982 to March 1988: "Specific Reports":
Offences by Government Agencies, including all Army and Police Units, and Zanu-PF Youth

Year	Dead X	Missing M	Detained D	Assault As	Rape R	TOTAL
1982	7	1	151	4	6	169
1983	18	3	15	10	4	50
1984	7			1		8
1985	9		6			9
TOTALS	41	4	172	15	10	242

There were NO REPORTS of property destroyed by government agencies, although "rioters" are acknowledged in 1985.
There were NO REPORTS of offences by any government agencies after 1985.
Total offences in country = 1 238

Table 7

The Chronicle: Jan 1983 – Dec 1986 "General Reports" on Dissident Atrocities

Released JAN 1984, but time span not clear:
58 ZANU officials killed
61 civilians killed
37 raped

JAN 1983-JAN 1984
120 murders
284 robberies
25 mutilations
47 rapes

JAN 1984-JULY 1984
45 civilians killed
37 rapes
253 robberies
No report on offences between July 1984 and Jan 1985

JAN 1985-JULY 1985
45 killed
40 raped
215 robberies

JULY 1985-JAN 1986
103 killed
57 raped
263 robberies plus millions in property damage

DURING 1986
116 civilians killed
57 raped 20 abducted
210 robberies, worth $47 000

1987 – NO GENERAL REPORT

Table 8

The Chronicle Database: Total Numbers of Offences "General Report" Totals Compared with "Specific Report" Totals for the Same Time Span

	General Reports	Specific Reports
TOTALS	Jan 1983-Dec 1986	Jan 1983-Dec 1986
Killed:	429	157
Property Loss:	1225	174
Assaults:	25 Mutilations	103
Rapes:	238	5
TOTAL:	1917	439

NOTE: "specific reports" totals here are lower than for the "district by district" analysis because they exclude offences before January 1983 and after December 1986 to correspond with dates of "general reports". Also excluded from "specific report" totals are those "dissident" offences which took place between January 1983 and December 1986 in other parts of the country: "general reports" always refer to Matabeleland and Midlands only, so "specific reports" here do the same.

Table 9

The Chronicle: Official References to Numbers of Dissidents in Operation, or Killed or Captured, June 1982 – Mar 1988

1982		1984	
June	1 killed	Jan	1 killed
July	Dissident numbers between 150 and 200 – Mugabe		175 armed clashes since July 1983
	1 killed, 1 captured	Feb	459 killed or captured "since operations began"
Aug	3 killed, 2 injured	Mar	41 killed since Jan
Sept	300 Ex-Zipras have deserted the army – Sekeramayi	May	3 killed
Oct	77 demobbed Zipras arrested – Kangai	June	5 killed
Dec	13 killed, 5 captured	July	16 killed since Feb curfew
			58 brought to trial
1983			191 armed clashes
Feb	Sekeramayi declines to give details of people killed:	Oct	100+ killed in 1984
	"A good number of dissidents and their		
	collaborators have been killed."	Nov	10 killed, 37 captured
	17 ex-Zipras desert – Mugabe	Dec	3 killed
	Nyoka refutes claims of atrocities and refuses		
	to give a figure on deaths.	**1985**	
Mar	Mnangagwa denies harrassment of civilians and says the	Jan – Dec	68 bandits killed in 1985 – Chief Supt T Gere
	infrastructure supporting dissidents must be destroyed.		
	"Several" dissidents and army deserters arrested in		
	Bulawayo.	**1986**	
	Sekeramayi calls stories of army atrocities "malicious."	Jan – Dec	45 dissidents killed, "specific reports" totalled.
	10 dissidents killed		
April	Munyaradzi denies many civilians are seeking	**1987**	
	medical help.	Jan – Dec	31 dissidents killed, "specific reports" totalled.
	Locals are reported to be capturing and killing dissidents.		Unity accord
	8 killed	**1988**	
Aug	4 killed		
Oct	3 killed, 1 injured	Feb	2 killed, 122 surrender

Total dissidents according to *The Chronicle*: 800 (approx)

NOTES – PART TWO

PART TWO, I
CASE STUDY ONE

1   While the term "village" has been used here, smallholdings in Tsholotsho are laid out in long, narrow lines, and are therefore frequently referred to by the residents themselves as "lines", rather than villages. For more on the origin of lines, see "Physical Torture", pp 39-40.

2   See Part Two, Chapter III, Table 5.

3   While *The Chronicle* figures for offences do not differ significantly from the HR Database, there remains the unexplained disparity between "Specific" and "General" totals, and the lack of cross-referability in the two databases: see Part One, II.

4   As mentioned in Part One, II, File H is a valuable source that provides thorough documentation of events in this particular region, but prefers to remain confidential.

5   See Part One, II, Methodology.

6   See Methodology, and the village by village summaries for process by which numbers of dead were calculated.

PART TWO, II
CASE STUDY TWO

1   Although *The Chronicle* attributes these two deaths to dissidents, LCFHR, op cit, reports witnesses who attributed them to security forces.

2   There is one recorded instance of a man who telephoned information about civilian deaths to mission staff being subsequently detained – the final outcome is not on record.

3   Information on the food embargo comes primarily from CCJP archives, which contained an 18-page closely typed statement on the situation in Matabeleland in Feb/March 1984. All information following on the embargo is from CCJP unless otherwise indicated.

4   CCJP archives, 23 March 1984. As the precise villages where these incidents occurred is not given, they are not included in the village by village summary which follows.

5   Information here on Bhalagwe is from J Alexander, op cit, p 9. One of the ex-ZIPRAs persecuted in 1:7 Battalion deserted after the camp was shut down and became a dissident.

6   All the following information on Bhalagwe is a composite of accounts given both in the 1980s and 1990s. These coincide to a remarkable degree and include a Commission of Inquiry sworn statement.

7   See above: specific references also follow in the village by village summary.

Part Two, III
Results

1   Interview with independent researchers, October 1996. They estimate far higher numbers of offence in all categories for Lupane and Nkayi than HR Database currently has on file.
2   CCJP archives.

PART THREE

IMPLICATIONS
OF RESULTS

I

ORGANISED VIOLENCE: ITS IMPLICATIONS

It is difficult to estimate the costs of the epidemic violence of the 1980s. Costs must be measured in physical injuries, psychological disorders, economic damage and social pathology. Some of these costs, such as the medical consequences of physical injury, can be estimated, at the least by inference and comparison. Psychological disorder can be also be estimated, as there is already a reasonably extensive literature on the effects of organised violence. The following chapter of this report (Legal Damages), makes some attempt to indicate the economic costs of the 1980s disturbances. There are, however, very few indications that social pathology can be easily measured.

As indicated in the previous chapters, the scale of violence was very large, and involved large numbers of people. The experiences reported by these people can be categorised, and it is the aim of this chapter to put the effects of the reported violence into a more human perspective.

Firstly, for each type of torture, we will begin with a definition and some examples as these are necessary, both for a clear understanding of the forensic approach involved, and for an interpretation of the reports from Matabeleland. Then we will look at a specific testimony from the 1980s disturbances illustrating the given category of torture.

Once we have gone through the six main categories of torture in this way, we will make some general observations about the physical and psychological consequences of organised violence, and of the likely situation now in Matabeleland for survivors. We will not attempt to quantify any of the categories for the 1980s, as this would be inappropriate in the absence of direct clinical measurement. We will, however, comment upon the likely prevalence of disorders, since direct comparison with other local and regional samples is possible. We will conclude with some suggestions for remediation of the ill-effects. Readers must bear in mind that the case testimonies which will be outlined in this chapter are merely illustrative, not conclusive evidence for any proposition.

1. EXISTING STUDIES ON VIOLENCE IN THE ZIMBABWEAN SETTING

There has been a series of studies into prevalence and effect of organised violence carried out at two small rural hospitals at Mount Darwin and Karanga, in the far north-eastern corner of Zimbabwe. Although this area was completely unaffected by events in the 1980s, it is an area that suffered extreme violence in the 1970s, and is the only area where the long-term consequences of organised violence for Zimbabweans have been studied. As no studies on the effects of the 1980s violence have yet been done, the Mount Darwin/Karanga study may provide some insight into the effects of organised violence in a Zimbabwean setting.

This suggestion is not made dogmatically, and one would expect cultural and historical differences to have made the 1980s experience discreet for its sufferers from the 1970s violence. Much of the data in the 1970s studies relates to war veterans, whereas in Matabeleland and the Midlands in the 1980s, it was civilians who were affected by the violence: there are problems in extrapolating from the former group to the latter. Even where Mount Darwin results relate to civilians, it must be remembered that in Matabeleland and the Midlands, people have now suffered two consecutive periods of violence, which has compounded the plight of survivors in these regions.

Interested readers are therefore referred to the list of references for this chapter, if they wish to pursue what is already known from the Mount Darwin/Karanga studies. As mentioned before in this report, the techniques of torture used by government agencies in the 1980s were not new in this country; such abuse was widespread in the 1970s.

2. DEFINITIONS OF ORGANISED VIOLENCE

The term "organised violence" derives from an initiative of the World Health Organization (WHO), and in southern Africa has been given a definition that both includes and extends the original definition given by the WHO. An International Conference, and a subsequent Regional Meeting, both held in Harare, gave the following definition:

> "Organised violence is the inter-human infliction of significant avoidable pain and suffering by an organised group according to a declared or implied strategy and/or system of ideas and attitudes. It comprises any violent action which is unacceptable by general human standards, and

relates to the victims' feelings. Organised violence includes *inter alia* 'torture, cruel, inhuman or degrading treatment or punishment' as mentioned in Article 5 of the UN Universal Declaration of Human Rights (1948). Imprisonment without trial, mock executions, hostage taking or any other form of violent deprivation of liberty also fall under the heading of organised violence. The effects of apartheid, destabilisation, civil war, the forced displacement of people, and political violence constitute organised violence. Violence which occurs in these situations as a direct consequence of political repression, although it may appear random, is of a structural nature, involves violation of basic human rights and can only disappear when human, social and political relationships are profoundly changed." (PAZ, 1991)

As can be seen from this definition, the term covers a very wide range of effects, from torture to displacement, from deliberate infliction of bodily harm to economic hardship. This may seem to some to be an unduly wide definition, but it does bear some relation to reality. It can also be seen that the events of the 1980s fall well within the definition of what constitutes organised violence.

There are other more restrictive definitions, mostly indicated in international conventions, declarations, and principles. The United Nations Convention Against Torture gives a very formal legal definition, as does the UN Declaration of Human Rights. The African Charter of Human and People's Rights gives a very simple and clearly understandable definition.

These legal definitions are mirrored in the definitions given by medical and forensic scientists, all of which emphasise the element of deliberate harm and violations of humanitarian principles. It is with these forensic perspectives that we examined the reports of violence in Zimbabwe in the 1980s.

In our review of the research and clinical studies, it became apparent that some clear categories emerge, both for types of violence and types of effects. We will describe these categories below in some detail.

3. FORMS OF ORGANISED VIOLENCE

It has become conventional in the study of organised violence to view violence as a kind of stress, albeit a very extreme form of stress. Where man-made stress is concerned, war, torture, riots, and psychological terror are sometimes considered to occupy a very similar position on the stress dimension. Despite their similarity, it is worth specifying the various forms, for although the intent behind the violence may be the same – to deliberately harm human beings – the effects found are by no means uniform.

Organised violence can be very simply classified into six main kinds:
- Physical torture
- Deprivation
- Sensory overstimulation
- Psychological torture – general
- Psychological torture – witnessing of death or torture
- Psychological torture – "disappearing" of people

These are by no means exclusive categories: it is usually not possible to separate clearly physical and psychological torture, except in the rare cases of psychological torture occurring in the absence of physical torture. It is fair to say that physical torture is always accompanied by verbal threats. In addition, people can suffer several types of physical torture simultaneously. A person might have been tortured, both physically and psychologically, have seen this happen to others, and have had a member of her family forcibly abducted and never seen again. Certainly, most interviewees providing data for this report suffered multiple types of abuse, as will be clearly illustrated by the cases used below.

A seventh category, wounds due to war, might also have been included, for these will clearly be found amongst people from Matabeleland and other victims of war, but this category is so obvious in its origin and its effects that it requires little discussion. Unfortunately, bullet wounds, or limbs missing due to landmine explosions, are all too often the only pathology examined by a society. Here we would point out that the First National Disability Survey, carried out in the early 1980s, is a good example of this point: injuries due to war are reported exclusively as physical injuries. We will thus concentrate on the original six areas.

A) PHYSICAL TORTURE
All methods of physical torture have the common element of causing extreme pain in a position of complete helplessness. This can be illustrated by a simple example in the difference between being hit by fists and boots in a fight as compared with being hit by fists and boots whilst being tied up.

Although it is generally futile to attempt any classification of types of physical torture, since man's creativity in this area seems to know no limits, the range of types may be illustrated by reference to the findings from an international study on torture victims (Rasmussen, 1990).

Types of physical torture (from Rasmussen, 1990)

Beating	99%
Severe beating	97%
Severe beating (head)	73%
Electrical torture	54%
Physical exhaustion	34%
Climatic stress	33%
Asphyxiation	29%
Falanga (beating of feet)	29%
Severe beating (genitals)	20%
Submarine ("wet")	19%
Standing	17%
Suspension by arms or legs	6%
Banging head	15%
Abnormal body position	13%
Torture by heat	13%
Suspension on bar	10%
Sexual torture	10%
Telephone	9%
Submarine ("dry")	6%
Sexual torture (rape)	3%
Nail torture	2%
Pushed down stairs, out of window	1%

Relating this to statements made to compilers of this report, all of the above types of physical torture, with the exception of the last two, occurred in the 1980s disturbances. The prevalence of various types of physical torture in different parts of the country varied, but research has not been analysed comprehensively enough at this stage to result in tables offering precise ratios for all these categories, although general trends can be commented upon.

Certainly, it is quite obvious that beating, severe beating and beating on the head were the most common forms of torture in the 1980s, in all regions for which records now exist. For named victims across all categories of physical torture, over 80% reported beatings. This number increases to more than 90% if unnamed victims involved in mass beatings are considered. In addition, the Matobo pilot study suggested that there were greater refinements in physical torture in 1984, and in particular that sexual torture was more common at this time. Further study will be needed to establish the precise ratios of these various types of abuse in the 1980s.

One form of physical torture which was reported from all districts on file as having occurred in the 1980s was the use of burning plastic: burning plastic bags would be dripped on to restrained victims. There are photographs on file of people scarred as a result of this form of torture.

It is common for different kinds of physical torture to be given at the same time: people can be beaten while being suspended or tied up in unusual positions; furthermore, physical torture can be accompanied by other kinds of torture. Almost every interview on record relating to the 1980s, reports the use of verbal abuse – psychological torture – in conjunction with one or more kinds of physical violence, either observed or personally experienced.

A considerable research effort has gone into identifying methods of physical torture, and new variations are found all the time. It is also apparent that methods seem to spread across the planet, and there is no form of physical torture that seems specific to any one culture. Not only the current study, but also the recent study of Zimbabwean war veterans in Mount Darwin endorses this, giving evidence of most of the forms of torture mentioned by Rassmussen.

In most torture studies, beatings of one kind or another are by far the most common methods of abuse. The beatings can be generally all over the body, but some countries show a preference for a particular kind of beating. Falanga, or beating the soles of the feet, has been frequently reported in Middle Eastern countries, but there are reports of its use in African countries too. Electrical torture is popular because of the extreme pain that it causes, as well as the few scars that it leaves. The point to grasp here is that any physical harm caused deliberately is torture, and thus any procedure or object can become torture or be used in torture.

Physical torture in the 1980s

As can be seen from the summary of the reports, many persons (65 per cent) experienced some form of physical torture. Beatings constitute about 80 per cent of the physical torture reported, with electrical shock, submarine, suspension, abnormal postures and rape all reported. The picture is actually little different to the kinds of abuse reported in other Zimbabwean studies. The following case, *Interview Case Number 1679 TD* illustrates a not-uncommon story.

On the 10th June 1983 at 4pm I was taken from my workplace in a Puma vehicle, along with two others who worked for another store in Tsholotsho. We were taken to Mbamba Police Camp, about 40–50km away. When we got there we were separated. My friend and I were accused of telephoning Bulawayo to warn our masters to stay away, because the killers (the 5 Brigade) were still there. The 5 Brigade had made it known that they wanted to kill my master, Y, and my friend's master, K. They had gone to hide in Bulawayo. I was beaten and lost four teeth on the spot, and 12 others after this. My friend was tied with his hands and feet together. They would hang him head down and feet up until he was paralysed in both hands and feet. He died from this in 1993. From 1983 he was on and off in hospital.

This individual received blows to the face, which were severe enough to cause the loss of teeth, and may well have resulted in further injuries. There would be queries about possible hearing loss, as well as possible minor brain injury. His friend experienced a severe form of suspension, which would have resulted in joint injuries, especially if he had experienced beatings at the same time as the suspension. The paralysis reported is unclear, but severe nerve damage is also a consequence of suspension. This case also illustrates the difficulty in separating out the different types of torture that these two men experienced. At the least we would have to consider physical torture, psychological torture, deprivation, and witnessing as possible experiences.

In addition to beating, some brief mention must be made of the other forms reported. Some survivors have reported the use of electrical shock, and this is a very severe form of abuse, which may result in physical damage in the form of lesions, and very frequently leads to long-standing psychological disorder. Here it is enough to point out the effects of what is termed "aversive conditioning".

Aversive stimulation, which is most frequently some form of electrical shock has been shown to have long-standing effects: one animal study of the effects of electrical shock showed complete suppression of all behaviour, including eating, in a squirrel monkey given very mild shock, and aversive conditioning has been used for the suppression of anti-social or disabling behaviour in the field of psychiatry. Under psychological torture following, there is mention of a persistent sexual disorder reported by one man in Mashonaland who had been sexually tortured through the use of electrical shock, and there are likely to be similar cases in

Matabeleland, as the following case from the *CCJP Confidential Report on Torture in Zimbabwe* illustrates:

> They then blindfolded and handcuffed me with my hands at the back and leg ironed me. Then they started beating me with a pick handle or some such stick. They beat me under the feet and on the back. I was lying face downwards as they were beating me. The pain was too severe for any description; I fainted in the process. When I gained consciousness, X, who was senior to the man beating me, came and gave orders that they use electric shock on me. They used the field electric telephone. The instrument works on battery power. Wires were tied to my genitals, then they would wind the machine. On winding the shock runs through the body and I was screaming. The shock threw me down but I could not remove the wires because I was handcuffed. While I was screaming, they would dip a large family-size towel in water and then tie it around my face covering the nose, so that I was breathing in water through my nose and mouth. This treatment caused me to faint. They poured water on me until I gained consciousness. Afterwards, that same day (at night) I was taken to Kadoma at Eiffel Flats. In the morning my feet were swollen so much and I could not pass urine, for my genitals were swollen and painful.[1]

This case illustrates how forms of torture are used simultaneously. This man suffered falanga, or beating of the feet, together with more general beating, sexual torture through use of electric shocks, and asphyxiation. Tying up, suspensions, being placed in abnormal positions; all are reported by the 1980s survivors, and the likely result is that many of them will have persistent joint injuries, which cause pain and suffering, affecting both their capacity to work and indulge in social activities. Certainly, survivors claim such injuries in their interviews, and many claim current medical records in support of ongoing health problems.

Here it is worth commenting that the data from studies of survivors from the Liberation War indicate that many persons are still suffering persistent pain more than two decades after the original abuse, so we cannot be complacent about the effects of human rights violations in the 1980s.

The Matabeleland reports show some differences too with the Mashonaland reports and war veteran reports. For example, as in the case above, there are on the 1980s records more cases of falanga, and this form of abuse produces very severe and crippling long-term effects.

Additionally, the medical records from Matabeleland show people with severe injuries due to beatings and other forms of physical abuse. It will be a matter of urgency to offer the proper physical rehabilitation for these survivors.

B) DEPRIVATION

Deprivation is separated from psychological torture in the southern African setting because it happens very frequently that people are detained in circumstances that lead to ill-treatment, but where the intention is not deliberately to use the detention as torture. For the victim, however, the effect of the deprivation can be the same as torture.

The point here is that torture is not just a matter of what was in the mind of the perpetrator or the person doing the detention, but it is also a question of what the victim believed was happening.

Deprivation should be understood as representing extreme stress, frequently causing exceptional discomfort or pain. Deprivation covers a variety of different experiences, summarised below.

Types of deprivation (from Reeler, 1995)
- Held incommunicado, minimal food and comfort: overcrowding for more than 2-3 days.
- Lack of water (more than 48 hours).
- Immobilisation, restraint, total darkness for more than 48 hours.
- Lack of sleep (less than 4 hours per night).
- Lack of needed medication or medical care.

Again this is not an exclusive list, but it covers the kinds of treatments that are forbidden by most human rights conventions or conventions relating to the treatment of prisoners or detainees. Furthermore, these forms of abuse can be very difficult to assess in many countries where the above forms of ill treatment are so common as to be felt that they are "normal" methods of treating prisoners. Patients will frequently be accustomed to these methods, or know that they are routinely practised, so that they will not remark upon them for themselves.

Deprivation in the 1980s
Deprivation has long-term effects, and we must mention both the specific deprivation suffered by those who were detained, and the more general effects of the food embargo and curfews. To deal with the first, we must here mention the effects of the detention in Bhalagwe, which was distinct from the interrogation centres such as Stops Camp. Detention on its own

may not have adverse consequences, but combined with psychological torture and deprivation, long-term adverse consequences become more likely. One obvious consequence for those who have experienced detention is a deep fear of authorities and places from where authorities exercise their power: police stations, offices and the like. Many survivors are likely to have strong anxiety at having to enter such places, or having to attend any official gatherings. Political rallies, voting, and similar events are quite likely to bring back strong post-traumatic responses. Furthermore, those who suffer psychological disorders as a consequence of their detention, may well retain traumatic memories of their detention, and these will be all the more powerful if detention was accompanied by torture or the witnessing of torture.

Bhalagwe Camp appears to be the one setting where specific deprivation occurred: conditions here were designed and enforced in a way to induce maximum discomfort. Those detained at Bhalagwe in the first day or two, before the camp was full, have reported that in spite of the fact that there were holding sheds standing empty, detainees were deliberately crowded in to a few sheds, to the point where there was virtually no space to sleep at night. Water and food were also rationed. The following sworn statement was made by a 19-year-old boy to CCJP on 8 March 1984.[2] Other archival statements and statements made in 1996 confirm and further detail conditions at Bhalagwe. (See Part Two, II and a further statement on Bhalagwe.)

On 7 February (1984) in the evening we were taken by truck to Bhalagwe Camp. We reached Bhalagwe around 5pm having left around 3pm. When we arrived we found many people at Bhalagwe, some of whom were being beaten.

We were separated, men from women, into barracks to sleep. In each barracks soldiers were counting up to 136 people, and if there were not 136 others would be brought in to make up the numbers.

We were arranged in three rows, two rows along the walls and one row in the middle of the building. We slept on our sides because we were told to squeeze since there was no room. We slept in our clothes with no blankets. We were not allowed to go out to the toilet at night, but in the morning we could do so under escort.

On Wednesday morning about 8am we were taken out one by one

to another barracks building where we were either beaten or given electric shocks. When the number got up to five we were then taken back to our barracks.

I myself was only beaten, but I saw others being given electric shocks, and when they fainted, water was thrown on them. What I saw is that they put a wire into the mouth of the victim which is secured by strings that are attached to his ears. The other wire is put at his back. This second wire is placed on and off the back of the person. Four people in army uniform, two men and two women did the electric torturing while the victim was lying down.

There were many barracks where they were taking people for beating and electric shock.

Six schoolboys, of whom I was one, plus two soldiers counted the women. This is how I came to know there were 856 women in the camp. This counting took place on 11 February in the morning. Later the same day four soldiers and six schoolgirls counted the men. After this the soldiers announced to us that the total number of men in the camp was 1 000, and that of women 856. The soldiers announced these final figures to everybody.

The prisoners from Sun Yet Sen were assigned to two barracks while those from Matopo, Plumtree, Gwanda and Belingwe (Mberengwa) were assigned one barracks each.

They brought us to Bhalagwe to get information about dissidents. Questions about this were asked during the beatings.

In the morning we used to dig graves, dig toilets, wash army clothes, wash pots, fetch firewood.

We were given food and water to drink only on alternate days, i.e. skipping one day when we got neither food nor water. The young men dug the graves, and the old people buried those who died each day in the camp. Those who died must have died because of beatings and electric shock. I saw two in my own sleeping barracks who were found dead one morning.

I was at the camp from 7–17 February. Until I left we were being beaten every day.

On 16 February, all schoolchildren were made to sit according to their respective schools and home areas, counted, and sent back to barracks. On 17 February, all schoolchildren were told that we were going home. Then trucks took us to our homes for going to school.

In Bhalagwe Camp the barracks had asbestos walls and asbestos roofs. Because I knew the place, I know that there were neither soldiers nor prisoners at this camp before the curfew was imposed in February. At the camp I pretended to be a student, although I had left school after Form 1, at the end of 1983, because I had heard in other areas the soldiers tended to treat scholars slightly better.

I came to Bulawayo by army Puma on 17 February because I had told them I was schooling in Bulawayo.

When I left home there was widespread hunger. Stores were closed; no buses were running except government transport. Soldiers were harassing people. I have since heard that some people were dying of hunger. I heard this from a teacher who had come to buy food at the end of February.

The data relating to Bhalagwe may bear some comparison with genocide survivors, such as those from the Nazi era or Cambodian survivors from the Pol Pot regime. The data from both these periods indicate very high rates of morbidity amongst survivors. However, those at Bhalagwe were usually detained for a few weeks or months, as opposed to years. Even within these few weeks detainees would suffer torture, deprivation, witness executions and torture, and suffer massive psychological abuse, ethnic in its focus. Their detention was also occurring in the context of a larger and more sustained attack on all living in their region at that time.

The most outstanding example of deprivation in the 1980s, because it affected so many people, was the use of the food embargo, denying access to food and other commodities and services during the early months of 1984. This resulted in the intimidation and near-starvation of 400 000 civilians. While drought is a common experience in Matabeleland, the food embargo clearly stands out in people's memories as a separate type of experience – that of state-induced hunger.

The curfew months were also accompanied by rallies at which specific threats were made: it is likely that many were deeply traumatised by these experiences, and it is probable that the whole process of drought relief that has been so commonplace in the southern parts of Zimbabwe brings back traumatic memories for many survivors. The following speech was made at a rally, three weeks after the food embargo had been in force. CCJP have it on file as a sworn statement, dated 8 March 1984.[3]

On Thursday, 23 February (1984), the soldiers called a meeting at Sibomvu (in Gwanda district, Mat South). I went there. The soldiers were under the shade of a big Ntenjane tree while the people sat around in the sun. The meeting was from 12 to 4pm. After that they told us there would be no curfew that evening because some people had come from very far.

Their leader told us that his name was Jesus. "I am one of the leaders of the Gukurahundi." he said.

These are some of the things he said at the meeting: he had some gallons of blood in his car. The blood came from people. His life is to drink human blood. He wanted more blood because his supply was running low. They had come to this place to kill, not to play. They had come to kill the maNdebele because the dissidents were found only in their area and not in Mashonaland.

Commander Jesus said he found his boys doing nothing – beating up people instead of killing them. He did not mind thousands of people being killed.

"You are going to eat eggs, after eggs hens, after hens goats, after goats cattle. Then you shall eat cats, dogs and donkeys. Then you are going to eat your children. After that you shall eat your wives. Then the men will remain, and because dissidents have guns, they will kill the men and only dissidents will remain. That's when we will find the dissidents.

Commander Jesus spoke in Shona while one of the soldiers translated into Ndebele. The ordinary soldiers are better. They go around nicely asking about dissidents and then they go their way. If these ordinary soldiers came we would be prepared to tell them the truth.

But with 5 Brigade, truth or lies, the result is the same.

Experiences at such rallies, or detention experiences, could very easily have caused Post Traumatic Stress Disorder (see section following) in the sufferers, both acutely at the time, and chronically in continued disorder since.

Apart from the deliberate policy of deprivation embodied in Bhalagwe and in the food embargo, there were instances in the 1980s when deprivation existed, but probably unintentionally so. As previously pointed out, "normal" detention conditions even when not deliberately worsened by the authorities, often resulted in deprivation and torture to those experiencing them. Those detained, for example at Stops Camp in Bulawayo, have reported appalling detention conditions, including overcrowding and lack of sanitation and food, but it cannot be concluded that this was the result of a deliberate policy: it was more likely the result of indifference to the situation of detainees.

Sleep deprivation was a consequence of the weekend long pungwes held in Matabeleland in 1983-84, although it is unlikely that rallies resulted in less than four hours' sleep a night. Mission staff reported their concern at the effect of these enforced gatherings on their school-age children, who were exhausted by Monday morning after a weekend of forced attendance at rallies, where they were not only deprived of sleep and recreational time, but were subjected to having to witness violence and verbal abuse (CCJP archives).

C) SENSORY OVERSTIMULATION

Sensory stimulation is often used as a method of torture of persons in detention, but it does not seem to be so common in community settings. The aim behind sensory stimulation, which is often erroneously termed "brain washing", is to cause mental confusion and distress, and psychological studies of sensory deprivation, one kind of sensory manipulation, have clearly demonstrated the damaging effects of such abuse. For example, people subjected to constant "white noise", or other forms of constant stimulation, rapidly show signs of stress, even to the point of beginning to hallucinate if it goes on long enough.

Types of sensory overstimulation (from Rasmussen, 1990)
- Constant noises
- Screams and voices
- Powerful lights. Constant lighting
- Special devices
- Drugs

All of these can be used deliberately, or can be part of the background to detentions. For example, many people have been tortured in settings where they can hear the sounds of others being tortured, and will talk about how terrible it was to hear the screams and voices of their comrades. This could have been a deliberate policy on the part of the torturers, but is frequently due to their indifference to whether other prisoners can hear or not.

The specific effects of overstimulation are difficult to produce in a community setting, since they require a controlled environment in which the perpetrator can exercise maximum control over the kinds of stimulation that a person can receive. Overstimulation is therefore reported only amongst those who were detained in interrogation centres or at Bhalagwe Camp. Deliberate deprivation is more commonly reported than overstimulation. This is similar to the findings from Mashonaland studies and those of war veterans.

Detainees have frequently recalled how having to listen to the screams of others being tortured added to their own terror, but it is not clear whether the keeping of people in close proximity to the torture cells was the result of indifference, or deliberation. The following account is taken from the *CCJP Report on Torture*:

> While at Stops Camp people were tortured. One boy was so badly beaten and bleeding in the face that I doubt if he is alive. People were being tortured and beaten until around 2am in the night and at 8am in the morning we heard screams and cries. They use electric shock and the water and cords for torture...

Those at Bhalagwe have also described how torture and interrogation began at 5.30am every day, and how from that time on, the camp resounded with screams. Apart from these types of reports, overstimulation as a method of torture does not seem to have been widely used.

A few high level political detainees have reported some of these more sophisticated forms of torture, such as being kept in continually lit cells.

D) PSYCHOLOGICAL METHODS

Psychological torture also defies easy description, but all forms identified share common elements in the creation of extreme fear in a situation of uncontrollability. However, uncontrollability is a factor common to most torture methods, and furthermore, it is difficult in practice to make clear distinctions between the effects of general psychological torture, and the specific anguish caused by "witnessing" and "disappearances."

The clearest distinctions can always be found between what are termed "impact torture" and "non-impact torture," where the presence of physical injuries is the major difference. As can be seen below in the findings reported by Rasmussen, the variety of forms of psychological torture is very wide.

Types of psychological torture (from Rasmussen, 1990)
- Threats   85%
- Threats of execution   60%
- Undressed   45%
- Threats towards family members   43%
- Sham execution   31%
- Sexual verbal assaults   20%
- Changing attitudes(hard/soft)   12%
- Noise torture   5%
- Excrement abuse   3%
- Nontherapeutic use of drugs   4%
- Torture via exposure to animals   1%

Physical torture in itself must always have psychological consequences, and psychological torture therefore is probably the most common form of torture used. Psychological torture is also frequently applied on its own, and can be very successful in causing both short-term and long-term damage to a person. Psychological torture should therefore not be seen as a lesser form of ill treatment.

Threats, verbal abuse, mock executions and the like are all intended to convey fear and instil obedience and, furthermore, usually convey some threat for the future.

Psychological torture in the 1980s
Entire communities consisting of thousands of people were subjected to psychological torture. The "Commander Jesus speech" above is a good example of the way 5 Brigade often prefaced their arrival in an area with dire threats against all residents of Matabeleland. Any subsequent meeting with 5 Brigade after such a speech would cause acute fear and anxiety for civilians. 5 Brigade also often used the salutary execution of randomly selected people as a threat of further executions in communities. People would also be detained and threatened with executions which were then not carried out.

Forced nudity was also a psychological weapon at times: the Tsholotsho case study reports the forced stripping of entire village communities before mass beating, and other cases where people were selectively stripped in front of their communities. The effectiveness of this strategy in causing extreme humiliation, anger and helplessness is evident from the interviews. In Matabeleland South in particular, there were frequently verbal sexual abuse and insults. Some interviews report 5 Brigade making sexual suggestions to naked victims, including suggesting forced sex between related family members, or between school children, or between people and animals. In addition, some political detainees were interrogated while naked.

The following statement is part of a far longer statement made to project personnel in October 1996 by a man who was 16 in 1984 – Interview Case Number 3737. He was detained with 12 others from his village on the day the curfew began, and was among the first ever to arrive at Bhalagwe. As in all the previous testimonies, his case serves to illustrate several types of physical and psychological torture: threatened execution is just one.

> The 5 Brigade herded everyone in our village together, about 70 or more people. From 6am until 11am we were beaten, including women and children, with sticks and fanbelts. Then they chose 12 people to come to Bhalagwe – four women and eight men. Two of the women were old and two were schoolgirls. Three of the men were schoolboys, including myself: I was sixteen.
>
> We were taken first to Kezi, and the 5 Brigade told us we were being taken there to be shot. When we arrived, they told us we would be taken two by two at 1pm and be shot. When one o'clock came, they told us they had decided to throw us down a mine instead. They then loaded us in a truck and drove off. We thought we were being taken to be killed, but we were brought to Bhalagwe...
>
> At Bhalagwe the charge office was full of blood. We had to sit in lines outside the office waiting our turn to be beaten. When you were in front of the line, you knew it was your turn next. The beatings started at 5.30am. I saw two people being shot, and seven being beaten to death. Very many died, but I helped to bury only these nine I saw die. I dug their graves. People were buried two or three to a grave...

There are large numbers of persons who reported witnessing others being abused. This is reported from the mass beatings, the pungwes, and the places of detention; both interrogation centres and Bhalagwe camp. The following case illustrates the point by reference to a pungwe. This case was recorded in the form of a sworn statement by a 31-year-old man from a village near Donkwe Donkwe, in Matobo, made to CCJP officials on 8 March 1984.[4]

In the morning of 5 February, 1984, soldiers came to our village and told us to go to Dingi Store. We were made to wriggle like snakes towards the store. When we got there I saw other people already gathered, and some of them were being beaten while lying down, by about 19 soldiers.

When we joined the gathering we were made to run around while being beaten; others were beaten lying down. There were men, women and children who could roughly fill two and a half buses [200?]. The soldiers hit us with mopane sticks and kicked us with their boots.

The soldiers were speaking Shona and through an interpreter they were saying, "You support dissidents."

We were being beaten at the shop from about sunrise until about 10am. Then afterwards we were all taken behind our houses to a spot about 100 metres away where there are two mopane trees and we were made to sit down. The soldiers asked for two picks and two shovels and they were brought to them. While some were being beaten, others were told to fight each other while at the same time being beaten by soldiers. Others were lying down while being beaten.

As this was going on soldiers were selecting six young men at random. Three were put on one side and three on the other side of the crowd. Two soldiers then shot dead the three in one group, and two other soldiers also shot dead the three young men in the other group. The other men and women and children who were sitting down were asked to sing while soldiers went among them beating them up. We were singing things like *"Pasi loNkomo, Pambili loMugabe."* Some songs were in Ndebele and others were in Shona.

The six killed were:
MM, aged 24 years – my brother
BD, aged about 24 years
BN, aged about 30 years
MB, aged about 31 years
ON, aged about 24 years
Z?, aged about 31 years

In two groups the older people were asked to dig two graves quickly or they themselves would be buried in the graves. The rest of the people in the meantime were being asked to sing and dance while being beaten.

I dug the grave in which my brother was buried – two faced one side and the other in the opposite direction. The graves were shallow, about thigh deep. They were buried in their clothes. The burial arrangements for the second grave were the same as for the first. We covered the graves after which we were made to join the others in the singing while being beaten.

At about 4pm a group of about 19 young men carried the bags of the soldiers and went away with the soldiers. These young men had come along with the soldiers in the morning. We were told by the soldiers to wait for five minutes after they left before we could go back to our homes.

My younger brother heard one shot as they left, and the following morning we heard that soldiers had killed GD near the store.

I arrived in Bulawayo on 11 February at about 2pm having left home on foot on 5 February at night. I was sick and bleeding through the mouth, and that is why it took me so long to get here. I used to sleep in the bush. I spent two days without food, and afterwards I would ask for food at kraals along the way.

There are a significant number of reports that mention being witness to an execution. This is also a factor that many survivors from the Chimurenga mention. In Mount Darwin, survivors of such multiple abuse were all found to be suffering from Post Traumatic Stress Disorder: the same would be expected for 1980s survivors.[5] People in Matabeleland and the Midlands have now been subjected to two successive periods of intense violence and the witnessing of violence. It is therefore important for the future that the effects of the massed, public violence be examined.

E) WITNESSING OF ORGANISED VIOLENCE

Some earlier workers in the field of traumatic stress argued that civilian populations were little affected by war. Rachman, for example, claimed that there was little evidence of increased psychological disorder during the Second World War in the United Kingdom (Rachman, 1986). However, there was little direct investigation of trauma in civilian populations until the last decade, and, following the invention of PTSD (see section following), there has been the continual demonstration of psychological disorder in populations in situations of war and civil conflict. These situations are usefully described by the term "High War Zone Stress", but can equally be described as "witnessing".

The term High War Zone Stress was originally applied to differentiate soldiers in combat settings from those in non-combat zones, and examined how frequent experience of military fighting, or proximity to people being killed, affected fears about oneself being killed. Sadly, High War Zone Stress is today not unique to military personnel, and describes the daily life of many civilians. It is particularly relevant to situations of guerrilla war, and obviously to southern Africa. Modern wars are distinguished by the strategic involvement of civilians: up to 80 per cent of the casualties of wars now are civilians, mostly women and children. Civilians world wide not only frequently suffer physically from conflicts, but inevitably they also witness violence and death.

Furthermore, deliberate massacres, executions, threats and abuse are frequently forced upon ordinary people by military and paramilitary forces in an attempt to remove support for guerrillas or political parties. This frequently leads to both sides terrorising civilians in order to prevent support for the other side. This creates a situation of sustained fear and stress for the ordinary person. The experience of being "The Man in the Middle"[6] was common in the Liberation War throughout Zimbabwe. And as this report has documented above, this situation was repeated in Matabeleland and the Midlands in the 1980s, with civilians trapped between the dissidents and the security forces.

Witnessing can vary in terms of the degree of resulting psychological torture depending on the element of controllability. A person among thousands of people at a mass rally where beatings are taking place, for example, could close his/her eyes or look the other way. However, such an option was not open to people in the rally described above, where proximity to the executions and the accompanying beatings and demands being made by the soldiers would have made witnessing of violence almost impossible to avoid, if one were lucky enough to avoid being beaten oneself. One should not minimize the seriousness of witnessing extreme violence, nor the depth of fear that it can create.

Witnessing in the 1980s
Forcing civilians to witness violence was a deliberate facet of 5 Brigade behaviour, both in Matabeleland North and the Midlands in 1983, and in Matabeleland South in 1984. Tens of thousands of civilians can be estimated to have observed violence, if one considers for example the high forced attendance at political rallies during these years, and the prevalence of public beatings at these rallies. In addition, possibly thousands witnessed

executions, particularly in 1983, when it was common practice for 5 Brigade to execute people in the village setting. All those who have reported their experiences at Bhalagwe in 1984 also witnessed killings in this camp, and if their experiences are typical, which they seem to be as they coincide to a remarkable degree, then thousands at Bhalagwe also witnessed executions. All the testimonies already included in this chapter give ample support for the prevalence of witnessed violence during these years.

F) DISAPPEARANCES

One very sinister form of psychological torture is the use of forced disappearances. This refers to the abduction of individuals, who may be kept in secret detention for long periods, but are often executed in secret. This is a strategy that has been growing in recent decades, and some of the most tragic examples can be found in Latin America. For example, about 10 000 individuals were "disappeared" in Argentina during the rule of the military junta in the 1970s. It is also a strategy that has been used in Zimbabwe, both during the Liberation War and the 1980s disturbances.

Disappearances are used for two reasons. Firstly, the disappeared person is usually some kind of an opponent of the government, and it serves a strategic purpose to get rid of opposition. Secondly, it puts extreme pressure on the targeted group and particularly the families of the disappeared. It creates enormous psychological and social problems for the surviving people, and this has been well documented by several Latin American groups who work with the families of disappeared persons. For example, in Argentina it has been argued that the life expectancy of the fathers of the disappeared is reduced below the national average, and it has also been shown that the surviving children often have marked psychological difficulties (Lagos, 1995).

In Africa, disappearances may have even more profound effects. Since death and misfortune are always events of extreme concern for the entire extended family, a disappearance that may or may not be a death creates a wide range of problems. African families are compelled by spiritual belief to undertake proper rituals for the burial of the dead, and anything that prevents this happening can leave the family with the expectation of future misfortune (Mupinda, 1995). For example, it was frequently observed in the refugee setting that many Mozambican refugees were preoccupied with worries about not having properly buried their dead when they fled into exile (Reeler, 1995).

It has also been observed in Zimbabwe that many families were deeply distressed by the non-return of family members from the Liberation War: large numbers of young men and women left home to join the guerrillas in

Mozambique, and many never returned. The families have no information about the fate of their relatives, and some have even engaged in lengthy searches to find out what happened, to find where they were buried if they died (Mupinda, 1995).

So disappearances in Africa can range from forcible abductions through disappearances in the sense of "missing in action", to disappearances in the sense of an individual never being heard of again. These seem to have identical effects on the surviving members of the family, and we need to understand much more about these effects.

Disappearances in the 1980s

Disappearances were a deliberate part of the state strategy in the 1980s, although to date there are only 354 named "disappeared" victims. Even this number is indicative of disappearance having been an official policy. Many dozens of others were picked up in midnight raids by mysterious Government agents, and held incommunicado for some months before their release. The manner of their removal from their homes, and the uncertainty this resulted in, generated intense psychological stress for their families. The timing of disappearances was also significant: they occurred in the months prior to Zimbabwe's general election, targeted opposition party officials, and generally added to the climate of fear and intimidation already prevalent at that time.

As mentioned above there are some reasons for considering disappearances to be an especially broad-reaching form of abuse. The effects of disappearances have been partially documented in Mashonaland (Mupinda, 1995). Anecdotal evidence and Richard Werbner's comments in *Tears of the Dead* suggest that the effects of disappearances are profound on surviving family members in Matabeleland and the Midlands.

There is evidence to suggest that disappearances cause long-term depression, family dysfunction, and even long-term community disruption. The number reported in this report is modest, but it should be borne in mind that this abuse targets whole families, and has long-term effects. For many of the families of the disappeared the burden of living without a death certificate for a loved one has been enormous – stopping them getting state-aided education for orphans, for example – and every encounter with the bureaucracy a reminder of the event. Bear in mind, further, that many disappearances took place in forcible abductions, often in very frightening circumstances.

The following statement, *Interview Case Number 1099*, is about an incident that took place in Tsholotsho in May 1985. It is typical of those on file:

Late at night, people knocked at our door, while we were all sleeping. I went to open and two men asked for my husband. I told them he was blind, and asleep. They asked for him and took him to the gate, where there were many others. I did not hear what they said to him, although I heard him reply that he did not know whatever it was they wanted to know.

They returned him to the house and said he should get his ID card and come back with me. This man in cross belts noticed I was in an advanced state of pregnancy. He ordered me back into the house and they went away with my husband.

The next morning we found my husband's ID card. It was 2km away from our home, and broken into two pieces. A little further on we found blood clots, sticks and vehicle tracks. The footprints ended here. We have not seen or heard of my husband since. We are destitute.

Internationally, disappearances have become the focus of major attention, with even the United Nations laying down principles to be applied in cases of disappearance. The long-term effects are only beginning to be understood, but it is continually stressed, by those working in this particular area, that the effects are exceedingly widespread and long-term. The disappearance of a person by the state strikes at the foundations of the state's trustworthiness: survivors seem rarely to feel any confidence or safety in the state's protection after this, and especially when no investigations take place to determine the legality of this behaviour. Various Argentinean and Chilean researchers have commented that corruption, increased violence, voter apathy and a climate of silence frequently follow undisclosed disappearances. We might speculate here on a reason for declining voting attendance at elections, and not just in Matabeleland, for the same comment might easily be made of all areas in Zimbabwe that have experienced epidemic violence.

4. CONSEQUENCES OF ORGANISED VIOLENCE

The consequences of repressive violence are many and complex, and include both physical and psychological effects. The psychological study of the effects of organised violence is a new field, and there are still controversies about the effects and how best to classify them. However, the physical effects of torture are generally more clear cut. Before considering the current findings, it is pertinent to consider some local and regional evidence as regards violence and its effects.

In Zimbabwe it is estimated that between 20 to 30 per cent of primary care patients are suffering from psychological disorders (Reeler and Todd, 1993; Reeler et al, 1991; Reeler, 1986), but there are no accurate estimates of the prevalence or incidence of disorders due to violence. However, one of the earlier studies of psychological morbidity, carried out by Hall and Williams at Karanda Mission Hospital in 1984, estimated morbidity at 39 per cent of all outpatients, and this was carried out in an area that experienced extreme violence during the Second Chimurenga. The Hall and Williams study has provided one of the highest estimates of psychological morbidity and, although the authors made no comment about violence, more recent observations at the same site suggest that disorders due to violence may explain this high rate (Reeler and Mupinda, 1995).

There are good grounds in Zimbabwe for already suspecting high rates of disorders due to organised violence, but there are no good estimates of the physical consequences of organised violence. This is a general comment of many observers of the effects of recent Zimbabwean conflicts, and there is nothing remarkable in this assertion.

Studies of Mozambican refugees and reports from the Zimbabwean community all indicate that many patients suffer from the effects of war, torture and ill-treatment, but all this data is drawn largely from the field of psychiatry, and the data that deals with physical sequelae is mostly self-report. There are therefore no good estimates to help in the assessment of likely morbidity as a result of the 1980s violence. However, comparisons with international studies, especially as regards physical effects, are possible.

A) PHYSICAL EFFECTS OF ORGANISED VIOLENCE

In general the physical effects of organised violence can be classified into two categories: one group of people who have a wide range of non-specific somatic complaints, and another group who describe specific symptoms corresponding to the type of violence they experienced (Juhler, 1992). To some extent this is an arbitrary classification, for some survivors can present with both types of complaints. We will briefly summarise the general findings here.

i) Non-specific somatic complaints

This refers to people showing signs of general stress, or psychological reactions to torture. As Juhler has commented (Juhler, 1991), the most frequent complaints come from four organ systems: the central nervous system (headaches), the musculo-skeletal system (joint and muscle pains), the cardio-vascular system (palpitations), and the gastro-intestinal system (abdominal pains). These are very common symptoms in Zimbabwean primary-care settings, but there are clear differences between general psychological disorders (due to ordinary stresses) and disorders due to organised violence.

The most important of these relates to musculo-skeletal symptoms. Studies carried out in Denmark have concluded that two main symptom clusters can be identified: those in joints due to over-stretching, and those in muscles, that are due to general stress. Joint pains are therefore an important different symptom in the complaints of survivors, but it is also clear that it is very difficult to find objective evidence of pathological lesions or injuries.

It is also clear that many survivors associate their pains with the torture or ill-treatment in an almost symbolic way, often as a consequence of the way in which the torture is delivered. Here we can give the example of electrical shocks given to the genitalia leading to later sexual dysfunction. It is rare that the sexual dysfunction is due to any physical lesion, but the conditioning effect is extremely powerful. This kind of conditioning effect is common to many forms of torture: rape is another good example.

ii) Specific symptoms

The more violent the torture the more likely there is to be sound evidence of physical damage such as brain injury, paralysis, fractures, damaged organs, and altered functions. There are a large number of studies that show the pathological damage of falanga, burnings, beatings, cutting, head injuries and the like.

In the current study there were a large number of interviewees who gave anecdotal evidence of deafness and partial blindness which they attributed to beatings in the 1980s. Such reports are in accordance with other studies, which report a high frequency of deafness in survivors who have been beaten on the head. There were also many reports of permanent damage to limbs and to reproductive and urinary functioning. While there is archival medical evidence for many injuries being suffered in the 1980s, the current medical status of those who suffered then still remains to be established.

As mentioned above, it is difficult years after the event to provide objective evidence of what originally caused a physical injury. It is enough to reiterate here that the only thing that distinguishes torture from other similar damage is the intent and the legal responsibility of the perpetrator.

B) PSYCHOLOGICAL EFFECTS OF ORGANISED VIOLENCE: POST TRAUMATIC STRESS DISORDER

These effects are perhaps not as well-known, but are certainly better understood than they were two decades ago. Post Traumatic Stress Disorder (PTSD) is the most commonly used current term to describe the psychological effects of organised violence, and it provides a catch-all description for all disorders and symptoms in which the stressor is of a "catastrophic" nature.

Earlier descriptions of these effects had been classified mainly by reference to the precipitating event, and "concentration camp syndrome", "post-Vietnam syndrome", and "rape trauma syndrome" are all well-known examples of this approach to classification (Rasmussen, 1990).[7]

The prevalence of PTSD is rather variable, and has been assessed in two ways: one approach has been to examine prevalence in the general population, whilst the other has been to examine prevalence in "at risk" groups. As Shay has commented, the prevalence rates for PTSD amongst Vietnam veterans is 32 times greater than the comparable prevalence rates amongst demographically similar civilians (Shay, 1996).

This is an extremely high prevalence, but data derived from studies of military veterans may not be directly useful for this report: many Vietnam veterans report both experiencing violence as well as perpetrating severe human rights violations themselves.[8] Thus, data from persons who are both victims and perpetrators may not be useful for the understanding of persons who are victims alone. This does not mean that we should not understand the perpetrators, merely that we are here concerned with victims alone.

Despite some conflicting findings, current research suggests a dose–response effect due to the magnitude of the stressor, and, according to this argument, torture will represent the most severe of all stressors, and the prevalence of PTSD should be highest in this population.

In terms of psychological torture and witnessing, if a stressful situation lasts an afternoon, or several weeks, or several years, its consequences for survivors should differ. In the 1980s, the situation of High War Zone stress lasted from 1982/3 until the Unity Agreement in 1987; although 5 Brigade, the most feared unit, was disbanded in 1986, civilians still felt under siege from multiple forces until December 1987. Indeed, some still do not rule out the return of persecution in the future.[9]

The way in which the violence developed exacerbated this: 5 Brigade's impact was unexpected, profound and unprecedented. Having once experienced the utterly unexpected, civilians in affected areas still believe it could happen again. The slow build up of violence which typified the

Second Chimurenga differed significantly from the sudden epidemic violence of 5 Brigade, and its psychological consequences can be expected to have differed accordingly, with the 1980s violence being perceived as worse by sufferers.[10]

Recent studies of Holocaust victims suggest clinical disturbance in third-generation survivors (Hardi and Szilagyi, 1993), but it is not clear that the disturbance measured in the grandchildren of concentration camp victims can be described as PTSD. Perhaps the significant aspect of these studies is that there is a pattern of disturbance in *descendants* of torture victims: this clearly has a bearing for the report on hand, and for other parts of Zimbabwe.

All of this epidemiological work has been substantially supported by empirical work. Studies of sleep show a wide range of differences between PTSD sufferers and other populations, both civilian and military, with PTSD sufferers showing greater problems with falling asleep and maintaining sleep.[11]

Some of the key features of PTSD – sleep disturbance, intrusive cognitions, psychological reactivity and physiological distress – seem to be supported empirically, and there is support for the notion of a specific disorder produced by trauma, and capable of being delineated from other disorders. It seems clear that exposure to violence has severe, persistent and delayed sequelae, with an apparent dose–response effect, but there still remain some difficulties, and some critics. The major critics come from amongst those working with torture survivors, who are critical of many aspects of the PTSD definition, and suggest that there may still be such a thing as a "torture syndrome" apart from PTSD.

C) Torture – psychological consequences

Torture clearly represents an extreme form of exposure to violence, in that the effects are premeditated and designed, the process usually involves attacks of both a physical and psychological nature, and, most importantly, torture has an explicitly political purpose in a clear socio-political context. One estimate sees "government-sanctioned torture" as being present in 78 countries in the world (Jacobsen and Vesti, 1992), whilst another estimate reckons that between 5 and 35 per cent of the world's refugees have suffered at least one torture experience (Baker, 1993).

It may seem to be hair-splitting to raise the socio-political in a consideration of psychopathology, but it is obvious that it is just this aspect of torture that sets it aside from disasters, catastrophes, wars, accidents and abuse. Torture and repressive violence are specifically targeted at individuals and groups with the specific intention of causing harm, forcing compliance, and destroying political will, frequently in the absence of war, but always in a situation of civil conflict (Somnier and Genefke, 1986).

The deliberate and systematic attack on people, and the attempt to destroy personality and political will, are felt to be such intrinsic features of torture that a narrow definition, such as PTSD, may miss this. In fact, torture survivors suffer a wide range of adverse consequences, and this frequently means that the process can carry on over a very extended time period. For this reason, many workers feel that "ongoing traumatic stress disorder" would be a much more accurate expression of torture (Straker, 1987).

> "The deliberate infliction of harm seems to place torture in the position of a distinct form of stressor, and the specific purpose behind torture makes it very different from random violence or catastrophe, whether natural or man-made. Furthermore, the violence is decidedly purposive, with the aim of the systematic destruction of individual and community identity, and it is very hard to know how to include in a definition what is surely a notion of 'evil', however unpalatable this notion might seem to a scientist."
> (Reeler, 1994)

The argument in support of a discreet and recognisable torture syndrome has been partially resolved by some recent British research (Ramsay et al, 1993; Gorst-Unsworth et al, 1993; Turner and Gorst-Unsworth, 1990). In Zimbabwe, this model has received partial validation in a study of war veterans (Reeler and Mupinda, 1996).

5. CONSEQUENCES OF ORGANISED VIOLENCE FOR SOCIETY

Repressive violence is not just an issue that affects individuals, but, as was pointed out above, much modern violence has the purpose of terrorizing whole communities. So we have to consider the consequences for society as a whole, and not just merely for the affected individuals. It is not a simple task, however, to identify the societal: not even attempts to explain the Nazi phenomenon have proved wholly satisfactory. Some general consequences can nonetheless be briefly indicated.

Firstly, there is frequently *a sustained climate of fear amongst the affected population,* and this is borne out by all contacts with persons who were involved during the various wars and disturbances in southern Africa. This affects all aspects of peoples lives, may be exaggerated during times of political disturbance, and profoundly affects peoples ability to live full, social lives. There is now a considerable literature from South Africa speculating on the consequences of decades of organised violence; the persistence of fear, helplessness and insecurity in social groups has been noted in many other national settings. One South African study, one of the best studies to date, followed up school children affected by the township violence of the 1980s, and found marked differences in how well the children adapted in later years (Straker et al, 1992).

Secondly, there may be *an increase in violent behaviour in the affected population.* Here the focus is not so much on the increase in violent crime per se, but in the increase in violence of a random or motiveless nature: reprisal killings, rampage killings, violent outbursts, etc. It is generally observed that sustained civil violence results in a general increase in all violence, not merely political violence. Northern Ireland provides a good case example here, where studies of children show a marked increase in child violence, violent attitudes amongst children, as well as higher levels of anxiety, depression and family pathology. South Africa is an even more relevant example, and all observers are agreed that the violence in South Africa is of epidemic proportions, and is not merely a political phenomenon (Michelson, 1994).

Thirdly, there is *the reappearance of silence in group situations,* which is usually related to fears about reprisals. This fear, seen as fear of speaking out in groups or fears about being overheard, can severely impair the ability to indulge in social and political activities. This can obviously have profound economic and political consequences, and it is worth noting that even the World Bank now views psychopathology as a significant impediment to social and economic development. Disorders due to violence should be included in the general category of psychopathology.

Fourthly, *there is a concern amongst human rights workers for the future,* albeit a speculative concern. It has been noted in several international meetings that the transition from strong repressive government to weak democratic government, which is the case for Zimbabwe, can often lead to highly destabilised situations in which violence increases rather than decreases. Here we should note carefully the recent events in the Balkans.

Clearly, none of these situations, especially the last, is desirable in the future, and suggests that, unless a determined effort is made to redress the wrongs and rehabilitate the survivors, there are likely to be long-term sequelae from war, destabilisation and human rights violations. At the societal level there is the need for action.

6. RELEVANCE TO MATABELELAND AND THE MIDLANDS

There are several conclusions that emerge from the reports on the violence in the 1980s. The first has to do with the way in which the violence developed. As was seen earlier, there was a massive escalation in violence in the early years (1982–84), with a marked decline in violence subsequently. This is very different to the violence seen during the Second Chimurenga, where the violence began at low levels and then increased over the years to reach the highest levels before the end of the war in 1980. It is fair to conclude that the violence in the 1980s was of an epidemic nature in which there was very widespread exposure to violence for many people.

There is a significant group of individuals, not fewer than 7 000, for whom active help may be needed now, and it is very probable that the total number is much higher. There are hospital records describing some of the injuries in the 1980s and their consequences, supporting the general assumption of epidemic violence made above. We should bear in mind here the findings from other settings and countries, which mostly suggest the dose–response effect – that there is an association between high levels of violence and the frequency and severity of disorders due to violence. There is an urgent need to investigate the current status of victims.

7. CONCLUSIONS

The findings of this report give much cause for concern. However, until it is possible to establish the numbers of people affected, the frequency and severity of the injuries sustained, and the range of long-term effects, all conclusions must be tentative. It is probable that the number of survivors is much higher than this study has indicated, and some epidemiological study is called for in the likely debate over numbers affected.

Torture and ill-treatment are the most common experiences reported, and these have severe long-term effects. Given that beatings were the most common experiences reported, there must be concern for the extent of the physical damage to the survivors, and this will require detailed medical examination by doctors and physiotherapists. Similarly, psychological disorders are also likely to be common, and we would expect PTSD, depression, and somatization disorders to be among the most common if the studies from other Zimbabwean settings are anything to go by. There has also clearly been a very high rate of witnessed violence in affected parts of the country, particularly in 1983 and 1984.

Thus, the possible effects – individual, familial and community – are serious indeed. There are those living now in our country that have been tortured, watched others being tortured, seen deaths by execution, and even had a close family relative abducted, never to be seen again. It is also pertinent to observe the very real poverty of many of these survivors, and to remember the findings on property loss. The general air of economic stress scarcely provides a climate for healing and rehabilitation, and may, worse than this, be a source of continued trauma, or what one South African worker has termed "continuous traumatic stress" (Straker, 1987).

There is very little in the reports of the survivors that is surprising or unusual, and very little that is not found in other settings in Zimbabwe, or even in other countries. There is little reason to expect that the findings from this investigation will be any different to previous findings. The survivors of Gukurahundi will show physical and psychological injuries and disorders, and will probably have little faith in these being addressed, given it is the same Government that inflicted the injuries that they must go to for help. As one Chilean worker has expressed this dilemma:

> "How can we continue to help to relieve others of their sorrow and liberate them from the sufferings of grief if society keeps shutting the door on truth and full redress? Is it at all possible to imagine peace of mind for a person if you force him/her completely to give up any hope of finding out the whereabouts of a son, a spouse, the most beloved? How do we succeed in making a survivor of cruel and inhuman torture feel completely rehabilitated if this society continues to disgrace the survivor and lets the torturer go unpunished?"
> (Simona Ruy-Peres, 1996)

Perhaps Zimbabwe can be different to Chile, and perhaps it will not take another ten years before we heal the wounds and assuage the grief. The task will be difficult, but not impossible with the will and commitment to change the future by acknowledging the past.

II

LEGAL DAMAGES

1. INTRODUCTION

It is not the purpose of this report to claim compensation on behalf of those who suffered. For the reasons spelt out below it would be very difficult to quantify accurately, or fairly, the compensation to be paid to individuals. It is necessary however to place the plight of the victims in the legal context of Zimbabwe. Furthermore, there is a danger that the statistics of dead people blur the actual cost to the survivors of the tragedy. Too often the cost of war is only illustrated in national budgets which detail how much has been spent on hardware and soldiers' salaries. This chapter seeks to illustrate how much victims have suffered in monetary terms; how much victims would have been able to claim had they had the opportunity to do so. In doing so it is hoped that the Government of Zimbabwe and the international donor community will realise how much is needed to redress the situation adequately.

2. ZIMBABWEAN LAW RELEVANT TO THE REPORT

The events we are concerned with took place when there was a State of Emergency throughout Zimbabwe. In connection with the military action it took in Matabeleland and the Midlands, the Zimbabwe Government sought to exonerate its officials and security forces of liability for any acts they might commit in connection with that action. The legislation in question was contained in the Emergency Powers (Security Forces Indemnity) Regulations 1982 (SI 487/1982, as amended by SI 159/1983), made by the President in terms of s 3 of the Emergency Powers Act [*Chapter 83 of 1974*]. Under s 4(1) of the Regulations:

No liability for damages shall attach to:
(a) the President or any Minister or Deputy Minister in respect of anything done in good faith by him or by any person referred to in paragraph (b) for the purposes of or in connection with the preservation of the security of Zimbabwe; or

(b) any member of the Security Forces or any person acting under the authority of any such member in respect of anything done in good faith by such member or person for the purposes of or in connection with the preservation of the security of Zimbabwe.

Under s 4(2), a Ministerial certificate to the effect "that any matter or thing referred to therein was done in good faith for the purpose of or in connection with the preservation of the security of Zimbabwe" was *prima facie* proof that the matter or thing was done in good faith. The immunity was made retrospective in its effect by subs (3), which provided that the limitation on liability applied whether the cause of action arose before, on or after the publication date of the Regulations (which was 23 July 1982).

Immunity from prosecution was similarly granted by s 4A.

This legislation was not new in concept; similar legislation had existed in the 1970s. The Indemnity and Compensation Act 45 of 1975, s 4(1), provided that:

No civil or criminal proceedings shall be instituted or continued in any court of law against

(a) the President or any Minister or Deputy Minister in respect of any act, matter or thing whatsoever advised, commanded, ordered, directed or done or omitted to be done by him or by a person referred to in paragraph (b) in good faith for the purposes of or in connection with the suppression of terrorism;

(b) any person who, at the relevant time, was

(i) a member of the Security Forces or employed in any capacity or appointed to any post by the State, whether for remuneration or otherwise; or

(ii) acting under or by the direction or with the approval of the President, any Minister or Deputy Minister or any person referred to in subparagraph (i);

in respect of any act, matter of thing whatsoever advised, commanded, ordered, directed or done or omitted to be done by him in good faith for the purposes of or in connection with the suppression of terrorism.

The above mentioned Act was repealed by the War Victims Compensation Act 22 of 1980.

The Supreme Court of Zimbabwe unanimously held in *Granger v Minister of State* 1984 (2) ZLR 92 that the good-faith provision of the Emergency Powers (Security Forces Indemnity) Regulations was unconstitutional. The Court ruled that the provision, which allowed for the reasonableness of an officer's act to depend solely on the *subjective* test of the good faith of the officer himself, was *ultra vires* s 13(5) of the Constitution, which requires an *objective* test for reasonableness.

The Government itself, in spite of the Court's decision, has consistently asserted that no compensation would be paid to victims of the Matabeleland conflict because the acts complained of were committed during "a State of Emergency". It is not clear whether the Government is thereby asserting that the acts were objectively reasonable or whether they are relying on prescription or any other legal point.

In the normal course, any claims that might have been brought against the Government would, by virtue of s 15(d) of the Prescription Act [*Chapter 8:11*], have been prescribed after three years. However, in 1994 and 1996, the Government conceded liability in two cases. In 1994, it paid the equivalent of US$3 500 compensation to the widow of Fraser Gibson Sibanda who remains missing but is presumed dead after his arrest by the police in 1985. In 1996, in the case of *June Hleza v Ministry of Home Affairs* (HC 3243-92), the Government agreed to a settlement of the equivalent of US$4 500 with the common-law wife (on behalf of her two children) of Tryagain Ndlovu who remains missing and who is also presumed dead after his arrest by the police and subsequent detention by the CIO and army in the years of the Matabeleland conflict.

Despite the apparent significance of these two cases, they are of limited legal value to victims of the Matabeleland conflict. Because both Mr Sibanda and Mr Ndlovu were officially "missing" and not "dead", the lawyers for their spouses were able to delay the running of the routine three-year prescription period on their claims by obtaining, before initiating their claims, official court declarations presuming the deaths of Mr Sibanda and Mr Ndlovu. From the date of the Court's declarations the respective prescription periods for each of their claims would then begin to run under s 6(1)(c) of the Prescription Act. In this way, *Sibanda* and *Hleza* serve as precedents only for the relatively small number of disappearance cases arising from the Matabeleland conflict.

The legal channels for claims in disappearance cases might arguably have been cleared by the Government's official response to the 52nd session of the UN Commission on Human Rights. While justifying the violence in the Matabeleland conflict on the grounds of a *de facto* war, the Zimbabwe Government nevertheless agreed, in its response to the Commission, to compensate the victims of such violence. As the Commission reported, the Government "decided to compensate all families with missing relatives, regardless of whether there were court proceedings concerning the circumstances of the disappearance[s]."

The case referred to on p 150 of the report is that of the late Fraser Gibson Sibanda referred to above. It is significant that the UN Commission on Human Rights was only aware of the one case and yet the Government of Zimbabwe appears to have given an undertaking to compensate all families, which contradicts statements made within Zimbabwe by President Mugabe and other high-ranking members of Government.[1] It may be argued that this decision constituted an acknowledgment of liability by the Government and a waiver of prescription. But this is not clear. In the normal course for waiver of prescription to be accepted, the waiver must be an express or implied acknowledgment of a liability, as opposed to an indebtedness. The statement by the debtor (in the legal sense) must amount to an admission that the debt is in existence and that the debtor is liable for it: *Benson and Anor* v *Walter and Ors* 1984 (1) SA 73 (A) at 86-87. A stated intention to pay compensation to unspecified persons in unspecified amounts would probably not be accepted as an acknowledgment of liability to pay specific persons with specific claims. An admission to a third person will not interrupt prescription: *Markham* v *SA Finance and Industrial Co Ltd* 1962 (3) SA 669 (A).

Secondly, in terms of the Prescription Act, claims of this kind prescribe after three years. It may be held that the effect of the act is that the debt is extinguished and cannot be revived, irrespective of the defendant's attitude. See *Wille's Principles of SA Law* 8 ed p 500; and see *Harry* v *Director of Customs and Excise* 1991 (2) ZLR 39 (H). However *if* the Government's statement can be construed as a waiver of prescription, and *if* waiver is legally possible, prescription would begin to run afresh "from the date on which the interruption [took] place" (Prescription Act s 18). The prescription period would in that event no longer stand as an obstacle for compensation claims by families of missing persons. However, it must be stressed that this argument is rather tenuous and the likelihood is that these claims have prescribed.

For relatives of persons killed; for victims of beatings, torture, or other physical or mental abuse; and for persons who suffered property damage who could not challenge the Government before the running of their prescription periods (whether because they did not dare to do so, because of the situation in Matabeleland, or for any other reason), though, the prescription period remains as an effective bar on legal claims. As such, the vast majority of victims of the Matabeleland conflict have no recourse for action under law. Because many people from rural Matabeleland remain ignorant of their legal rights, and lack the resources to pursue or even gain access to legal counsel, those relatively few persons who do have recourse for action (i.e. relatives of missing persons) are unlikely to make claims for the compensation they may now be entitled to under law.

Notwithstanding these legal and practical impediments to the realisation of claims in disappearance cases and the legal impasse which the prescription period poses on claims for beatings, torture, property damage and murder cases, compensation for *all* victims of the Matabeleland conflict should, in our view, be offered. Victims of violence or aggression against their person or property would be entitled to compensation under both Zimbabwean law (if prescription were not a problem) and international standards of justice (see, for example, section 8 of the Annex to the United Nations Declaration of Basic Principles of Justice for Victims of Crime and Abuse of Power). Logistical impediments or legal technicalities should not get in the way of victims of the Matabeleland conflict receiving compensation for the injury they suffered, and in some cases, continue to suffer as a result of the physical and psychological harm inflicted upon them.

The technical legal obstacles to realising such compensation could be overcome by amending Section 4 of the War Victims Compensation Act [*Chapter 11:16*] in s 2 (the definite section), so that the phrase "the war" would apply to the Matabeleland conflict; and in s 4, so that the Act would apply to any injury to a person, the date of which was before the 1st March *1988,* rather than 1990, as the Act presently stands.

Through such amendments, the formal avenues to compensation for victims of the Matabeleland conflict would be opened. Those 1980s victims of the MNR in eastern and northern Zimbabwe would also be able to claim compensation. This would not, however, give the right to bring legal action through the courts.

The real-life logistical impediments to the realisation of potential compensation claims, however, would still remain. This chapter, through ten individual case studies, seeks to illustrate and exemplify the kind of abuses committed (beatings, killings, torture, detentions, destruction of property), persons victimised (fathers, mothers, children, the elderly), and compensation claims that could theoretically be made. In each case study, legal damages representing the amount of compensation victims would be entitled to claim under Zimbabwean delict law (disregarding any problems posed by prescription periods) are quantified.

3. METHODOLOGY

To realise meaningful quantification figures, legal damages have been tabulated in US dollars for the years in which the incidents of each particular case occurred. Because the case studies analysed span the years 1983 to 1987, years in which the Zimbabwe dollar experienced great devaluation, the more stable US dollar provides a better benchmark against which the quantifications of the different case studies can be compared and understood. Where valuations of goods or awards were available for the relevant years of incidents in Zimbabwe dollars or South African Rand, they are simply converted to US dollars using the June month exchange rates published in First Merchant Bank of Zimbabwe Limited's *Quarterly Guide to the Economy.* Where valuations were not available for the relevant years, they are adjusted for inflation using the June month Consumer Price Index (CPI) published in the *Quarterly Digest of Statistics* of the Central Statistics Office, then converted to US dollars using the relevant exchange rate.

Prices of goods taken from relevant year June month editions of *The Chronicle,* for example, are converted according to the appropriate exchange rate, while prices of goods taken from Brian MacGarry's *Rural Poverty Datum Line* (measured in Hurungwe, February 1996 and based on Verity Mundy's 1995 *The Urban Poverty Datum Line in Zimbabwe)* or from current-price surveys of supermarkets and other stores are adjusted for inflation using the CPI index before conversion to US dollar amounts. Awards from precedents in relevant Zimbabwean or South African case law are similarly adjusted for inflation before conversion to US dollar amounts.

The income of rural households, necessary for calculations of loss of support and opportunity, is based on a range of minimum wages prescribed in statutes from 1983 (Statutory Instruments 15, 19 and 300 of 1983). In this report, the income of a rural household in 1983 is valued at Z$125 per month and indexed according to the CPI when needed for other years. The income of a rural household in 1987, for example, is adjusted to Z$210 per month in Case Study One. In US dollar terms, the wage of a breadwinner in a rural household turns out to hold at US$0.78 per hour across the years 1983-87. The value of a rural household breadwinner's work is not readily quantifiable, and this report errs on the side of conservatism by imputing the least amount of income deemed necessary for survival.

Loss of support calculations are based on the tables and formulas provided in Robert J Koch's *Damages for Lost Income* (Juta and Co Ltd, 1984), referred to by the Supreme Court of Zimbabwe in *Minister of*

Defence v *Jackson* 1990 (2) ZLR1.

"Opportunity cost" calculations are made when quantifying the value of destroyed huts and granaries. The building materials for a hut are valued at US$127.46 (100 bundles of grass at US$0.62 per bundle; log poles at US$20.62; one door at US$15.46; one window at US$8.76; cement, clay, or mud for the walls at US$20.62) and US$67.01 for a granary (100 bundles of short grass at US$0.42 per bundle; log poles and stones at US$16.70; cement, clay, or mud at US$10.31). Time spent rebuilding huts and granaries, however, is time lost from routine value-earning activity. Opportunity costs are thus included. Assuming conservatively that it requires 60 hours of labour to rebuild a hut and 30 hours of labour to rebuild a granary, the opportunity cost for rebuilding a hut is valued at US$46.80 (60 x US$0.78) and at US$23.40 (30 x US$0.78) for rebuilding a granary. Huts, then, are valued at US$174.26 (US$127.46 + US$46.80), while granaries are valued at US$90.41 (US$67.01 + US$23.40).

Information from victims as to property lost is sometimes vague and unspecific. Victims often reported, for example, that a certain number of their wardrobes were destroyed without specifying what their wardrobes consisted of, or that their kitchens were destroyed, without specifying what items they kept in their kitchens. For such difficulties, a composite wardrobe for both males and females and a typical set of kitchenware are conservatively constructed:

Male Wardrobe (in US dollars)

4 pairs trousers	4 x 5.15	20.60
4 shirts	4 x 4.64	18.56
4 jackets	4 x 8.25	33.00
4 pairs of socks	4 x 0.72	2.88
4 pairs of underwear	4 x 0.93	3.72
2 pairs of overalls	2 x 10.00	20.00
1 pullover		2.58
1 manyatera (sandals)		1.03
1 handkerchief		0.31
1 belt		0.72
1 pair of leather shoes		7.22
1 pair of heavy-duty gumboots		8.00
	US$	118.62

Female Wardrobe (in US dollars)

4 bras	4 x 2.68	10.72
3 dresses	3 x 14.02	42.06

2 jerseys	2 x 8.25	16.50
1 pair of pants		1.24
1 Zambia (apron)		2.06
1 scarf		1.96
1 pair of leather shoes		10.93
1 pair of canvas shoes		3.30
		US$ 88.77

Kitchenware (in US dollars)

6 large plates	6 x 1.04	6.24
6 small plates	6 x 0.57	3.42
6 mugs	6 x 0.93	5.58
6 knives	6 x 1.35	8.10
6 tablespoons	6 x 0.49	2.49
6 teaspoons	6 x 0.17	1.02
2 dishing spoons	2 x 0.44	0.88
2 badzas (hoes)	2 x 2.64	5.28
1 table and chair set		56.70
1 large cooking pot		10.30
1 small cooking pot		3.19
1 battery-operated torch		4.00
1 transistor radio		5.00
1 bowl		3.40
1 grate		4.02
1 iron		7.11
1 bucket		1.24
1 box of washing soda		0.56
1 towel		1.65
1 stirrer		1.13
		US$ 131.91

At other times, information provided by victims as to property lost is specific, but ostensibly incomplete. In such cases, damages are quantified only as to what is specified by the victims.

4. CASE STUDIES

CASE 1
Reference Number: 1711 X
Name of Deceased: MN

Sex:	Male
Year of Birth:	1931
Occupation:	Kraal Head
Dependants:	1 surviving spouse; 9 surviving children
Wife's Year of Birth:	1943
Source of Information:	Wife
Place of Incident:	Mlagisa Line, Tshino School, Tsholotsho

On February 11 1987, at approximately 4pm, a group of Shona-speaking men in combat uniform entered the home of MN. The men, carrying AK-47s, asked MN and his wife for information about dissidents. When MN explained that he did not know the whereabouts of any dissidents, the men pushed him down on the floor and beat him with a hoe handle. They then dragged him into the kitchen which they proceeded to set on fire. MN broke out of the kitchen, but was severely burned from head to shoulder. The men tried to grab him, but he escaped. They also shot at him, but missed. Eight months later, MN died from the injuries and burns he had suffered.

DAMAGES

Beating

During the eight months he survived, MN would have been entitled to compensation for the beating he suffered. General damages would be awarded for pain, suffering, shock, contumelia (loss of dignity), disfigurement, discomfort and disability. MN's case resembles that of the plaintiff's in *Joseph* v *Esterhuizen* HB-46-93 where the plaintiff was awarded Z$20 000 in general damages from the defendant who had beaten him senseless without a weapon. MN, like Joseph, suffered serious physical injuries to his head (broken nose, black eye) and chest. MN's case is even stronger, however, because he was beaten with a weapon (a hoe handle) and also died directly from the injuries inflicted by the beating. An award of Z$20 000 in general damages is thus at least a minimum amount which MN would be entitled to. Taking into account the rate of inflation, MN's claim in 1987 would have been equivalent to Z$6 380.49 or US$3 810.43. See also *Chadwich* v *Chard* HH-262-91 (the plaintiff was awarded Z$5 000 for a single punch thrown by his employee for pain and suffering, loss of dignity and disfigurement).

Burns

MN is also entitled to general damages for the burns he suffered. In *Oosthuizen* v *Homegas (Pty) Limited* (Orange Free State Provincial

343

Division: Case 539/86 13 July 1989), the plaintiff was awarded R45 000 general damages for the pain, suffering, inconvenience, disfigurement and loss of amenities of life he suffered as a result of the severe burns to his face, scalp, ears, hand, and upper back. Because MN died from his burns within a year, his burns were even more severe than those suffered by the plaintiff in the Oosthuizen case. At the very least, then, a general damage award of R45 000 here would be reasonable and fair as well. Taking into account the rate of inflation, the equivalent judgment in 1987 would have been Z$48 883.25 or US$29 193.08.

Property

MN and his dependants may also claim compensation for the destruction of their kitchen and all the items within it. A typical kitchen (a separate hut) is valued at US$174.26 and kitchenware is valued at US$131.91.

Funeral expenses

MN's dependants are entitled to funeral expenses and loss of support compensation for the death of their breadwinner. In *Munhumutema* v *Zimnat Insurance Co Ltd* HH-249-91, the plaintiff was awarded Z$2 860 in expenses for the funeral of his 20-year-old son who was killed by the defendant in an automobile accident. The court held that funeral expenses can be recovered provided that they are reasonable under the circumstances: these circumstances may include the cost of local customs such as the slaughtering of an ox or a cow. See also *Rondalia Assurance Corp* v *Britz* 1976 (3) SA 243.

Given that the income of a rural household in 1987 is valued in this report at Z$210 per month, an award of Z$2 860 for funeral expenses would probably be too high for the circumstances. Taking into account the cost of a coffin and the costs of hosting relatives and friends in accordance with local customs and traditions, a reasonable figure for MN's family to conduct a proper burial in 1987 would be at the reduced figure of Z$750 or US$447.90.

Loss of Support

With respect to loss of support, MN's expectation of working life at the date of his death in 1987 based on his birth date in 1931 was 7.67 years (Koch 316). Annuity for 8 years at 1.5% is 7.486 (Koch 322). Family income is Z$210 x 12 = Z$2 520. Assuming the wife and children's share of his income would be 80% and deducting 5% for contingencies, the family's share of his income would be Z$2 520 x 0.95 x 0.80 = Z$1

915.20. So the value of loss of support in 1987 would have been Z$l 915.20 x 7.487 = Z$14 339.10 or US$8 563.31.

Total damages

Beating	3 810.43
Burns	29 193.08
Property	256.17
Funeral Expenses	447.90
Loss of Support	8 563.31
TOTAL	US$ 42 420.89

CASE 2

Reference Number:	1325 MD
Name of Missing Person:	JN
Sex:	Male
Year of Birth:	1954
Occupation:	ZNA
Income:	Z$200/month
Political Affiliation:	ZAPU – former ZIPRA combatant
Dependants:	1 surviving spouse and 1 invalid father
Source of Information:	Brother
Place of Incident:	Mbamba Shopping Center – Tsholotsho

On December 9, 1983, JN's 16-year-old brother received a parcel from the Fellowship Bus Company which contained belongings of JN. JN's brother and his invalid father went to the bus company for an explanation. A bus driver revealed that on July 8 1983 at the Mbamba Shopping Center, heavily armed men wearing combat fatigues and red berets boarded a Fellowship Bus and took JN away. The bus driver said some of the armed men spoke Shona, while others spoke a language he did not recognise. He also noted that some of the men were darker than most Zimbabweans. JN's brother was told to bring documents which would identify JN to the Tsholotsho police station. The following day, December 10, JN's brother went to the police station with JN's ZNA identification card and bank book, as well as some letters JN had written while he was in the ZNA (these were the items sent to JN's brother in the parcel). Tsholotsho police officers G.V.M and Sgt. G took JN's items and told JN's brother to go home and JN would follow. A week later, JN was still missing. JN's brother went back to the police and was told JN had been taken to Bulawayo to get clearance to return home. JN never returned home, and the police never returned JN's ZNA identification card, bank book, or personal letters to JN's brother.

DAMAGES
Loss of support
JN's dependants are entitled to loss of support compensation. JN's expectation of working life at the date of his death in 1983 based on his birth date in 1983 was 28.76 years (Koch 316). Annuity for 29 years at 1.5% is 23.376 (p 322). Family income is Z$200 x 12 = Z$2 400. Assuming the wife and invalid father's share of his income would be 80% and deducting 5% for contingencies, their share of his income would be Z$2 400 x 0.95 x 0.80 = Z$1 824. So the value of loss of support in 1983 would have been Z$1 824 x 23.376 = Z$42 637.82 or US$42 880.86.

Total damages
Loss of Support   42 880.86
TOTAL   US$ 42 880.86

CASE 3

Reference Number:	442 X
Name of Deceased:	JN
Sex:	Male
Year of Birth:	1933
Political Affiliation:	ZAPU
Dependants:	1 surviving spouse, 5 surviving children (dates of birth: 1965, 1967, 1969, 1971, 1973)
Wife's Year of Birth:	1947
Source of Information:	Wife
Place of Incident:	Jowa Line – Tsholotsho

On October 15 1983, three Shona-speaking men armed with AK-47s and bayonets and wearing combat fatigues and red berets drove up to the house of JN, entered the house, and took JN away by force. He was kept in the bush under guard for two days. On the third day, the men brought JN back to his homestead, and executed him in front of his wife and two of his children. The men then ransacked JN's house, destroying a bed, table, four chairs, and the shirts, trousers and dresses belonging to the family before departing. The next day, JN was buried by his family and neighbours.

DAMAGES
Detention
J.N. is entitled to general damages for his two-day detention in the bush. In *Muchenje* v *Chinyanganya and Ors* HH-95-94, the plaintiff was awarded Z$9 000 for his detention by armed officers. Mr Muchenje, an opposition party leader, was arrested by police and held in a cold and grimy cell for 29 hours. The court did not rule on whether the arrest was lawful, but held nonetheless that Mr Muchenje was entitled to Z$4 000 for physical discomfort and Z$5 000 for contumelia. JN's similar situation would justify a claim for Z$9 000 in general damages. It should be noted that Z$9 000 is a conservative claim. In *Masawi* v *Chabata and Minister of Home Affairs* HH-60-91, the plaintiff was awarded Z$3 000 for less than three hours of detention, despite the court's determination that no malice, mistreatment or physical force was involved. In his decision, Greenland J explained that being compelled to leave your family at night is degrading and that "liberty is a sacrosanct fundamental human right which must be meaningfully protected by the courts." The claim here does not adopt the generous Z$1 000 an hour rate of compensation awarded in *Masawi*, but instead relies on the far more conservative compensation sum of Z$9 000 awarded in *Muchenje*. Taking into account the rate of inflation, an equivalent judgment in 1983 would have been US$1 408.96. See also *Ellison* v *Rusike and Anor* HB-40-95 (the plaintiff was awarded Z$12 500 for his illegal arrest and compulsion to pay Z$500 fine to avoid detention and the seizure of his vehicles); *Nheta and Ors* v *Fernandes* HB-29-94 (the plaintiff was awarded Z$10 000 in general damages for malicious arrest and prosecution).

Property
J.N. is also entitled to compensation for the destruction of his property. Among his property destroyed were one table and chair set (US$56.70), one bed (US$70), and the wardrobes for all of his family (three male wardrobes + four female wardrobes = 3 x US$118.62 + 4 x US$88.77 = US$710.94). Altogether, JN's loss of property totals US$126.70 + US$710.94 or US$837.64.

Funeral expenses
JN's dependants are entitled to funeral expenses and loss of support compensation for the death of their breadwinner. A reasonable figure for

JN's family to conduct a proper burial in 1983 would be at the reduced figure of Z$450 or US$452.57 (see the reasoning in Case 1, above).

Loss of support

With respect to loss of support, JN's expectation of working life at the date of his death in 1983 based on his birth date in 1933 was 12.19 years (Koch 316). Annuity for 12 years at 1.5% is 10.908. Family income is Z$125 x 12 = Z$1 500 (Koch 322). Assuming the wife and children's share of his income would be 80% and deducting 5% for contingencies, the family's share of his income would be Z$1 500 x 0.95 x 0.80 = Z$1 140. So the value of loss of support in 1983 would have been Z$1 140 x 10.908 = Z$12 425.12 or US$12 506.

Total damages

Detention	1 408.96
Property	837.64
Funeral Expenses	452.57
Loss of Support	12 506.00
TOTAL	US$15 305.17

CASE 4

Reference Number:	445 X
Name of Deceased:	AN
Sex:	Male
Year of Birth:	1958
Occupation:	Clerk at Sipepa Hospital
Income:	Z$150/month
Political Affiliation:	ZAPU
Dependants:	1 surviving spouse, 2 surviving children (dates of birth: 1977, 1982)
Source of Information:	Brother and hospital staff
Place of Incident:	Sipepa – Tsholotsho

In February 1983 two armed soldiers wearing red berets entered the Sipepa Hospital looking for AN, an ex-ZIPRA. When they found AN, they shot him. AN ran to the police compound for help, but found none. As a result, he bled to death. AN's brother was called to collect the body of AN for burial.

DAMAGES

Funeral expenses

AN's dependants are entitled to funeral expenses and loss of support compensation for the death of their breadwinner. Taking into account the cost of a coffin and the costs of hosting relatives and friends in accordance with local customs and traditions, a reasonable figure for AN's family to conduct a proper burial in 1983 would be at the reduced figure of Z$450 or US$452.57 (see the reasoning of Case 1 above).

Loss of support

With respect to loss of support, AN's expectation of working life at the date of his death in 1983 based on his birth date in 1958 was 32.03 years (Koch 316). Annuity for 32 years at 1.5% is 25.267. Family income is Z$150 x 12 = 1 800 (Koch 322). Assuming the wife and children's share of his income would be 80% and deducting 5% for contingencies, their share of his income would be Z$1 800 x 0.95 x 0.80 = Z$1 368. So the value of loss of support in 1983 would have been Z$1 368 x 25.267 = Z$34 565.26 or US$34 762.28.

Total damages

Funeral Expenses   452.57
Loss of Support   34 762.28
TOTAL   US$ 35 214.85

CASE 5

Reference Number:	637 X
Name of Deceased:	SS
Year of Birth:	1957
Political Affiliation:	ZAPU
Dependants:	1 surviving spouse, 2 surviving children (dates of birth: 1981, 1983), and 1 widowed mother
Source of Information:	Mother
Place of Incident:	Ngamo Kraal – Tsholotsho

In September 1983, SS went to Ngamo Kraal to visit his sister. Soldiers from the 5 Brigade found him, accused him of being at a kraal which was not his home, and shot him dead. The 26-year-old breadwinner SS was survived by his wife, two infant children, and widowed mother.

DAMAGES

Funeral expenses

SS's dependents are entitled to funeral expenses and loss of support compensation for the death of their breadwinner. Taking into account the cost of a coffin and the costs of hosting relatives and friends in accordance with local customs and traditions, a reasonable figure for SS's family to conduct a proper burial in 1983 would be at the reduced figure of Z$450 or US$452.57.

Loss of support

With respect to loss of support, SS's expectation of working life at the date of his death in 1983 based on his birth date in 1957 was 31.21 years (Koch 316). Annuity for 31 years at 1.5% is 24.646. Family income is Z$125 x 12 = Z$1 500 (Koch 322). Assuming the wife and children and widowed mother's share of his income would be 80% and deducting 5% for contingencies, their share of his income would be Z$1 500 x 0.95 x 0.80 = Z$1 140. So the value of loss of support in 1983 would have been $1140 x 24.646 = Z$28 096.44 or US$28 256.59.

Total damages

Funeral Expenses   452.57
Loss of Support   28 256.59
TOTAL   US$28 709.16

CASE 6

Reference Number: 1211 P
Name of Victim: EN
Sex: Female
Year of Birth: 1915
Source of Information: Self
Place of Incident: Tshinu Line – Tsholotsho

EN was resting under a tree in her yard when a group of armed men surrounded her house and jumped her fence. The men wanted information about dissidents. When EN replied that she had none, one of the men cocked his gun and accused her of providing food and shelter for the dissidents. EN then watched as the men set her house and granary on fire. As a result of the fire, EN's family lost a four-piece sofa, 4 beds, 2 gallex radiograms, 1 table, 4 chairs,

7 wardrobes, 7 bags of nyawuthi (a type of grain), 1 bicycle, 7 blankets, and all their kitchenware.

DAMAGES
Inconvenience/Displacement
EN is entitled to general damages for the inconvenience and discomfort that she suffered due to the destruction of her house. In *Tshuma-Matingwende* v *Matare* HB-39-92, the defendant and her thirteen children were illegally evicted from their house by the plaintiff who had only paid for the house in part. The court held that the defendant was not only entitled to damages for unlawful occupation, but to delictual damages of Z$6 000 as well for the inconvenience and discomfort her family had to experience due to the loss of their house. A claim for Z$6 000 here, then, is conservative because EN could not even recover her house or possessions since they were destroyed in the fire set by the soldiers. Taking into account the rate of inflation, the equivalent judgment in 1983 would have been US$1 465.79.

Property
EN is also entitled to compensation for loss of property. Among her property destroyed: a homestead which, for a family of seven, includes at least 4 huts (4 x US$174.26 = US$697.04); 1 granary (US$90.41); 1 four-piece sofa (US$300); 4 beds (4 x US$70 = US$280); 2 radios (2 x US$50 = US$100); 1 bicycle (US$65); 7 blankets (7 x US$6 = $42); 7 wardrobes (3 male wardrobes + 4 female wardrobes = 3 x US$118.62 + 4 x US$88.77 = US$710.94); 7 bags of nyawuthi (7 x US$25 = US$175); and kitchenware valued at US$131.91.

Total damages
Inconvenience/Displacement	1 465.79
Property	2 392.21
TOTAL	US$ 3 858.00

CASE 7

Reference Number:	1255 P
Name of Victim:	PS
Sex:	Male
Year of Birth:	1952
Source of information:	Self
Place of Incident:	Kalane Line – Tsholotsho

PS was forced to watch as soldiers set his property on fire. Among PS's belongings destroyed in the fire: 6 houses, 2 granaries, 4 beds, 1 sewing machine, a four-piece sofa, 1 centre table, 4 side tables, 2 bicycles, 1 wheelbarrow, 2 ploughs, 15 bags of maize, 30 bags of nyawuthi, 12 bags of sorghum, 9 bags of monkey nuts, 4 bags of groundnuts (peanuts), 2 bags of beans, clothing for 7, blankets for 7, 2 pressing irons, 1 harrow, 2 shovels, and 2 picks.

DAMAGES
Inconvenience/displacement
PS is entitled to general damages for the inconvenience and discomfort that he suffered due to the destruction of his house. A claim for Z$6 000 here as awarded in *Tshuma-Matingwende* v *Matare*, HB-39-92, is conservative because PS could not even recover his house or possessions since they were destroyed in the fire set by the soldiers. Taking into account the rate of inflation, the equivalent judgment in 1983 would have been US$1 465.79.

Property
PS is also entitled to compensation for the destruction of his property: 6 houses (6 x US$174.26 = US$1045.56), 2 granaries (2 x US$90.41 = US$180.81), 4 beds (4 x US$70 = US$280), a four-piece sofa (US$300), 1 sewing machine (US$150), 1 centre table (US$20), 4 side tables (4 x US$5 = US$20), 2 bicycles (2 x US$65 = US$130), 1 wheelbarrow (US$48), 2 ploughs (2 x US$62 = US$124), 15 bags of maize (15 x US$14.50 = US$217.50), 30 bags of nyawuthi (30 x US$25 = US$750), 12 bags of sorghum (12 x US$24 = US$288), 9 bags of monkey nuts (9 x US$24 = US$216), 4 bags of groundnuts (4 x US$30 = US$120), 2 bags of beans (2 x US$30 = US$60), 3 male wardrobes (3 x US$118.62 = US$355.86), 4 female wardrobes (4 x US$88.77 = US$355.08), 7 blankets (7 x US$6 = US$42), 2 pressing irons (2 x US$7.11 = US$14.22), 1 harrow (US$1.53), 2 shovels (2 x US$8.50 = US$17), and 2 picks (2 x US$8.43 = US$16.86), All together, the value of his property destroyed was US$4 752.42.

Total damages
Inconvenience/displacement   1465.79
Property   4 752.42
TOTAL   US$6 218.21

CASE 8

Reference Number:	1714 ASP
Name of Victim:	ST
Sex:	Male
Year of Birth:	1931
Source of Information:	Self
Place of Incident:	Hlabekisa Line – Tsholotsho

On February 11 1983, five armed men approached ST for information regarding the whereabouts of dissidents. When ST said that he had not seen any dissidents, he was instructed by a soldier to open the doors of his houses for inspection. Upon entering one of the houses with ST, the soldiers struck ST with a stick across his shoulders. They then forced him and his sister to lie flat on the floor. One soldier continued to beat ST and his sister, while the other soldiers searched the other houses. Only when the search was completed did the beatings cease; ST and his sister were then released to watch the soldiers set their family's three houses on fire. Among their property destroyed in the fire: a three-piece sofa, a bed, a radiogram, nine suitcases, and all the family's clothing. As a result of the beating, moreover, ST lost his two front teeth, can no longer bend his right index finger, and suffers persistent pains in his left hip.

DAMAGES
Beating

ST is entitled to compensation for the beating he suffered. General damages would be awarded for pain, suffering, shock, loss of dignity, disfigurement, discomfort and disability. ST's case resembles that of the plaintiff's in *Joseph* v *Esterhuizen* (referred to above, in Case No 1). ST, like Mr Joseph, suffered serious blows to his head (lost teeth) and torso. ST's case is even stronger, though, because he was beaten with a weapon. An award of Z$20 000 in general damages is thus a minimum amount which ST would be entitled to. Taking into account the rate of inflation, ST's claim in 1983 would have been equivalent to US$3 828.25. See also *Chadwich* v *Chard,* also referred to in Case 1; *Bhebhe and Anor* v *Mukhomi and Anor* HB-9-93 (plaintiff awarded $13 000 for 5% permanent disability of a dislocated right hip from a traffic accident); *Munro* v *National Employers Insurance Co Ltd* – Durban and Coast Local Division 6 December 1988 (plaintiff awarded R50 000 for severe pain, disfigurement, and future operation for complications from hip replacements).

Property
As for the destruction of his property, ST may claim US$1 209.17 in compensation: 3 homes (3 x US$174.26 = US$522.78), a three-piece sofa (US$225), 1 bed (US$70), a radio (US$50), 9 suitcases (9 x $18 = US$162), 1 male wardrobe (US$118.62), and 1 female wardrobe (US$88.77).

Inconvenience/discomfort
ST is also entitled to general damages for the inconvenience and discomfort that he suffered due to the destruction of his house. A claim for Z$6 000 here, as was awarded in *Tshuma-Matingwende* v *Matare* above, is conservative because H could not even recover his house or possessions since they were destroyed in the fire set by the soldiers. Taking into account the rate of inflation, the equivalent judgment in 1983 would have been US$1 465.79.

Total damages
Inconvenience/displacement	1 465.79
Beating	3 828.25
Property	1237.17
TOTAL	US$ 6 531.21

CASE 9

Reference Number:	1342 AS
Name of Victim:	LFM
Year of Birth:	1918
Source of Information:	Self
Place of Incident:	Tshabanda School – Tsholotsho

On 4 July 1983, a group of armed Shona-speaking men wearing combat uniform and red berets entered the town of Tshabanda and forced all its residents into the compound of the local primary school. The villagers were instructed to lie down on the ground and were subsequently beaten with sticks. After they were beaten, those who could walk returned home while those who could not were carried away by relatives. A month later, the same brigade of men returned. They approached LFM demanding to know the whereabouts of his son-in-law. When LFM asked which son-in-

law they were referring to, LFM was accused of brewing beer for dissidents and beaten.

After the beating, the 65-year-old LFM was left for dead. A neighbour treated LFM with warm water and helped him back to his house. LFM cannot afford hospital care and suffers today from a total loss of hearing, continuous headaches and persistent coughing.

DAMAGES

Beating

LFM is entitled to compensation for the beating he suffered. General damages would be awarded for pain, suffering, shock, loss of dignity, disfigurement, discomfort and disability. LFM's case resembles that of the plaintiff's in *Joseph* v *Esterhuizen* (referred to in Case 1). LFM, like Mr Joseph, was severely beaten. LFM's case is even stronger, though, because he was beaten with a weapon. An award of Z$20 000 in general damages is thus a minimum amount which LFM would be entitled to. Taking into account the rate of inflation, LFM's claim in 1983 would have been equivalent to US$3 810.43. See also *Chadwich* v *Chard* (referred to in Case 1).

Loss of hearing

LFM may also receive compensation for the total loss of hearing he suffers as a result of the beating. In *Nyathi* v *Tshalibe* H-B-158-88, the plaintiff received Z$2 200 in general damages for deafness in one ear caused by a succession of blows during an assault. Taking into account the rate of inflation, LFM's claim in 1983 would have been equivalent to US$1 228.65. See also *Baso* v *Minister of Police and Anor* 1969 (Eastern Cape), where the plaintiff was awarded R400 for shock, pain and suffering, and R700 for loss of amenities for the rupture of one ear drum.

Total damages

Beating	3 810.43
Loss of Hearing	1 228.65
TOTAL	US$ 5 039.08

CASE 10

Reference Number:	1697 TP
Name of Victim:	AS
Sex:	Male

Year of Birth:	1950
Occupation:	Veterinary Assistant
Political Affiliation:	ZIPRA
Source of Information:	Self
Place of Incident:	Nyamandlovu – Tsholotsho

AS was at home in Zimdabuli Resettlement Scheme when the army entered the town. For four days, AS witnessed atrocities committed by the army. After his father failed to return home one day and after seeing, among other things, his neighbour killed, AS left the area and went to Bulawayo to report the army's activities to his superiors at the regional veterinary offices. He stayed in Bulawayo for two months before he was sent to Nyamandlovu by his superiors to provide veterinary services to the Cold Storage Commission (CSC). In August of 1985, CIO agents picked up AS and accused him of being a dissident. He was ordered to dig up weapons they alleged he had buried in the cattle quarantine camp of the CSC. When AS explained that he was not a dissident and knew of no firearms buried in the quarantine camp, the CIO agents commenced a program of beatings and systematic water torture in which AS's head was stuffed in a sack of water to bring him to the brink of death by suffocation, often rendering him unconscious. After three days of beatings and water torture, AS was released. He went immediately to Mpilo, the Government hospital in Bulawayo, to be treated for his physical wounds. AS, however, still suffers from acute back pain and spasms incurred from the CIO torture and beatings. The CIO torture and beatings also traumatised AS such that he remained afraid to return home for three years. When he did return in 1988, he found the windows of his home smashed and all his furniture stolen.

DAMAGES

Detention

AS is entitled to general damages for his two-day detention in the bush. A figure of Z$9 000 is suggested, on the same basis as Case 3 above. Taking into account the rate of inflation, the equivalent judgment in 1985 would have been US$1 167.07

Beating

In addition to being detained, AS was also beaten and tortured, for which general damages would be awarded. See *Joseph* v *Esterhuizen* HB-46-93 where Z$20 000 was awarded. Taking into account the rate of inflation, AS's claim in 1985 would have been equivalent to US$3 171.10. See also *Chadwich* v *Chard* HH-262-91 above.

Total damages

Detention	1 167.07
Beating	3171.10
TOTAL	US$ 4 338.17

5. CONCLUSION

These case studies, though illustrative, do not permit one to make any meaningful extrapolation of overall damages. There is a huge number of variables, even among the ten case studies. The statistical summaries in Part Two, III, and even the village by village summaries, are too sparse to allow the detailed case studies to be applied without further particulars. Further, the village by village summaries were confined to two areas: Tsholotsho and Matobo. Military activity and, it would seem, atrocities took place in other areas which are not examined in any detail in this report. Without such detailed examination, it would be quite impossible to even guess at the level of damages. Nonetheless, it is clear that the overall damages would be an enormous figure. For example, these ten case studies alone could have resulted in compensation being paid in the sum of US$ 190 515.60 or Z$ 1 964 215 (at 1996 exchange rates).

Extrapolation/suppositionary

While the following extrapolation is of academic interest only, what is apparent is that the violence which occurred in Matabeleland and the Midlands, which this report only partially documents, has cost surviving civilian victims hundreds of millions of Zimbabwean dollars.

This report estimates no fewer than 3 000 deaths: if conservative loss of support for dependants is assumed at US$ 10 000 and funeral expenses are assumed at US$ 450 in all cases, US$ 31 350 000 could be claimed by families of the deceased.

This report has estimated 7 000 cases of beatings: if conservative damages of US$3 500 were assumed to apply in all these cases, US$ 24 500 000 could have been claimed, by beating victims alone.

This report has estimated 10 000 detentions: if conservative damages of US$ 1 000 were assumed to apply in all these cases, US$ 10 000 000 could have been claimed, by detainees.

This report has estimated no fewer than 680 burnt homesteads: if conservative damages in lost property of US$2 000 and US$ 1400 for inconvenience/displacement were assumed to apply in all cases, US$2 312 000 could have been claimed by families who lost homesteads.

The suppositionary damages listed above, which is far from a complete listing of likely damage suffered in the 1980s disturbances, already add up to US$ 68 162 000, or Z$ 661 125 000 at current estimated exchange rates.

APPENDIX A
CONSUMER PRICE INDEX (CPI)
Source: Quarterly Digest of Statistics, Central Statistics Office

Year	CPI
1980	100
1981	113,1
1982	125,2
1983	154,1
1984	185,2
1985	200,9
1986	229,7
1987	258,3
1988	277,5
1989	313,3
1990	362,1
1991	445,5
1992	634,4
1993	809,7
1994	989,9
1995	1184,4
1996	1480,5

APPENDIX B
EXCHANGE RATE (June)
Source: Quarterly Guide to Economy, First Merchant Bank of Zimbabwe Limited

Year	US$	Rand
1983	1,0057	1,1011
1984	0,8425	1,1338
1985	0,6390	1,2587
1986	0,5754	1,4356
1987	0,5972	1,2211
1988	0,5617	1,2603
1989	0,4644	0,7589
1990	0,4084	0,9276
1991	03016	1,1172
1992	0,2017	0,5588
1993	0,1529	0,3088
1994	0,1230	0,4483
1995	0,1170	
1996	0,1031	

III

HUMAN REMAINS –
RECOMMENDATIONS ON
POSSIBLE RECOVERY

Interviews with civilians resident in Matabeleland North and South made it clear not only that there are mass graves in these parts of Zimbabwe as a result of the 1980s disturbances, but also that this is an issue of concern to residents and affected families. It is also known that there are likely to be unrecovered bodies in the Midlands. The full nature and causes of the disturbances have been covered elsewhere in this report. This section will therefore concentrate on the likely types of human remains at this point and how best to deal with them.

1. "DEAD" AND "MISSING"

In this report, people are referred to as "Dead" if their deaths were witnessed. In most cases in Matabeleland North, this also means that what happened to their remains is known, even if all that is known is that the bodies were taken away on trucks. While the current location of the remains of the "Dead" is often known in Matabeleland North, this is less often the case in Matabeleland South.

"Missing" refers in most cases to people who were known to have been taken from their homes at night in mysterious circumstances, or known to have been detained, and never seen again. There is no indication in these cases as to where bodies might now be.

As the vast majority of victims can be classified as Dead rather than Missing, the possibility of identifying and recovering human remains for many victims is positive. In this Zimbabwe is more "fortunate" than Argentina for example, where approximately 10 000 disappeared, or Guatemala, where 50 000 people have disappeared in recent decades.

The recovery and identification of those who died in the 1980s might also be more easily accomplished than for those who died in the 1970s civil war in what was then Rhodesia, as many of these victims went missing outside of the country, or were killed and buried in regions of Zimbabwe far from their own districts. In spite of the difficulties, many victims of the 1970s war have been successfully recovered and reburied in the years since Independence, and the reburial exercise continues.

The establishing of a pre-mortem data base on all Missing victims, containing as much physical information on each victim as possible, would dramatically improve chances of identification. The structure of the computer data base currently used in Argentina could be adapted to the Zimbabwean situation.

2. THE BEARING OF PERPETRATOR ON BODY DISPOSAL

Murders in the 1980s were perpetrated by both Government agencies and dissidents. The case studies in Part Two illustrate that approximately 98 per cent of deaths and disappearances in the communal lands were at the hands of Government agencies, and 2 per cent were murders by dissidents. In Tsholotsho, for example, 18 murders by dissidents were claimed by civilians, while a further 900+ deaths and disappearances, mainly perpetrated by 5 Brigade, were identified, most occurring in February 1983.

In addition to murders in communal lands, dissidents murdered people living in the sparsely populated commercial farming areas. Approximately 70 deaths in these regions were at the hands of dissidents, not government agencies.

Dissidents would typically murder one or two civilians in the communal lands in any one incident, almost invariably people they believed to be sell-outs. The victims would be murdered and the dissidents would then make a hasty departure before the authorities arrived. This meant that families of victims were able to give their deceased traditional burials.

Other dissident victims were typically commercial farmers and their families or employees, who would also be murdered in hit-and-run raids or ambushes. These victims, too, would be left behind and were accorded proper funerals. There are a few notable exceptions here, namely the six tourists who were abducted and buried in shallow graves, in July 1982. There was also an abduction of two commercial farmers in Bubi, one of whose remains were only recovered years later. Such cases of abduction were not common. In both these cases, the remains were ultimately recovered and identified.

Those in mass graves, and those who were not given decent burials are the civilians killed by state agencies, in particular 5 Brigade. Part Two, III, indicates 1 437 killings and 354 disappearances in which the names of victims are known. Of these, 1 134 deaths and 169 disappearances were perpetrated by 5 Brigade.

These figures are known by researchers to be incomplete, with substantial indications on record of large numbers of dead in areas not extensively researched for this report, in particular in Lupane and Nkayi, where mass graves and bodies in mine shafts have been reported. Matabeleland South, including Matobo, Gwanda and Bulilimamangwe, also have mass graves and reports of bodies down mine shafts.

3. DISPOSAL OF BODIES

It has been previously stated in this report that it was a characteristic of 5 Brigade to insist that there was no mourning for the dead. In some cases the family of the dead victims were themselves shot because they wept. It was also characteristic, particularly of the early weeks of 1983, for victims to be buried in mass graves. In some cases, 5 Brigade would shoot people and pass on with no concern for what happened to the dead, and in these cases, families were able to bury their own dead, although full burial rites and full attendance by family members were not possible because of the prevailing conditions in those weeks. This part of the report will concern itself with cases in which no proper burial took place. The way in which bodies were disposed of in such cases can be categorised as follows:

• Bodies left where they were killed and burial forbidden.
• Bodies buried in mass or individual graves in villages but not in the culturally accepted place or manner.
• Bodies left inside huts in cases where people were burnt to death in huts.
• Bodies buried in mass or individual graves at 5 Brigade camps.
• Bodies dumped into mine shafts.

4. CHANCES OF RECOVERY IN EACH CATEGORY

A) BURIAL DENIED

In Lupane in particular, but also in parts of Tsholotsho (see Pumula Mission section), burial was on occasion forbidden, and relatives of the dead were reportedly forced to observe the remains of their dead rotting away and being scavenged. In these cases, bones were sometimes buried months or years later, and in other cases, bones were removed by the 5 Brigade, who came past in trucks and collected them. In cases where bones were removed by 5 Brigade, chances of recovery now are almost non-existent.

B) MASS GRAVES

There are reports of mass graves throughout most of Matabeleland North and South. Compilers of this report personally visited a few such sites. Photographs and video clippings also exist of these graves. What is notable is the careful way in which these graves have been demarcated by civilians in the area: they have often been fenced off with logs, or covered with boulders. In some cases most or all of the actual victims in a grave are still known to those in the area, and in other cases, those buried were strangers to the area, and are completely unknown. In most cases, victims in mass graves were shot dead.

If it was the will of affected communities, relatives of the deceased and the authorities, such graves would provide ideal sites for forensic investigations. The possibility of identifying at least some, or even all, of the victims in such cases would be extremely high. It would also be likely that cause of death could be established.

C) PEOPLE BURIED UNDER HUTS

There are several incidents of people burnt to death in huts in Tsholotsho, and also reports that this happened in Lupane. In Tsholotsho, there are on record, nine cases where people were burnt to death in huts (see Pumula Mission section). Numbers of victims ranged from one to 30, with at least two villages experiencing hut burnings involving large numbers of people. These bodies were not removed from the huts, but were given a makeshift burial where they lay, with soil being mounded over the remains, and the area then being fenced. It is not clear how many hut burnings resulting in deaths happened in Lupane, although at least two are on current records.

If it was the will of affected communities, relatives of the deceased and the authorities, these hut sites would also provide ideal cases for forensic investigation, although cause of death can be harder to establish in the case of burnings (see "cause of death" following).

D) GRAVES IN 5 BRIGADE CAMPS

Those detained at Bhalagwe in Matobo report the existence of burial grounds within the camp. Ex-detainees, particularly from the early weeks, report the daily digging of graves as one of their chores. Almost every interview about Bhalagwe alludes to daily deaths in the camp, as a result of beatings or shootings. Who victims were is not clear, nor exact numbers (see previous discussion in part Two, III for more details).

However, it seems clear that some, if not all, of the graves at Bhalagwe were dug up and the bodies removed, while the camp was still in operation.

The policy of disposing of bodies changed, or became supplemented within a few weeks, with the throwing of bodies down mine shafts. Visits to Bhalagwe in November of 1996 showed the grave sites to have been dug up, although the position of the graves is still clearly visible. Eye witnesses involved in the burial procedure recount how at the time of burial, bodies were covered with asbestos sheeting before the soil was added, and then further sheeting demarcated the graves clearly. Pieces of this sheeting are still in the now-empty graves. This could suggest that the graves were only ever intended as a temporary measure, and were designed in such a way as to facilitate later identification of the sites and removal of the bodies. Certainly, the use of the asbestos sheeting is not a normal burial procedure in Zimbabwe, nor was it used in Matabeleland North, where people had been murdered by 5 Brigade the previous year.

E) MINE SHAFTS

There are reports of human remains in mine shafts in both Matabeleland North and South, though these are more common in Matabeleland South where such shafts abound. In two instances in the 1990s, human remains have been found in mine shafts. In the first instance, they were found in Old Hat Mine No. 2, in Silobela in the Midlands, and remains were also found at Antelope Mine, near Bhalagwe camp in Matobo. Interviews on record, both archivally and recently, refer to the nightly departure of trucks from Bhalagwe, taking away bodies. Accounts by villagers living near the mine confirm that this was the destination.

Those interviewed in Matabeleland South also mentioned Legion Mine, near Sun Yet Sen in the far south of Matobo, as a possible site for the dumping of bodies. Sun Yet Sen was used as an interrogation and detention centre by 5 Brigade in 1983 and 1984.

Bones were found in Old Hat Mine in 1992, and CCJP attended their exhumation. Unfortunately, this was not done by forensic anthropologists, and the bones were disturbed by the police, thus destroying potential evidence. The identification of eight individuals was possible, two women and six men, but their precise identification was not possible.

Bodies of guerrillas are known to have been thrown down mine shafts in the 1970s by the Rhodesian army and the first response of the government to finds in the 1990s was that these were Rhodesian victims. However, post-Independence minted coins found in the pockets of the deceased, dated the remains in Antelope Mine to the 1980s.

It is unlikely that positive identification of particular victims would be possible if bones were exhumed from mine shafts. This is a consequence of the fact that so little is known about precisely who was dumped into particular shafts. However, such exhumation could be important in terms of validating historical claims. Evidence of peri-mortem trauma (i.e. trauma at point of death) might be detectable on the remains. Items such as coins could also help date time of dumping. It is not unlikely that any extensive exploration of mine shafts would also result in the exhumation of victims from the 1970s, although again, precise identification of victims would be difficult.

5. REGIONAL DIFFERENCES IN BODY DISPOSAL

There seem to be regional differences in body disposal between Matabeleland North and South. In 1983, killings in Matabeleland North were more open and the repression was generally more visible, but in 1984 in Matabeleland South the *modus operandi* became more clandestine, with victims more frequently dying in 5 Brigade camps than in the village setting. There were also fewer killings in 1984.

The disposal of bodies seems to reflect this change in strategy. In 1983 in Matabeleland North, bodies were more commonly disposed of in individual or mass graves in or near villages, or inside burnt huts. At the end of 1983 and in 1984 in Matabeleland South, bodies were disposed of in mine shafts and mass graves located inside 5 Brigade camps, in particular at Bhalagwe, but also at Sitezi and other bases.

The change in body disposal suggests that the 5 Brigade *modus operandi* deliberately became more secretive in 1984 than it had been in 1983, particularly where killings were concerned. This change in strategy might have been related to growing pressure from local and international press and human rights groups, including from CCJP who were operating within the country, and had made several appeals to Government by this stage. This observation might be modified in the light of future evidence.

To summarise the regional differences:
Burials forbidden are reported to date only in Matabeleland North.
Mass graves in village settings are reported in all districts, but are more common in Matabeleland North.
Hut burnings resulting in deaths have to date only been reported in Matabeleland North, mainly from western Tsholotsho and Lupane.
Deaths in 5 Brigade camps are reported in all areas, but in Matabeleland North such deaths are not common: method of disposal in

Matabeleland North is also not clear. In Matabeleland South, deaths and temporary burials mainly at Bhalagwe and also at camps in Gwanda and Bulilimamangwe are reported.

Mine shaft disposal is reported mainly in Matabeleland South, but there are also reports of this in Matabeleland North.

6. OBJECTIVES OF EXHUMATION AND RECOVERY OF HUMAN REMAINS

Exhumation assists the relatives of the victims in their right to recover the remains of their dead or missing loved ones, so that they can carry out the customary funeral rights and mourn their dead. Families and affected communities may see the procedure of identification of their dead, or even the willingness to attempt this, as a necessary step towards their own emotional healing. Exhumation can provide physical evidence to help in the historical reconstruction of events, and to validate one version of events over another. Forensic investigations can end historical controversies.

The evidence can be used in court if necessary.

National awareness and acknowledgment of events would follow revelations from the exhumations, which could further help the process of healing for survivors.

A) CAUSE OF DEATH

Forensic anthropologists only deal with skeletal remains. Therefore, if the cause of death did not affect the skeleton, then there is no way of establishing the cause of death with certainty. For example, in cases of hut burnings, it may well be that not all, or even none, of the skeletons will show signs of burning. However, some hut burnings were allegedly accompanied by shooting of victims trying to escape, in which case there might be skeletal evidence of bullet wounds. There will also be circumstantial evidence, such as testimonial evidence and the finding of burned elements associated with the remains, such as charred clothing.

Fatal gunshot wounds are likely to involve human bones, particularly shots to the head or thorassic regions, which is where fatal gun shot wounds are typically found. However, shots to the abdominal region will not necessarily cause skeletal damage, and can cause death.

B) IDENTIFICATION OF HUMAN REMAINS

The process of identification of victims is a physical one. Physical or pre-mortem information about the victims when they were alive (such as height, age, dental records) and peri-mortem information relating to the time of their death obtained from those who witnessed their death, can be compared with exhumed skeletal remains. For example, if a certain person was witnessed to die from a shot to a particular part of the body, and a skeleton shows corresponding damage, this helps differentiate this victim's skeleton from others in the same grave.

In cases where there are no existing dental records for victims, and no witnesses to help with precise causes of death, it is very difficult to identify bodies. Bodies exhumed from 5 Brigade camps and bodies from mine shafts would have a poor chance of positive identification, as there are no witnesses who can say with certainty who was buried where.

In the case of bodies in mass graves and burnt huts, the prospect of identification is high, as names of victims are largely known already, and deaths were witnessed. There should be good peri-mortem or circumstantial evidence to confirm cause of deaths.

7. FORENSIC ANTHROPOLOGY AND HUMAN RIGHTS INVESTIGATIONS – A BRIEF HISTORY AND OUTLINE

Forensic sciences are a group of interrelated disciplines which utilise different scientific methods to analyse physical evidence related to legal cases. When working on legal cases involving skeletal remains, forensic anthropology is among the main disciplines involved. Considering the time elapsed and the condition of burial sites recently observed, forensic investigation could be useful in Zimbabwe.

Forensic anthropology consists of the application of methods and techniques from physical anthropology and forensic medicine to legal cases in which skeletal or mainly skeletonised remains are involved. It is considered a branch of physical anthropology.[1] The physical anthropologist applies his/her knowledge about how bodies vary over time and place to a legal or forensic context. There are several other disciplines involved in this task. In order to recover the remains in the proper way, the use of forensic archaeology is crucial. This simply consists of the "application of standard archaeological techniques slightly modified to meet the requirements of crime scene processing where a skeleton(s) or buried body(ies) is present."[2] Other skills involved are forensic pathology, odontology, ballistics, radiology and genetics, among others.

The use of forensic anthropology in the investigation of human rights violations started in Argentina in 1984. Argentina returned to democracy in December 1983. The newly elected President Dr Raul Alfonsin, created the National Commission on the Disappearance of Persons (CONADEP). The Commission established that at least 10 000 people had been disappeared under the previous military regime (1976–83). Bodies had been dumped from aeroplanes into the sea, illegally cremated or buried in anonymous graves in cemeteries.

In order to ensure impartiality and expertise, a group of American forensic scientists under the leadership of Dr Clyde Snow was assembled, and several forensic teams in South America were trained over the next ten years. These are the Guatemalan Forensic Anthropology Team, the Chilean Forensic Anthropology Team and the Argentinean Forensic Team. In the USA, the Physicians for Human Rights and the American Association for the Advancement of Sciences (AAAS) continue to promote and assemble teams of experts for specific missions. They work internationally in interdisciplinary teams, as expert witnesses or international consultants invited by local judiciaries, or by intergovernmental bodies such as the United Nations War Tribunals and the United Nations Commissions of Inquiry, to help resolve human rights issues. These teams of forensic anthropologists are all non governmental and non-profit making.

Since 1984, forensic anthropology has been used in investigations in Argentina, Chile, Brazil, Bolivia, Colombia, Venezuela, El Salvador, Guatemala, Panama, Honduras, Haiti, Mexico, The Philippines, Iraqi Kurdistan, Romania, Croatia, Bosnia, Rwanda and Ethiopia.

Procedure used in forensic anthropological investigations:

A) PRELIMINARY INVESTIGATION
This involves the gathering of historical information about the case under investigation, including official records, eye witness accounts, etc. Pre-mortem data is also collected: physical information about victims, such as medical and dental records, old X-rays, height, etc. Peri-mortem information is also gathered, that is information on injuries sustained at the time of death.

B) ARCHAEOLOGICAL WORK
The archaeological approach provides a rational way to recover and reconstruct events, ensuring evidence is not damaged, recovery is complete, and that documentation is adequate.

C) LABORATORY ANALYSIS
Using techniques from physical anthropology and medicine, it is possible

to establish stature, sex, age at death, ancestry, pathologies and lesions, dental features, etc, of the exhumed skeletal remains. Pre-mortem and peri-mortem data is then compared with skeletal remains to try to establish their identities. In countries where the affected populations are largely poor with little access to medical and dental check ups and where there is therefore little pre-mortem data, new genetic methods involving the extraction of DNA material from remains and comparing them with DNA material from likely relatives can help identify victims.

8. RECOMMENDATIONS

1. The Will of Affected Communities. It is essential that no steps be taken without consultation with communities and relatives of the deceased. Some may wish for exhumation, while in adjacent areas, others may not, for cultural or personal reasons.
2. Judicial Proceedings. Exhumations should be done through the intervention of judges in order to keep a legal record of the proceedings and findings, even in situations where no legal prosecutions are to follow on findings (such as in Zimbabwe).
3. Exhumations must be professional. There are teams of forensic anthropologists and organisations around the world who are expert at this type of work. They have accomplished successful exhumations in several Latin American countries, and also in the former Yugoslavia, Iraq, Ethiopia and Rwanda, among other places.[3]
4. A short exploratory mission. A first mission by an international forensic team, lasting two or three months, would ideally include different types of cases to fit the categories of human remains listed above. For example, one burnt hut and one mass grave could each be excavated. A mine shaft identified as having a high likelihood of remains could be excavated, and a 5 Brigade camp could be examined.
5. Depository for Human Remains. In cases where exhumed remains are not identified:
   i. establish a general data base in the hope that identification might ultimately be possible, and keep the remains available at a specific centre and under control;
   ii. if it is not possible to keep remains unburied, do not rebury underground, but keep them in an above-ground sepulchre, so that remains will not be affected by the organic activity of the soil. If this is not possible, due to economic or cultural constraints, remains should be reburied in the hardest possible container so that they could be retrieved and re-analysed if necessary.

6. Protection of the sites. Sites should be protected from tampering. Those living close to sites should know who to inform if there is a sudden interest in them.

7. Establishment of a Symbolic Shrine. The existence of a place where the remains of missing or disappeared or unidentified people are buried or commemorated has a symbolic value in many countries. Relatives of victims often express the strong need to have a place where they can remember their loved ones, pray, or follow other cultural practices of mourning. Communities in Zimbabwe may – or may not – decide after consultation that they would like to establish such a shrine, or shrines. The establishment of such public places has, in other countries, implied a social and national recognition of what happened: in Zimbabwe, the current clandestine or abandoned graves do not allow for this. The lack of broader acknowledgment is apparently a source of deep disturbance for the relatives and witnesses of the tragic events. Such a shrine would break the secrecy. The unspeakable, currently limited to secret memories, would be brought out into the realm of historical and social reality.

In summary, the process of exhuming and identifying human remains is one that should aim to show a respectful acknowledgment of events, and to commemorate the suffering of the survivors. The process also serves as a testimony to other sectors of the population and is a reminder to future generations. The suffering of victims and survivors should also be placed in a broader social and historical arena.

NOTES – PART THREE

PART THREE, I
ORGANISED VIOLENCE: ITS IMPLICATIONS

1   Case quoted from CCJP report on torture, presented to Robert Mugabe in January 1987.
2   Presented to the Chihambakwe Committee, March 1984.
3   Presented to the Chihambakwe Committee, March 1984.
4   Presented to the Chihambakwe Committee, March 1984.
5   More than 80% of one Mount Darwin sample had witnessed torture, and 60% had witnessed an execution.
6   CCJP has a video and a book of this name, documenting the plight of civilians in the 1970s.
7   Some workers in the field have defined differing types of trauma-related disorders, and are investigating the likelihood of a "torture" syndrome discrete from other types of PTSD, but this debate will not be explored here.
8   For the same reason, published data on Zimbabwe war veterans has not been used in this chapter.
9   This perception is explored in Part One, III.
10 Numerous statements on record show this perception, as do comments in Werbner's book, op cit.
11 Further studies into effects of particular words on PTSD sufferers show key words can interfere with cognitive activity: eg "bodybag" produces a response in Vietnam vets, while "germs" does not: McNally *et al*, 1990.

PART THREE, I
REFERENCE LIST

Allodi, F (1980): "The psychiatric effects in children and families of victims of political persecution and torture", *Danish Medical Bulletin*, 27, 229-32.

APA (1980): *The Diagnostic and Statistical Manual of Mental Disorders*, 3 ed, New York: American Psychiatric Association.

APA (1987): *The Diagnostic and Statistical Manual of Mental Disorders*, 3 ed (rev), New York: American Psychiatric Association.

Baker, R (1993): "Psychosocial consequences for tortured refugees seeking asylum and refugee status in Europe", in Basoglu, M (ed): *Torture and Its Consequences: Current Treatment Approaches*, Cambridge: Cambridge University Press.

Danieli, Y (1988): "Confronting the Unimaginable: Psychotherapists' reactions to victims of the Nazi Holocaust", in Wilson, JP, Harel, Z & Kahana, B (eds): *Human Adaptation to Extreme Stress*, New York: Plenum.

Dawes, A (1994): "The Emotional Impact of Political Violence", in Dawes, A & Donald, D (eds): *Childhood and Adversity*, Cape Town: David Philip.

Feinstein, A & Dolan, R (1991): "Predictors of post-traumatic stress disorder: An examination of the stress criterion", *Psychological Medicine*, 21, 85-91.

Genefke, IK (1982): "Morbidity spectrum amongst torture victims", *Acta Neurologica Scandinavica*, 65, 320.

Gorst-Unsworth, C, Van Velsen, C & Turner, S (1993): "Prospective pilot study of survivors of torture and organised violence: Examining the existential dilemma", *Journal of Nervous and Mental Disorders*, 181, 263-64.

Haedi, L & Szilagyi, J (1993): "Holocaust survivors and their descendants", Paper presented to VI International Symposium on Torture as a Challenge to Doctors and Other Health Professionals, Buenos Aires, October 1993.

Jacobsen, L & Vesti, P (1992): *Torture Survivors: A new group of patients,* Copenhagen: IRCT.

Juhler, M (1991): "Diagnosis and Treatment of Torture Survivors" in *The International Handbook of Traumatic Stress Syndrome.*

Kulka, RA, et al (1988): *National Vietnam Veterans Readjustment Study (NVVRS): Description, current status, and initial PTSD estimates,* Research Triangle Park, NC, Research Triangle Institute.

Michelson, CL (1994): "Township violence, levels of distress, and post-traumatic stress disorder, among displacees from Natal", *Psychology in Society,* 18, 47-56.

Mupinda, M (1995): "Loss and Grief among the Shona: The Meaning of Disappearances", Paper presented to VII International Symposium on Torture as a Challenge to the Medical Profession, Cape Town, November 1996.

McNally, R (1993): "Psychopathology of post-traumatic stress disorder (PTSD): Boundaries of the syndrome", in Basoglu, M (ed): *Torture and Its Consequences: Current Treatment Approaches,* Cambridge: Cambridge University Press.

Psychiatric Association of Zimbabwe (1991): *Regional Workshop Report on the Consequences of Organised Violence in Southern Africa,* Harare: PAZ.

Psychiatric Association of Zimbabwe (1990): *Report on an International Conference on The Consequences of Organised Violence in Southern Africa,* Harare: PAZ.

Ramsay, R, Gorst-Unsworth, C & Turner, SW (1993): "Psychiatric morbidity in survivors of organized state violence including torture: A retrospective series", *British Journal of Psychiatry,* 162, 55-59.

Rassmussen, OV (1990): "Medical Aspects of Torture: Torture types and their relation to symptoms and lesions in 200 victims, followed by a description of the medical profession in relation to torture", *Danish Medical Bulletin, 37,* 1-88.

Rassmussen, OV & Lunde, I (1980): "Evaluation of 200 torture victims", *Danish Medical Bulletin, 27,* 241-43.

Reeler, AP (1995): "Community-based care of survivors: The AMANI experience in Mount Darwin, Zimbabwe", paper presented to VII International Symposium on Torture as a Challenge to the Medical Profession, Cape Town, 14-17 November 1995.

Reeler, AP (1995): *Assessment of the Consequences of Torture and Organised Violence: A manual for field workers,* Harare: AMANI.

Reeler, AP (1995): "Surviving Torture: A Zimbabwean Experience", in Irmler, D (ed): *Old Ways – New Theories: Traditional and Contemporary Family Therapy Connect in Africa,* Harare: CONNECT.

Reeler, AP (1991): "Psychological disorders in primary care and the development of clinical services: An African perspective", *The Psychologist*, 4, 349-53.

Reeler, AP (1986): "Psychological disorders in Africa I: Issues of Prevalence", *Central African Journal of Medicine*, 32, 298-303.

Reeler, AP and Mupinda, M (1995): "Community-based rehabilitation for survivors of organised violence: Some preliminary findings", Paper presented to an International Conference on Mental Health in Africa: A Multidisciplinary Approach, Harare, 3-7 April 1995.

Reeler, AP and Todd, CH (1995): "An overview of psychological disorders and psychiatric services in Zimbabwe", in Pillay, Y and Bhana, A (eds): *Proceedings of a Primary Mental Health Care Workshop*, Durban: University of Durban-Westville.

Reeler, AP, Williams, H & Todd, CH (1993): "Psychopathology in Primary Care patients: A four-year study in rural and urban settings", *Central African Journal of Medicine*, 39, 1-8.

Ruy-Peres, S. (1996): "Celebrating the 10th Anniversary of CINTRAS", *Torture*, 6, 98-99.

Sarantidis, D et al (1996): "Long-term effects of torture of victims during the period of dictatorship in Greece", *Torture*, 6, 16-19.

Shay, R (1996): "Shattered Lives", *Networker*, 46-54.

Solomon, Z et al (1989): "Delayed onset PTSD among Israeli veterans of the 1982 Lebanon war", *Psychiatry*, 52, 428-36.

Somasundaram, DJ & Sivayokan, S (1994): "War trauma in a civilian population", *British Journal of Psychiatry*, 165, 524-27.

Somnier, R & Genefke, IK (1986): "Psychotherapy for victims of torture", *British Journal of Psychiatry*, 149, 323-29.

Straker, G (1993): "Exploring the effects of interacting with survivors of trauma", *Journal of Social Development in Africa*, 8, 33-47.

Straker, G (1987): "The continuous traumatic stress syndrome – the single therapeutic interview", *Psychology in Society*, 8, 48-78.

Terr, L (1983): "Chowchilla revisited: The effects of psychic trauma four years after a school-bus kidnapping", *American Journal of Psychiatry*, 140, 1543-50.

Turner, SW (1993): "Exploring the limitations of the anxiety concept in work with survivors of repressive violence", *Torture*, Supp No., 19-21.

Turner, SW & Gorst-Unsworth, C (1990): "Psychological sequelae of torture, a descriptive model", *British Journal of Psychiatry*, 157, 475-80.

PART THREE, II
LEGAL DAMAGES

1   Commission Report, pp 1–7 and 85 can be found as Appendix C I.

PART THREE, III
HUMAN REMAINS

1   Stewart, TD: *Essentials of Forensic Anthropology*, Charles Thomas Publisher, Springfield, Illinois.
2   Morse, D et al: "Forensic Archaeology" in Buikstra and Radhnoum (eds): *Human Identification*, 1980.
3   See final section of this chapter for more on these teams.

PART FOUR
RECOMMENDATIONS

"Peace is not the absence of tension; it is the presence of justice."

Martin Luther King

This report is not simply a history of what happened in Matabeleland North, South and Midlands provinces between 1982 and 1988. Parts Two and Three of the report catalogue the present, continuing suffering of victims. It is not merely a report about the dead; it outlines the legacy of war that still has to be endured by the living. In certain respects the history is irrelevant: both the victims and the perpetrators already know what happened. To that extent all the historical aspect of this report does is bring their existing knowledge to the attention of the wider community, to the attention of those of us who were not directly affected by what happened.

On the surface it would appear as if there is peace in these provinces. It might appear to outsiders that people have forgotten, or at the very least forgiven, what happened years ago. The Unity Accord signed between ZAPU and ZANU PF in 1987 brought about the end of hostilities and people may be excused for thinking that it ushered in true peace. However one does not have to dig deep to find that, not surprisingly, the victims have not forgotten what happened. Some victims have tried to have their story told three to four times. Some gave evidence to the Chihambakwe Commission in 1984, to the New York Lawyers' Committee in 1985, to Bulawayo Legal Projects Centre paralegals in the early 1990s and again, finally, when the detailed case studies were conducted. Thirteen years have gone past and for many the recounting of their tales has to date achieved little.

Some people in Zimbabwe may want to sweep everything that occurred under the carpet; it may be genuinely believed that the injury and hurt has dissipated. The harsh reality is that the Unity Accord did not bring about meaningful reconciliation among the common people of Zimbabwe; the Unity Accord largely brought about an accommodation of interests between political leaders. Thousands of interviews conducted during the research leading to this report revealed that there is still deep-rooted fear, anger and distrust at grassroots of society. The unity accord brought a superficial peace but has not dealt with these innermost emotions.

Interviews also show that the people living in the communal areas in Matabeleland North, South and Midlands provinces have been psychologically crushed. To that extent the military objective expressed by Colonel Dyke has been achieved. It would be foolhardy to think that these people will always feel crushed. The events of the last few years in Bosnia and Sri Lanka are testimony to the fact that unresolved ethnically based conflict can come back to haunt a country years, even decades, later. The horrifying events that have unfolded in Bosnia in the last few years find their roots in ethnic conflict which happened over forty years ago. The conflict that happened then was never resolved satisfactorily and the results were horrific. Accordingly, for very practical reasons, it is vitally important to deal with the emotions of people now before they fester and a monster is created which cannot be controlled in future.

Some may argue that this report will simply reopen wounds and should not see the light of day. It may be argued that this chapter of our history should be buried in the hope that if there is any residual hurt or suffering, that will dissipate over time. This line of argument assumes that wounds have healed or that the residual suffering is minor. But the evidence given by over a thousand witnesses contradicts that notion: the wounds have not healed; indeed many of the wounds are festering and need sunlight and treatment if they are to heal.

It is in this context that Martin Luther King's words referred to above are particularly pertinent. The apparent absence of tension in the region today should not deceive us as a nation. If we desire to bring about true peace and true healing to our nation the events of the 1980s must not be left unattended. It is in the desire to bring about true healing in our nation that we make the following recommendations. By doing so we acknowledge that we do not have a monopoly over wisdom; accordingly these recommendations are not meant to be definitive; they are merely suggestions as to how our nation can move forward and recover from this painful episode.

1. NATIONAL ACKNOWLEDGMENT

The suffering endured by Zimbabweans during the Liberation War was fairly uniform and as a result there is mutual empathy between people throughout Zimbabwe regarding the agony caused during that period. However, the human rights abuses documented in this report were largely confined to three provinces. The remaining provinces in Zimbabwe were untouched. At the time when the people of Matabeleland North, Matabeleland South and Midlands provinces were facing tremendous hardship, people in other provinces were enjoying the fruits of peace. At the same time, because of the curfew and the tight control of the media within Zimbabwe, there was limited reporting on what was actually going on. As a result most people in the remainder of the country do not know what happened during this period. Indeed if they believed the Government line, many people would have been of the view that victims of human rights violations recorded in this report supported insurrection within Zimbabwe and to a certain extent deserved the violence they suffered.

In the circumstances it is not surprising that civilians residing outside Matabeleland North, Matabeleland South and Midlands provinces cannot today begin to understand the true feelings of the victims who still carry the burden of that period with them. Until there is knowledge of what happened throughout Zimbabwe there cannot be genuine empathy for those who suffered; and without empathy there cannot be true reconciliation and nation building.

The problem that we all face, as Zimbabweans, is that of discerning the truth. How is it possible to convey what actually happened to Zimbabweans in affected regions? It is likely the Government will not agree with some of the factual findings of this report and as a result it may question the veracity of its findings. If Government questions the veracity of this report it may object to this report being the last word regarding what actually happened. This however should not deter Zimbabwe as a nation from finding out the truth of what happened. It is vital that the truth be revealed and examined so that the process of reconciliation can begin. What we have to strive to achieve then is to establish the truth in a manner that is acceptable to all. Once we have done so there can be a national acknowledgement of what happened and the resultant national empathy for those who suffered.

In this context we make the following recommendations:
a) That this report be published and be made available to the general public in Zimbabwe.
b) That the Government's own Chihambakwe Commission report (1984) be published and be made available to the general public.
c) That, if the Government disputes the veracity of this report, a joint fact-finding enquiry be commissioned to enable interested parties to make submissions in public.
d) That nationwide discussion, involving all ethnic groups, be encouraged to promote reconciliation amongst all the peoples of Zimbabwe.

2. HUMAN RIGHTS VIOLATORS

The amnesty declared in 1988 has ensured that all those responsible for human rights violations, be they dissidents or security forces, are immune from prosecution. Whilst we have grave reservations about amnesties of this nature, given the lapse of time between 1988 and now and the fact that those responsible for the (more numerous) human rights violations which occurred during Zimbabwe's liberation struggle are also immune from prosecution, we do not suggest that human rights violators be prosecuted. However, it is important that those who were directly responsible for human rights violations be removed from positions which may enable them to violate human rights again in the future. History shows us that the retention of the human rights violators in positions of authority can lead to those same people reverting to their old ways.

Accordingly we recommend that all those members of the Government security forces and dissidents who were responsible for violating human rights during the period of this report and who presently hold positions of authority be removed from these positions of authority.

3. LEGAL AMENDMENTS

Many families throughout Zimbabwe suffered abuses and losses of life and property at the hands of the colonial regime in the 1960s and 1970s. However, some legal mechanisms were created after Independence in terms of which people who were victims before Independence can claim compensation. The War Victims Compensation Act [*Chapter 11:16*] is a major channel through which pre-1980 victims can be recompensed.

President Mugabe has stated, in the last few years, that far too much focus has been placed on the human rights violence that occurred in the 1980s. This position overlooks the fact that the victims of the Liberation War have been able to claim compensation whereas no such mechanisms exist to provide help for those who suffered losses during the years between 1980 and 1988. In terms of existing legislation, the opportunity to lodge claims against any other party, including the Government, lapses after three years. Furthermore, those victimised during the 1980s were in a state of continuing persecution, largely at the hands of the State, and often were too intimidated to seek legal redress. In many cases the opportunity to claim has long since lapsed. In addition this report reveals that most of the victims are poor, uneducated, rural people who have had little recourse to justice for their entire lives, especially during the period when these violations occurred. For reasons outlined in the Legal

379

Damages chapter, the payment of compensation to individuals is fraught with problems. The same chapter also reveals that had these victims been able to bring claims of compensation the Zimbabwean Courts would have, in all probability, ordered Government to pay out millions of dollars in compensation.

Whilst Government has stated on several occasions that it has no intention of offering compensation to the 1980s victims, these statements have been contradicted by payments made by Government in recent cases concerning the late Fraser Gibson Sibanda and Tryagain Ndlovu. In addition, the Government's undertaking given to the United Nations in January 1996 that compensation would be paid appears to indicate a change of heart. Accordingly not only has a precedent for paying compensation been set in the two cases mentioned above, but the Government has also given an unequivocal undertaking to the United Nations, which it presumably intends honouring. It is important that Government should introduce mechanisms to facilitate the payment of compensation if this is its desire.

This report also reveals that many victims are still battling with day-to-day problems as a result of abuses that occurred many years ago. Victims battle to have births and deaths registered as a direct result of the death or disappearance of spouses years ago. In addition many rural farmers who obtained Agricultural Finance Corporation loans prior to the onset of hostilities in the 1980s are unable to repay those loans due to the destruction of their homes, grain, bins and the like. In many cases those loans remain outstanding and this in itself causes immense hardship today – another legacy which is unresolved.

It is apparent that the Government needs to introduce legislation to smooth the path of those who need compensation, births and deaths registered and outstanding Agricultural Finance Corporation loans cancelled.

In the circumstances we make the following recommendations:
a) That the Government should publicise its undertaking, given to the United Nations in January 1996, that it will pay compensation to victims.
b) That the Government should devise appropriate mechanisms to process claims made by victims of human rights violations.
c) That the Government should amend sections 2(1) and 4(a) of the War Victims Compensation Act [Chapter 11:16] by:
   (i) the deletion (in section 2 under the definition of "the war") of "29th February 1980" and the substitution thereof by "27th December 1987";

   (ii) the deletion (in section 4) of "1st March 1980" and the substitution thereof by "1st March 1988".

d) That the Government should amend the War Victims Compensation Act to extend the types of compensation that can be claimed by victims.

e) That the Government and other non-governmental organisations publicise, and educate, regarding any amendments introduced to enable and assist victims to claim compensation.

f) That the Government should conduct an enquiry into the present provisions of the Births and Deaths Act [Chapter 5:02], the regulations made in terms of section 26 of that Act and the Registrar General's policy with a view to making recommendations to ease the problems faced by victims in registering births and deaths.

g) That the Government should amend the Agricultural Finance Corporation Act, [Chapter 18:02], and relevant regulations made in terms of section 64 of that Act cancelling all extant debts incurred by communal land farmers in Matabeleland North, Matabeleland South and Midlands provinces which such farmers can prove (the onus being on them) remain unpaid as a result of human rights violations which occurred prior to the 27th December 1987.

4. IDENTIFICATION AND BURIAL OF THE REMAINS OF MISSING PERSONS AND REMAINS BURIED IN UNMARKED GRAVES

This report documents that hundreds of people went missing during the period covered by the report. Thousands more were shot in front of witnesses and many of these were then buried in unmarked graves. Whilst in the latter cases the identity of the victims so buried is sometimes known by their surviving loved ones it is still depressing to affected communities that grave sites have not been properly marked and that deceased people have not been buried properly. Furthermore there is great distress presently being experienced by entire communities in these regions who only know that the remains of their kith and kin are lying somewhere in mine shafts and unmarked graves. The chapter on missing persons and unmarked graves confirms that communities must be consulted prior to decisions being taken regarding the identification and reburial of the remains of missing persons. Likewise communities must be consulted if remains are to be exhumed from known mass graves and given appropriate reburial. It is not in our mandate to make any recommendations in the above regard, as that would be premature and presumptuous. What is apparent, however, is that Government and others have made mistakes when remains have been discovered (as happened at Antelope Mine in 1992) and these mistakes have compounded the anguish felt by surviving relatives and communities. This chapter also reveals the skill required in effectively identifying remains of missing persons.

In the circumstances we make the following recommendations:
a) That a neutral team of anthropologists and psychologists conduct research in Matabeleland North, South and Midlands provinces to determine the desires of the communities affected by the still-existent problem of missing persons and mass graves.
b) That Government should undertake to protect and leave undisturbed all mass grave sites and mine shafts in which the remains of victims lie pending the outcome of the research mentioned above, and (if so recommended) the employment of expert forensic teams to find and identify missing persons and to exhume the remains of persons buried in mass graves.
c) That Government should not hinder or prevent suitably qualified forensic teams from conducting work to find and identify the remains of missing persons and to assist in the reburial of the remains of persons buried in mass graves and mine shafts, if it is the desire of the communities affected to bring in such forensic teams.

5. HEALTH

The chapter on the psychological consequences of the human rights violations reveals that entire communities in Matabeleland North, Matabeleland South and Midlands provinces have suffered, and are still suffering, severe psychological trauma. Likewise many human rights violators, be they dissidents or security force members, are likely to be still suffering from psychological trauma. This is another continuing legacy of the human rights abuses that ended in 1988. Trauma of this nature cannot be ignored and must be remedied by professional counsellors and medical practitioners. Indeed one of the most important components of bringing about reconciliation will be through psychological healing.

In the circumstances we recommend:
a) That Government and donors provide the necessary financial and logistical support to enable professional teams and counsellors/

psychologists/medical practitioners to work in affected communities.

b) That those non-governmental organisations already doing work in this field in Zimbabwe send teams to work in affected communities forthwith.

6. COMMUNAL REPARATION: THE "RECONCILIATION / UXOLELWANO TRUST"

It is clear that even if the War Victims Compensation Act were amended and expanded, and some of the other recommendations referred to above were implemented, compensation for all individuals would be an impossible task. Too much time has lapsed and, in many cases, fundamental evidence in support of claimed abuses no longer exists. Ignorance of legal processes, destruction of documentary proof of loss, continued fear and conflicting interests within communities would probably prevent most individuals from obtaining satisfactory redress. In addition, because of the sheer scale of the human rights violations, the Government would not be able to afford to pay out hundreds of millions of dollars in compensation to individuals.

It is also apparent from the report that whole communities have suffered human rights violations. In many cases violence was directed towards communities and not individuals as such. Whilst individuals were singled out for abuse it was in fact the entire community that was being targeted. In view of all these factors the concept of reparation to communities as a whole, therefore, seems sensible.

The most important gesture the State could make to entire communities is to acknowledge complicity in their suffering. Many victims have volunteered this as an important step towards alleviating their bitter memories and towards convincing them that the State will never again inflict organised violence on thousands of civilians. If reparation is made in this manner entire communities will be restored and healed; the healing of individuals will inevitably follow.

Civil society in the regions affected is still somewhat nascent and this may pose a difficulty in distributing fairly any reparations that may be forthcoming. A further problem is that many of these communities still have an inherent distrust of Government and its motives. Likewise Government and donors may not wish to pour millions of dollars into organisations that cannot be held financially accountable.

In addition, some of the recommendations made in this report cannot be implemented by Government or the affected communities themselves because of lack of expertise and other factors such as the need for neutrality. For example there may well be a need for the neutral body to facilitate and organise psychological counselling of victims, the identification of the remains of missing persons and persons buried in mass graves by forensic experts, the construction of memorials and shrines and the provision of scholarships for the dependants of those who have died.

Financial assistance to whole communities, in the form of improved infrastructures, educational scholarships for impoverished families, irrigation schemes, financial help for ceremonies to appease the dead and the missing – these are some ways in which reparation could now be offered. If the State itself does not have funds at its disposal, it could consider facilitating the process of approaching donors willing to finance such projects. Once the Government has shown itself as prepared to act in good faith, dialogue between the Government and affected communities would become possible, freeing people of fear and empowering them to put forward proposals based on their own assessment of priorities.

Accordingly it is suggested that a Trust be established with the primary object of facilitating reconciliation and peace between the communities affected by the human rights violations and other sectors of Zimbabwean society. As will appear from the proposed Trust Deed annexed to this report, the Trust will have the power to raise funds from Government and donors to implement "reconciliation projects" in affected communities. The Trust will be administered by a board of trustees comprising equal numbers of Government representatives, non-governmental organisations and community representatives.

In the circumstances we recommend that the "Reconciliation/ Uxolelwano Trust" be formed. (*Uxolelwano* being the Ndebele word for reconciliation).

7. CONSTITUTIONAL SAFEGUARDS

We as Zimbabweans need to ensure that what happened in Matabeleland North, Matabeleland South and Midlands Provinces in the 1980s will never happen again anywhere in Zimbabwe. If we pride ourselves in being a democracy, a leader amongst nations, then we must conduct much self analysis to understand why it was that such horrendous atrocities could occur after our hard fight for independence. Why was it that these human rights violations could occur on our very doorstep without most of us knowing about it? Why is it that it has taken so long for victims to be heard?

Our belief is that many of the answers to these questions lie in our constitution. It is not the purpose of this report to advocate constitutional reform. That would require a separate report in itself. What is clear however is that constitutional safeguards must be introduced to prevent a recurrence of what happened in Matabeleland North, Matabeleland South and Midlands Provinces in the 1980s.

In the circumstances we recommend that Government, citizens of Zimbabwe and civil society in general begin an urgent debate to consider what constitutional safeguards are necessary to prevent widespread human rights violations occurring again in Zimbabwe in future.

8. THE FUTURE

In many ways this report must be viewed as a preliminary contribution to what we hope will be a serious and all-embracing debate. Undoubtedly further studies will have to be conducted. Government may wish to conduct its own investigations to qualify this report's findings. Affected communities may feel we have been too conservative in our findings. In any event because of major financial constraints, this report at best can only paint part of the picture.

Our hope is that this report will provoke all Zimbabweans to deal with this immediate past and sorry chapter of our history. It is imperative that we learn from our mistakes and move forward. However, we can only learn from our mistakes if a tolerant atmosphere for debate is encouraged by all. As difficult as it is, human rights victims and violators – and those indirectly responsible for the events detailed in this report – must try to create conditions within Zimbabwe conducive to all being able to work through the issues raised in this report.

In the circumstances we recommend that Government, universities, churches, non-governmental organisations, political parties and all citizens of Zimbabwe restrain themselves from making inflammatory comments and instead do everything in their power to promote sensible dialogue to achieve true reconciliation amongst all Zimbabweans.

APPENDIX A
INTERVIEW FORMS

AI

CATHOLIC COMMISSION FOR JUSTICE AND PEACE IN BULAWAYO: EXAMPLE OF A COMPLETED INTERVIEW FORM

CASE 281 M
Transcribed as follows:
Covering Note:

> Chief M
> District Gwanda
>
> Dear Sir/Madam
> Will you please attend CN's matter. He will say ever thing about his father. He want to have birth certificate.

Statement, Page 2:

> Four members of CIO from Guyu came to our village at Ntalale and asked my brother where his rifle was. They also searched the house and found a rifle belonging to J's grandfather a .22. They then took J to his grandfather's home at Garanyemba and asked if the people there knew J. The people said they did. They also asked if he did not go for training outside the country. These CIO told his grandfather that they were not going to see J again. We later heard that these men had killed him on the way to Gwanda at Setchane. One of the CIO members was called M.

> Page 4:
> WAS DEATH REPORTED: No, because of fear.
> WAS A DEATH CERTIFICATE ISSUED: No.
> WAS THERE A WILL, OR WAS DECEASED'S ESTATE ADMINISTERED, HOW/BY WHOM: No, his dues from sick contractors were never collected.
> WHAT ARE THE PROBLEMS FACED BY SURVIVING DEPENDANTS: Birth certificates, schooling, clothing, food.

Ward 9.
Chief N
District Rwanda.

Dear Sir/Madam.
   Will you please attend C   N
matter. He will say a ever thing about
his matter. He want to have birth
certificate.

389

CATHOLIC COMMISSION FOR JUSTICE AND PEACE IN BULAWAYO

MISSING PERSON ---*J*----*N*----------------------------------

DATE --------*1984 CURFEW*----------------------------

NAME OF INTERVIEWEE ---*L*--------*N*----------------------

RELATIONSHIP TO DECEASED/MISSING/INJURED PERSON --*BROTHER*--

----

AGE --*36 YEARS*---

MARITAL STATUS ---*MARRIED*------------------------------

CONTACT ADDRESS --*GARANYEMBA SECONDARY SCHOOL*----------

NAME OF DECEASED/MISSING/INJURED PERSON -------------------

------*J*--*N*---

DATE OF BIRTH ---*All PARTICULARS TAKEN BY CIO*----------

IDENTITY CARD NUMBER --*TAKEN BY CIO*--------------------

MARITAL STATUS AT TIME OF INCIDENT --*MARRIED*-----------

SURVIVING SPOUSE --*E!*--------*N*----------------------

NAMES OF SURVIVING CHILDREN AND AGE -*C*----*N*----*23 YRS*

--*V*----*N*----*21 YRS* M--------*18 YRS* T----*12 YRS*

--*K*----*9 YRS* K----*7 YES*---------------------------

EMPLOYMENT STATUS/EARNING AT TIME OF INCIDENT --*JOINTER WITH*

Sisk Builders $280=00 p.m-----------------------------

POLITICAL AFFILIATION/ACTIVITY OF DECEASED/MISSING/INJURED

PERSON (IF ANY) ---*Z.A.P.U MEMBER*----------------------

PARTICIPATION IN LIBERATION WAR (RECRUITED/TRAINED WHERE.

ACTIVE WHERE, UNIT, CHUMURENGA NAME, ANY OTHER DETAILS (IF ANY):

N/A

STATEMENT OF THE INCIDENT WHEN PERSON WAS KILLED/WENT MISSING/INJURED:

THIS IS TO INCLUDE DATE/TIME/PLACE OF THE INCIDENT. DETAILS OF WITNESSES INCLUDING NAME AND PRESENT ADDRESSES. DESCRIPTION OF PEOPLE RESPONSIBLE I.E. LANGUAGE, UNIFORM, NUMBER, WEAPONS, VEHICLES. UNIT - CIC, ZRP, ZNA, 5 BRIGADE, PLAIN CLOTHES, DISSIDENTS. NAME OF EXACT CIRCUMSTANCES STEP-BY-STEP.

STATEMENTS

Four members of CIO from Guyu came to our village at Ntalale and asked my brother where his rifle was. They also searched the house and found a rifle belonging to J grandfather a .22. They then took J to his grandfathers home at Gobanyemba and asked if the people there knew J. The people said they did. They also asked if he did not go for trainings outside the country. These CIO told his grandfather that they were not going to see J again.

We later heard that these men had killed him on the way to Gwanda at Setchane.

One of the C.I.O. members was called Matavana.

DESTRUCTION OF PROPERTY (WHAT WAS DESTROYED, HOW, ITS VALUE)

DECEASED PERSON

WAS DEATH REPORTED _No Because of Fear_____

WAS A DEATH CERTIFICATE ISSUED ___No_____

WAS THERE A WILL, OR WAS DECEASED'S ESTATE ADMINISTERED, HOW
/BY WHOM.
____ No. His Dues From Sick Contractors
Were Never Collected_____

WHAT ARE THE PROBLEMS FACED BY THE SURVIVING DEPENDANTS OF
THE DECEASED. (FINANCIAL, PROPERTY, SCHOOLING, BIRTH
CERTIFICATES).
__Birth Certificates, Schooling, Clothing,_____
__Food_____

HAVE THEY APPLIED FOR AN ORDER TO MISSING MISSING ACT?
                                        No

INJURED PERSON

N/A

WHERE/WHO TREATED HIM/HER ------------------------

N/A

IS THERE A MEDICAL REPORT ------------------------

IF YES, PLEASE ATTACH IT ------------------------

EXPENSES INCURRED FOR TREATMENT ------------------------

ANY DISABILITY RESULTING FROM THE INJURY ------------------------

----

IS THERE DISABILITY PERMANENT --------- N/A

IS CONTINUED MEDICAL TREATMENT REQUIRED NOW, AND WHAT COSTS
ARE INCURRED:

N/A

N/A

394

AII

BULAWAYO LEGAL PROJECTS CENTRE: EXAMPLE OF A COMPLETED MISSING PERSONS QUESTIONNAIRE

CASE 729 AG

Cross refer CASES 730 X, 731 X: SILWANE INCIDENT: describes some of the events on this day when 52 people died here, all in the vicinity of their homes.

Transcribed as follows:
Statement, Page 2:

It was at 3pm on 6/2/83 when 15 armed men arrived at the homestead of A. The armed men had AK guns and spoke Shona. They wore red berets and had soldier combat. On their arrival the armed men said they had come to kill everybody. A and the other two neighbours who were with him – LM and HM – tried to show the armed men their IDs but they ignored them. The armed men started shooting. A was shot on the right hip, L was shot in the mouth and he died instantly, H was shot on the stomach and he too died shortly. A says he tried to put back the intestines of H who had recovered a bit, but failed because he was seriously injured. A says the armed men thought he was dead and he heard them talking about the people they had shot that day and they numbered eight. A was the only one who survived among the eight who were to be killed on that particular day. A was later picked up by the ambulance from St Luke's, and the others MN and the other lady he could not remember her name.

Witnesses – 3 names given.

Medical Report – attached

This is to certify that AM from   was admitted to this hospital on 7 February 1983 after sustaining a gun shot wound through his right hip crushing the head of the femur and the osileum of the pelvis. He remained an in-patient until 20 March 1983 and eventually made a good recovery.

729AG.PL
730x.PL
731x.PL

Date: 24/7/95

Name of Interviewee: mr A m

Relationship to Deceased/Missing/Injured Person (D/M/I) .... Self

Age: 34   Marital status: married

Contact address: Silwane school
                  Box 3
                  Lupane

****

Name of Deceased/Missing/Injured person: ....

Date of birth: .... ID No. ....

Marital status at time of incident: ....

Surviving spouse: ....

Surviving children (names/ages now): ....

Employment status/earnings at time of incident: NiL

Political affiliation/activity of D/M/I person (if any): NIL

Participation in liberation war (recruited/trained where, active where, unit, chimurenga name, any other detail (if any):

did not participate

Statement of the incident when person was killed/went missing/injured:

This is to incluue date/time/place of the incident.
Details of witnesses including names and present addresses.
Description of people responsible i.e. language, uniform, number, weapons, vehicles, unit - CIO,ZRP, ZNA,
5 Brigade, plain clothes, dissidents.
Name of others killed/went missing/injured in the same incident.
Description of exact circumstances step-by-step.

STATEMENT

It was at 3 Pm on the 6/2/83 when 15 armed men arrived at the homestead of A   . The armed men had AK guns and spoke shona. They more red berets and had soldier combat, On they arrival the armed men said they had come to kill everybody, A   and other two neighbours who were with him - L   m and H   M   tried to show the armed men their I.Ds but they ignored them. the armed men started shooting, A   was shot on the right hip, L   was shot in the mouth and he died instantly, H   was shot on the stomach and he too died shortly, A says he tried to put back the intestines of H   who had recovered a bit but failed because he was shadgone seriously injured. H   says the armed men thought he was dead and he heard them talking about the people they had shot that day and they numbered 9. H   was the only one who survived among the eight who were to be killed on that particular day. H was later picked by the ambulance from ST. Lukes, and the others M   N   and the other lady he could not remember her name

1. Mr M   N   Gokwana School
2. Mr P   . M   Box 3 Lupane

PS. He claims a sum of $10 000 for the injury

397

Destruction of property (what was destroyed, how, its value):

....
....
....
....

Was the incident ever reported? (Police, priest, other) And is there any record of this report?

It was not possible to report in
fear of being killed

....
....

DECEASED PERSON

Was death reported: ....

Was a death certificate issued: ....

Was there a will, or was deceased's estate administered, how/by whom :

....
....
....
....

What are the problems faced by the surviving dependents of the deceased:
(Financial, property, schooling, birth certificates)

....
....
....
....

MISSING PERSON

What are the problems faced by the surviving dependents of the missing person (obtaining death/birth certificates, financial, schooling, etc.)

....

....

....

....

Have they applied for an order to Missing Persons Act ? If yes, where and when

....

....

....

....

INJURED PERSON

Nature of injury: Gun shot throug the right ~~Gun~~ hip .

Where/who treated it: ST. Lukes — Davis

Is there a medical report? attached   If yes, please attach

Expenses incurred for treatment   it was free

Any disability resulting from the injury? as shown on the m/report

Is the disability permanent? N.C

Is continued medical treatment required now and what costs are incurred?

NC

Statement taken by: ....

Date: 24/7/95

St Luke's Hospital
P Bag 12 53 14. Byr
21. 7. 1995

To Whom It May Concern

This is to certify that A___ M___ from ___ was admitted to this Hospital on 7. February 1983 after sustaining a gunshot wound through his Right hip crushing the head of the femur and the Os ileum of the pelvis. He remained an inpatient until 20th March 1983 and eventually made a good recovery.

M.D.

Medical Superintendent.

ST. LUKES HOSPITAL
21 JUL 1995
P.BAG R5341 BULAWAYO

400

AIII

BULAWAYO LEGAL PROJECTS CENTRE: EXAMPLE OF COMPLETED HUMAN RIGHTS FACT SHEET

CASE 3344 ASD
Transcribed as follows:
Statement, Page 3:

> We were taken from our homes to Sun Yet Sen Mine Camp.
> The people were tortured there using logs.
> I went through this beating for 3 months.
> I lost one of my eyes completely and can bare see with my left eye.
> I have marks on my back, particularly shoulder blades were damaged.
> I can no longer work for myself and family.
> I only went to hospital 1992 when my right eye was falling out.
>
> Page 4:
> DAMAGES SUSTAINED: Personal injuries or permanent disability:
> Pain over both shoulder blades and loss of my sight.

HUMAN RIGHTS FACT SHEET

File reference: 3344 ASD.   Cross-references: _____

Original file name: _____

DESCRIPTION OF HUMAN RIGHTS VIOLATION (Murder, disappearance, assault/injury, unlawful detention,

property destruction): _____ assault   detention _____

DEVELOPMENTS IN CASE (state action, court ruling, other relevant developments) _____

_____

_____

VICTIM INFORMATION

SURNAME: M_____   FIRST NAMES: T_____   _____

Date of birth: 13.12.32.   Sex (M/F): M   ID No. _____

Address at time of incident: ST. MARY PRIM. SCHOOL

P. O. MAPHISA — SIGANGATSHA AREA

Employment status and earnings at time of incident: _____ No _____

_____

Political affiliation/activity of victim (if any): Branch Organizing Secretary

ZAPU

Participation in liberation war (if any):

    1. Where recruited/trained: _____

    2. Where active: _____

    3. Unit: _____

    4. Chimurenga name: _____

    5. Other involvement: _____

_____

_____

SOURCE OF INFORMATION: _Self_

DETAILS OF INCIDENT

Date: _10. 02. 84_ Approximate time: _around 3 p.m_

Location of incident (give address or directions): _Mbume - St. MARY'S_
Pr. School

Administrative district of location: _Matebo_

Place where events occurred (at home, at work, at an army base, etc.): _at home._

Description of persons responsible:

1. Clothing: _Combat - red & black_
berrets

2. Language spoken: _SHONA_

3. Weapons, vehicles, or other equipment: _A.K., PUMA_

4. Unit (if identifiable, such as CIO, ZRP, ZNA, (5 Brigade) plain clothes, dissidents, etc.):

5. Other details: _F____m____and many_
others I don't remember

GANGA - CEM.

Others involved in same incident: _____

Other documents attached or on file (death certificate, medical report, police statement, etc.): _____

Documents needed: _____

- We were taken from our homes to Sun Yet Sen mine camp.
- The people were tortured there using logs.
- I went through this beating for 3 months
- I lost one of my eyes completely and can bare see with my left eye.
- I have marks on my back particularly shoulder blades were dammaged.
- I can no longer work for myself and family.
- I only went to hospital 1992 when my right eye was falling out.

INTERVIEWEE INFORMATION

If source was based on an interview or listed witnesses to the offence, complete this section.

Surname: _____ First names: _____

Date of birth: _____ Sex (M/F): _____ ID No.: _____

Relationship to victim: _____

Marital status: _____

Contact address: _ST. Mary's Pr. School_
P.O. Maphisa.

Names of witnesses (if any) and present addresses: _As above_
_____
_____
_____
_____

DETAILS OF DEPENDENTS OF VICTIM

Marital status at time of incident: _____

Type and date of marriage: _____

Surviving spouse(s) and date(s) of birth: _____
_____

Surviving children (list names and dates of birth): _____
_____
_____
_____
_____

DAMAGES SUSTAINED

Personal injuries or permanent disability: _Pain over both_
shoulder blades and loss of
my sight .

405

Details of property destroyed or stolen: _____

_____

_____

Loss of support for dependents: _____

_____

_____

Estimate of monetary damages (include expenses incurred for treatment of injuries, expenses for continuing treatment, value of property destroyed or stolen, and financial problems faced by surviving dependents):

_____

_____

Non-monetary needs of dependents (such as birth or death certificates): _____

_____

406

BLPC: HUMAN RIGHTS MEDIA REPORTS: EXAMPLE OF A COMPLETED MEDIA FORM

HUMAN RIGHTS MEDIA REPORTS

Reference No.: _30(i).SH_ Cross-reference(s): _____

Newspaper: _The Chronicle_____

Date of publication: _June 22, 1982_____ Page No.: _1_____

Headline: _Bandits hit seven buses in province_____

Type of reporting ((article,) editorial, letter): _____

Name of author (if available): _____

Date of incident: _June 17, '82 (Thurs.)_____

Location of incident: _Kumalo communal land_____
_____

Nature of incident: _Robbery_____

Victims: _Dope Store_____

Perpetrators (include description, if any): _one armed man_____
_____

Witnesses: _____
_____

Other information: _Store was robbed of $40. The gunman_____
_fired one shot, but no one was hurt_____
_____
_____
_____
_____
_____
_____
_____

Report taken by: _____ Date: _Jun 15, '95_

APPENDIX B
INTERVIEW FORMS

I   MEDICAL RECORD: LIST OF PATIENTS ADMITTED TO
    HOSPITAL WITH INJURIES AFFLICTED BY MEMBERS
    OF THE ARMY

II EXAMPLE OF A LETTER WRITTEN TO CCJP OFFICIAL
    IN 1985

BI

MEDICAL RECORD: LIST OF PATIENTS ADMITTED TO HOSPITAL WITH INJURIES AFFLICTED BY MEMBERS OF THE ARMY

Hosp. No.	Date	Age	Sex	Name	Place	Injury
612	25.1.83	54	M		Malunku	Frt. R.arm &ribs.
664	26.1.83	60	M		Mateteni	assault R knee
665	26.1.83	26	M		~eteteni	G.S.W. neck
714	30.1.	15	F		Manasse	Severe bruises but
717	30.1.	52	M		Manasse	Multiple bruises
782	30.1.	65	M		Manasse	Necroticing Buttoc
841	5.2.	37	M		Mzola 8	G.S.W. neck
864	6.2.	10 f	F		Silwana	Haematoma on head
866	6.2.	43	F		Silwana	Frt.R Humerus thi
867	6.2.	16	F		Silwana	G.S.W. R.hand &
868	6.2.	5	M		Silwana	Bruises on chest
869	6.2.	14	M		Silwana	Haematoma R.eye Fract.Elbow.
870	6.2.	2+	M		Silwana	Multiple bruises
871	6.2.	13	M		Silwana	Fract.R thumb
872	6.2.	20	M		Siwana	Multiple bruises
873	6.2.	24	M		Silwana	Br.both arms & Ear
874	6.2.	21	F		Silwana	Multiple bruises
875	6.2.	23	F		Silwana	Haematoma buttocks
876	6.2.	21	F		Silwana	" Buttocks
877	6.2.	23	F		Silwana	Multiple bruises
878	6.2.	22	M		Silwana	Bruises,Frt finge:
881	6.2.	58	M		Ndamuleni	G.S.".Frct.Lforea:
882	7.2.	35	M		Silwana	G.S.W. R. shoulder a: upper
883	7.2.	13	F		Silwana	Frct.L arm
886	7.2.	55	F		Silwana	G.S.W. R.shoulder
891	7.2.	30	F		Silwana	G.S.W. L elbow
892	7.2.	16	F		Silwana	G.S.".R arm& thora:
893	7.2.	16	F		Silwana	G.S.W.Back L foot
900	7.2.	18	M		Silwana	G.S.". R.Elbow
901	7.2.	8	F		Silwana	G.S.W. L arm
902	7.2.	3	F		Silwana	G.S.W. L arm &ches:
905	7.2.	15	F		Silwana	G.S.W. Fct.L femur
906	7.2.	16	F		Keswe	G,".". axilla,fem.
907	7.2.	53	M		Silwane	Frct.Tibie Lac.hea
908	7.2.	30	F		Silwane	G.S.". L arm
909	7.2.	24	M		Silwane	G.S.". R.hip Frct.
910	7.2.	14	F		Silwane	G.S.W. Lfem & eg F
911	7.2.	7	F		Silwane	G.S.". L cheek
912	7.2.	26	F		Silwana	G.S.".chest
913	7.2.	10	M		Silwane	G.S.". lower leg

No	Hosp. No.	Date	Age	Sex	Name	Place	Injury
41	914	7.2.	60	F		Silwana	G.S.W.in pelvis
42	915	7.2.	23	F		Zwananzi	G.S.W.Multiple fracture
43	918	8.2.	3	M		Silwana	G.S.W. L foot
44	919	8.2.	7/12	F		Silwana	G.S.W. R buttock
45	920	8.2.	24	M		Mtupane	Bruises
46	931	8.2.	16	F		Somgoro	Bruises
47	933	8.2.	18	F		St.Paul's	Bruises. Fct.L arm
48	934	8.2.	61	M		Malunku	Bruises
49	935	8.2.	17	F		Malunku	Bruises
50	936	8.2.	18	F		Malunku	Bruses & Lacerations.Su
51	937	8.2.	50	F		Malunku	Fract.both forearms.
52	938	8.2.	23	M		Malunku	G.S.W. L check,R arm
53	939	8.2.	26	F		Silwana	G.S.W. R radius
54	940	8.2.	19	M		Lake Alice	G.S.W. Frct.R knee
55	941	8.2.	62	M		Malunku	Bruises
56	945	8.2.	16	F		Madotye	Frct.both forearms,R.th
57	950	8.2.	14	F		a Silwana	G.S.W. L.cheek,L back
58	951	8.2.	17	F		Jiba Jiba	G.S.W. Frct. L arm.
59	954	8.2.	33	M		Kabela	G.S.W. Chest, R thigh,d
60	955	8.2.	25	M		Dibudibu	G.S.W. Both legs,L hip
61	959	9.2.	40	F		Keswa	Bruises
62	960	9.2.	27	F		Keswa	Bruises,Frct.L hand
63	961	9.2.	35	F		Keswa	Bruises. R eye
64	967	9.2.	29	M		Sibangani	Bruises,Frct.R hand
65	969	9.2.	40	F		Lupane	Bruises
66	971	9.2.	29	M		Lupanda	Bruises.perforated eard
67	972	9.2.	25	M		Lake Alice	Bruises
68	975	9.2.	69	M		Lupane	Bruises, Frct.R ulna
69	991	9.2.	27	F		Sipopoma	Pregnant;Bruises
70	992	9.2.	54	F		Sipopoma	Burns,escaped from hut
71	993	9.2.	25	F		Sipopoma	Bruises:Buttocks arms
72	994	10.2.	28	F		Tshebe Thsebe	Bruises,Septic Haema
73	998	10.2.	55	M		Gandangula	Bruises
74	1006	10.2.	60	M		Bembezwana	Burns
75	1009	10.2.	22	M		Forestry	Bruises
76	1013	10.2.	16	F		Daluka	Bruises
77	1015	10.2.	25	M		Daluka	Bruises
78	1016	10.2.	26	M		Daluka	Bruises
79	1017	10.2.	40	M		Daluka	Bruises,severedamage
80	1018	10.2.	40	M		Daluka	Lacerations,Sutured

412

Hosp. No.	Date	Age	Sex	Name	Place	Injury
1021	10.2	60	F		Zwanenzi	G.S.W.shoulder& face
1022	10.2	31	M		Msewele	GSW R hip
1027	11.2	35	M		Geleza	Bruises
1029	11.2	31	M		Thayamatole	GSW R cheek
1034	11.2	23	F		Bembezi Bridge	Bruises Frct.R arm
1037	11.2	2	M		Silwana	GSW R shoulder,L leg
1043	11.2	25	F		Msewele	Bruises,buttocks
1044	11.2	22	F		Msewele	Bruises.buttocks
1047	11.2	65	M		Keswa	Bruises
1048	11.2	57	F		Keswa	Bruises
1050	12.2	5/12	F		Mateteni	Knifed on brim of nose
1055	12.2	55	F		Manasse	Bruises
1077	12.2	40	F		Gandangula	Bruises
1075	12.2	60	F		Nkulumane	Fractures both arms
1078	13.2	50	M		Lupanda	Bruises
1096	13.2	14	F		Gandangula	Bruises
1106	14.2	21	F		Sibangani	Bruises
1124	15.2	48	M		Bembezi Forest	Bruises
1131	15.2	38	M		Lake Alice	Frct.L arm, R leg
1152	17.2	15	M		Lake Alice	Bruises
1153	17.2	20	F		Mateteni	Perforated Ear drums
1159	17.2	22	F		Madotwa	Bruises
1165	17.2	14	M		Lake Alice	Frct.L arm
1167	17.2	43	FF		Bembezi Wireless	Bruises
1168	17.2	36	F		Bembezi	Bruises
1170	17.2	19	M		Bembezi	Frct arm Bruses
1171	17.2	17	M		Bembezi	Bruises
1172	17.2	27	M		Bembezi	Bruises
1179	17.2	70	M		Mzola	Frct.lower orbit R ey
1202	18.2	60	F		Mzola	Burns in face & butto
1203	18.2	17	F		Mzola	Bruises Buttocks & Le Breastfee
1204	18.2	25	F		Mzola	Burnt breast & buttoc
1229	20.2	65	M		Lake Alice	Frct.L arm both bones
1260	22.2	61	M		Kabela	Bruises
1268	22.2	55	M		Malonga	Frct.both arms
1276	22.2	14	F		Mafa	Bruises
1277	22.2	42	F		Mafa	Compound Frct R arm
1283	22.2	32	M		Lake Alice	Bruises
1288	23.2	32	M		Sibombo	GSW Frct R.tibia
1317	23.2	38	M		Bembezi Forest	Bruises in face

413

	Hosp. No.	Date	Age	Sex	Name	Place	Injuries
1	1329	24.2.	15	F		Somgoro	Bruises
2	1377	24.2.	30	F		Somogoro	Bruises
3	1378	26.2.	46	F.		Somgoro	Bruises,Frct R hand
4	1379	26.2.	44	F		Somgoro	Bruises,Frct.R arm
5	1416	28.2.	52	F		Somgoro	Haematoma on chest
6	1477	3.3.	66	M		Bembezi Wrs.	Frct R arm
7	1479	3.3.	23	M		Mzola	GSW R knee Frct.femur
8	1486	3.3.	28	M		Lupane	GSW R.knee,soft tissue
9	1607	8.3.	61	M		Bembeswana	Bruises to the chest
0	1651	10.3.	39	M		Gandangula	Extensive bruises
1	1720	12.3.	30	M		Jibe Jibe	Bruises
2	1850	17.3.	38	M		Insuza	Bruises
3	1886	19.3.	50	M		Insuza	Frct R arm
4	1940	22.3.	40	F		Insuza	Frct both forearms
5	2027	27.3.	21	M		Jotjolo	Bruises
6	2073	30.3.	60	M		Dongamuzi	Severe tissue necrosis
7	2125	1.4.	15	F		Sivalo	Severe injuries both t. g
8	2191	5.4.	20	F.		Jibe (Bembezi)	Severe br.buttocks &t;
9	2381	15.4.	65	M		Gumede	Bruises on chest
0	2633	26.4.	23	M		Shashi	Bruises back
1	2667	28.4.	34	M		Mzola 60	Bilateral gluteal tiss necro
2	2741	1.5.	60	F		Insuza	Frct L arm
3	2768	2.5.	17	F		Sibombo	Threatened abortion beaten up
4	2775	2.5.	19	M		Mzola 60	Bruises.
5	2792	2.5.	16	F		Ndimibili	Bilat.glut.tissue necr
6	2836	2.5.	46	M		Lupanda	Frct.L forearm
7	2873	4.5.	62	M		Nzaligwa	Bruises & hip
8	2911	5.5.	49	M		Insuza	Multiple Bruises
9	2960	8.5.	57	M		Lupanda	Bruises to chest
0	2967	8.5.	24	F		Mzola 2	Frct.R arm
51	3052	10.5.	58	M		Sipemba	Bruises
52	3161	14.5.	24	M		Dlobolobo	Bruises
53	3162	14.5.	24	M		Mpikiwa	Bruises
54	3192	15.5.	20	M		Sipopoma	2nd degree burnsR leg
55	3222	15.5.	16	M		Lupenda	2nd degree Burns both thighs
56	3237	16.5.	20	M		Mbanyana Line Sipepa.	GSW on 9,3. in chest left unattended incl;

414

157	3486	25.5.	M	40	Jiba School	Fract. arm, hemat.
158	3487	25.5.	F	21	Jiba School	Buttock hematomas
159	3488	25.5.	F	24	Jiba School	Bruises on back
160	3589	29.5.	M	20	Mzola 5	GSW, comp.fract. leg
161	3605	30.5.	M	52	Gandangula	Bruises on back
162	3635	31.5.	M	27	Daluka	Bruises on chest
163	3657	1. 6.	M	44	Lupane	Bruises on back
164	3665	1.6.	F	31	Daluka	Buttock necrosis
165	3674	2.6.	M	40	Somgoro	Perf. L eardrum, lac.
166	3679	2.6.	F	25	Janke	Multiple bruises
167	3686	2.6.	M	42	Janke	Bruises on back
168	3712	3.6.	F	43	Somgoro	Buttock bruises
169	3783	5.6.	F	38	Malonka	Multiple bruises
170	3740	5.6.	F	33	Malonka	Buttock necrosis
171	3912	11.6.	M	22	Forestry	Bruises on legs, butt
172	3973	13.6.	M	68	Makhuyana	Bruises on skull
173	4015	15.6.	M	54	Silwane	2^0 Burn on face,neck
174	4204	22.6.	M	46	Sindombe	Fract. R ribs
175	4275	26.6.	M	39	Manasa	Lacer. hemat. L knee
176	4306	26.6.	M	60	Kabela	Died on next day
177	4314	27.6.	M	62	Ndimimbili	Fract. R forearm
178	4377	29.6.	M	32	Madojwa	2^0 Burn R hand
179	4535	4.7.	M	18	Dandanda	Wheals multiple
180	4571	5.7.	M	30	Jibajiba	Subdural hematoma
181	4582	6.7.	M	54	Zinaphi	Buttock necrosis
182	4649	10.7.	M	30	Ngombane	Buttock necrosis

BII

EXAMPLE OF A LETTER WRITTEN TO CCJP OFFICIAL IN 1985

Transcribed as follows:

Dear Brother in Christ

I think you are fine and had a very good Easter. Well my journey back home was excellent and I had a tremendous Easter Weekend at Catholic Hall with Father presiding over the mass. I spent the weekend contented and confidential although there were some disturbances on my mind which are still worrying me day and night.

Well, Brother, it was unfortunate that when I arrived in town I received sad news that my father was kidnapped by armed men in February at night. This really disappointed me that if I think of it tears fall like heavy rains falling from the sky. He was kidnapped with eight farmers and he was the ninth. Even today we haven't heard anything about them whether they are alive or dead nobody knows. We have tried to dig information but there is nothing to be heard. The problem is that if we tell the Police about it, they reply us harshly that we are sometimes promised a bullet. They take no notice about the kidnap. It was reported the day when it happened and they came to ask my mother and that was all, no action was taken by both the police and army yet it was reported that the kidnap was done by the bandits.

But what worries me is that all witnesses say that after every kidnap a sound of a truck is heard and the other thing is that this kidnapp happened in tribal grounds that is Ndebele speaking people were the only ones kidnapped.

So I have sleepless nights nowadays because mother says they took father saying they wanted him to show them the way and at the main gate of the farm she heard father crying very loud and this cry suddenly stopped in a serious way. So we still haven't got any information about their whereabouts.

I have thought it best to share my sympathy with you and I am fully convinced that the present and other Christians shall assist in praying that we may see our fathers again and share our joys.

To me this is like reading an interesting book and find that the last chapter is torn and could not complete with interest. I have been doing very well at school and now I am cut off from my progress. I do not know whether I will manage next term because I can't see any reason why I am living in such a country without freedom.

Well, Brother there is nothing we can do, thus the trend of life we are living in. There is mine I can share with you but now my heart is wounded.

Yours
Distressed
XX

P.O. Mp OPOMA
BULAWAYO
15 - 04 - 85.

Dear Brother in Christ

I think you are fine and had a very good Easter. Well my journey back home was excellent and I had a tremendous Easter weekend at Entumi and Catholic Hall with Father ___ presiding over the mass. I spent the weekend contented and confidential although there were some disturbances in my mind which are still worring me day and night.

Well, Brother, it was unfortunate that when I arrived in town I received sad news that my Father was kidnapped by armed men in February at night. This really disappointed me that if I think of it tears fall like heavy rains falling from the sky. He was kidnapped with other 8 farmers and he was the nineth. Even today we haven't heard anything about them, whether they are alive or dead nobody knows. We have tried to dig information but there is nothing to be heard. The problem is that if we ask the Police about it, they reply us harshly that we are sometimes promised a bullet. They take no notice about the kidnap. It was reported the day when it happened and they came to to ask my mother and that was all no action was taken by the Police and army yet it was reported that the kidnap

418

was done by the bandits.

But what worries me is that all witnesses say that after every kidnapp a sound of a truck was heard and the other thing is that this kidnapp happened in Tribal grounds that is Ndebele speaking, were the only ones kidnapped.

So I have sleepless nights nowardays because mother says they took father saying that they want him to show them the way and at the main gate of the farm she heard father crying very loud and this cry suddenly stopped in a serious way so we still haven't got any information about their whereabouts.

I have thought it best to share my sympathy with you and I am fully convinced that the present and other fellow christians shall assist in praying that we may see our fathers again and share our joys.

To me this is like reading an interesting book and find that the last chapter is tone and could not complete the interest. I have been doing very well at school and now I am cut off from my progress. I do not know whether I will manage next term because I can't see any reason why I am living in such a country without freedom.

Well Brother there is nothing we can do, thus the trend of life we are living in. There is more I can share with you but now my heart is wounded.

Greetings from the family

Yours
Distressed

419

APPENDIX C
FINDINGS

I UNITED NATIONS COMMISSION ON HUMAN RIGHTS:
REPORT OF THE WORKING GROUP ON ENFORCED OR
INVOLUNTARY DISAPPEARANCES: 15TH JANUARY
1996 pp 1–7, 85

II THE RECONCILIATION/UXOLELWANO TRUST DEED

CI

UNITED NATIONS COMMISSION ON HUMAN RIGHTS: REPORT OF THE WORKING GROUP ON ENFORCED OR INVOLUNTARY DISAPPEARANCES: 15TH JANUARY 1996 PP 1–7, 85

UNITED
NATIONS

E

 Economic and Social Council

Distr.
GENERAL

E/CN.4/1996/38
15 January 1996

ENGLISH ONLY*

COMMISSION ON HUMAN RIGHTS
Fifty-second session
Item 8 (c) of the provisional agenda

QUESTION OF THE HUMAN RIGHTS OF ALL PERSONS SUBJECTED TO ANY
FORM OF DETENTION OR IMPRISONMENT

QUESTION OF ENFORCED OR INVOLUNTARY DISAPPEARANCES

Report of the Working Group on Enforced
or Involuntary Disappearances

* In view of its length, the present document is being issued in the
original language only, the Conference Services Division of the United Nations
Office at Geneva having insufficient capacity to translate documents that
greatly exceed the 32-page limit recommended by the General Assembly (see
Commission resolution 1993/94, para. 1).

GE.96-10218   (E)

CONTENTS

CONTENTS (continued)

CONTENTS (<u>continued</u>)

Introduction

1.   The present report of the Working Group on Enforced or Involuntary Disappearances is submitted pursuant to Commission on Human Rights resolution 1995/38 entitled "Question of enforced disappearances". 1/ In addition to the specific tasks entrusted to the Working Group by the Commission in this resolution, the Group has also taken into account other mandates stemming from a number of resolutions adopted by the Commission, entrusted to all special rapporteurs and working groups. These are explained in chapter I, section A, "Legal framework for the activities of the Working Group". All these tasks have been given due attention and consideration by the Working Group in the course of 1995.

2.   During the year under review, the Working Group continued to carry out the activities it has undertaken since its establishment. Its original role which it has described in previous reports, is to act as a channel of communication between families of the disappeared persons and the Governments concerned, with a view to ensuring that sufficiently documented and clearly identified individual cases are investigated and the whereabouts of the disappeared persons clarified. Since its inception, the Working Group has analysed thousands of cases of disappearance and other information received from Governments and non-governmental organizations, individuals and other sources of information from all over the world in order to ascertain whether such material falls under the Working Group's mandate and contains the required elements; entered cases into its database; transmitted those cases to the Governments concerned, requesting them to carry out investigations and to inform the group about their results; forwarded the Governments' replies to relatives or other sources; followed up investigations carried out by the Governments concerned, as well as the inquiries made by the relatives or other agencies or organizations; maintained a considerable correspondence with Governments and the sources of information in order to obtain details on the cases and the investigations; and examined allegations of a general nature concerning specific countries with regard to the phenomenon of disappearances.

3.   In addition to its original mandate, the Working Group has been entrusted by the Commission with various other tasks. In particular, the Working Group is to monitor States' compliance with their obligations deriving from the Declaration on the Protection of All Persons from Enforced Disappearance. States are under an obligation to take effective measures to prevent and terminate acts of enforced disappearance, by making them continuing offences

---

1/ Since its creation in 1980, the Working Group has submitted a report to the Commission annually, starting at the Commission's thirty-seventh session. The document symbols of the last 14 reports are as follows: E/CN.4/1435 and Add.1; E/CN.4/1492 and Add.1; E/CN.4/1983/14; CN.4/1984/21 and Add.1 and 2; E/CN.4/1985/15 and Add.1; E/CN.4/1986/18 and Add.1; E/CN.4/1987/15 and Corr.1 and Add.1; E/CN.4/1988/19 and Add.1; E/CN.4/1989/18 and Add.1; E/CN.4/1990/13; E/CN.4/1991/20 and Add.1; E/CN.4/1992/18 and Add.1; E/CN.4/1993/25 and Add.1; E/CN.4/1994/26 and Corr.1 and 2 and Add.1; E/CN.4/1995/36.

under criminal law and establishing civil liability. The Declaration also
refers to the right to a prompt and effective judicial remedy, as well as
unhampered access of national authorities to all places of detention, the
right to habeas corpus, the maintenance of centralized registers of all places
of detention, the duty to investigate fully all alleged cases of
disappearance, the duty to try alleged perpetrators of disappearance before
ordinary (not military) courts, the exemption of the criminal offence of acts
of enforced disappearance from statutes of limitations, special amnesty laws
and similar measures leading to impunity. The Working Group reminded the
Governments of these obligations not only in the context of clarifying
individual cases, but also by taking action of a more general nature. During
the year under review, it drew the attention of Governments and
non-governmental organizations to the general or specific aspects of the
Declaration; it discussed with representatives of Governments and
non-governmental organizations how to solve specific problems in the light of
the Declaration and how to overcome obstacles to its implementation.

4.   As in previous years, the Working Group has continued to apply the urgent
action procedure in cases that allegedly occurred within three months
preceding the receipt of the report by the Group, and has also promptly
intervened with Governments in cases in which relatives of missing persons, or
other individuals or organizations which have cooperated with the Group, or
their legal counsel, have been subjected to intimidation, persecution or other
reprisals.

5.   The total number of cases being kept under active consideration as they
have not yet been clarified now stands at 43,508. In 1995, the Working Group
received some 824 new cases of disappearance in 27 countries. The number of
countries with outstanding cases of alleged disappearances was 63 in 1995.

6.   As in the past, the present report reflects only communications or cases
examined before the last day of the third annual session of the Working Group,
which was 17 November 1995. Urgent action cases which may have to be dealt
with between that date and the end of the year, as well as communications
received from Governments after 17 November 1995, will be reflected in the
Working Group's next report.

7.   In 1995, the Working Group continued to undertake a review of its methods
of work, which it had begun in 1994, bearing in mind, in particular, its
responsibilities under the Declaration on the Protection of All Persons from
Enforced Disappearance. It was guided by resolution 1995/38, paragraph 20, in
which the Commission on Human Rights requested the Working Group to again
identify obstacles to the realization of the provisions of the Declaration, to
recommend ways of overcoming those obstacles and to pursue, in this respect,
its dialogue with Governments and institutions concerned. The Group's general
recommendations and comments are contained in chapter I.F on the
implementation of the Declaration. Its country-specific observations, if any,
are to be found at the end of the respective country chapters in part II of
the present report. The Commission will find the Group's revised methods of
work in annex I to this report.

8.   One member of the Group, Mr. Diego García-Sayán, carried out a visit to
El Salvador in order to continue a process, begun last year, of examining,

428

with the Governments concerned, what to do with the large number of very old
cases of disappearance which remain pending on the Group's books, taking into
account, of course, the legitimate human rights concerns of the families. The
Working Group intends to pursue such discussions with other Governments in the
future.

9.   Finally, the Working Group feels obliged to draw the Commission's
attention to another matter. The Group fully understands, particularly in a
situation of serious financial crisis, the efforts of the United Nations to
reduce unnecessary costs and expenditures. In a spirit of cooperation, the
Group agreed, therefore, to reduce its forty-seventh session from eight
working days to five, and to postpone its visit to Colombia from 1995 to 1996.

10.   The Working Group has no understanding, however, of the way in which the
decision to reduce costs is being implemented. If one wishes to save money by
reducing the size of the reports of working groups, special rapporteurs and
other expert bodies established by the Commission, there should, first of all,
be clear guidelines on the page length which take into account the different
natures and types of work of the different mandates. While 32 pages may be a
reasonable limit for certain reports, it is certainly not the case for the
report of this Working Group, which deals with almost 70 countries. Secondly,
these guidelines should be brought to the attention of the respective entities
before they start to draft their reports to the Commission.

11.   It is unacceptable to the Working Group to be told a few days before the
adoption of its report that a 32-page limit for reports may now be enforced,
when this had never been the case in the past. In showing once again its
willingness to cooperate, the Group made great efforts to cut its report down
to some 100 pages. Any further reduction would have been irreconcilable with
its duty to carry out its mandate and to report to the Commission in a
responsible manner.

the Yemen Socialist Party and who reportedly disappeared in August 1994. This case was clarified in 1994 when the person concerned was reported to have been released.

454. At its forty-sixth session, a representative from the Permanent Mission of Yemen to the United Nations Office at Geneva met with the Working Group and confirmed the willingness of his Government to cooperate with the Group. He said that his country attached a great deal of importance to the 97 outstanding cases of disappearance in Yemen. The Government understood the anguish of the family members and was aware of the social and humanitarian implications families of the disappeared have to deal with. In this regard the representative informed the Working Group that his Government had taken several measures to alleviate the suffering of individual families, such as providing them with financial assistance and subsidies.

Zaire

455. During the period under review, no new cases of disappearance were transmitted by the Working Group to the Government of Zaire.

456. The majority of the 24 reported cases of disappearance occurred between 1975 and 1985 and concerned persons suspected of being members of a guerrilla group known as the Parti de la révolution populaire or of being political activists. More recent cases concern a journalist who was allegedly abducted from his home in 1993 by members of the Division spéciale présidentielle and the civil guard, and interrogated on the premises of the State radio station, Voix du Zaïre, and four men who were allegedly arrested in Likasi by soldiers and detained for almost two months before being transferred to Kinshasa; since then their whereabouts have remained unknown.

Zimbabwe

457. During the period under review, no new cases of disappearance were transmitted by the Working Group to the Government of Zimbabwe.

458. The one outstanding case occurred in 1985 in the context of the armed conflict between government forces and political opponents in Matabeleland. It concerned a member of the Zapu political party who was reportedly arrested by four men (two of them in police uniform) while attending a church service and taken away in a police vehicle.

459. During the period under review, the Government provided information on the one case of disappearance in which it stated that, pursuant to the signing of the unity accord in 1987, it had decided to compensate all families with missing relatives, regardless of whether there were court proceedings concerning the circumstances of the disappearance. The subject's family was therefore awarded compensation and his case had been settled through the High Court. It further stated that since his disappearance occurred during the armed conflict, it was impossible to carry out an investigation as no documents had been kept from this period.

430

II

NOTARIAL DEED OF TRUST RECONCILIATION/ UXOLELWANO TRUST

Be it hereby known that on the   day of   in the year of our Lord, 1997, before me   , legal practitioner and notary public by lawful authority admitted and sworn, in the presence of the subscribed witnesses, personally came and appeared (hereinafter referred to as "the founder trustees") and the appearers declared that:

WHEREAS thousands of Zimbabweans resident in Matabeleland North, Matabeleland South and Midlands Provinces suffered human rights violations between the 1st June 1982 and the 1st March 1988 as a result of civil unrest in those provinces;

AND WHEREAS entire communities in these provinces are still suffering as a result of these human rights violations;

AND WHEREAS the Government of the Republic of Zimbabwe, Zimbabwean Non Governmental Organisations and the communities affected themselves are desirous of creating a Trust to promote reconciliation within these affected communities through the implemention of developmental, educational, spiritual and health projects;

AND WHEREAS the Trustees desire that the purposes and objects of the Trust and the provisions for the management and conduct of the Trust, including the administration of its assets, be set forth in a Trust Deed.

NOW THEREFORE these present witness that;

1. NAME

A Trust called the Reconciliation/Uxolelwano Trust (hereinafter referred to as "the Trust") is hereby founded and established.

2. OBJECTIVES OF THE TRUST

The main object for which the Trust is established is to promote reconciliation between the peoples of Matabeleland North, Matabeleland South and Midlands Provinces and the remainder of the Republic of Zimbabwe by implementing projects in Matabeleland North, Matabeleland South and Midlands Provinces which will heal physical and mental wounds of victims of human rights violations who reside in those Provinces.

Consistent with the aforesaid main objective of the Trust, it is the further objective of the Trust;

(a) to act as an institution of public character;

(b) to utilise the assets, the rights and property of the Trust from time to time for charitable purposes of a public nature within Zimbabwe;

(c) to promote an understanding amongst all Zimbabweans of what happened in Matabeleland North, South and Midlands Provinces between 1982 and 1988 through educational programmes, debates scientific projects, research and studies;

(d) to encourage dialogue between human rights victims and human rights violators with a view to bringing reconciliation between communities;

(e) to identify and engage suitably qualified psychologists, medical practitioners, anthropologists, archaeologists and counsellors to provide health care and counselling for victims and to assist in the identification and reburial (if so desired by surviving relatives) of the remains of missing persons and the remains of persons buried in unmarked mass graves;

(f) to provide educational scholarships for children of impoverished families in Matabeleland North, Matabeleland South and Midlands Provinces;

(g) to utilise the whole or such part of the income of the Trust fund as the Trustees may in their sole discretion think necessary for the purposes of supporting agro/industrial/irrigation activities as implemented by any organisation, institute or association, or for the benefit of any person or group of persons interested or involved in agricultural, rural or industrial development in Matabeleland North, Matabeleland South and Midlands Provinces;

(h) to provide financial assistance for the erection of shrines and memorials and for the reburial of the remains of victims;

(i) to receive gifts and donations provided that all donations made to and accepted by the Trust shall be irrevocable and the Trust shall not accept or be party to any agreement or arrangement or any donation which directly or indirectly may be revocable by the donor or any other person, and to undertake the activities designed to raise funds and to be utilised for the purposes of the Trust;

(j) purchase movable and immovable properties so as to achieve the objectives of the Trust herein provided;

(k) to invest the assets of the trust fund in such a manner as the Trustees shall deem fit;

(l) to do all things and to engage in all activities generally which are incidental to any of the aforegoing specified objectives of the Trust or which the Trustees from time to time consider will serve to promote the main or any of the further objectives of the Trust.

3. BOARD OF TRUSTEES

The Trust shall be administered by a Board of Trustees which shall consist of not less than six (6) Trustees, two of whom shall be nominated by the Government of the Republic of Zimbabwe, two of whom shall be nominated by the Catholic Commission for Justice and Peace and the Legal Resources Foundation and two of whom shall be permanently resident in any communal land within the boundaries of Matabeleland North or South Provinces. There shall be no more than ten (10) Trustees. The founder Trustees shall be

4. POWERS OF THE BOARD OF TRUSTEES

The Board shall have power to do all things pertaining, conducive, or incidental to the objects of the Trust, and without prejudice to the generality of the aforegoing, the Board shall have the power:

(a) to solicit for funds from the Government of the Republic of Zimbabwe and other Government and international donor agencies to implement projects undertaken by the Trust;

(b) to purchase, take on, lease or exchange, hire or otherwise deal in any movable or immovable property and make payment therefore out of the funds of the Trust;

(c) to maintain, repair, improve, manage, develop, exchange, lease, mortgage, sell, donate, dispose of, invest and otherwise deal with all or any part of the property and the rights of the Trust;

(d) to enter into contracts of insurance and indemnity of every description;

(e) to accept and apply for the purposes of the Trust any donation or bequest for money or property in accordance with the terms of such donation or bequest provided its terms are in accordance with the aforesaid purposes;

(f) to open accounts at any bank, building society or post office savings bank, to operate the same through the agency of such member if the board, secretary, treasurer or other employee of the Trust as the board may from time to time determine;

(g) to invest any monies of the Trust in such investments or securities as the board may choose, and to receive, hold and disburse the funds of the Trust for the fulfilment of the purposes of the Trust as aforementioned;

(h) to ask, demand, sue for and recover all debts, goods, effects and things whatsoever due and belonging to the Trust, to discharge, compromise and settle all claims and matters in dispute relating to the Trust and to submit the same to arbitration, to commence, prosecute, defend and oppose any action or other proceeding in law relating to the Trust in any Court;

(i) to appoint a secretary and/or treasurer to the Trust in any other offices or staff which the board may consider necessary for the carrying out of the purposes of the Trust, to define and regulate their duties and to pay them a suitable remuneration and to dismiss them;

(j) to appoint an executive committee to run projects developed and implemented by the Trust, to define and regulate their duties or to pay them a suitable remuneration and dismiss the members of the executive committee;

(k) to establish and maintain or procure the establishment of maintenance of any contributory or non-contributory pension or super annuation fund for the benefit of any persons who are or were at the time in the employment or service of the Trust;

(1) to delegate all or any of its powers of duties, to employ legal practitioners or agents to set up committees and regulate their proceedings;

(m) to charge fees, to award bursaries for efficiency and studies, exercise or games, and to provide scholarships;

(n) to enter into any arrangement for co-operation, joint ventures, union of interests or amalgamation with any person, company or trust whose purposes are similar to those of the Trust or who is engaged in carrying on any business which is capable of being conducted so as directly or indirectly to benefit the Trust and further its purposes;

(o) to subscribe for, take or otherwise acquire and hold capital, shares, stock, ventures or any other securities or any other trust, person or company having a purpose similar to that of the Trust and to acquire and undertake the whole or any part of the assets and liabilities of such trust, person or company;

(p) to sell, donate, or otherwise dispose of the whole or any part of the assets and undertakings of the Trust and/or any trust or company whose purpose is similar to that of the Trust;

(q) to indemnify all or any of the members of the time being of the board out of the funds of the Trust against any loss occasioned by the *bona fide* exercise of their power or performance of the duties recited in this deed;

(r) to dismiss from office by majority of vote of all the Trustees any Trustee herein appointed or subsequently appointed in terms of Clause 4(s) *infra,* and by majority vote of all the Trustees to elect a new Trustee in place of any Trustee who may die, resign from office or otherwise become incapable of acting, or be dismissed from the office of Trustee in terms hereof, subject to the condition that such new Trustees shall only serve the unexpired term of office of the former Trustee whom he or she is replacing;

(s) to elect, by unanimous vote of all the trustees, any new trustees.

5. DUTIES OF BOARD OF TRUSTEES

The Board shall:

(a) do all things necessary or desirable for the proper fulfilment of the objects and purposes of the Trust;

(b) cause accounts of the Trust to be prepared annually in respect of the period from time to time fixed by the Board as the financial year of the Trust and shall cause such accounts to be audited and shall make them available to any person from whom the Trust has borrowed money, if so required;

(c) apply the income and property of the Trust solely towards the fulfilment and promotion of the objects and purposes of the Trust, including payment in good faith, remuneration, bonus, pension, allowance or gratuity to any officer, servant, legal practitioner, auditor or agent of the Board and just or proper reward to any member of the Board for services contracted for by the Board and reasonable and proper interest and money lent to the Trust and property rent from the premises let to the Trust;

(d) meet at least twice a year for the transaction of business of the Trust;

435

(e) pay special attention to:
  (i) the proper investment of funds of the Trust not immediately required to be expanded;
  (ii) the preservation of the property of the Trust;
  (iii) the attraction of donations and bequests to the Trust;
  (iv) the maintenance of high ethical standards in all business transactions and personal dealings conducted by the Board;
  (v) the employment and conditions of service of staff in accordance with Christian principles, which should recognise that the people working for the Trust are its greatest assets;
(f) at its first meeting, and thereafter at its first meeting in each calendar year, appoint a chairman and vice-chairman;
(g) prepare proper minutes of all meetings of the Board, and records of all Trust transactions, keep the same and send copies of the same to all Trustees.

[NUMBERS 6 AND 7 OMMITTED IN FIRST EDITION]

8. QUORUM/TERM OF OFFICE

A quorum of the Board shall consist of at least three members being present. The Chairman, or in his absence the Vice-Chairman, shall preside at all meetings of the Board. Questions arising at any meeting shall be decided by a majority of votes and in the event of the equality of votes, the Chairman of the meeting shall have a second or casting vote. If at any meeting neither the Chairman nor the Vice-Chairman is present, the members present shall choose one of their members to be the Chairman of the meeting. The term of office of Trustees shall be three years from the date of his or her appointment or co-option, but any persons ceasing to be a member of the Board by reason of expiration of his or her term of office in terms hereof may be co-opted to serve further terms.

9. DISQUALIFICATION

In the event of any member of the Board becoming disqualified from acting as a Director of Companies by virtue of the provisions of Section 173(1) of 173(2) of the Companies Act, Chapter 24:03, such Trustee shall be deemed to have tendered his or her resignation as a member of the Board and the Board shall have power to accept such resignations as if it had been voluntarily tendered.

10. REGULATIONS

The Board shall have power to make regulations consistent with the spirit and object of this Trust:

(a) determining the procedure at meetings of the Board;
(b) providing for procedure whereby special meetings of the Board can be held and convened;
(c) providing for the appointment of an executive committees, or sub-committees of the Board to perform individual functions of the Board;
(d) providing for the keeping of minutes and recordings of all resolutions and proceedings of all meetings of the Board;
(e) regulating any other matters necessary or desirable for the smooth and efficient continuance and operation of the Trust and the achievement of its objects.

11. SECURITY

The Trustees shall not be required to give security for the due and faithful administration of the Trust Deed, or for the due discharge of their Trust, and any Master or Masters of the High Court of Zimbabwe, or any corresponding or like official or officials having jurisdiction are hereby directed to dispense with such security.

12.

The Trustees shall be charged with only such assets, securities and investments as are actually paid or handed over to them, and shall be answerable or accountable only for their own account, receipts or defaults, and shall not be answerable for the defaults of any agent, broker or banker into whose hands any assets, securities or investments may from time to time be deposited in the ordinary course of the administration of the Trust.

13. PERSONAL LIABILITY

The Trustees shall not incur any personal liability by reason of any loss or damage sustained in or about or in any consequence of:

(a) the failure, depreciation or loss of any investments made, assets, security or investment retained, administered or realised by them in good faith;

(b) any mistake or omission made in good faith;

(c) the exercise (whether negligently or otherwise) by them in good faith of any of the powers or discretion vested in them under this Deed or law except wilful and individual fraud on the part of that Trustee who is thought to be held liable.

14. PAYMENT FOR SERVICES

While it is contemplated that the Trustees will generally serve as such on an honorary basis, any Trustee may be entitled to be paid a fee for his or her services, at the discretion of the Trustees. Such fees shall be charged against the Trust Funds. It shall be competent for Trustees to determine special or *ad hoc* fees or remuneration to be paid to Trustees who may from time to time give special or extraordinary time and attention to the affairs of the Trust. The Trustees may also be entitled to receive reimbursement for expenses incurred in connection with the services he or she provides to the Trust.

15. ARBITRATION

If any difference or dispute shall at any time arise in regard to the interpretation of this Trust Deed or the respective rights of any person hereunder, then and in such event, the matters in dispute shall be referred to arbitration in accordance with the succeeding provisions:

(a) the arbitration proceedings shall be held on an informal basis, it being the intention that a decision should be reached as expeditiously as possible, subject only to the due observance of the principles of natural justice;

(b) each party to the dispute shall be entitled to be represented at such arbitration proceedings by his or her legal representatives and/or any expert or specialist retained by him or her.

(c) the arbitrator shall be such person having an appropriate knowledge as may be agreed upon between the parties, and failing agreement, as may be nominated by the President of the Law Society of Zimbabwe, or failing him, the Vice-President;

(d) the decision of the arbitrator shall be final and binding on the parties hereto.

16. PROPERTY

All improvements and movable property of any sort and description which is acquired by the Trust by virtue of the provisions of this Deed or may hereafter be acquired, shall be vested in and become the property of the Trustees hereby appointed, or their successors in office in terms of Clause 4 *supra* in Trust for the purposes and use of the Trust, and the Trustees when authorised thereto by the Board shall have power to buy and sell, take, give, transfer or grant or take leases of property and pledge or mortgage such property and exercise any of the powers of the Board in relation to such property or any portion thereof, and shall generally be and become owners in Trust for the said Trust.

17. AMENDMENTS

This Deed may be amended, added to, altered or varied at any time by agreement by resolutions supported by the majority of all Trustees being present at a meeting of which at least seven days' written notice has been given; the full wording of the resolution must be contained in the written notice and if passed must be enacted by way of a Deed of Amendment.

18. DISSOLUTION

The Trust may be dissolved at any time by a two-third majority vote of all members of the Board. If on dissolution there remains any surplus funds or property after all debts and liabilities of the Trust have been discharged such surplus shall be handed over, in the discretion of the Board, to any Trust or organisation in Zimbabwe which is not for the gain and has objects similar to this Trust.

19. ACCEPTANCE OF TERMS

The Trustees appointed herein do hereby accept appointment subject to and in terms of the provisions of this Deed. Any new Trustees appointed in terms of Clause 4 *supra* shall only be appointed if they accept the provisions of this deed and the appointment itself is subject to the provisions of this Deed.

THUS DONE AND EXECUTED on the day, month and year first aforewritten in the presence of the undersigned witnesses and of me the Notary.

_____

_____

_____

AS WITNESSES:

1.

2.

QUOD ATTESTOR

_____

LEGAL PRACTITIONER
NOTARY PUBLIC